Holistic Game Development with Unity

Holistic Game Development with Unity

An All-in-One Guide to Implementing Game Mechanics, Art, Design, and Programming

Penny de Byl

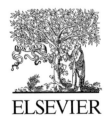

AMSTERDAM • BOSTON • HEIDELBERG • LONDON
NEW YORK • OXFORD • PARIS • SAN DIEGO
SAN FRANCISCO • SINGAPORE • SYDNEY • TOKYO

Focal Press is an imprint of Elsevier

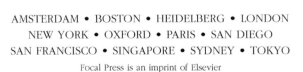

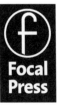

ELSEVIER

Focal Press

Focal Press is an imprint of Elsevier
225 Wyman Street, Waltham, MA 02451, USA
The Boulevard, Langford Lane, Kidlington, Oxford, OX5 1GB, UK

Notices

Knowledge and best practice in this field are constantly changing. As new research and experience broaden our understanding, changes in research methods, professional practices, or medical treatment may become necessary.

Practitioners and researchers must always rely on their own experience and knowledge in evaluating and using any information, methods, compounds, or experiments described herein. In using such information or methods they should be mindful of their own safety and the safety of others, including parties for whom they have a professional responsibility.

To the fullest extent of the law, neither the Publisher nor the authors, contributors, or editors, assume any liability for any injury and/or damage to persons or property as a matter of product liability, negligence or otherwise, or from any use or operation of any methods, products, instructions, or ideas contained in the material herein.

Library of Congress Cataloging-in-Publication Data
Application submitted

British Library Cataloguing-in-Publication Data
A catalogue record for this book is available from the British Library.

ISBN: 978-0-240-81933-4

For information on all Focal Press publications
visit our website at www.elsevierdirect.com

11   12   13   14   5   4   3   2   1

Printed in the United States of America

Working together to grow
libraries in developing countries

www.elsevier.com | www.bookaid.org | www.sabre.org

ELSEVIER   BOOK AID International   Sabre Foundation

Contents

Contents

Contents

Preface

About This Book

I decided to write this book when I found existing literature for budding game designers, artists, and programmers tended to focus on only one specific vein of games development—that being a design, artistic, or programming book. Those with artistic talents and ideas for games could not find a good resource to ease them into programming. However, programming texts tend to be dry and ignore the visual aspect.

With the face of the game development industry rapidly changing from a small number of large development teams to much more of a cottage industry consisting of small multiskilled teams, it is more imperative that individuals are skilled in both art and programming.

Game development tools are also not what they used to be, and rapid game development tools such as Unity are making it a possibility for individuals to make complete games from scratch.

To address these issues, this book is written for the artist who wants to program and the programmer who wants some pointers about using game art. In the beginning I started writing just for artists but soon came to realize the content was equally as relevant to those wanting to learn how to start programming games.

How This Book Is Organized

This book has been written with *artists who want to learn how to develop games* and *programmers who want to learn about using art in games* in mind. It approaches game development in a unique combination of teaching programming, keeping in mind the design; for programming, a game's graphical user interface is entirely different from making it look good. Learning about how design impacts on programming and vice versa is a logical way to introduce both sides of the game develop coin to game creation.

All chapters focus on sets of mechanical functions existing within games:

- Chapter One, The Art of Programming Game Mechanics, explains the roles both art and programming play in creating games and explores the limitations of having one without the other. In addition, the complementary nature of digital art and programming is established.
- Chapter Two, Real-World Mechanics, examines the branch of physics dealing with the study of motion. Motion is a fundamental idea in all of science that transcends the computer screen into virtual

environments. This chapter examines kinematics, which describe motion, and dynamics, which examine the causes of motion with respect to their use in computer games. It introduces the physical properties of the real world and demonstrates how a fundamental understanding of mathematics, physics, and design principles is critical in any game environment. Composition, rules of animation, and design principles are introduced in parallel with technical considerations, mathematics, and programming code, which controls and defines the movement of characters, cameras, environments, and other game objects.

- Chapter Three, Animation Mechanics, studies the technical nature of 2D and 3D animated models. The reader will develop skills with respect to the programmatic control of their own artwork, models, and/or supplied assets in a game environment. Elementary mathematics, physics, and programming concepts are introduced that demonstrate the concepts of keyframes, animation states, and development of dynamic character movement and sprite animation.
- Chapter Four, Game Rules and Mechanics, introduces common generic game mechanics such as matching, sorting, managing, and hitting. Examples of how each of these is represented visually in a game and the programming that controls them are explained in depth. Common algorithms and data structures used for each mechanic are worked through with the reader integrating, where appropriate, key art assets.
- Chapter Five, Character Mechanics, explains simple artificial intelligence algorithms to assist the reader in creating his or her own believable nonplayer characters. Animation states and techniques covered in Chapter 3 are integrated with game-specific data structures and algorithms to control the behavior of characters from flocking of birds to opponents that follow and interact with the player.
- Chapter Six, Player Mechanics, presents the code and artwork deployed to develop graphical user interfaces and maintain player states. It includes details about the development of inventory systems, heads-up displays, and character–environment interaction.
- Chapter Seven, Environmental Mechanics, reveals the fundamental concepts in creating and optimizing game environments. It covers techniques from adding detail to environments to make them more believable to tricks for working with large maps and weather simulations.
- Chapter Eight, Mechanics for External Forces, examines issues related to developing games while keeping in mind the new plethora of input devices, social data, GPS locators, motion sensors, augmented reality, and screen sizes. Included is practical advice on using Unity to deploy games to iPhone, iPad, and Android mobile devices that leverage touch screens, accelerometers, and networking.

The Companion Web Site

The Web site accompanying this book is http://www.holistic3d.com. It contains all the files referred to in the workshops, finished examples, and other teaching and learning resources.

Acknowledgments

First I thank my editor, Sara Scott, who has kept my project on track. Her encouragement and enthusiasm in the book have been highly motivational. In addition, thanks must go to Mark Ripley of Effervescing Elephant Interactive who acted as technical editor and provided valuable insight on game programming with Unity.

Next, I acknowledge Unity3d who have developed a truly inspirational game development tool and all the forum contributors who have freely shared their ideas and code to answer all conceivable game development questions. The forums at http://forums.unity3d.com are an invaluable knowledge base.

Finally, I thank my family, Daniel, Tabytha, Deefa (Labrador 15 years old), and Merlin (Labrador <1 year old). Daniel has been an absolute rock. His knowledge of Microsoft Word formatting still leaves me amazed, and his proofreading and testing of all the workshops have saved so much time (i.e., if the code in this book doesn't work for you—blame him! ☺). Tabytha has been as patient as a 6–7-year-old can be when it seems your mother's every waking moment is spent in front of the iMac. As always, Deefa has provided moral support, sitting constantly under the desk at my feet, and Merlin, the little voice in the back of my mind, wondering which pair of shoes he was dining on given his obvious absence from the room.

To me, game development is the quintessential seam where the tectonic plates of programming and art meet. It is where both domains really start to make sense. If you are reading this, I hope you feel the same.

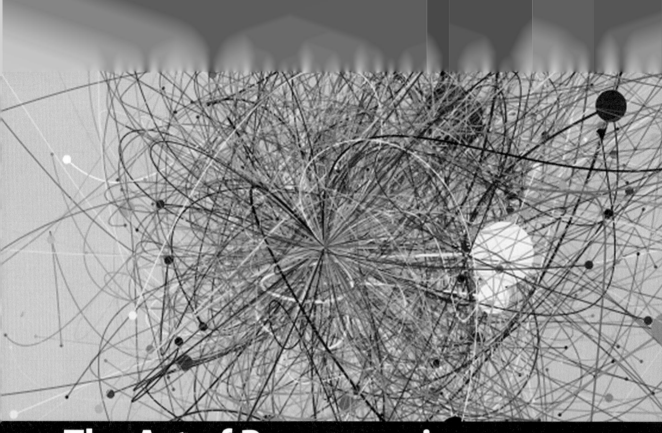

The Art of Programming Mechanics

Everyone can be taught to sculpt: Michelangelo would have had to be taught how not to. So it is with the great programmers.

Alan Perlis

1.1 Introduction

In 1979, art teacher Betty Edwards published the acclaimed *Drawing on the Right Side of the Brain*. The essence of the text taught readers to draw what they saw rather than what they *thought* they saw. The human brain is so adept at tasks such as pattern recognition that we internally symbolize practically everything we see and regurgitate these patterns when asked to draw them on paper. Children do this very well. The simplicity in children's drawing stems from their internal representation for an object. Ask them to draw a house and a dog and you'll get something you and they can recognize as a house and dog or, more accurately, the icon for a house and

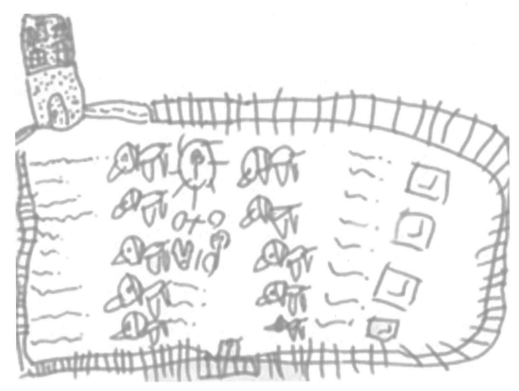

FIG 1.1 Dogs in the yard of a castle by Tabytha de Byl aged 4.

dog, but something far from what an actual house and dog look like. This is evident in the child's drawing in Figure 1.1. The title of the book, *Drawing on the Right Side of the Brain*, also suggests that the ability to draw should be summoned from the side of the brain traditionally associated with creativity and that most *bad* drawings could be blamed on the left.

Different intellectual capability is commonly attributed to either the left or the right hemispheres. The left side being responsible for the processing of language, mathematics, numbers, logic, and other such computational activities, whereas the right deals with shapes, patterns, spatial acuity, images, dreaming, and creative pursuits. From these beliefs, those who are adept at computer programming are classified as left-brained and artists as right-brained. The segregation of these abilities to either side of the brain is called *lateralization*. While lateralization has been generally accepted and even used to classify and separate students into learning style groups, it is a common misconception that intellectual functioning can be separated so clearly.

In fact, the clearly defined left and right brain functions are a *neuromyth* stemming from the overgeneralization and literal isolation of the brain hemispheres. While some functions tend to reside more in one side of the brain than the other, many tasks, to some degree, require both sides. For example, many numerical computation and language activities require both hemispheres. Furthermore, the side of the brain being utilized for specific tasks can vary among people. Studies have revealed that 97% of right-handed people use their left hemisphere for language and speech processing and 70% of left-handed people use their right hemisphere.

In short, simply classifying programmers as left brainers and artists as right brainers is a misnomer. This also leads to the disturbing misconception that programmers are poor at art skills and that artists would have difficulty understanding programming. Programming is so often generalized as a logical process and art as a creative process that some find it inconceivable that programmers could be effective as artists and vice versa.

When Betty Edwards suggests that people should use their right brain for drawing it is in concept, not physiology. The location of the neurons the reader is being asked to use to find their creative self is not relevant. What is important is that Dr. Edwards is asking us to see drawing in a different light—in a way we may not have considered before. Instead of drawing our internalized symbol of an object that has been stored away in the brain, she asks us to draw what we see. To forget what we *think* it looks like. In the end this symbolizes a switch in thinking away from logic and patterns to images and visual processing.

There is no doubt that some people are naturally better at programming and others at art. However, by taking Edwards' *anyone can draw* attitude, we can also say *anyone can program*. It just requires a little practice and a change of attitude.

1.2 Programming on the Right Side of the Brain

While it is true that pure logic is at the very heart of all computer programs, it still requires an enormous amount of creativity to order the logic into a program. The process is improved greatly when programmers can visualize the results of their code before it even runs. You may liken this to a scene from *The Matrix* where the characters look at screens of vertically flowing green numbers and text but can visualize the structure and goings on in a photorealistic, three-dimensional virtual reality. To become a good computer programmer you need to know the language of the code and be able to visualize how it is affecting the computer's memory and the results of running the program.

Learning a computer language is one key to being able to program. However, understanding how the language interacts with the computer to produce its output is even more important. Good programmers will agree that it is easy to switch between programming languages once you have mastered one. The fundamental concepts in each are the same. In some languages, such as C, C++, C#, Javascript, Java, and PhP, even the text and layout look the same. The basic code from each aforementioned language to print *Hello World* on the computer screen is shown in listings 1.1 through 1.6.

Listing 1.1 C

```c
#include < stdio.h>
main()
{
      printf("Hello World");
}
```

Listing 1.2 C++

```cpp
#include < iostream >
using namespace std;
void main()
{
      cout < < "Hello World" < < endl;
}
```

Listing 1.3 C#

```csharp
public class HelloWorld
{
      public static void Main()
      {
            System.Console.WriteLine("Hello World");
      }
}
```

Listing 1.4 JavaScript (in Bold) Embedded in HTML

```html
<html>
      <head>
            <title > Hello World</title>
      </head>
      <body>
            <script type = "text/javascript">
                  document.write('Hello World');
            </script>
      </body>
</html>
```

Listing 1.5 Java

```
class helloworld
{
        public static void main(String args[])
        {
                System.out.println("Hello World");
        }
}
```

Listing 1.6 PHP

```
<?php
        echo "Hello World";
?>
```

Umberto Eco, the creator of *Opera Aperta*, described the concept of art as mechanical relationships between features that can be reorganized to make a series of distinct works. This too is true of programming. The same lines of programming code can be reorganized to create many different programs. Nowhere is this shared art/programming characteristic more obvious than in fractals.

Fractals are shapes made up of smaller self-similar copies of themselves. The famous Mandelbrot set or *Snowman* is shown in Figure 1.2. The whole shape is made up of smaller versions of itself. As you look closer you will be able to spot tens or even hundreds of smaller snowman shapes within the larger image.

A fractal is constructed from a mathematical algorithm repeated over and over where the output is interpreted as a point and color on the computer screen. The Mandelbrot set comes from complex equations, but not all fractal algorithms require high-level mathematical knowledge to understand.

The Barnsley fern leaf is the epitome of both the creative side of programming and algorithmic nature of art. Put simply, the algorithm takes a shape, any shape, and transforms it four times, as shown in Figure 1.3. It then takes the resulting shape and puts it through the same set of transformations. This can be repeated infinitum; however, around 10 iterations of this process give a good impression of the resulting image (see Figure 1.4).

Creating images with these types of algorithmic approaches is called *procedural* or *dynamic generation*. It is a common method for creating assets such as terrain, trees, and special effects in games. Although procedural generation can create game landscapes and other assets before a player starts playing, procedural generation comes into its own *while* the game is being played.

FIG 1.2 The Mandelbrot set and
periodicities of orbits.

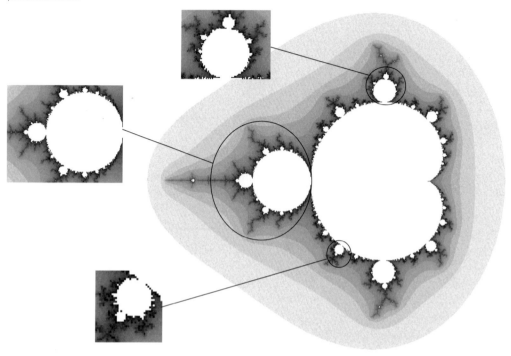

FIG 1.3 Transformations of Barnsley's
fern leaf.

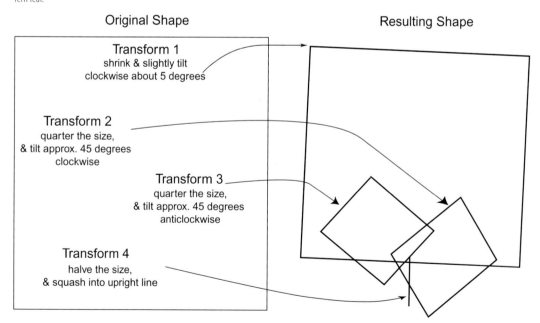

Original Shape

Resulting Shape

Transform 1
shrink & slightly tilt
clockwise about 5 degrees

Transform 2
quarter the size,
& tilt approx. 45 degrees
clockwise

Transform 3
quarter the size,
& tilt approx. 45 degrees
anticlockwise

Transform 4
halve the size,
& squash into upright line

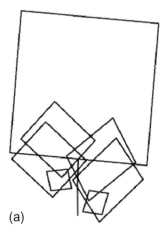
(a)

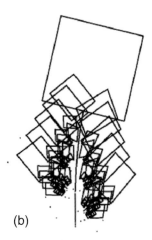
(b)

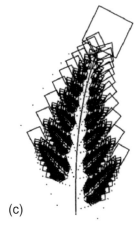
(c)

FIG 1.4 Three iterations of Barnsley's fern leaf transformations after (a) 2 iterations, (b) 5 iterations, and (c) 10 iterations.

Programming code can access the assets in a game during run time. It can manipulate an asset based on player input. For example, placing a large hole in a wall after the player has blown it up is achieved with programming code. This can only be calculated at the time the player interacts with the game, as beforehand a programmer would have no idea where the player would be standing or in what direction he would shoot. The game *Fracture* by Day 1 Studios features dynamic ground terrains that lift up beneath objects when shot with a special weapon.

⦿ For Research
Procedural Generation in Unity
The Unity Web site has a project with numerous procedural generation demonstrations. At this point in your game development learning journey, you may not be able to understand the underlying code, but the examples will show you what is possible and the types of things you will be able to achieve by the end of this book. The Unity project can be downloaded from http://unity3D.com/support/resources/files/Procedural.zip.

A purpose-built programming language for creating art is *Processing*. The syntax of the code is not unlike JavaScript and contains all the fundamental programming concepts you will learn about in Section 1.4. The image in Figure 1.5 was created with Processing by randomly plotting circles and drawing a series of curves from a central location to each circle. Art created by Casey Reas, shown in Figure 1.6, created with Processing has been displayed at Gallery [DAM] Berlin.

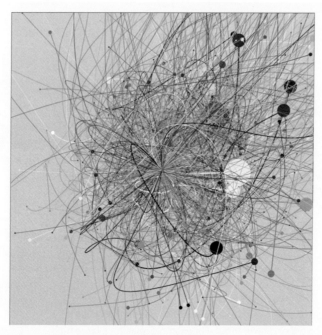

FIG 1.5 An image created with Processing.

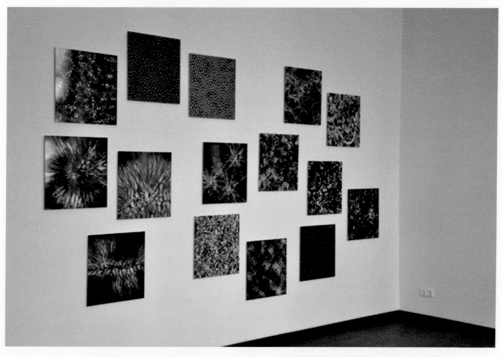

FIG 1.6 Artwork created by Casey Reas using Processing as exhibited at Gallery [DAM] Berlin.

1.3 Creating Art from the Left Side of the Brain

Most people know what they like and don't like when they see art.
However, if you ask them why they like it they may not be able to put their
thoughts into words. No doubt there are some people who are naturally
gifted with the ability to draw and sculpt and some who are not. For the
artistically challenged, however, hope is not lost. This is certainly Betty
Edwards' stance.

A logical approach to the elements and principles of design reveals rules
one can apply to create more appealing artwork. They are the mechanical
relationships, alluded to by Umberto Eco, that can be used as building blocks
to create works of art. These fundamentals are common threads found to
run through all good artwork. They will not assist you in being creative and
coming up with original art, but they will help in presentation and visual
attractiveness.

The elements of design are the primary items that make up drawings,
models, paintings, and design. They are *point*, *line*, *shape*, *direction*, *size*,
texture, *color*, and *hue*. All visual artworks include one or more of these
elements.

In the graphics of computer games, each of these elements is as important
to the visual aspect of game assets as they are in drawings, painting, and
sculptures. However, as each is being stored in computer memory and
processed by mathematical algorithms, their treatment by the game
artist differs.

1.3.1 Point

All visual elements begin with a point. In drawing, it is the first mark put on
paper. Because of the physical makeup of computer screens, it is also the
fundamental building block of all digital images. Each point on an electronic
screen is called a *pixel*. The number of pixels visible on a display is referred to
as the *resolution*. For example, a resolution of 1024×768 is 1024 pixels wide
and 768 pixels high.

Each pixel is referenced by its *x* and *y* Cartesian coordinates. Because
pixels are discrete locations on a screen, these coordinates are always in
whole numbers. The default coordinate system for a screen has the (0,0)

pixel in the upper left-hand corner. A screen with 1024×768 resolution would have the (1023,767) pixel in the bottom right-hand corner. The highest value pixel has x and y values that are one minus the width and height, respectively, because the smallest pixel location is referenced as (0,0). It is also possible to change the default layout depending on the application being used such that the y values of the pixels are flipped with (0,0) being in the lower left-hand corner or even moved into the center of the screen.

1.3.2 Line

On paper, a line is created by the stroke of a pen or brush. It can also define the boundary where two shapes meet. A line on a digital display is created by coloring pixels on the screen between two pixel coordinates. Given the points at the ends of a line, an algorithm calculates the pixel values that must be colored in to create a straight line. This isn't as straightforward as it sounds because the pixels can only have whole number coordinate values. The *Bresenham line algorithm* was developed by Jack E. Bresenham in 1962 to effectively calculate the best pixels to color in to give the appearance of a line. Therefore, the line that appears on a digital display can only ever be an approximation to the real line as shown in Figure 1.7.

FIG 1.7   A real line and a Bresenham line.

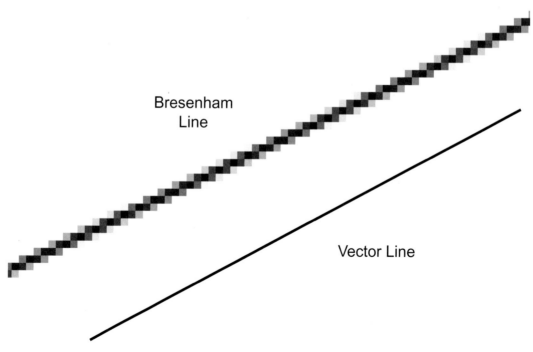

10

1.3.3 Shape

A shape refers not only to primitive geometrics such as circles, squares, and triangles, but also to freeform and nonstandard formations. In computer graphics, polygons are treated as they are in geometry; a series of points called *vertices* connected by straight *edges*. By storing the coordinates of the vertices the edges can be reconstructed using straight line algorithms. A circle is often represented by as a regular polygon with many edges. As the number of edges increases, a regular polygon approaches the shape of a circle.

Freeform objects involve the use of curves. To be stored and manipulated by the computer efficiently, these need to be stored in a mathematical format. Two common types of curves used include Bezier and nonuniform rational basis spline (NURBS).

A Bezier curve is constructed from a number of control points. The first and last points specify the start and end of the curve and the other points act as attractors, drawing the line toward them and forming a curve, as shown in Figure 1.8. A NURBS curve is similar to a Bezier curve in that it has a number of control points; however, the control points can be weighted such that some may attract more than others.

In computer graphics, a polygon is the basic building block for objects, whether in 2D or 3D. A single polygon defines a flat surface onto which texture can be applied. The most efficient way to define a flat surface is through the use of three points; therefore, triangles are the polygon of choice for constructing models, although sometimes you will find square polygons used in some software packages. Fortunately for the artist, modeling software such as Autodesk's 3DS Studio Max and Blender do not require models to be handcrafted from triangles; instead they automatically construct any objects using triangles as a base as shown in Figure 1.9.

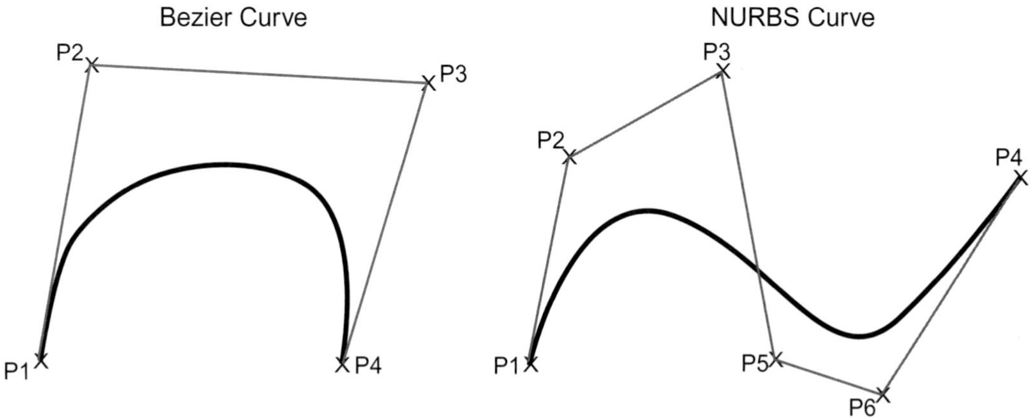

FIG 1.8 A Bezier and a NURBS curve.

Bezier Curve

NURBS Curve

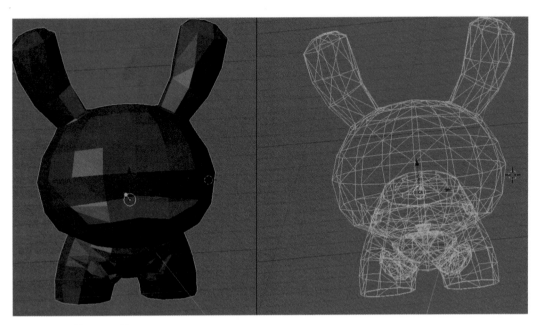

FIG 1.9 A 3D model constructed from triangles in Blender.

The wireframe model that represents a 3D object is called a *mesh*. The number of polygons in a mesh is called the *polycount*. The higher the polycount, the more triangles in the model and the more computer processing power required to render and manipulate the model. For this reason, computer game artists must find a balance between functionality and visual quality, as a high-resolution model is too costly with respect to making the game run slowly. The models must be dynamically processed and rendered in real time. In contrast, animated movie models can be much higher quality, as they are not rendered in real time. Next time you are playing a game, take a closer look at how the models are constructed.

1.3.4 Direction

Direction is the orientation of a line. Depending on its treatment, it can imply speed and motion. A line can sit horizontal, vertical, or oblique. In computer graphics, physics, engineering, and mathematics, a *Euclidean vector* is used to specify direction. A vector stores information about how to get from one point in space to another in a straight line. Not only does it represent a direction, but also a distance, otherwise called its *magnitude*. The magnitude of a vector is taken from its length. Two vectors can point in the same direction but have different magnitudes, as shown in Figure 1.10a. In addition, two vectors can have the same magnitude but different direction, as shown in Figure 1.10b. A vector with a magnitude of one is *normalized*.

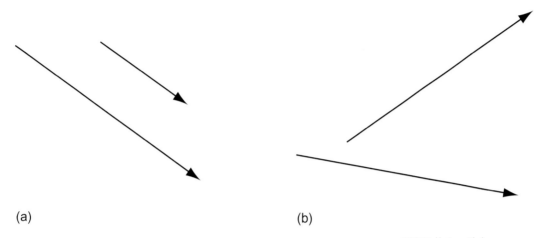

(a) (b)

FIG 1.10 Vectors with the same direction but different magnitudes (a) and vectors with the same magnitude but different directions (b).

Vectors are a fundamental element in 3D games as they describe the direction in which objects are orientated, how they are moving, how they are scaled, and even how they are textured and lit. The basics of vectors are explored further in Chapter Two.

1.3.5 Size

Size is the relationship of the amount of space objects take up with respect to each other. In art and design it can be used to create balance, focal points, or emphasis. In computer graphics, size is referred to as *scale*. An object can be scaled uniformly or in any direction. Figure 1.11 shows a 3D object (a) scaled uniformly by 2 (b), by 3 vertically (c), by 0.5 horizontally (d), and by −1 vertically (e).

Note in Figure 1.11d how scaling by a negative value flips them vertically. They can also be achieved uniformly or horizontally using negative scaling values.

Depending on coordinates of an object, scaling will also move it. For example, if an object is centered around (0,0), it can be scaled remaining in the same place. However, if the object is away from (0,0), it will move by an amount proportional to the scale. This occurs as scaling values are multiplied with vertex coordinates to resize objects. A vertex at (0,0) multiplied by 2, for example, will remain at (0,0), whereas a vertex at (3,2) multiplied by 2 will move to (6,4). This is illustrated in Figure 1.12.

1.3.6 Texture

In art and design, texture relates to the surface quality of a shape or object. For example, the surface could be rough, smooth, or highly polished. In computer games, texture refers not only to the quality, but also to any photographs, colors, or patterns on the surface where the surface is defined by a polygon.

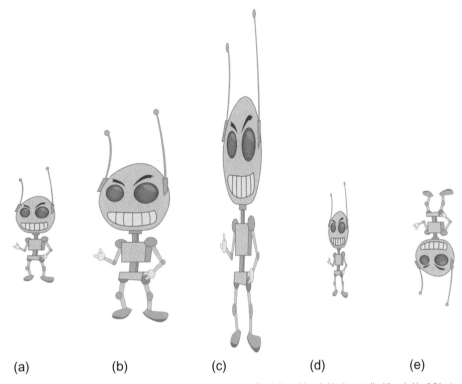

(a) (b) (c) (d) (e)

FIG 1.11 A 3D object scaled in multiple ways: (a) the original object, (b) scaled uniformly by 2, (c) scaled by 3 vertically, (d) scaled by 0.5 horizontally, and (e) scaled by −1 vertically.

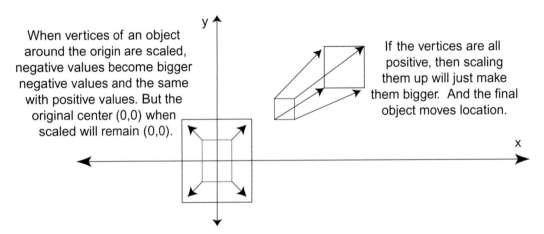

When vertices of an object around the origin are scaled, negative values become bigger negative values and the same with positive values. But the original center (0,0) when scaled will remain (0,0).

If the vertices are all positive, then scaling them up will just make them bigger. And the final object moves location.

FIG 1.12 How scaling can move an object.

In games, textures are created using image files called *maps*. They are created in Adobe Photoshop or similar software. The image that gives an object its color is called a *texture map*, *color map*, or *diffuse coloring*. All images are mapped onto an object, polygon by polygon, using a technique called *UV*

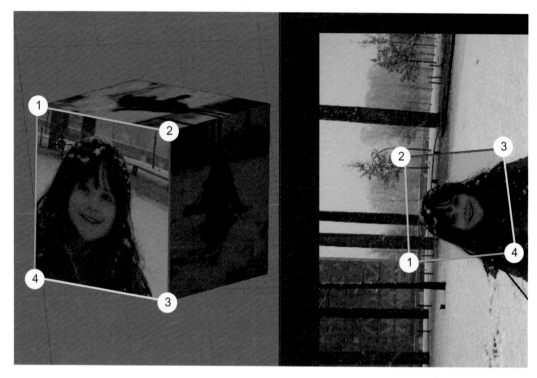

FIG 1.13 The UV mapping process. Vertices of a polygon on an object are mapped to locations on a 2D image.

mapping. This aligns points on an image with vertices of each polygon. The part of the image between the points is then stretched across the polygon. This process is shown on a square polygon in Figure 1.13.

To add a tactile look to the surface of a polygon enhancing the base texture, *bump mapping* is applied. This gives the object an appearance of having bumps, lumps, and grooves without the actual model itself being changed. Bump mapping is often applied to add more depth to an object with respect to the way light and shadow display on the surface. Figure 1.14 illustrates the application of a color and normal map on a soldier mesh taken from Unity.

A variety of other effects also add further texture to a surface. For example, *specular lighting* can make an object look glossy or dull, and *shaders*, small programs that manipulate the textures on a surface, can add a plethora of special effects from bubbling water to toon shading. A closer look at these will be included in later chapters.

1.3.7 Color

In the theory of visual art involving pigments, color is taught as a set of primary colors (red, yellow, and blue) from which all other colors can be created. The color perceived by the human eye is the result of light being

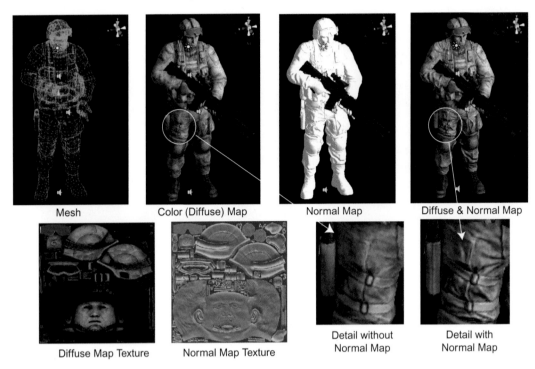

Mesh | Color (Diffuse) Map | Normal Map | Diffuse & Normal Map

Diffuse Map Texture | Normal Map Texture | Detail without Normal Map | Detail with Normal Map

FIG 1.14 A soldier mesh with and without a color map and normal map.

reflected off the surface of the artwork. When all of the light is reflected, we see white. When none of the light is reflected, we see black. The resulting color of a mixture of primaries is caused by some of the light being absorbed by the pigment. This is called a *subtractive* color model, as the pigments subtract some of the original light source before reflecting the remainder.

The light from a digital display follows an additive color model. The display emits different colors by combining the primary sources of red, green, and blue light. For this reason, color is represented in computer graphics as a three or four numbered value in the format (red, green, blue, alpha). In some formats, the alpha value is not used, making color a three value representation.

Alpha represents the transparency of a color. When a surface has a color applied with an alpha of 0, it is fully transparent; when it has a value of 1 it is totally opaque. A value of 0.5 makes it partially transparent. Values for red, green, and blue also range between 0 and 1, where 0 indicates none of the color and 1 all of the color. Imagine the values indicate a dial for each colored lamp. When set to 0 the lamp is off and when set to 1 it is at full strength—any values in between give partial brightness. For example, a color value of (1,0,0,1) will give the color red. A color value of (1,1,0,1) will give the color yellow. The easy way to look up values for a color is to use the color picker included with most software including MS Word and Adobe Photoshop. The color picker from Adobe Photoshop is shown in Figure 1.15.

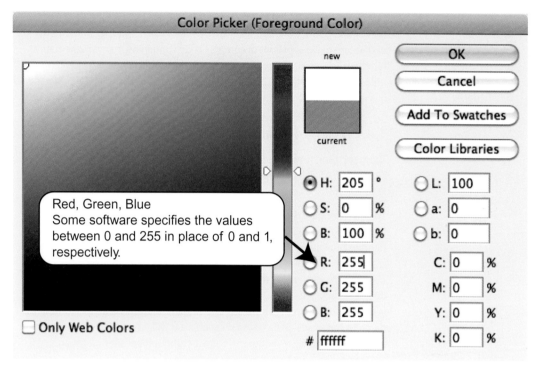

FIG 1.15 The Adobe Photoshop color picker.

- **Note**

An alternate way to set the value of a color is with values between 0 and 255 instead of between 0 and 1. It depends on the software you are using. In programming, values are usually between 0 and 1 and more commonly between 0 and 255 in color pickers.

Also included with most color pickers is the ability to set the color using different color models. The one shown in Figure 1.15 includes a Hue, Saturation, and Brightness model, as well as a CMYK model. For more information on these, check out http://en.wikipedia.org/wiki/Color_model.

1.4 How Game Engines Work

A game engine takes all the hard work out of creating a game. In the not so distant past, game developers had to write each game from scratch or modify older similar ones. Eventually game editor programs started to surface that allowed developers to create games without having to write a lot of the underlying code.

The game engine takes care of things such as physics, sound, graphics processing, and user input, allowing game developers to get on with the creation of high-level game mechanics. For example, in Unity, physical properties can be added to a ball with the click of a button to make it react to gravity and bounce off hard surfaces. Driving these behaviors, embedded in the engine, are millions of lines of complex code containing many mathematical functions related to real-world physics. The game developer can spend more time designing what the ball looks like and even selecting the type of material it is made from without having a background in Newtonian physics.

1.4.1 A Generic Game Engine

To understand how a game engine works, we will first look at a simple illustration of all its components. A conceptualization is shown in Figure 1.16.

The game engine is responsible for the running of a variety of components that manage all the game resources and behaviors. The *Physics Manager* handles how game objects interact with each other and the environments by simulating real-world physics. The *Input Manager* looks after interactions between the player and the game. It manages the drawing of graphical user interfaces and the handling of mouse clicks and the like. The *Sound Manager* is responsible for initializing and controlling how sound is delivered from the game to the player. If 3D sound is called for it will ensure that the right sound at the right volume is sent to the correct computer speaker.

FIG 1.16 Parts of a generic game engine.

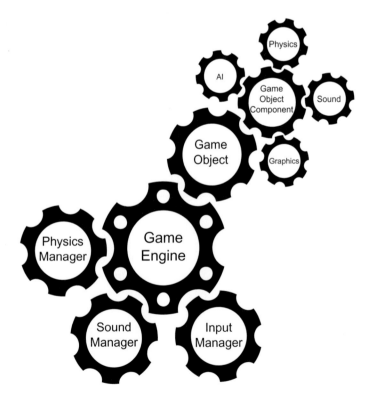

In addition to these managers are game objects. Game objects represent all the assets placed in a game environment. These include the terrain, sky, trees, weapons, rocks, nonplayer characters, rain, explosions, and so on. Because game objects represent a very diverse set of elements, they can also be customized through the addition of components that may include elements of Artificial Intelligence (AI), sound, graphics, and physics. The AI component determines how a game object will behave. For example, a rock in a scene would not have an AI component, but an enemy computer-controlled character would have AI to control how it attacks and pursues the player. A sound component gives a game object a sound. For example, an explosion would have a sound component whereas a tree may not. The physics component allows a game object to act within the physics system of the game. For example, physics added to a rock would see it roll down a hill or bounce and break apart when it falls. The graphics component dictates how the game object is drawn. This is the way in which it is presented to players on the screen. Some game objects will be visible and some will not. For example, a tree in a scene is a visible game object, whereas an autosave checkpoint, which may be a location in a game level, is not.

1.4.2 The Main Loop

All games run in the same way, as illustrated in Figure 1.17. There is an initialization stage in which computer memory is allocated, saved information is retrieved, and graphics and peripheral devices are checked. This is followed by the *main game loop* or *main loop*. The main loop runs continuously over and over again until the player decides to quit the game. While in the main loop the game executes a cycle of functions that processes user input messages; checks through all game objects and updates their state, including their position; updates the environment with respect to game object positions, user interaction, and the physics system; and finally renders the new scene to the screen.

Essentially each loop renders one frame of graphics on the screen. The faster the loop executes, the smoother the animation of the game appears. The more processing that needs to be performed during the main loop, the slower it will execute. As the number of game objects increases, the amount of work the main loop has to do also increases and therefore slows down the time between frames being rendered on the screen. This time is called *frames per second* (FPS).

Game developers strive for very high FPS, and for today's computers and consoles, FPS can extend beyond 600. In some circumstances, however, such as on mobile devices with less processing power, FPS can become very low with only several game objects, and the animation will flicker and user controls are nonresponsive. Having said this, beginner game developers need to be aware of this issue as even on a very powerful computer, adding a lot of highly detailed game objects can soon bring the FPS to a grinding halt. Anything below 25 FPS is considered unacceptable, and as it approaches 15 FPS the animation starts to flicker.

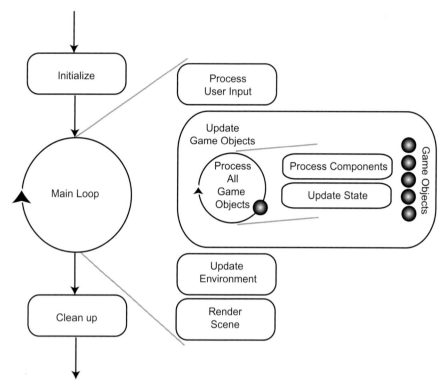

FIG 1.17 How a game runs.

◁ Unity Specifics
Game Objects

Game objects are the fundamental building blocks for Unity games. It is through the addition, modification, and interaction of game objects that you will create your own game. After adding a game object in Unity (which you will do in the next section), a variety of components can be added to give the game object different functionalities. In all there are seven component categories. These are explored thoroughly throughout this book. In short, they are *mesh, particles, physics, audio, rendering, miscellaneous,* and *scripts* as shown in Figure 1.18. A game object can have all, none, or any combination of these components added. The game object exemplified in Figure 1.18 has at least one of each of these component types added.

A Mesh component handles the drawing of an object. Without a Mesh component, the game object is not visible. A Particles component allows for a game object to have a particle system added. For example, if the game object were a jet fighter, a particle system could be added to give the effect of afterburners. A Physics component gives the game object real-world physical properties so it can be collided with and affected by gravity and other physics effects. An Audio component adds sound or sound effects to a game object. For example, if the game object were a car, the noise of a car engine could be added. A Rendering component adds special effects to a game object such as emitting light. Miscellaneous components include a variety of effects for the game objects that do not fit within other categories. In Figure 1.18, the Wind Zone component is shown as a type of miscellaneous component. In brief, this causes the game object to become a source of wind for interaction within the physics system. Finally, Scripts are components that contain programming code to alter the behavior of a game object. Scripts can be used for a large variety of purposes and are fundamental to developing game mechanics and tying an entire game together.

In Unity, scripts added to game objects can be written in JavaScript or C#. This book uses JavaScript, as it requires less background knowledge in programming to get started and the syntax is more forgiving than C#.

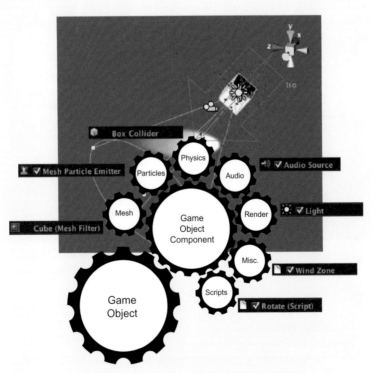

FIG 1.18 Components that can be added to a game object in Unity.

● Unity Hands On

Getting to Know the Unity3D Development Environment

Step 1. To begin, download Unity by visiting http://unity3D.com/ and clicking on *Download*. Unity has a free version that lacks some functionality, but never expires. The free version is still quite powerful and is certainly enough for the first-time game developer. Once you have downloaded the software, follow the installation instructions to get Unity up and running.

Step 2. Running Unity for the first time reveals the multiwindowed editing environment shown in Figure 1.19. The tabs and windows can be dragged around to suit your own preferences.

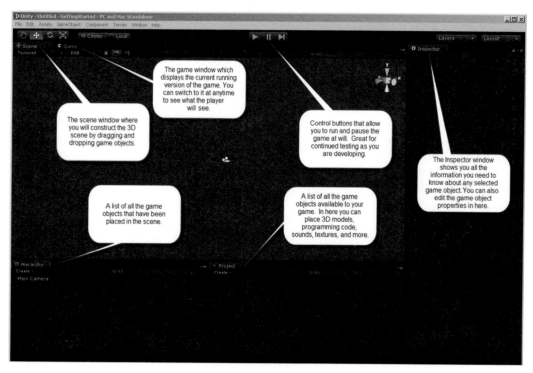

FIG 1.19 The Unity 3 editing environment.

● On the Web

Navigating the Unity Editor Interface

Visit the Web site for a short video demonstrating some best practices for finding your way around in the Unity Editor.

Step 3. After starting Unity, create a new project by selecting File > New Project. Note the project name and directory used to save the project are one and the same; by default, this is "New Unity Project." **Step 4.** To create a simple scene, select GameObject > Create Other > Cube from the main menu. All objects added to a game scene are called *GameObjects* in Unity. A cube will appear in the Hierarchy, Scene, Game, and Inspector windows.

● Note
From this point in the text, these windows will be referenced just by their capitalized names.

Step 5. If the cube appears very small, place your mouse in the Scene and use the scroll wheel to zoom in. Note that your viewing position and angle in the Scene do not affect the look of the final game or change the attributes of any game objects. This initial Scene is shown in Figure 1.20. The Inspector shows all the properties of the cube. This includes its position, rotation, scale, the 3D mesh representing it, and a physics collider. We will look at these properties in more detail later.

FIG 1.20 A single cube in a scene.

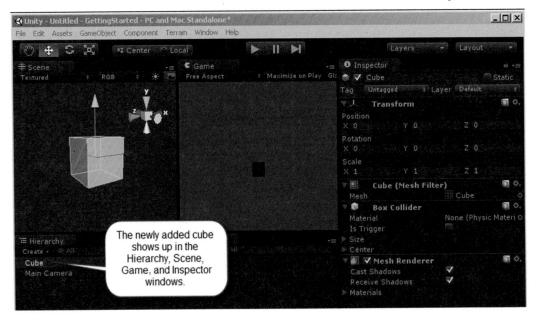

Step 6. At this time, press the play button. As you have not added any functionality at this stage when running, all the game will do is display a static cube.

Step 7. Although lighting is a subject usually delayed for more advanced topics in game development, the author always like to add a light to scenes to give them more depth and bring them alive. In the Scene, the cube is already shaded, as this is the default method of drawing. However, in the Game, the cube is a lifeless, flat, gray square. To add a light, select GameObject > Create Other > Directional Light from the main menu. A light displaying as a little sun symbol will appear in the Scene and the cube in the Game will become brighter.

Step 8. Now because we are looking at the cube front on in the Game, it still appears as a little square. Therefore, we need to transform it for viewing. A transformation modifies the properties of position, rotation, and scale of a GameObject. The specifics of transformation are discussed later, but for now you can transform the cube quickly using the W key for changing position, the E key for rotating the objects, and the R key for scaling it. Before pressing any of these keys, ensure that the cube is selected in the Hierarchy window. When it is selected, it will have a green and blue wireframe displayed on it.

Step 9. In W (position) mode, the cube will be overlaid with red, green, and blue arrows. These represent the x, y, and z axes of the object. Clicking and dragging from any of the arrowheads will move the object along that axis. To move the object freely, click and drag from the central yellow box.

Step 10. In E (rotate) mode, the cube will have red, green, and blue circles drawn around it. Click and drag any of these circles to rotate the cube in the associated directions.

Step 11. In R (scale) mode, the red, green, and blue axes will include small cubes on the ends. Clicking and dragging any of these will change the scale of the object in the respective directions. You may also click and drag the central small cube to resize the object in all directions uniformly. Note that while you are moving, rotating, and scaling the cube that it changes in the Game window accordingly. You will also notice that values in the Transform part of the Inspector change too. Move and scale the cube so that you can see it clearly in the Game window.

Step 12. The color of a GameObject comes from an associated material. To create a material, click on Create in the Project window and select Material. New material will appear in the Project window and, when selected, its properties in the Inspector are as shown in Figure 1.21.

FIG 1.21 Creating new material.

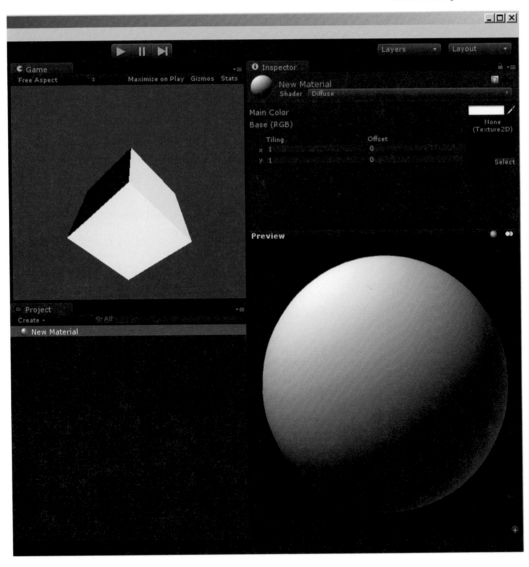

Step 13. To change the color of this material, click on the white box next to Main Color in the Inspector. Select the color you want from the Color Popup and then close it. The large sphere view of the material in the Inspector will change to your chosen color. To change the name of the material, click on New Material once in the Project window. Wait a moment and then click on it again slowly. This will place you in editing mode for the material name. Type in a new name and hit the Enter key.

Step 14. To add material to the cube, drag and drop your material from the Project window onto the cube in the Scene. Alternatively, you can drag and drop the material from the Project window and drop it onto the cube listed in the Hierarchy window. Both will achieve the same effect. The cube will be colored.

Step 15. In the Project window, select Create and then JavaScript. The JavaScript created will be called *NewbehaviorScript*. Change this, by slow clicking on it, as you did with the material, to *spin*.

● **Note**

When you create a new JavaScript file, you only give it a name. Do not add *.js* on the end. Unity will do this for you automatically. However, in the Project, *spin.js* will only appear in the list as *spin*, without the *.js* on the end.

Step 16. Double-click on it and a code/text editor will open for entering code. In the code editor type:

```
function Update()
{
        transform.Rotate(Vector3.up * 10);
}
```

The code must be EXACTLY as it appears here. Ensure that you have the correct spelling and capitalization, as otherwise it may not work. For large spaces, for example, before the word *transform,* insert a tab. When you are done, save your code in the text editor.

● **Note**

The code in Step 15 contains the Unity function *Update()*. Whatever code you place inside *Update()* will be run once each main loop. Therefore, the code in Step 15 will run over and over again for the entire time the play button is down.

Step 17. Return to Unity and drag and drop the spin code from the Project window onto the cube in the Hierarchy window. You'll notice that if you select the cube, the spin script will appear as a component added to the cube in the Inspector as shown in Figure 1.22.

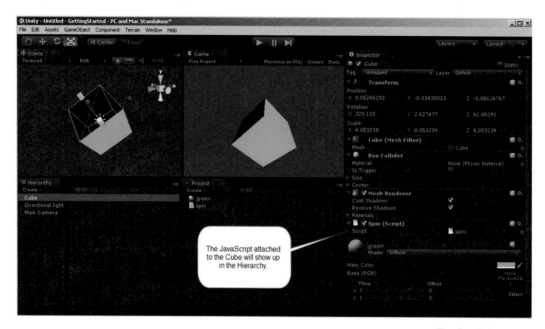

The JavaScript attached to the Cube will show up in the Hierarchy.

FIG 1.22 The cube with the spin script attached.

Step 18. Press the play button and watch as the cube spins.

Step 19. To save the application, select File > Save Scene from the main menu. In the dialog that pops up, give the scene a name such as *spinningCube*. Next, select File > Save Project from the main menu.

Each project you create can have multiple scenes. Scenes are saved inside projects. For example, an entire game application would be a single project. However, inside the game there would be multiple scenes, such as Main Menu, Help Screen, Map View, and 3D View. Single scenes can also be imported from one project to another.

1.5 A Scripting Primer

Hard-core programmers do not strictly consider scripting as programming, as it is a much simpler way of writing a program. Scripting languages have all the properties of programming languages; however, they tend to be less verbose and require less code to get the job done. For example, the JavaScript and Java shown in Listings 1.4 and 1.5, respectively, demonstrate how the scripting language JavaScript requires much less code to achieve the same outcome as Java. The major difference between programming and scripting is that programming languages are compiled (built into a program by the computer) and then run afterward and a scripting language is interpreted by another program as it runs. This book refers to the JavaScript you are about to learn as being *compiled*, when in reality at the technical level it isn't really.

When a program is compiled, it is turned into machine code the computer can understand. Compilation checks through the code for errors and then builds it into a program. Don't worry if you get lots of errors when you start programming. It is a normal part of the learning process. Some of the error messages will also seem quite vague and ambiguous for what they are trying to tell you. However, a quick search on Google will often reveal their true meaning.

JavaScript is used in this book as the primary means of programming. Although it is strictly a *scripting* language, it will be referred to in terms of programming, as it will be used to add computational functionality to games developed in Unity. Its syntax and constructs are also closely related to C++, C#, and Java; therefore, as a beginning language to learn it is ideal. It also provides a very powerful and yet simple way to develop game mechanics in Unity and many other game-editing environments.

Several fundamental constructs in programming are required to fully understand a programming language. These are variables, operations, arrays, conditions, loops, functions, and objects. However, the most fundamental and important concept that underlies everything is logic.

1.5.1 Logic

At the heart of all computers are the electronic switches on the circuit boards that cause them to operate. The fact that electricity has two states, on or off, is the underlying foundation on which programs are built. In simplistic terms, switches (otherwise known as relays) are openings that can either be opened or be closed, representing on and off, respectively. Imagine a basic circuit illustrated as a battery, electric cable, light switch, and lightbulb shown in Figure 1.23.

When the switch is open, the circuit is broken and the electricity is off. When the switch is closed, the circuit is complete and the electricity is on. This is exactly how computer circuitry works. Slightly more complex

FIG 1.23 A very basic electric circuit.

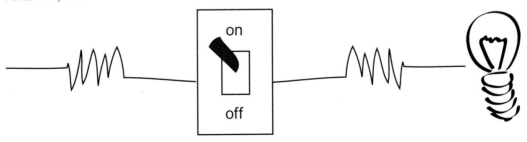

switches called *logic gates* allow for the circuit to be opened or closed, depending on two incoming electrical currents instead of the one from the previous example.

In all, there are seven logic gate configurations that take two currents as input and output a single current. These gates are called AND, OR, NOT, NAND, NOR, XOR, and XNOR. The AND gate takes two input currents; if both currents are on, the output current is on. If only one or none of the input currents is on, the output is off. This is illustrated in Figure 1.24.

In computer science,[1] the operation of combining two currents or signals into one is called *Boolean algebra*[2] and logic gate names (i.e., AND, OR) are called *Boolean functions*, although the *on* signal in computer science is referred to as TRUE or the value 1 and *off* is FALSE or 0. Using this terminology, all possible functions of the AND gate can be represented in *truth tables* shown in Table 1.1. It should be noted from Table 1.1 that truth tables can be written in a number of formats using 1s and 0s or TRUEs and FALSEs.

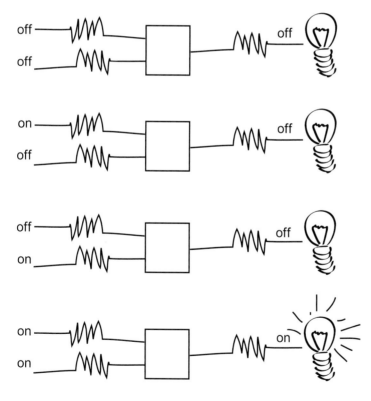

---

[1] And mathematics, physics, information technology, etc.
[2] Named after George Boole, the 19th-century mathematician who first defined algebraic systems of logic.

TABLE 1.1 Truth table for the Boolean function AND

Format 1			Format 2		
Input		*Output*	*Input*		*Output*
A	**B**	**A and B**	**A**	**B**	**A and B**
1	1	1	TRUE	TRUE	TRUE
1	0	0	TRUE	FALSE	FALSE
0	1	0	FALSE	TRUE	FALSE
FALSE	FALSE	FALSE	FALSE	FALSE	FALSE

Each Boolean function has its own unique truth table. They work in the same way as the AND function does. They have two input values of TRUE and/or FALSE and output a value of TRUE or FALSE.

If you are just learning about programming for the first time right now, these concepts may seem a bit abstract and disconnected from real programming. However, as you learn more about programming, you'll realize how fundamental knowing these truth tables is to a holistic understanding. It will become much clearer as you begin to write your own programs.

● Quick Reference

Boolean Algebra

Function	Boolean algebra syntax	JavaScript	Truth table		
AND	A · B	A && B	**INPUT**		**OUTPUT**
			A	B	A AND B
			0	0	0
			0	1	0
			1	0	0
			1	1	1
OR	A + B	A || B	**INPUT**		**OUTPUT**
			A	B	A OR B
			0	0	0
			0	1	1
			1	0	1
			1	1	1

NOT	$\overline{A}$	! A	INPUT	OUTPUT
			A	NOT A
			0	1
			1	0

NAND	$\overline{A \cdot B}$	!(A && B)	INPUT		OUTPUT
			A	B	A NAND B
			0	0	0
			0	1	1
			1	0	1
			1	1	0

NOR	$\overline{A + B}$	!(A || B)	INPUT		OUTPUT
			A	B	A NOR B
			0	0	1
			0	1	0
			1	0	0
			1	1	0

XOR	$A \oplus B$	(A && !B) || (!A && B)	INPUT		OUTPUT
			A	B	A XOR B
			0	0	0
			0	1	1
			1	0	1
			1	1	0

XNOR	$A \odot B$	(!A && !B) || (A && B)	INPUT		OUTPUT
			A	B	A XNOR B
			0	0	1
			0	1	0
			1	0	0
			1	1	1

● On the Web Site
Interactive Boolean Algebra Logic Gates
Navigate to the book's Web site for an interactive Unity version of Boolean algebra.

1.5.2 Comments

Comments aren't actually programming code. They are, however, inserted lines of freeform text totally ignored by the compiler. They allow you to insert explanations about your code or little reminders to what your code does. They are *very* useful when you write some ground-breaking code, leave it for 6 months, and then come back to it, having forgotten what it does. The author's advice is to use comments as frequently as possible. It is common practice to place comments at the top of each program file to give an overview of the entire code, as well as above each function. Another programmer may also insert comments if he makes a change. Some examples are shown in Listing 1.7.

Listing 1.7 A Short Program with Comments

```
/*Program: spin.js
Description:     Will rotate any game object around the y axis
Author:         Penny de Byl
Date:           12/08/2010
*/
function Update()
{
       //rotate around the vertical axis with a speed of 10
       transform.Rotate(Vector3.up * 10);

}
```

There are two types of comments. The first is a way to block out an entire paragraph. It begins with a /* and ends with a */. You can write anything you want between these characters and it will be totally ignored by the compiler. The second type is a one liner. A line starting with // will also be ignored by the compiler, but only until the end of the line. Therefore, you could write this:

```
       /* Here are some comments about my program I wrote
   to control a spinning cube in Unity. I used the code I
   found in the Script Reference after doing a search for the
   word Rotate.*/
```

or this:

```
       //Here are some comments about my program I wrote to
   control a
       //spinning cube in Unity. I used the code I found in the
       //Script Reference after doing a search for the
   word Rotate.
```

Use comments wisely and as you see fit. It is quite legitimate to write an entire program without comments; however, be warned, when you come back to code several months later you'll be glad you did.

1.5.3 Functions

A *function* is a block that bundles a number of lines of code together to form a specific operation. It contains prewritten code that can be reused over and over again, saving programmers the stress of reinventing the wheel each time they write a program. Programmers can also write their own functions.

Whenever the author thinks of functions, she visualizes them as food processing machines. You put vegetables in, they get processed, and you get chopped, mashed, or minced vegetables out.

The most common newbie function taught is *print()* or a derivative thereof. This function takes input and prints it to the screen. For example,

```
print("Hello Unity");
```

will print

```
Hello Unity
```

on the screen or console.

Functions available to you as a programmer will depend on the programming language. JavaScript has numerous standard functions but also takes on added ones depending on the context. For example, when JavaScript is embedded into the HTML of a webpage,

```
document.write("Hello Unity");
```

will display the text on the webpage when viewed inside a browser. To define your own function in JavaScript, the format is that shown in Listing 1.8.

Listing 1.8 Code Syntax for an Empty Function

```
function myFunctionName(input list)
{
}
```

A function declaration begins with the *keyword* function, followed by its name and then a list of input values.

While functions are a programming element usually introduced to new programmers further down the track, they are fundamental to writing JavaScript code for Unity and therefore are being explained up front.

◁ **Unity Specifics**
Functions

Several essential JavaScript functions need to be included in your script to talk to Unity. As Unity is running your game, it will look through code attached to all game objects for functions it needs to execute at any particular time. For example, the *Update()* function runs once each main loop. If there are five game objects each with *Update()* functions in their scripts, then all five *Update()* functions will be executed.

Another useful function is *Start()*. This function runs just once during the lifetime of the game object. Think of it as an initialization method for a game object. You can use it to set initial states and values for a game object. It does not run over and over again like the *Update()* function and therefore is a good place to put code that does not need to run for the life of the game object. For example, if you want to constantly rotate an object like that in Listing 1.7, then it makes sense for the rotation to occur each loop. However, if you want to set the color of a game object to red, coding it in an *Update()* function will just cause the same command to run over and over again. Once the object is red, there is no need to keep setting it to red. A more suitable place to make an object red would be in the *Start()* function. It is set to red just once.

Remember, code inside *Update()* runs each main loop and each line of code in the main loop will cause it to run slower, albeit a minute amount, but superfluous code can soon add up to huge drops in frame rates.

● **For Research**
More Unity Functions

More Unity-specific functions will be revealed throughout the book as needed. If you are interested in other available functions, go to the *Script Reference*, type *Monobehavior* in the search, and have a look at the *Overridable Functions*. These are the ones you can use in your JavaScript.

1.5.4 Variables

A *variable* is the name of a piece of computer memory allocated for your program. Think of it as a storage box that you can put things into, take things out of, add to, and change. A variable in programming is similar to a variable in algebra that holds a numerical value. However, in programming, pretty much anything can be placed into a variable. In the line of code,

```
x = 50;
```

x is the name of the variable and it has a value of 50. If you continued with

```
y = x + 30;
```

another variable called y is being given the value of x (50) plus 30. The value of y in this case would be 80.

The differing types of information that can be stored in variables are called *data types*. These include integers (whole numbers, e.g., 5), floating point numbers (numbers with decimal values, e.g., 3.14), characters (a single alphanumeric value), strings (words and texts, e.g., "hello"), Boolean values (e.g., true and false), and other data types made from mixtures of the aforementioned.

Variables don't just exist automatically in computer memory. They must be *declared*. The process of declaring a variable gives it a name, initial value, and a size. Some examples are shown in Listing 1.9.

Listing 1.9 An Example of Declaring Variables of Differing Types

```
var x: int = 10;    //an integer called x with the value 10
var y: float = 5.6; //a float called y with the value 5.6
var isSpinning: boolean = true; //a Boolean value set to true
var ch: char = 'a'; // a character called ch with a value 'a'
// a string called myName with the value Penny
//Note: the datatype starts with a Capital "S"
var myName: String = "Penny";
```

If you don't know what value should be placed into a variable you do not need to assign one. For example,

```
var x: int;
```

will create an integer variable called *x* and the value will be set to 0 automatically.

Variables in computer memory can be conceptualized as boxes in a large storage space. The different types of variables have different sized boxes. The smallest box is a Boolean, as you only need to store a value of 1 or 0 inside it. A character is the next size up. It would hold all the alphanumeric characters such as those appearing on the keys of your keyboard and a couple of miscellaneous others. The integer size box is even bigger, holding numbers between −32,768 and 32,767 and a float box bigger again holding numbers with seven decimal digits of significance between 0.000000×10^{-95} and 9.999999×10^{96}. The exact size of the boxes will change depending on operating system and computer processor,[3] but the relative sizes remain the same. A conceptualization of memory allocation from variable declarations is shown in Figure 1.25.

---

[3] If you are interested in exploring this topic more, see http://en.wikipedia.org/wiki/Primitive_data_type.

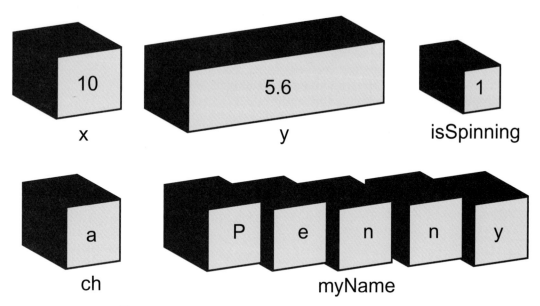

FIG 1.25 A conceptualization of the memory allocation, which occurs from Listing 1.9.

One thing to note from Listing 1.9 is the way characters and strings are given values. A single character is enclosed in single quotes and a string in double quotes. The reason being that if they were not, the compiler would consider them to be other variable names.

This brings us to another matter about naming variables. Variables can be named anything you like, keeping in mind the following. Variable names

- must start with a letter or number (e.g., myNumber, x, 7number, name10)
- cannot contain spaces (e.g., my Number)
- cannot be the same as a reserved word [these are the key words used in the programming language (e.g., var, for, function, transform)]
- cannot be the same as another variable unless it's in a different function (e.g., `var x:int = 10; var x: char = 't'`)

Also keep in mind that variable names can make your code more readable and can reduce the need for comments. For example,

```
x = 10;
```

is ambiguous, whereas

```
accountBalance = 10;
```

has more meaning.

You will notice the use of capital letters in some of the variable names shown beforehand. This is just one convention of using several words in the

36

one name. The capital makes the variable name more readable as single words are easier to read. A variable name could also be written

```
account_Balance
```

using the underscore to separate words. This is a totally personal preference and makes no difference to the compiler; however, naming conventions[4] are recommended. For example, if programming in JavaScript, camel casing for variable names is recommended with the first letter being in lowercase. Because conventions can vary slightly between languages, it will not be covered in this book.

JavaScript Variables

Variables in Unity JavaScript usually appear at the top of the code file. Although they could be placed in a variety of locations, the best place is at the top because they are easy to find. We will examine other types of variables in later sections.

Consider the script in Listing 1.10.

Listing 1.10 JavaScript to Change the *x* Axis Scale of a GameObject on Game Start

```
private var objScaleX: float = 0.5;
function Start ()
{
      transform.localScale.x = objScaleX;
}
```

The line showing the variable declaration is shown in **bold**. Note, do not use bold in your own code; this is for illustrative purposes only. The keyword *private* forces the variable to remain hidden for use inside the JavaScript file in which it is declared. It cannot be seen for use by other code files. You can add many JavaScript files into the same Unity application, and sometimes you will want to be able to share the variable contents between these. In this case, you would declare an *exposed* variable. In this example, the code would be the same as Listing 1.10, except the *private* keyword would be removed.

When a variable becomes exposed, it also appears in the Inspector of the Unity Editor where values can be entered manually. The difference is illustrated in Figure 1.26.

---

[4]For more information about naming conventions, see http://en.wikipedia.org/wiki/Naming_convention_(programming).

FIG 1.26 A private and exposed variable in the Inspector.

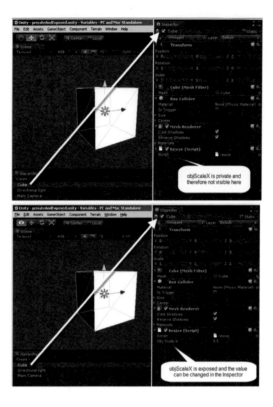

⊙ Unity Hands On
JavaScript Variables

In this hands-on session you will create variables of your own to modify the scale of a cube and explore the differences between private and exposed variables. The starting file is supplied on the Web site for download.

Step 1. Download *Chapter One/Variables.zip* from the Web site; unzip. Run Unity and open the project by using File > Open Project, select *Open Other*, and browse for the *Variables* directory. In the Project, double-click on *cubeResize* to open the scene. In the Scene you will see a white cube. Attached to the cube is the script from Listing 1.10. The objScaleX variable is private and therefore not visible in the Inspector when the cube is selected.

Step 2. Highlight Cube in the Hierarchy and look at the resize script in the Inspector at the very bottom. You'll notice that there are no variables visible. Press play to watch the *x* scale of the cube change. Remember to press stop when finished.

Step 3. Double-click on *resize.js* in the Project to open with a code editor. Note that the objScaleX variable has the keyword *private* at the beginning of the declaration.

Step 4. Remove the *private* keyword and save the file.

When saving a script in the external editor there is no need to close the editor. If you keep it open and just click on the Unity window to switch back it becomes quicker to edit and re-edit script files. You only need to click back and forth between the Unity and script editor windows to move between programs. Just remember to save the script file before switching back to Unity. Unity will automatically reload any script changes you have made.

> **Step 5.** Highlight Cube in the Hierarchy and look at the *resize* script in the Inspector at the very bottom. You will notice that the variable has become exposed.

◐ **Note**
Remember that variable names cannot have spaces. However, because the variable name in this case is constructed with capital letters in it, Unity has made it look like three separate words in the Inspector. *objScaleX* has become *Obj Scale X*. This is only for readability purposes. Your variable is still called *objScaleX* in the script.

> **Step 6.** In the Inspector, click on the 0.5 value for Obj Scale X. This will put the variable into editing mode. Change the value to 0.1 and press play. The cube will now become very narrow.

◐ **Note**
When a variable's value is changed in the Inspector, it does not change in the script. Opening the resize.js in the script editor will review the *objScaleX* variable to still have an initial value of 0.5. Any value you type into the Inspector for a variable will override what you have initialized the variable within the script. This can quickly become confusing when you start changing variable values in the script and expect them to affect the game when nothing seems to happen. If this occurs it is most likely because the variable is exposed and has a value set in the Inspector.

> **Step 7.** Switch back to the script editor. If you have closed this window, it can be reopened by double-clicking on *resize.js* in the Project. Change the value of *objScaleX* to 2.0. Don't forget the semicolon after the value.
> **Step 8.** Save the script and switch back to Unity. The Inspector will still have 0.1 as the value. Playing at this point will give the same results as before. The Inspector value of 0.1 will override the value in your code.
> **Step 9.** To update the Inspector values to those in the script file, click on the wheel/cog icon drop down to the very right next to *Resize (Script)* and select from the list *Reset*. Note that the value of *objScaleX* has been synchronized with the code in the script file.
> **Step 10.** Play the application to see the cube resized to double its width.

Step 11. Switch back to the script editor. Take a look at where the value of *objScaleX* is being used. It is changing the *X* value of the *Scale* in the *Transform* component of the GameObject the script is attached to, which in this case is the cube. This linkage is illustrated in Figure 1.27 showing Unity in play mode and the modified *X* scale in the Inspector.

FIG 1.27 How script links to the values of components attached to Game Objects.

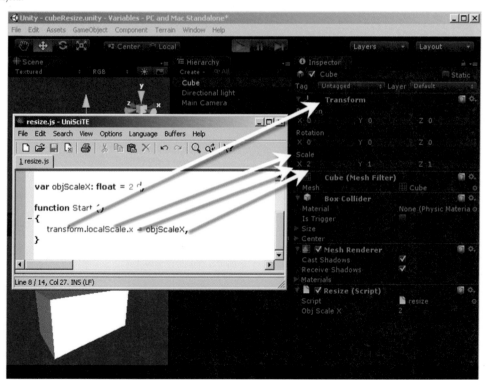

Step 12. In the script, add two more variables for adjusting the *Y* and *Z* scales and some code to link these values to the cubes transform component. The full listing of the new code is shown in Listing 1.11. Modifications are shown in **bold**.

> ● **Note**
>
> *Do not* use **bold** in your own code. Scripting should have no font effects whatsoever. Any coloration or bolding put in by the editor is for your own readability. It is put in automatically. Make use of this coloration and bolding to check that you have keywords spelled correctly.

Listing 1.11 A Script to Modify *X*, *Y*, and *Z* Scales of a Game Object

```
var objScaleX: float = 2.0;
var objScaleY: float = 0.2;
var objScaleZ: float = 0.5;
function Start ()
{
        transform.localScale.x = objScaleX;
        transform.localScale.y = objScaleY;
        transform.localScale.z = objScaleZ;
}
```

Step 13. Save the script, return to Unity, and play to see the changes take effect. Change the values of these scales in the Inspector to experiment with the shape of the cube as the differing scales are changed.

> ● **Note**
>
> When you start programming it is extremely common to make typing errors and to leave out parts of code such as semicolons on the end of lines or missing brackets. If you make a mistake, Unity will detect it and give an error message. It shows up in red at the very bottom of the Unity window, as shown in Figure 1.28. If you get an error, double-click on the red message and Unity will take you to the line in the script editor where the error occurred. From there you can fix it, save the file, and return to Unity to try again.

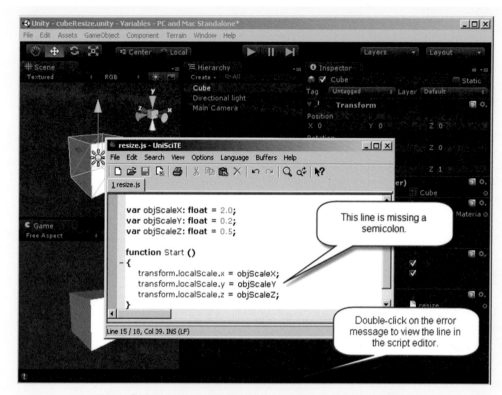

FIG 1.28 The Unity error message displayed when a semicolon is missing from a line of code.

1.5.5 Operators

There are two main types of operators in programming: *arithmetic operators* perform mathematical operations between variables and values and *relational operators* compare variables and values.

Arithmetic Operators

Basic math operators are shown in Table 1.2.

The assignment operator you may be more familiar with as an equal sign and the multiplication and division operators are a little different to those used in traditional math. Note from the JavaScript examples in Table 1.2 that values are placed into variables using the assignment operator. To use values already stored in a variable you simply refer to them in the equations using their name. It is exactly the same as high school algebra. More complex equations can also be created, such as

$$x = (y + z) / 3 + 8;$$

where parentheses work for order of precedence as they do in traditional algebra (e.g., the $y + z$ between the parentheses would be calculated first).

TABLE 1.2 Common math operators used in all programming languages

Operator	Arithmetic performed	Example in JavaScript	Value of x from example
=	Assignment	x = 2;	2
+	Addition	y = 5; x = y + 3;	8

-	Subtraction	y = 15;
		z = 5;
		x = z - y;
			−10

*	Multiplication	y = 15; x = x * 3;	45

/	Division	y = 15;
		z = 5;
		x = y/z;
			3

Relational Operators

Unlike arithmetic operators that can calculate a plethora of values, relational operators make comparisons that result in Boolean values (TRUE or FALSE). The most common operators are given in Table 1.3.

TABLE 1.3 Common relational operators used in all programming languages

Operator	Arithmetic performed	Example in JavaScript	Value of x from example

>	Greater than	y = 5;
		z = 2;
		x = y > z;
			TRUE

<	Less than	y = 10;
		z = 3;
		x = y < z;
			FALSE

>=	Greater than or equal to	y = 4;
		z = 4;
		x = z >= y;
			TRUE

<=	Less than or equal to	y = 3;
		z = 1;
		x = z <= y;
			TRUE

==	Equal to	y = 12;
		z = 16;
		x = y == z
			FALSE

!=	Not equal to	y = 12;
		z = 16;
		x = y != z
			TRUE

An important thing to note in Table 1.3 is the use of = versus ==. One equal sign means *assign* or place a value into a variable, and the double equal sign means *compare* two values. First-time programmers often get these mixed up but with practice the differences become clear.

◉ Unity Hands On
Operators

Step 1. Download *Chapter One/Operators.zip* from the Web site, unzip, and open in Unity. In the Project, double-click on *dynamicResize* to open the scene. In the Scene you will see a small white sphere. Attached to the sphere is the script called *grow.js*.

Step 2. Double-click on *grow.js* in the Project to open the script editor. Note that there is already a variable added called *growthRate*. Modify the script to reflect the one in Listing 1.12.

Listing 1.12 Script to Grow a Game Object by 0.05 in Scale in Each Game Update

```
var growthRate: float = 0.05;
function Update ()
{
        transform.localScale.x
            = transform.localScale.x + growthRate;
        transform.localScale.y
            = transform.localScale.y + growthRate;
        transform.localScale.z
            = transform.localScale.z + growthRate;

}
```

Step 3. Save the script and play in Unity. Note how the sphere grows slowly in size. This will continue until you stop playing. The Update function continues to run over and over again while the application is playing. Functions will be explored in depth later. For now, a simplistic explanation of what is happening is that the growthRate is continually being added to the current value of the localScale, thus updating it.

Step 4. Click on the Sphere in the Hierarchy. Ensure that you can see the Scale part of the Transform component in the Inspector. Now press play and watch as the *x, y,* and *z* values of the scale change constantly.

Step 5. In the Project, select *Create* and add a new JavaScript file. Call it *revolve*. To the file add the code in Listing 1.13.

Listing 1.13 A Script to Move a Game Object in a Circle

```
var radius: float = 5;
function Update ()
{
      transform.position.x =
          radius * Mathf.Sin(Time.fixedTime);
      transform.position.y =
          radius * Mathf.Cos(Time.fixedTime);
}
```

Step 6. This new JavaScript file can be added to the Sphere while the *grow* script is still attached. Select *revolve* in the Project and drag and drop it onto the Sphere in the Hierarchy. Select Sphere in the Hierarchy and check the Inspector to see that *revolve* is attached. If it is not attached, try the drag and drop process again.

Step 7. Play the application. The Sphere will resize slowly while moving in a circular motion.

● **Note**

The parametric form for a circle is used in Listing 1.13 to move a sphere around the circumference of a circle. These equations are based on modifying the *x* and *y* positions with cosine and sine functions and the time. The value of *Time.fixedTime* is a built-in Unity variable holding the time in seconds since the application started running. It is therefore a dynamic and constantly changing value. Unity also contains functions for all mathematical operations, such as *Mathf.Sin()* and *Mathf.Cos()*.

It is not expected at this early stage in learning Unity to know this type of information. However, it can be handy to know where to find it, and the most **invaluable resource** you should have at your disposal is the *Unity Scripting Reference*. To access this information, while in Unity, select Help > Script Reference from the main menu. In the Web site that opens, try searching for *Mathf* and *Time* to see what is available to you.

1.5.6 Conditional Statements

Conditional statements allow the flow of a program to change when certain conditions are met (or not met). They rely on Boolean algebra for making decisions on which way code should flow. Conditional statements can divert code to other parts of code or can make the same statement of code repeat over and over.

Conditional statements, which are essentially the programmed form of Boolean algebra, cannot operate on their own. They need constructs around them to assess their value. The simplest form of these is an *if-else statement*.

Used quite a lot in simple artificial intelligence programming, if-else statements make an assessment of a statement and do one thing if that statement is true and another (or nothing) if it is false. The if-else statement was used in the logic circuit application mentioned earlier in the chapter. Think of it as the type of logic you might use in deciding whether or not to wear a raincoat, thus:

```
if it is raining
wear a raincoat
otherwise
don't wear a raincoat
```

The if-else statement in JavaScript looks like that in Listing 1.14.

Listing 1.14 An if-else Statement

```
if (test)
{
        //if the value of test is true do this bit;
}
else
{
        //if the value of test is false do this bit;
}
```

For example, consider the script in Listing 1.15.

Listing 1.15 An Example Script Using an if-else Statement

```
var x:int = 5;
var y:int = 10;
if( x > y)
{
        print("X is greater than.Y");
}
else
{
        print("Y is greater than or equal to X");
}
```

This program will print out "Y is greater than or equal to X" because the conditional statement inside the parentheses of the if statement will equate to false. If X were given a value of 20, the program would print out "X is greater than Y".

⊙ Unity Hands On

if-else Statements

Step 1. Download *Chapter One/ifelse.zip* from the Web site, unzip, and open in Unity. In the Project, double-click on *falling* to open the scene. In the Scene you will see a small white sphere. Attached to the sphere is the script called *fallandgrow.js*.

Step 2. Play the application. The sphere will appear to fall as its *y* position is changed constantly by the script.

Step 3. Open the *fallandGrow.js* script and make the changes shown in Listing 1.16.

Listing 1.16 Making a Game Object Fall to a Certain Position and Then Stop

```
var speed: float = 0.1;
var groundLevel: int = -4;
function Update ()
{
        if(transform.position.y > groundLevel)
        {
                //keep moving down
                transform.position.y = transform.position.y - speed;
        }
}
```

Step 4. Save and play. Watch as the sphere moves down the screen until it stops. What is occurring is that the *y* position is constantly being reduced by 0.1. While the value of the *y* position remains larger −4, the code inside the if statement will continue to be processed. As point *y* becomes greater than or equal to the *groundLevel*, that line of code is skipped and thus the sphere no longer has its *y* position modified.

Step 5. We are now going to modify the code to make the sphere start to grow when it stops moving. We know it will stop moving when the conditional statement in Listing 1.16 becomes false; therefore, by adding some growth code into an else we can have it execute, but only when the sphere stops moving. Update the fallandGrow.js script to reflect Listing 1.17.

Listing 1.17 A Script to Make a Game Object Fall Down to a Certain Height and Then Grow

```
var speed: float = 0.1;
var growthRate: float = 0.01;
var groundLevel: int = -4;
function Update ()
{
        if(transform.position.y > groundLevel)
        {
          //keep moving down
          transform.position.y = transform.position.y - speed;
        }
        else
        {
          transform.localScale.x =
              transform.localScale.x + growthRate;
        }
}
```

Step 6. Save and play. When the sphere reaches a *y* position of −4 it will stop moving and start to grow along its *x* axis.

The other programming construct that handles condition statements is a *loop*. A loop is a segment of code that runs over and over again until an ending condition is met. There are several types of loop constructs, but for now we are going to have a look at just one, the *for loop*.

Consider the code in Listing 1.18.

Listing 1.18 JavaScript for Printing Numbers between 1 and 5

```
var i = 1;
print(i);
i = i + 1;
print(i);
i = i + 1;
print(i);
i = i + 1;
print(i);
i = i + 1;
print(i);
i = i + 1;
```

The output from this code would be

```
12345
```

as the variable *i* starts with a value of 1, is then printed, has one added to the value, and is printed again five times. Imagine printing out all the numbers between 1 and 100. It would be a lot of code.

Enter the for loop. The for loop reduces such repetitive tasks down into a few simple lines. The basic format of a for loop is shown in Listing 1.19.

Listing 1.19 A for Loop

```
for( initialize variable; test value; update value)
{
       //perform some action while the test is true
}
```

The first part of the for loop declares a variable and gives it an initial value. The second part performs a Boolean test on the value of the variable. If the test comes back true, the loop performs the code inside the parentheses. After the contents of the parentheses are finished, the variable value is updated and the test is performed again; if true, the inside part runs again. This continues until the test becomes false and the loop quits.

A for loop to perform the same action as Listing 1.18 is shown in Listing 1.20.

Listing 1.20 A for Loop to Print out Numbers between 1 and 5

```
for( var i:int = 1; i <= 9; i++)
{
       print(i);
}
```

● Note

Listing 1.20 introduces a new type of arithmetic used as a shortcut in programming. Writing

```
i++
```

is identical to writing

```
i = i + 1
```

It is a shortcut for adding one to the value of a variable. You can also write

```
i--
```

which will take one away from the variable i. More shortcut arithmetic is shown in Table 1.4.

TABLE 1.4 Shortcut arithmetic operations and their equivalent longhand

Shortcut	Longhand	Description
i++	i = i + 1	Adds one to the value of the variable and replaces the original value with the new one
i--	i = i - 1	Takes one away from the value of the variable and replaces the original value with the new one
i += 2	i = i + 2	Adds two to the value of the variable and replaces the original value with the new one
i -= 2	i = i - 2	Takes two away from the value of the variable and replaces the original value with the new one
i *= 2	i = i * 2	Multiplies the value of the variable by two and replaces the original value with the new one
i /= 2	i = i / 2	Divides the value of the variable by two and replaces the original value with the new one

⚙ **Unity Hands On**

for Loops

Step 1. Download *Chapter One/forloop.zip* from the Web site, unzip, and open in Unity. In the Project, double-click on *stacked* to open the scene. The Scene will appear empty. Attached to the Main Camera is the script called *stackedSpheres.js*. Play the file. A vertical stack of spheres will appear in the Game.

Step 2. Open *stackedSpheres.js* with the script editor. The code used to create the stack of spheres is inside the Start function. Each sphere is created individually and its *y* position is changed by 1 with each new sphere.

Step 3. Modify each line like this

```
sphere = GameObject.CreatePrimitive(PrimitiveType.Sphere);
```

to this

```
sphere = GameObject.CreatePrimitive(PrimitiveType.Cube);
```

Step 4. Save the script and replay the application. The stack of spheres will be replaced with a stack of cubes.

Although the sphere is being changed to a cube, note that the variable called *sphere*, which is being assigned the Game Object, does not need to be changed. This is because the name of a variable as far as the compiler is concerned is not important. It is only named sphere in this case for readability. It could have easily been called *aPrimitive* or *aP*.

Step 5. Imagine that you now need to add another 50 cubes on top. This would be a big cut and paste and editing job as the *y* position would need to be incremented for each new cube. Instead we will replace all the code with just three lines (and a couple of parentheses) that will allow you to make the stack any height you like. Modify *stackedSpheres.js* to the code shown in Listing 1.21.

Listing 1.21 Creating a Stack of Cubes with a for Loop

```
function Start ()
{
        var aP : GameObject;

        for(var i:int = 1; i <= 9; i++)
        {
                aP = GameObject. CreatePrimitive(PrimitiveType.
                        Cube);
                aP.transform.position.y = i;
        }
}
```

● **Note**
Although the variable *aP* in Listing 1.21 does not have the keyword *private* included, it *will not* become exposed. Variables declared inside functions are called *local variables* and are only visible inside the function that created them.

Step 6. Save and play the application. It will produce the same result as the previous version. Note how the value of the variable *i* is being used to set the *y* position of each cube? Just another advantage of using a for loop.

Step 7. To put even spaces between each cube, change the line

```
        aP.transform.position.y = i;
```

to

```
        aP.transform.position.y = i * 2;
```

Step 8. Save and play to see the spaces created between the cubes.

Step 9. To create another set of cubes horizontally in the Game, add another for loop as shown in Listing 1.22. Note the use of the new variable *j* as the *x* position.

Listing 1.22 A Script That Creates One Column and One Row of Cubes

```
function Start ()
{
        var aP : GameObject;

        for(var i:int = 1; i <= 9; i++)
        {
                aP = GameObject.
                        CreatePrimitive(PrimitiveType.Cube);
                aP.transform.position.y = i * 2;
        }

        for(var j:int = 1; j <= 9; j++)
        {
                aP = GameObject.
                        CreatePrimitive(PrimitiveType.Cube);
                aP.transform.position.x = j * 2;
        }
}
```

Step 10. Save and play. The result will look like that in Figure 1.29. You may need to move the camera around to see all the cubes.

Step 11. A few readjustments to this code can give you the power to create a matrix of 9 × 9 cubes. By placing one for loop inside the other, the nine repetitions of the horizontally placed cubes are compounded by the nine repetitions of the vertical cubes. Modify your code to that in Listing 1.23. On the first pass of the outer loop, the inner loop runs nine times. Then the outer loop moves onto its second pass. At this time the inner loop runs nine times again. This continues until the outer loop has finished its nine passes.

Listing 1.23 A Matrix of Cubes Created Entirely with Script

```
function Start ()
{
        var aP : GameObject;
        var numRows: int = 9;
        var numCols: int = 9;
```

```
for(var row:int = 1; row <= numRows; row++)
{
      for(var col:int = 1; col <= numCols; col++)
      {
            aP = GameObject.
                  CreatePrimitive(PrimitiveType.Cube);
            aP.transform.position.x = col * 2;
            aP.transform.position.y = row * 2;
      }
}
}
```

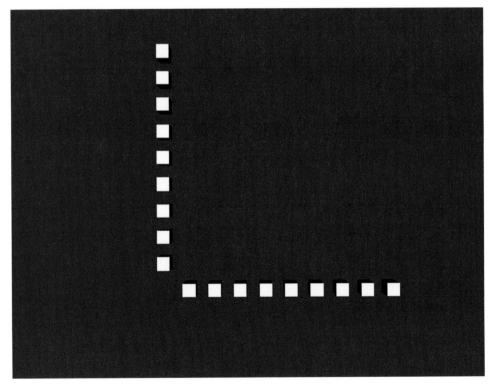

FIG 1.29   A column and row of cubes created entirely with script.

Step 12. Save and play to see the matrix of cubes as shown in Figure 1.30.

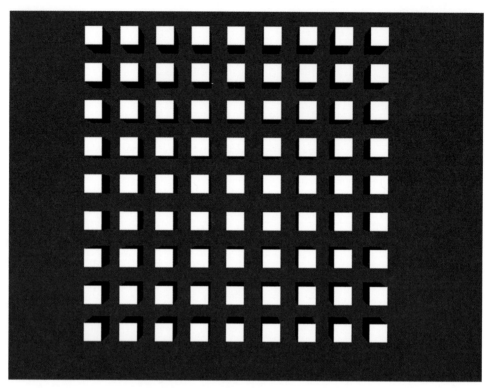

FIG 1.30 Game view of a matrix of cubes created with Listing 1.23.

1.5.7 Arrays

Sometimes a single variable is a less efficient way of storing data and objects. For example, consider changing the color of each of the cubes created in Listing 1.21, not initially at the beginning of the program, but randomly and constantly while it is running. In Listing 1.21, a single variable is used to create nine cubes. However, the variable itself only ever holds one cube at a time. Each time a new cube is created, the variable is overwritten with a new one. This means that after a new cube is created and assigned to *aP*, it is no longer possible to access the properties of the previous cube. Even the ability to change its position is gone. Therefore, we need the variable *aP* to hold not just one GameObject, but nine.

This can be achieved by making *aP* into an *array* as shown in Listing 1.24.

In Listing 1.24, the variable *aP* is no longer a single Game Object but an array. An array can store anything, including integers, floats, and Game Objects. If the original *aP* was a single storage box in memory, this new *aP* is a row of storage boxes where each box has its own index number.

Listing 1.24 Storing Game Objects in an Array

```
function Start ()
{
      var aP:Array = new Array(9);

      for(var i:int = 0; i < 9; i++)
      {
            aP[i] = GameObject.
                        CreatePrimitive(PrimitiveType.Cube);
            aP[i].transform.position.y = i + 1;
      }
}
```

The first box in the array is indexed with a 0. To refer to each box individually, their names are *aP[0], aP[1], aP[2], aP[3], aP[4], aP[5], aP[6], aP[7],* and *aP[8]*. This is the reason for changing the for loop in Listing 1.24 to begin counting at 0. The variable *i* can be used as the array index. The first time the loop runs, *aP[i]* is equivalent to writing *aP[0]*.

Because the *y* position of the first cube was initially 1 and *i* now starts at 0, the position must be set with *i* +1 to keep this consistent.

◉ Unity Hands On
Arrays

> **Step 1.** Download *Chapter One/Arrays.zip* from the Web site, unzip, and open in Unity. In the Project, double-click on *coloredCubes* to open the scene. The Scene will appear empty. Attached to the Main Camera is the script called *stackedColors.js*. Play the file. A vertical stack of colored cubes will appear in the Game as shown in Figure 1.31.
>
> **Step 2.** Open *stackedColors.js* in the script editor. Note that in the *Update()* function only four of the cubes are assigned a color. Also, the array declaration has been moved to the top of the script. This is to make *aP* a global variable available to all functions, not just *Start()*.
>
> **Step 3.** Modify *stackedColors.js* to the code shown in Listing 1.25.

Listing 1.25 Setting an Array of Cubes to the Color Red

```
private var aP:Array = new Array(9);
function Start ()
{
      for(var i:int = 0; i < 9; i++)
      {
```

```
                aP[i] = GameObject.
                            CreatePrimitive(PrimitiveType.Cube);
                aP[i].transform.position.y = i + 1;
        }
    }
    function Update ()
    {
        for(var i:int = 0; i < 9; i++)
        {
                aP[i].renderer.material.color = Color.red;
        }
    }
```

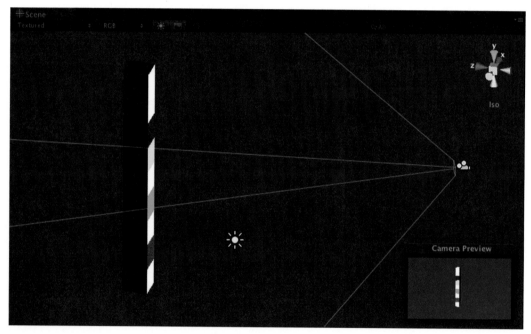

FIG 1.31 A stack of colored cubes
created entirely with script.

Step 4. Save and play. The cubes created will have turned red. If you
want to keep the cubes red, the code in the *Update()* function of
Listing 1.25 would be better served inside the bottom of *Start()* as
there would be no need to keep setting them to red in each main
loop. However, we are now going to modify them to change to
random colors.

Step 5. Modify the Update() function in your code to that in Listing 1.26.

```
function Update ()
{
    for(var i:int = 0; i < 9; i++)
    {
        aP[i].renderer.material.color =
            new Color(Random.Range(0.0,1.0),
            Random.Range(0.0,1.0),
            Random.Range(0.0,1.0));
    }
}
```

Step 6. Save and play. The cubes will change colors constantly. An explanation of the Color function is given in later sections.

1.5.8 Objects

Objects are complex data types. They consist of a bunch of variables (sometimes called *properties*) and functions (sometimes called *methods*). In most of the previous examples, you've already worked with objects. A Game Object is an object. A cube is an object. Most of the items you work with when coding that aren't integers, floats, strings, or characters are objects. A *class* defines the data type of an object.

Let's assume we have a simple class called *Square*. The class definition acts as a template for making many *Square* objects. Figure 1.32 illustrates how

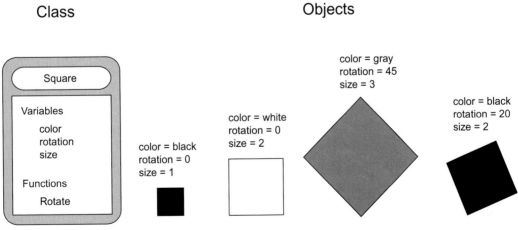

FIG 1.32 A Square class and four instances of the class.

57

the variables of the class can be set to create differing objects. Each object is called an *instance* of the class. In this case, setting the variable values for *Square* allows for a variety of *Square* objects to be created. So although they all look different, they are still squares and retain the essence of a square, which is to have four equal sides and 90° angles.

The functions of an object can be used to set the values of the variables or change the behavior. For example, the *Rotate* function in the *Square* class might update the *rotation* variable and thus change the orientation of the object.

◉ Unity Hands On
Objects

Step 1. Download *Chapter One/objects.zip* from the Web site, unzip, and open in Unity. In the Project, double-click on ChangeObjects to open the scene. The Scene will appear empty. Attached to the Main Camera is the script called *createObjects.js*. Play the file. A capsule will appear in the Game.

Step 2. Open *createObjects.js* in the script editor. Note that *gameObj* is a private variable created to hold a Game Object. In the *Start()* function, it is assigned a *PrimitiveType.Capsule*. The capsule is a complex game object where the attached components are also objects. For example, *Transform* is an object. *Position*, which is a part of *Transform*, is also an object.[5] Visualizations of the Game Object, Transform, and Position classes, along with their locations in the Unity Editor, are shown in Figure 1.33.

◉ On the Web Site
Game Object Definition

All of the variables and functions attached to a Game Object are listed in the script reference at http://unity3D.com/support/documentation/ScriptReference/GameObject.html.

Step 3. To change the location of the capsule you can access the *x*, *y*, and *z* position coordinates via the Transform component of the Game Object. Modify the script to that in Listing 1.27. Save and play.

---

[5] Actually, Position is a *structure*. This is another data type with complex variables and functions. It acts so much like an object that we will just treat it as one rather than complicate matters.

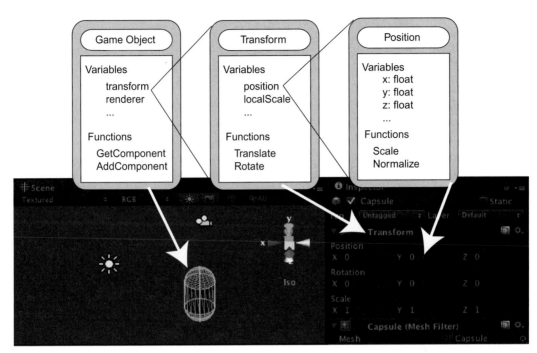

FIG 1.33 The Game Object class containing a Transform class that contains a Position class.

Listing 1.27 Changing the Location of a Game Object with Script

```
private var gameObj : GameObject;
function Start()
{
     gameObj = GameObject.CreatePrimitive(PrimitiveType.Capsule);
     gameObj.transform.position.x = 1;
     gameObj.transform.position.y = 5;
     gameObj.transform.position.z = 2;
}
```

● **Note**

You can always change the location of a Game Object by typing values into the Transform component in the Inspector, although this can't be done while the game is playing. That is why scripting is more powerful.

Step 4. One of the functions available to the Game Object is *AddComponent()*. This script performs the same task as selecting the Game Object in the Editor and choosing an item from Component in the main menu. To add a physics component to the Game Object, modify your code to that in Listing 1.28. Save and play.

Listing 1.28 Adding a Rigidbody to a Game Object Using Script

```
private var gameObj : GameObject;
function Start()
{
        gameObj = GameObject.CreatePrimitive(PrimitiveType.Capsule);
        gameObj.transform.position.x = 1;
        gameObj.transform.position.y = 5;
        gameObj.transform.position.z = 2;

        gameObj.AddComponent("Rigidbody");
}
```

Step 5. The Rigidbody component is used by the physics system. As you play your new script, the capsule will fall due to gravity until it hits the plane in the scene. The collision event will cause the capsule to stop dead in its tracks. If you examine the capsule in the Inspector while the script is playing, you will notice that the capsule has a Collider component. This is used by the physics system to determine the boundary area of the object in order to calculate collisions. You can access the collider and change its values in the script. Modify your script to that in Listing 1.29.

Listing 1.29 Modifying the Physics Material of a Game Object

```
private var gameObj : GameObject;
function Start()
{
        gameObj = GameObject.
                    CreatePrimitive(PrimitiveType.Capsule);
        gameObj.transform.position.x = 1;
        gameObj.transform.position.y = 5;
        gameObj.transform.position.z = 2;

        gameObj.AddComponent("Rigidbody");

        var material = new PhysicMaterial();
        material.bounciness = 1;
        gameObj.collider.material = material;
}
```

Step 6. Save and play. We will examine physics in more depth later in the book. For now, just accept that this new code makes the capsule bouncier, and the physics engine will cause it to bounce when it collides with the plane. *PhysicsMaterial* in Listing 1.29 is another type of object. Note the use of the keyword *new* as it is being assigned. On this line a new variable called *material* is being created and assigned a new *PhysicsMaterial*. The *new* keyword creates an instance of the object. After an instance is created the values can then be manipulated via referencing the variable to which it has been assigned—in this case, *material*.

Step 7. So far we have modified a game object via a script attached to the camera. Scripts can also be attached directly to a game object. From the main menu select GameObject > Create Other > Sphere. A sphere will appear in the Scene. Select the sphere in the Hierarchy and press the W key. Use the axes in the Scene to move the sphere above the plane.

Step 8. In the Project, select Create > JavaScript. Rename the script *spherePhysics*, attach it to the sphere by dragging and dropping it from the Project onto the sphere in the Hierarchy, and open it in the script editor. Add the script in Listing 1.30.

Listing 1.30 Script to Modify Properties of a Game Object to Which It Is Attached

```
var myColor: Color = Color.red;
function Start()
{
        this.gameObject.AddComponent("Rigidbody");

        var material = new PhysicMaterial();
        material.bounciness = 0.5;
        this.collider.material = material;
        this.renderer.material.color = myColor;
}
```

Step 9. Save and play. Now the script is attached to a game object; it can directly reference the object with the keyword *this*. There is no need to create the object because it already exists in the scene. Because the variable *myColor* is exposed, you will be able to change it in the Inspector.

Step 10. From the main menu select GameObject > Create Other > Cube. A cube will appear in the scene. Position it above the plane and to one side of the sphere. Attach the *spherePhysics* script to the new cube.

Step 11. Play. Note that the new cube behaves in the same way as the sphere. This is because the script in *spherePhysics* applies itself to the object to which it is attached. As a result, the cube turns red and falls with the same physics attributes at the sphere. Generic script like this can be added to any game object.

Step 12. Because the *myColor* variable is exposed, it can be changed in the Inspector before playing. Select the cube from the Hierarchy and change *myColor* in the Inspector to green.

Step 13. Play. Note that the sphere remains red but the cube is now green. Both are using the same script but different versions of it. You could also expose the variable for the bounciness and set it to different values for the sphere and cube in the Hierarchy, as shown in Listing 1.31.

Listing 1.31 Exposing a Variable for Bounciness

```
var myColor: Color = Color.red;
var bouncyAmount: float = 0.5;
function Start()
{
        this.gameObject.AddComponent("Rigidbody");

        var material = new PhysicMaterial();
        material.bounciness = bouncyAmount;
        this.collider.material = material;
        this.renderer.material.color = myColor;
}
```

● **Note**

Bounciness in the physics engine is a float that only takes values between 0 and 1 where 0 is not bouncy and 1 is fully bouncy.

1.6 A Game Art Asset Primer

This primer *will not* teach you how to *create* game assets. Such topics are books on their own. It will, however, point you in the right direction to get started creating your own assets, as well as where to find already made ones. Most importantly, this primer will introduce you to the different types of assets and how to get them into a Unity game.

When it comes down to it, there are two types of art assets used in games: 2D and 3D. Two-dimensional art assets are the most used, as everything in the game has a 2D visual element. From trees to buildings, terrain to explosions, and characters to user interfaces they all include 2D art. In addition, normal maps and shading maps are also 2D images.

1.6.1 The Power of Two Rule

Since the inception of computer graphics, people have been trying to create superior and higher resolution images. The quality has not been restricted by the ability of art to create, but by the computer hardware's ability to process. In the mix with computer games is the need to quickly render frame after frame of real-time animation that changes with game flow influenced by user input. Unlike an animated movie in which the contents of each frame are known from the outset, the interactive nature of a computer game means that the artist will never know what will be in any particular frame. The game itself needs to render frames on the fly. This requires a lot of processing power. This is why, over the years, as hardware performance has improved, so too has the quality of game graphics.

However, as a game developer you will still want to push the boundaries of quality and knowing a few simple tricks can help you optimize your art assets to get the best out of the graphics processing. One such trick is to follow the *power of two* rule.

Computers continuously process data in cycles in order to push it through the processors, whether it be the central processing unit or, more commonly for graphics, the graphical processing unit. Processors can only handle so much data in one cycle and therefore it is chunked into packages of certain sizes.

Earlier in this chapter we examined the most elementary values in computing. They were 0 for on and 1 for off. These values are the basis for binary code that is used to encrypt all values in computer memory. The smallest amount of computer memory is a *bit*. It can store either a 0 or a 1. If we put two bits together they can store four values: 00, 01, 10, or 11. Three bits can store eight values: 000, 001, 011, 010, 011, 100, 101, or 111. In fact, the number of values that can be stored is 2 to the power of the number of bits or $2^{number\ of\ bits}$. Therefore, eight bits (called a byte) can store 2^8 or 256 values.

A computer processor has a limited number of bytes it can push through in one cycle. By making an image file a power of two in dimensions, it optimizes the number of cycles required to process it. For example, if an image were nine bytes in size and the processor could process four bytes per cycle, the first two bytes of the image could be processed in two cycles. On the third cycle the ninth byte would be processed. This would mean three whole empty bytes of space wasted during the third cycle.

Imagine it as though you have a dishwasher that can hold four plates. You need to wash nine plates. You would do two full cycles and then have only one plate in the third cycle. For the same amount of dishwashing you could have invited another three guests to dinner! This illustration is exacerbated as file sizes become larger.

If you sacrifice processing cycles, you will sacrifice quality and speed. Ideally, images should have width and height values that are a power of two, for example, 2, 4, 8, 16, 32, 64, 128, 256, etc. The image does not need to be square; for example, the width could be 16 and the height 128. Making an image this size in dimension will lead it to occupy a space in computer memory that is also a power of two in size.

A digitized image is not just the size of its width and height, but also its depth—its *color depth*. The color depth is defined as the number of bits required to store the color values of each pixel. When a pixel is colored according to its red, green, blue, and alpha values that take up 8 bits (1 byte) each, it is said to have a color depth of 32 bits.

Therefore, an image that is 16×32 pixels with a color depth of 32 bits is 16,384 bits in total size. This is equal to 2^{14}; a power of two! Because computer memory processes in chunks whose sizes are also a power of two, it will result in an optimized use of each processing cycle.

But what happens if your texture is not a power of two? Your image will be resized or rescaled. If it is rescaled, the game engine will make it into an image with a power of two width and height closest to that of the original. This means the original image will be squashed or stretched to fit into the new space. This could result in undesirable distortions in the texture. If the image is resized, the original could be cut off or extra blank space added around the edges in order to make it fit into a power of two texture. Either way, the result could be something that you don't want as it may misalign your UV mapping.

◁ Unity Specifics
Textures
Unity will accept nonpower of two images as textures but it will rescale them. It accepts widths and heights of 2, 4, 8, 16, 32, 64, 128, 256, 512, 1024, or 2048 pixels. The majority of image file formats are accepted, including psd, tiff, jpg, tga, png, gif, bmp, iff, and pict. A multilayered psd file created with Photoshop will appear flattened inside the Unity Editor; however, the layers will still be there and editable when reopened in Photoshop.

Unity Hands On
Adding Textures to a Model

 Step 1. Download *Chapter One/Texturing.zip* from the Web
 site, unzip, and open in Unity. In the Project, double-click on
 texturedemo to open the scene. The Scene will open with a shaded
 female model. In the Hierarchy, click on the little triangle next
 to the word Female to expose the entire mesh hierarchy. You
 will now see that the submeshes of eyes, face, hair, pants, shoes,
 and top are listed beneath the parent of Female as shown in
 Figure 1.34.

FIG 1.34 Project view showing
shaded model and mesh hierarchy.

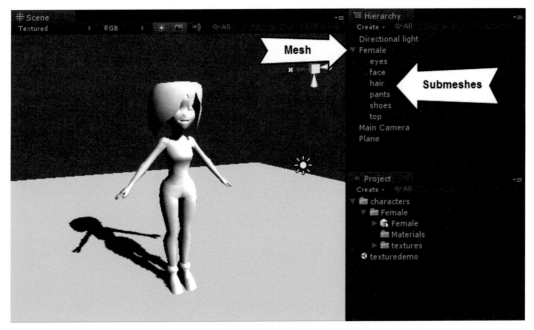

 Step 2. In Project, select Create > Folder and call it Materials.
 Highlight the Materials folder and select Create > Material from the
 small drop-down menu. Rename the material to *top*.
 Step 3. With *top* in Project highlighted, at the very top of the
 Inspector select the *Shader* drop-down list and click on *Bumped
 Diffuse*. The Inspector will reveal the properties of *Main Color*, *Base
 (RBG)*, and *Normalmap* as shown in Figure 1.35.

FIG 1.35 A Bumped Diffuse
Shader opened in the Inspector.

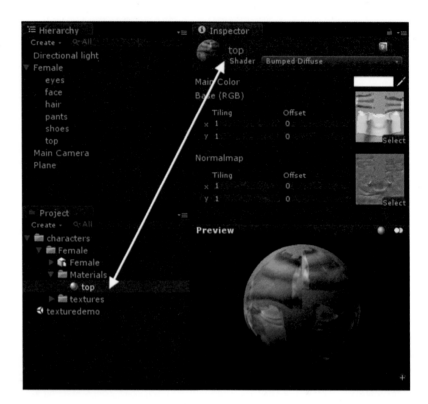

Step 4. The Main Color is a color added to the color of the texture. If you leave it as white it will have no effect. For now leave it as white. In the texture box to the right of Base (RGB) click Select. From the image picker that pops up select the *female_top-1_green*. For the Normalmap, click on Select for the texture box and pick out *female_top-1_normal* by double-clicking on it. If the full name of the texture is not displayed beneath it, clicking once on the image will reveal the full name at the bottom of the picker, as shown in Figure 1.36.

Step 5. Drag the *top* material from Project and drop it onto the *top* mesh in the Hierarchy. In the Scene and Game the model will now appear with texturing on the top of the body.

Step 6. Repeat the process for the face, hair, pants, and shoes submeshes (not eyes), selecting appropriate Base (RGB) and Normalmaps from the texture picker.

Step 7. Create a new material for the eyes. In the Inspector, set the shader for this material to Specular. Select an eye image for the Base (RGB) Gloss (A) texture. The *Specular Color* property for this shader sets the color that is reflected from the surface on any shiny parts. The Shininess value changes the surface value from highly glossy to dull.

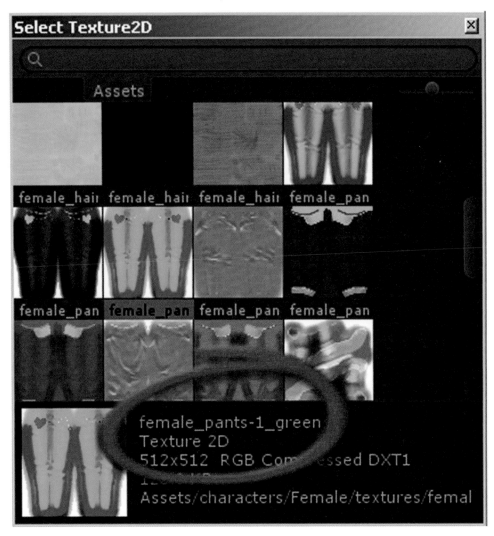

FIG 1.36 Unity's Texture Picker with Image Full Name Selected.

Add the material to the eyes submesh and change the specular color and shininess values to see their effect.

Step 8. To give the ground plane a texture, open a browser window and search Google for "seamless grass texture." Switch the search to *Images*. A seamless texture is one that neatly tiles both horizontally and vertically across a surface where the patterns meet exactly at the seams. Large areas such as terrains use seamless textures as it is less costly than one very large texture. From the search, locate a texture that is a power of two in size (and free to use), as shown in Figure 1.37. Download it to your desktop.

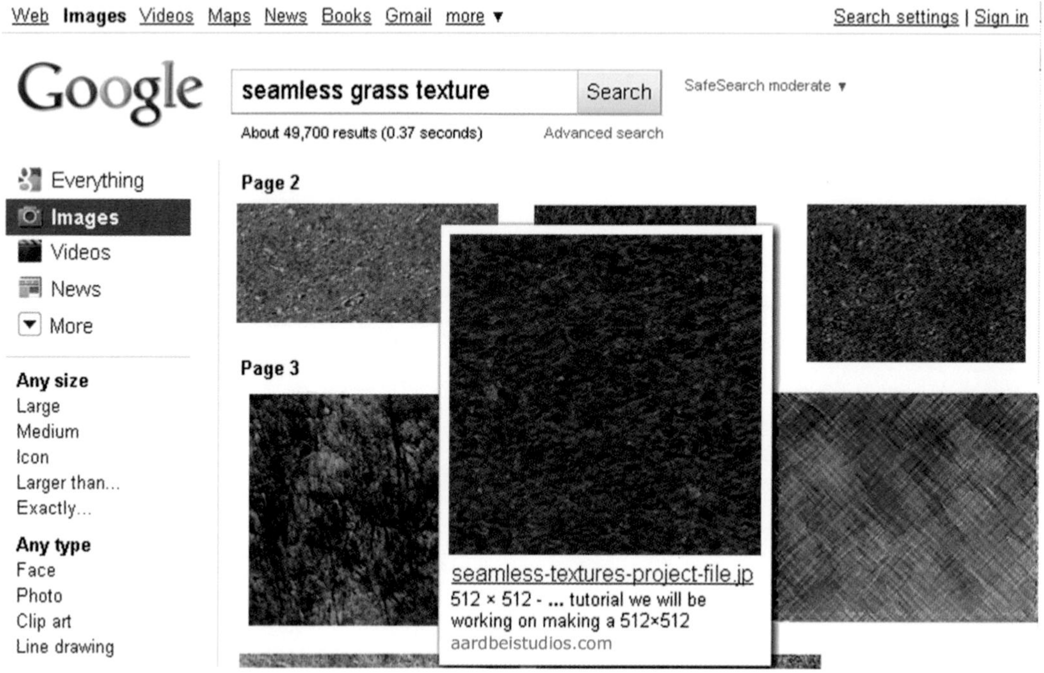

FIG 1.37 A search for seamless grass textures in Google image search.

Step 9. Drag the image file from your desktop and drop it into the Project. Unity will load it for you automatically.

Step 10. Create a new material called *grass*. Leave the shader as the default *Diffuse*. Drag and drop the grass material onto the ground plane. Select Plane from the Hierarchy and find the grass material in the Inspector. Beneath Base (RGB) are Tiling values. These set the size and alignment of the texture on the surface. For example, setting Tiling's *x* to 5 will cause the texture to repeat five times across the surface. The bigger the tiling values, the smaller the tiles. Try setting the Tiling values to see the effect in the Scene.

1.6.2 Using Other People's Art Assets

Sometimes it's not worth your time recreating 3D models and textures when they are available on the Web. For example, if it will cost you a week's worth of work to create a model that someone is selling on the Web for $50, then it is worth purchasing if you can afford it. There are also many free 3D models available for use under a variety of licensing formats. Others are royalty free, which means that you pay for them once and then use them as many times as you like under the terms of the license.

There are many online Web sites for which you can freely sign up and download models for use in your own games. Some of the better ones include:

- TurboSquid: http://turbosquid.com
- Exchange 3D.com: http://exchange3D.com
- 3D Cafe: http://3Dcafe.com/

The model format used most widely and accepted in game engines is 3Ds. This was the original file format created by Autodesk's 3D Studio DOS release. This format can also be created and modified by Autodesk's 3D Studio Max, Maya, and Blender.

● Unity Specifics
3D Models
Unity's native 3D model format is fbx. This can be created with Autodesk's 3D Studio Max. It will also import and use max files, but only if 3D Studio Max is installed on the same machine. The native files produced by Blender are also highly compatible and can be added seamlessly to projects, as can 3Ds formats. To add a model into your project, simply drag and drop it and any associated textures into the Project.

● Unity Hands On
Adding a Model to a Unity Project
Step 1. Create an account on TurboSquid by visiting http://turbosquid.com and following the prompts.

Step 2. Search on Turbosquid for "car" or something else if you wish. Ensure that you set the filter to *3D Models* and sort by *Lower Prices* to have the free models appear first.

Step 3. Look through all the models and select one you like. Note that the file format type is listed beneath the image of the model. Look for a 3Ds, fbx, or blend file. Download the file to your desktop.

Step 4. If the files are zipped, unzip them. Some files will be single mesh files such as a 3Ds; others may have textures with them. Three freely downloaded models and how they unzipped are shown in Figure 1.38: a Ferrari model created with Blender, a 3Ds model of an alien with a texture, and a Mini Cooper Blender model in its own folder.

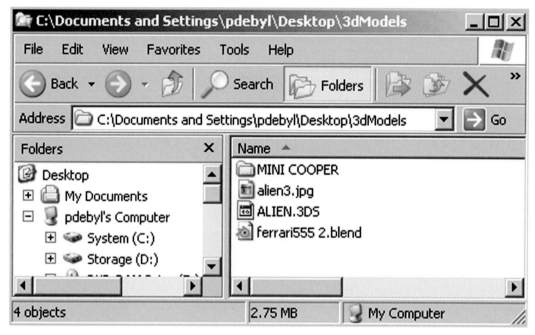

FIG 1.38 How three model files downloaded from TurboSquid appeared with unzipped.

Step 5. To import the models into Unity, select all the files associated with the model and drag and drop into the Project. If the model contains textures, ensure that you have the model file and the texture file in your selection. If the model and associated files are in a folder, drag the entire folder into Unity. The way they will appear is shown in Figure 1.39. Don't worry if you receive a couple of Unity error messages.

Step 6. Using free models is mostly a potluck as to the ones that will work in Unity. Sometimes they will be too big (Unity only allows 65,000 vertices per mesh), inside out, or just missing textures. If the model you get appears this way, go back and find another model.

● **On the Web Site**
A Model That Works
If you are having difficulty finding a model that works, one can be downloaded from the book Web site under *Chapter One/tyrannosaurus_rex.zip.*

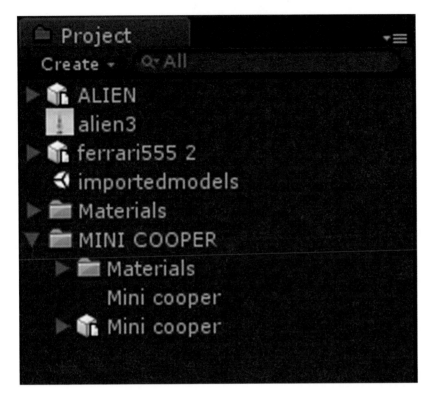

FIG 1.39 A view of the Project after importing three downloaded models.

FIG 1.40 Models imported and viewed in Unity.

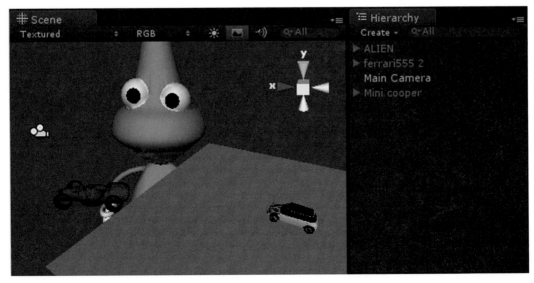

Step 7. Once the models are in the Project, find ones with a small cube icon next to them. Drag these into the Hierarchy or Scene to add them into the application. The three models shown in Figure 1.39 are imported into Unity as shown in Figure 1.40. In this case, the Ferrari model was too big and parts of the wheel are missing, the alien model was okay, and the Mini Cooper included a ground plane. Also note that the scaling for each mesh is different. This will be due to the scaling the original modeler used.

Step 8. To resize the models, select them and use the Inspector to change their scale component. Alternatively, press the "R" key and use the resizing axes in the Scene. If you get a model without any texturing, but have an image for the texture, create your own material, select the texture for it, and apply the material to the mesh.

1.7 Summary

Game art and game programming are two sides of the same coin. This chapter examined the complementary nature that both art and programming play and suggested that anyone can learn to program and anyone can understand the logic behind art. While you may not become fluent in both art and programming, you will gain knowledge, and appreciation for both domains is important for working in the games industry. In addition, it is absolutely necessary for artists working in the area to appreciate the technical limitations placed on their artwork by game engines and computer hardware. Some simple planning ahead and modeling within the restrictions of a games platform can eliminate a lot of future time, money, and heartache.

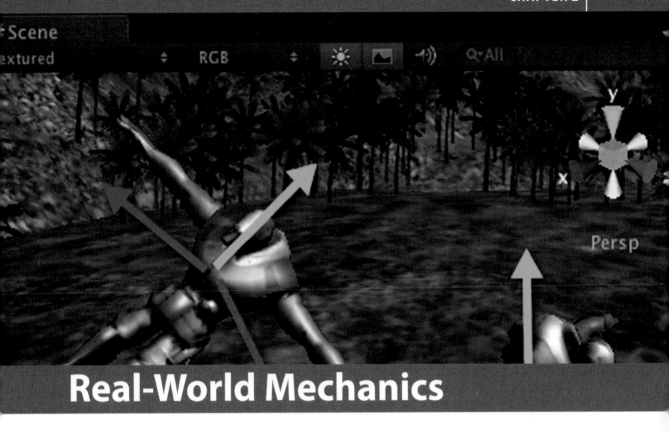

CHAPTER 2

Real-World Mechanics

The player's primary logic operates within the known possibilities of physics. Keep in mind gravity, weight, mass, density, force, buoyancy, elasticity, etc. Use this as the starting point, but do not be limited by it.

Matt Allmer

2.1 Introduction

An understanding of motion and the driving forces thereof is crucial in understanding games. Most objects in games move. That is what makes them dynamic. Whether it be a 2D character such as the original Mario or a fully fledged 3D character such as *Halo's* Master Chief, they and their game environments are in constant motion.

To grasp the concept of motion, especially with respect to computer games, a development of foundation knowledge in vector mathematics is required. Vectors are used extensively in game development for describing not only positions, speed, acceleration, and direction but also within 3D models to specify UV texturing, lighting properties, and other special effects.

Before leaping into the use of vectors in games for defining motion, a crash course in essential vector mathematics for game environments is presented in the next section.

2.2 Principles of Vectors

In Chapter One, a vector was introduced as a line with a length (magnitude) and a direction (indicated by an arrow). Vectors can be used to represent measurements such as displacement, velocity, and acceleration. In 2D, a vector has x and y coordinates. In 3D, it has x, y, and z coordinates. In pure mathematics, a vector is not a point in space, but a set of changing coordinate instructions. It can be likened to the instructions on a fictional pirate's treasure map, for example, take three steps to the west and seven steps to the south. As shown in Figure 2.1, the instructions three steps to the west could be interpreted as the vector (3,0), meaning move 3 in the positive x direction and nothing in the y direction. The instructions move seven steps to the south become the vector $(0, -7)$, meaning move only 7 in a negative y direction.

To determine the final location, vector x and y values are added to the starting point x and y values. For example, in Figure 2.1, the pirate ship lands at (4,8) and moving (3,0) will place them at $(4 + 3, 8 + 0) = (7,8)$. Then moving $(0,-7)$ will put them at $(7 + 0, 8 - 7) = (7,1)$. They can also take a shortcut by going directly in a straight line to the treasure. In this case, the two instruction vectors (3,0) and $(0,-7)$ are added together and become $(3,-7)$. By taking the starting location and adding this new vector, they will end up in the same location [i.e., $(4 + 3, 8 - 7) = (7,1)$].

FIG 2.1 A pirate's treasure map illustrating the use of vectors.

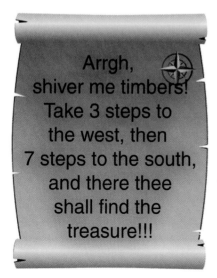

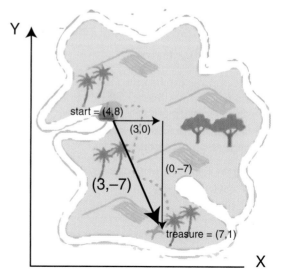

To travel from the treasure back to the ship, the pirates can follow the same line but in the opposite direction. This is achieved by flipping the vector such that all coordinate values are multiplied by −1. In this case, to get back to the ship they follow the vector (−3,7).

It might also be useful for the pirates to know how far the treasure is from the ship. The length of a vector, *v*, called its *magnitude* and written |*v*|, is found using Pythagoras' theorem shown in Equation (2.1).

$$|v| = \sqrt{v \cdot x^2 + v \cdot y^2} \qquad (2.1)$$

For the pirates, it means that their journey is a length of 7.62 (kilometers, if the units being used are kilometers), that is, $\sqrt{3^2 + (-7)^2}$.

Sometimes it is necessary to scale a vector so that it has a length equal to 1. The process of scaling the length is called *normalizing*, and the resultant vector, which still points in the same direction, is called a *unit vector*. To find the unit vector, each coordinate of the vector is divided by the vector's length. In the case of the pirate's journey, this would equate to (3/7.62, −7/7.62) = (0.39,−0.92). If the pirate takes 0.39 steps to the west and 0.92 steps to the south, he will end up a distance of 1 from his starting position, right on the original vector, as shown in Figure 2.2. As can be seen, the vectors (3,−7) and (0.39,−0.92) are parallel and the magnitude of (0.39,−0.92) is 1. The unit

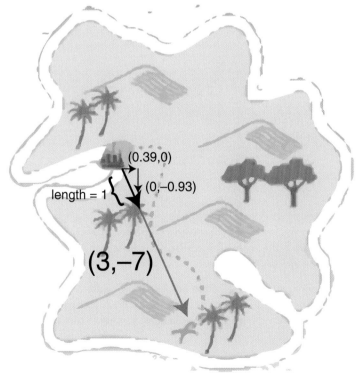

FIG 2.2 A normalized vector has a length of 1.

vectors for north, south, east, and west as they would be overlaid on a map of the earth[1] are (0,1), (0,–1), (–1,0), and (1,0).

Two further important calculations can be performed with vectors. These are the *dot product* and the *cross product*. The use of these in computer graphics and games programming will become overwhelmingly clear later. Among other things, the dot product can be used to calculate the angle between two vectors and the cross product can be used to determine the direction.

The dot product is calculated by taking two vectors, *v* and *w,* and multiplying their respective coordinates together and then adding them. The dot product results in a single value. It can be calculated using Equation (2.2).

$$v \cdot w = v_x \times w_x + v_y \times w_y \qquad\qquad (2.2)$$

Given the vectors *v* = (1,0) and *w* = (3,–7), the direction the pirate is facing and the direction to the treasure (shown in Figure 2.3), the dot product will be $1 \times 3 + 0 \times -7 = 3$.

But what does this mean? The most useful application of the dot product is working out the angle between two vectors. In a moment we will work out the actual value of the angle, but for now by just knowing the value of the dot product you can determine how the vectors sit in relation to each other. If the dot product is greater than zero, the vectors are less than 90° apart; if the dot product equals zero, then they are at right angles (perpendicular); and if the dot product is less than zero, then they are more than 90° apart.

To find out the exact angle the pirate must turn to face the treasure, the arccosine of the dot product of the unit vectors is calculated. The unit vector for (3,–7) is (0.39,–0.92) as already established and (1,0) is already a unit vector. This result for the angle between the vectors is therefore:

= arcos((1,0).(0.39,0.92))
= arcos((1 × 0.39) + (0 × 0.92))
= arcos(0.39)
= 67°

You can always check the result of your calculation by looking at a plot of the vectors and measuring them with a protractor. In this case, by taking a visual estimate, the angle is larger than 45 and less than 90; therefore, the calculation appears to be correct.

Now imagine the pirate is told to turn 67° and walk for 7.62 kilometers to get to the treasure. Which way does she turn? The image in Figure 2.3 shows that a decision needs to be made as whether to turn to the right or the left.

---

[1] This is only for a land map. For 3D coordinates, there are no such equivalents.

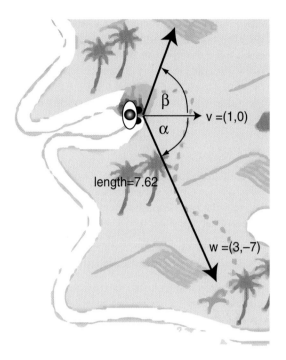

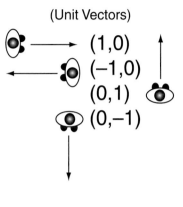

(Unit Vectors)

(1,0)
(−1,0)
(0,1)
(0,−1)

FIG 2.3 A pirate facing (1,0) and the vector to the treasure.

In computer graphics, a positive value for an angle always indicates an anticlockwise turn. An anticlockwise turn in this case would have the pirate facing away from the treasure. When calculating the angle between vectors using the dot product, the angle is always positive. Therefore, you need another method to determine the turn direction. This is where the cross product comes into play.

The cross product of two vectors results in another vector. The resulting vector is perpendicular (at 90°) to both the initial vectors. This sounds odd working in 2D as a vector at right angles to two vectors in 2D would come right out of the page. For this reason, the cross product is only defined for 3D. The formula to work out the cross product is a little obtuse and requires further knowledge of vector mathematics, but we will try to make it as painless as possible.

The cross product of two vectors, **v** and **w**, denoted **v** × **w** is shown in Equation (2.3):

$$v \times w = (v_y w_z - v_z w_y)(1,0,0) + (v_z w_x - v_x w_z)(0,1,0)$$
$$+ (v_x w_y - v_y w_x)(0,0,1)$$

(2.3)

The equation is defined in terms of standard 3D unit vectors. These vectors are three unit length vectors orientated in the directions of the x, y, and z axes. If you examine Equation (2.3) you will notice that there are three parts added together. The first part determines the value of the x coordinate of the vector, as the unit vector (1,0,0) only has a value for the x coordinate. The same occurs in the other two parts for the y and z coordinates.

To find the cross product of two 2D vectors, the vectors first need to be converted into 3D coordinates. This is as easy as adding a zero z value. For example, $\mathbf{v} = (1,0)$ will become $\mathbf{v} = (1,0,0)$ and $\mathbf{w} = (0.39,-0.92)$ will become $\mathbf{w} = (0.39,-0.92,0)$. The value of $\mathbf{v} \times \mathbf{w}$ would equate to $(0 \times 0 - 0 \times -0.92)(1,0,0) + (0 \times 0.39 - 1 \times 0)(0,1,0) + (1 \times -0.92 - 0 \times 0.39)(0,0,1) = 0(1,0,0) + 0(0,1,0) + -0.92(0,0,1) = (0,0,0) + (0,0,0) + (0,0,-0.92) = (0,0,-0.92)$. This vector only has a z coordinate and therefore is directed along the z axis. It is therefore coming out of the page.

An interesting thing to note about the cross product is that if the order of the equation is reversed, the resulting vector is different. $\mathbf{w} \times \mathbf{v}$ would equal $(0,0,0.92)$ (check this out!), which is a vector the same length as the one produced by $\mathbf{v} \times \mathbf{w}$, but traveling in the exact opposite direction. This differs from the calculation of the dot product that yields the same answer no matter what the order of the vectors.

How does this help the pirate determine the direction in which to turn?

If he starts by facing in the direction of $\mathbf{v}$ and wishes to turn to face $\mathbf{w}$, we can calculate $\mathbf{v} \times \mathbf{w}$. If we examine Figure 2.3 it can be seen that w would be on the pirate's right and therefore would require a clockwise turn. We know from the previous example that a clockwise turn between two vectors produces a cross product result with a negative z value. The opposite is true for an anticlockwise turn. Therefore, we can say that if z is positive it means an anticlockwise turn and if z is negative, a clockwise turn.

The pirate now knows to turn to his right 67° clockwise and travel 7.62 kilometers in a straight line to reach the treasure.

This may all seem obvious by looking at the map. However, objects in a game environment that have no visual point of reference, such as artificially controlled bots or vehicles, require these very calculations in order to move around successfully in a virtual environment.

◁ Unity Specifics
Vectors
Every object in Unity has a number of vectors associated with it. A Game Object's transform component has three: position, rotation, and scale. Figure 2.4 shows the layout of a typical game environment with a car model as a game object. Usually, in 3D, the y axis represents up, the x axis to the side, and the z axis forward. Both the environment and all game objects have their own transforms. The axes are displayed in the Scene as red, green, and blue arrowed lines, as shown in Figure 2.4. The y/up axis is green, the x/side axis is red, and the z/forward axis is blue.

The environment has its own axes, and the orientation is set by the way you change the scene around to look at different objects. In the Game,

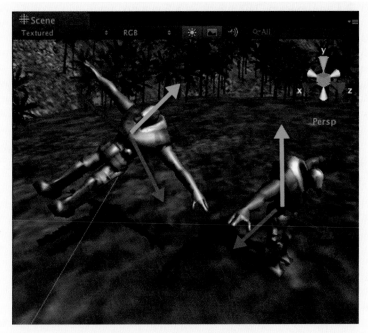

FIG 2.4 Vectors in the Unity 3D environment.

the orientation is dependent on the camera's orientation. Each game object has its own local orientation depicted by a set of axes appearing in the Scene when the object is selected. So while the y axis for the world may be vertical in a scene, it could be horizontal locally for an object that is lying down.

In Unity, there are two vector classes: Vector2 and Vector3. A game object's position, rotation, and scale values are stored as Vector3. Vector2 is useful for storing 2D vector information.

A game object also has a vector for each of its x, y, and z axes: Vector3.left, Vector3.up, and Vector3.forward, respectively. These are useful for moving an object along its axes without needing to know its orientation.

On the Web Site
Vector2 and Vector3 Class Definitions
Detailed information about the Unity vector classes can be found in the Script Reference here: http://unity3d.com/support/documentation/ScriptReference/Vector2.html and http://unity3d.com/support/documentation/ScriptReference/Vector3.html.

2.3 Defining 2D and 3D Space

Whether it is in 2D or 3D space the principles of vectors are applied in the same way. As we explored with vectors, the difference between a 2D coordinate and a 3D coordinate is just another value. In 3D game engines, such as Unity, 2D games are created by ignoring one of the axes. In the rocket ship application shown later in this chapter, all game objects are positioned in the same plane, having a *y* position value initially set to 0. All movements thereafter only move and rotate the objects in *x* and *y*. This is the same principle as moving objects around on a flat tabletop. In the rocket ship game, the camera is positioned directly above the game objects and perspective is removed to give the illusion of a truly 2D world.

The camera in a game is a critical component as it presents the action to the player. It is literally the lens through which the game world is perceived. Understanding how the camera moves and how to set what it looks at is essential knowledge.

2.3.1 Cameras

The camera in a game defines the visible area on the screen. In addition to defining the height and width of the view, the camera also sets the depth of what can be seen. The entire space visible by a camera is called the *view volume*. If an object is not inside the view volume, it is not drawn on the screen. The shape of the view volume can be set to orthographic or perspective. Both views are constructed from an eye position (representing the viewers' location), a near clipping plane, the screen, and a far clipping plane.

An orthographic camera projects all points of 3D objects between the clipping planes in parallel onto a screen plane, as shown in Figure 2.5. The screen plane is the view the player ends up seeing. The viewing volume of an orthographic camera is the shape of a rectangular prism.

A perspective camera projects all points of 3D objects between the clipping planes back to the eye, as shown in Figure 2.6. The near clipping plane becomes the screen. The viewing volume of a perspective camera is called the *frustum* as it takes on the volume of a pyramid with the top cut off. The eye is located at the apex of the pyramid.

The result of using a perspective and orthographic camera on the same scene in Unity is illustrated in Figure 2.7. A perspective camera is used in Figure 2.7a. The way in which perspective projections best show depth is evident from the line of buildings getting smaller as they disappear into the distance. This is not the case for the orthographic camera shown in Figure 2.7b. Depth can only be determined by which objects are drawn in front. The buildings appear to be flattened with no size difference between buildings in the distance. Figures 2.7c and 2.7d illustrate the way in how the camera view volume is displayed in Unity's Editor Scene. If an object is not inside the view volume in the Scene, it will not appear on the screen in the Game.

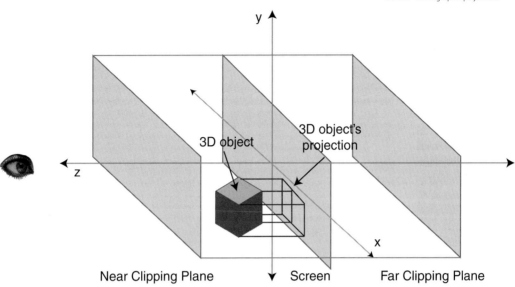

FIG 2.5 Orthographic projection.

y

z

x

3D object

3D object's projection

Near Clipping Plane   Screen   Far Clipping Plane

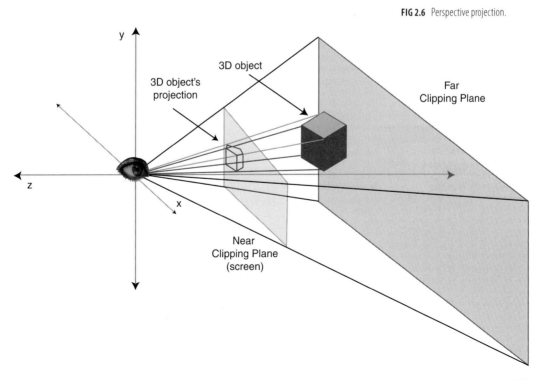

FIG 2.6 Perspective projection.

y

z

x

3D object

3D object's projection

Far Clipping Plane

Near Clipping Plane (screen)

81

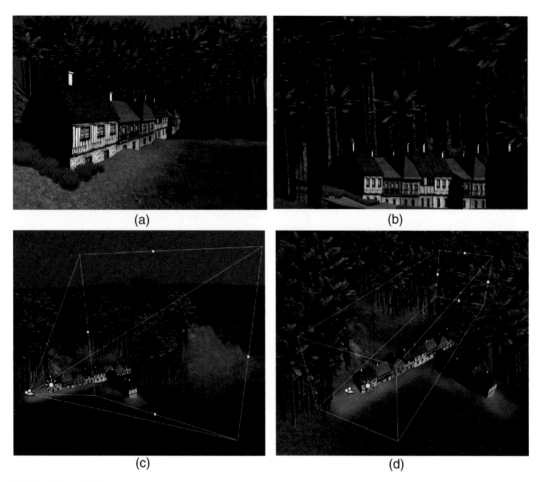

(a) (b)

(c) (d)

FIG 2.7 A 3D scene in Unity using a perspective camera (a) and an orthographic camera (b). (c) The perspective camera's frustum as displayed in the Unity Scene. (d) The orthographic camera's frustum as displayed in the Unity Scene.

◁ Unity Specifics
Cameras

When you first create a new project in Unity it will come with a Main Camera in the Hierarchy. Selecting a camera reveals the settings in the Inspector. Examples for orthographic and perspective cameras are shown in Figures 2.8a and 2.8b, respectively.

While setting the camera values for the near and far planes in the Inspector, the resulting frustum can be watched in the Scene. To change the width and height of the viewing volume, the *field of view* (FOV) is modified for a perspective camera. The greater the field of view, the more the player will be able to see around his immediate area. To get a feel for the field of view, hold your arms out to the side and look straight ahead as if to make a cross figure with your body. Slowly bring your arms around to your front until you can just see both hands out of the corners of your eyes (while looking straight ahead). When your hands come into

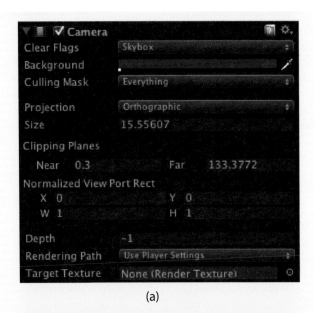

(a)

(b)

FIG 2.8 Settings for the Unity camera.

your peripheral vision, the angle your arms make is your field of view. The average human forward-facing field of view is close to 180° while some birds are capable of almost 360°.

The complementary field of view for the orthogonal camera in Unity is set by the size property.

◉ **Unity Hands On**

Getting Comfortable behind the Camera

Step 1. Download *Chapter Two/CameraPlay.zip* from the Web site, unzip, and open in Unity. In the Project, double-click on *street* of the *Scenes* folder to open the scene. The Scene will appear with a row of medieval houses on a terrain.

Step 2. Modify the window tabs if necessary to enable viewing of the Game and Scene at the same time. Select Main Camera from the Hierarchy. Zoom in or out in the Scene so that the camera and its frustum are in full view. If you can't find the camera, double-click on it in the Hierarchy to bring it into the center of the Scene.

◉ **Note**

To set the Game view camera to look at the environment from the same location set in the Scene, select the Main Camera in the Hierarchy and GameObject > Align with View from the main menu. This repositions the camera to be looking at the scene from your point of view.

To move independently around in the Scene, leaving the camera where it is, hold down "Q" and drag the mouse to pan and hold down "ALT" and drag the mouse to rotate.

Step 3. Locate the Camera component for it in the Inspector. Find the Field of View slider. Move the slider forward and back to change the viewing angle. Take note how the frustum is affected in the Scene and the resulting Game view.

Step 4. Set the Field of View to 60°. This is a popular setting for the FOV in many games. This setting is half the total viewing angle. In this case it gives you 120°.

Step 5. Change the Far clipping plane to 90. Note that half of the background trees are missing in the Game. This is because they are now beyond the far plane and outside the frustum. The background color you see is set by the *Background* property in the camera settings.

Step 6. To watch the effect of changing the far plane distance continually, place the mouse over the word Far, hold down the right mouse button, and drag it left and right to decrease and increase the value in the Far box. This method can be used for changing the values of most properties in the Unity Editor.

Step 7. Now, do the same for the Near clipping plane and observe how the view in the Game is modified.

Step 8. Change the camera to Orthographic by changing the Projection property of the Camera component. Try modifying the size property to see how it affects the Game view.

Step 9. Change the camera back to a perspective projection. Set the FOV to 60 and the Near and Far planes to 1 and 200, respectively.

Step 10. Create a sphere game object and position it at (620,15,715).

Step 11. Select GameObject > Create Other > Camera from the main menu. Rename it to SphereCam. This camera will become the viewing camera automatically.

Step 12. Locate the Depth property in the SphereCam's Camera component. If this property is larger than the depth for the Main Camera, it will be the one that is drawn in the Game. Change the depth for both cameras so that the SphereCam's depth is –1 and the Main Camera's depth is 2. The Main Camera will take control again.

Step 13. Set the SphereCam's position to (0,0,0).

Step 14. Drag and drop the SphereCam onto Sphere in the Hierarchy as shown in Figure 2.9.

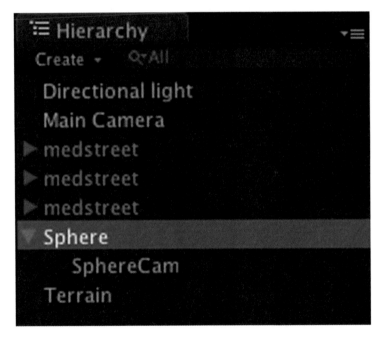

FIG 2.9 SphereCam attached to the Sphere.

Step 15. If you try to play the scene at this point there will be an error reported saying "There are 2 audio listeners in the scene. Please ensure there is always exactly one audio listener in the scene." This is because there is an audio listener attached to all cameras by default. As with the *Highlander*, in the end there can be only one … in your game. The audio listener is the component that listens out for audio sources in the game environment and ensures that they play at the right volume and in the correct speakers. To resolve the error, remove the audio listener from the SphereCam.

Step 16. Create a new JavaScript file and call it *orbit*. Enter the code in Listing 2.1.

Listing 2.1 Script to Make a Game Object Move in a Circular Path Around Its Starting Position

```
private var radius: float = 30;
private var startPosition: Vector3;
private var speed: int = 3;
function Start()
{
     startPosition.x = this.transform.position.x;
     startPosition.z = this.transform.position.z;
}
function Update ()
{
      transform.position.x =
     radius * Mathf.Sin(Time.fixedTime * speed) + startPosition.x;
      transform.position.z =
     radius * Mathf.Cos(Time.fixedTime * speed) + startPosition.z;
}
```

Step 17. Attach the JavaScript to the Sphere.

Step 18. Select SphereCam from Hierarchy such that the Camera Preview window opens in Scene.

Step 19. Ensure that you can see both Game and Scene views and press play.

Step 20. The camera preview for the SphereCam will display a moving scene as the Sphere moves about within the environment.

Step 21. Create a Plane and position and orientate it as shown in Figure 2.10.

Note: Steps 22–25 are only possible in the Pro version of Unity as the free version does not have the option *Render Texture*.

Step 22. In Project, select Create > Render Texture. Rename it to sphereCamView.

Step 23. Select SphereCam in the Hierarchy and in the Target Texture property of the Camera component select and set sphereCamView. If you select sphereCamView from the Project, you will see the view captured by SphereCam on this new texture's surface in the Inspector.

Step 24. Drag and drop the sphereCamView render texture onto the new plane in the Scene.

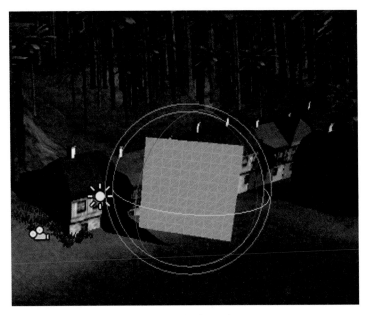

FIG 2.10 Adding a new plane to the scene.

Step 25. Play to see the view from SphereCam play out on the big screen in your scene. This technique can be used in your games for surveillance cameras, minimaps, or reflections in mirrors or water.

While cameras can be used to create a number of different visual effects, they are also important for optimizing a game's performance. For example, the camera's view volume should not be considered a trivial setting. As mentioned previously, all objects inside the view volume get drawn to the screen. The more objects to be drawn, the slower the frames per second. Even objects behind other objects and not noticeably visible will be considered by the game engine as something to be drawn. So even though an object doesn't appear on the screen, if it is inside the camera's view volume it will be processed. Therefore, if you have a narrow back street scene in a European city where the player will never see beyond the immediate buildings, the camera's far plane can come forward to exclude other buildings that cannot be seen anyway.

Whether the camera is looking at an orthographic or a perspective view, the coordinate system within the game environment remains the same.

2.3.2 Local and World Coordinate Systems

There are two coordinate systems at work in game environments: local and world. The local system is relative to a single game object, and the world system specifies the orientation and coordinates for the entire world. It's like having a map for the local layout of a city versus the longitude and latitude system used for the entire earth.

A game object can move and rotate relative to its local coordinate system or the world. How it moves locally depends on the position of the origin, the (0,0,0) point, within the model. Figure 2.11a shows a 3D model in Blender with the origin situated at the tip of the head, and Figure 2.11b shows it in

FIG 2.11 The effect of transformations based on local coordinates. (a) A model in Blender with the origin at the center top, (b) a model in Blender with the origin in the abdomen, (c) translation axes positioned in Unity for the model in a, (d) translation axes positioned in Unity for the model in b, (e) both models positioned at the world origin in a Unity Scene, and (f) both models rotated 90° about their local x axes.

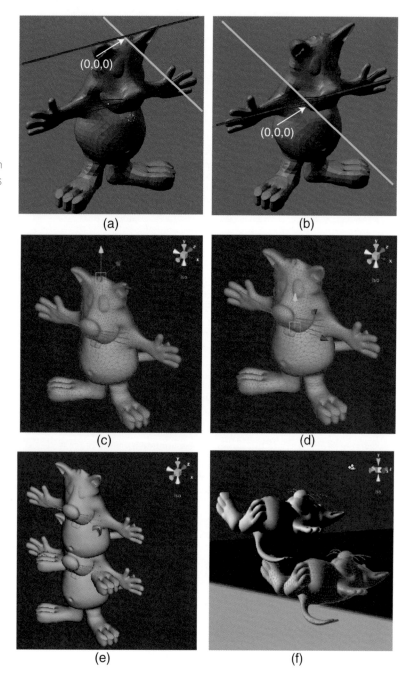

(a)

(b)

(c)

(d)

(e)

(f)

the center of the body. In Blender the default vertical axis is the *z* axis. The red and green lines in Figure 2.11a and 2.11b represent the *x* and *y* axes, respectively. When imported into Unity, the software automatically flips the *z* axis for you, making *y* the new vertical axis. As shown in Figure 2.11a and 2.11b, the origin of the model is carried across into Unity. When a model is selected, its origin is evident by the location of the translation handles used for moving the model around in the Scene. The location of the model's central point becomes an issue in Unity when positioning and rotating it. In Figure 2.11e, both models are placed in the world at (0,0,0) as set by the Inspector. As you can see, the models are placed in differing positions relative to their own central points. Figure 2.11f demonstrates how rotation is also affected by the model's origin. The model from Figure 2.11a rotates about the point in the center top of the head, whereas the model in Figure 2.11b rotates about its abdomen.

In Figure 2.12, the effect of rotations on local and world coordinate systems is illustrated. Any object at the world origin when rotated will orientate in the same way around local and world axes. However, when the model is not at the world origin, a rotation in world coordinates will move as well as reorient the model. Local rotations are not affected by the model's location in the world.

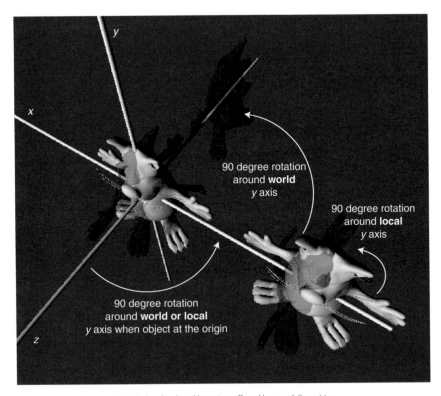

FIG 2.12 Local and world rotations affected by a model's position.

2.3.3 Translation, Rotation, and Scaling

Three transformations can be performed on an object whether it be in 2D or 3D: translation, rotation, and scaling.

Translation refers to moving an object and is specified by a vector in the same way the pirate in the previous section moved across the island. A translation occurs whenever the x, y, or z values of an object are modified. They can be modified all at once with a vector or one at a time. To move an object in the x direction by 5, the Unity JavaScript is:

```
this.transform.position.x += 5;
```

To move the object by 3 in the x, 5 in the y, and 8 in the z, in Unity JavaScript it could be written:

```
this.transform.position.x += 3;
this.transform.position.y += 5;
this.transform.position.z += 8;
```

or

```
this.transform.Translate(3,5,8);
```

Several examples of the Translate function are shown in Figure 2.13.

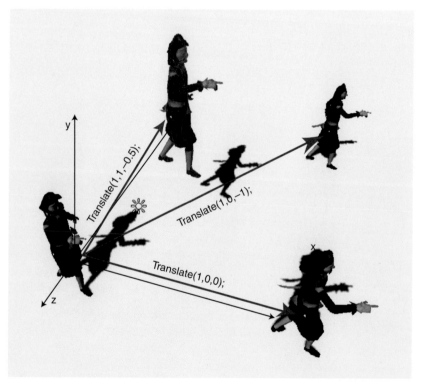

FIG 2.13 Using the Translate function to modify the position of a game object.

Rotation turns an object about a given axis by a specified number of degrees. An object can rotate about its x, y, or z axes or the world x, y, or z axes. Combined rotations are also possible. These cause an object to rotate around arbitrary axes defined by vector values. The Unity JavaScript to rotate an object about 90° about the y axis is

```
this.transform.Rotate(Vector3.up, 90);
```

To rotate 90° around the x axis, the script is

```
this.transform.Rotate(Vector3.right, 90);
```

and to rotate 90° around the z axis, the script is

```
this.transform.Rotate(Vector3.forward, 90);
```

Some of these rotations are illustrated in Figure 2.14.

Finally, scaling changes the size of an object as shown Figure 2.15. An object can be scaled along its x, y, or z axis. This can be achieved in Unity JavaScript by setting each scale value individually, thus:

```
this.transform.localScale.x = 3;
this.transform.localScale.y = 0.5;
this.transform.localScale.z = 10;
```

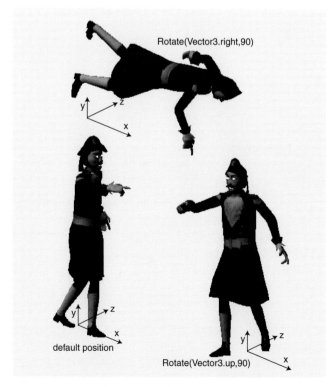

FIG 2.14 Rotating a game object with the Rotate function.

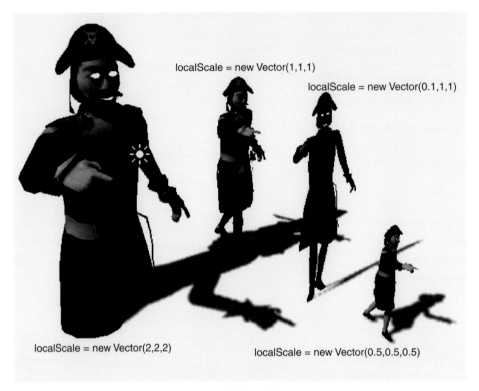

localScale = new Vector(1,1,1)

localScale = new Vector(0.1,1,1)

localScale = new Vector(2,2,2)

localScale = new Vector(0.5,0.5,0.5)

FIG 2.15 Scaling an object.

or all at the same time using a vector like this:

```
this.transform.localScale = new Vector3(3,0.5,10);
```

Values for the scale are always multiplied against the original size of the object. Therefore, a scale of zero is illegal. If a negative scaling value is used, the object is flipped. For example, setting the y axis scale to −1 will turn the object upside down.

Taking some time to orient yourself with both 2D and 3D space is necessary to understanding how objects will move around within your game. Fortunately, Unity takes the hard mathematics and hides it behind many easy-to-use functions. However, when something goes wrong in your game, it's nice to have some idea where to start looking.

2.3.4 Polygons and Normals

Chapter One introduced polygons as the small shapes, usually triangles and sometimes squares, that make up 2D and 3D meshes (or models). A polygon in a mesh also represents a *plane*. A plane is a 3D object that has a width and height but no depth. It is completely flat and can be orientated in any direction, but not twisted.

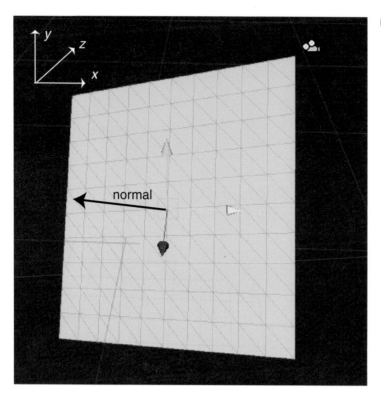

FIG 2.16 A plane and its normal.

The sides of planes are defined by straight edges between vertices. Each vertex has an associated point in space. In addition, planes only have one side. This means that they can only be seen when viewed from above. To see this, open Unity and create a plane game object. Rotate the plane around to the other side. It will become invisible, but it will still be there.

In order to define the visible side of a plane, it has an associated vector called a *normal*. This is not to be confused with normalization of a vector into a unit vector. A normal is a vector that is orthogonal (90°) to the plane as shown in Figure 2.16.

Knowing the normal to a plane is critical in determining how textures and lighting affect a model. It is the side the normal comes out of that is visible and therefore textured and lit. When a model is created in a 3D modeling package such as Blender the normals are usually facing outward from the object. Figure 2.17 shows a model in Blender with the normals for each plane shown in blue.

The angle that a normal makes with any rays from light sources is used to calculate the lighting effect on the plane. Figure 2.18 illustrates the vectors and normal used in calculating the effect of light on a plane. The closer the normal becomes to being parallel with the vector to the light source, the brighter the plane will be drawn. This lighting model is called Lambert shading and is used in computer graphics for diffuse lighting. Further elucidation of shading is presented in later chapters.

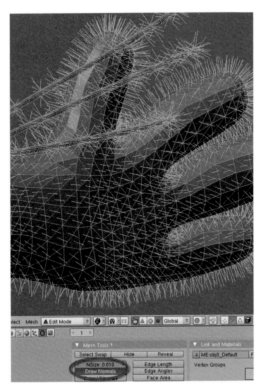

FIG 2.17 A 3D model in Blender showing normals for each plane in blue. To turn this on, select the object and, in Edit Mode, click on Draw Normals in the Mesh Tools 1 panel.

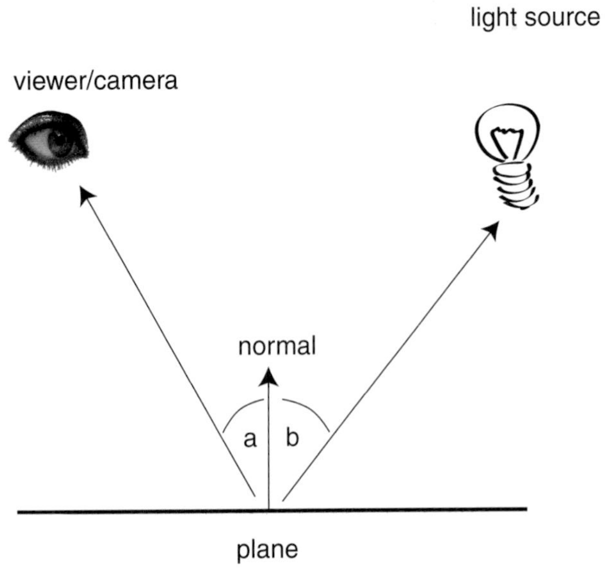

light source

viewer/camera

normal

a | b

plane

FIG 2.18 Vectors used in calculating the strength of lighting on a plane; a vector to the viewer, the normal and a vector to the light source.

◉ Unity Hands On
Meshes and Normals

Step 1. Download *Chapter Two/PolyNormals.zip* from the Web site, unzip, and open.

Step 2. In the Scene, create two plane objects and place them side by side.

Step 3. Add a directional light and rotate it so the light is hitting the planes at about 30°.

Step 4. Take the *CrumbleMesh.js* script and attach it to both planes.

Step 5. Select one of the planes in the Hierarchy, and tick the box next to *Recalculate Normals* of the *Crumble Mesh Script* component in the Inspector.

Step 6. Play. You will be able to see the planes deforming as shown in Figure 2.19.

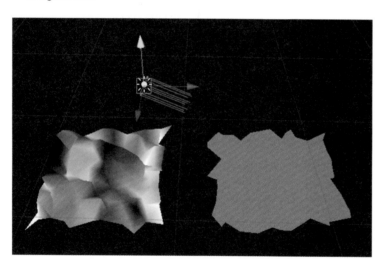

FIG 2.19 Two planes, a directional light, and a script to deform the surfaces. The plane on the left has its normal recalculated.

Step 7. Examine the CrumpleMesh script in the editor. Although the code itself is complex for a beginner programmer, there are a few lines of significance to point out. First, the script uses a class called *Perlin()*. The complete code for this can be found in the Plugin folder in the Project. The specifics of this at this time are not important but it is the cause of the smooth deformation movement of the planes. It is essentially a fractal algorithm for a random yet smooth movement. Each vertex of the plane's mesh is captured and translated using a value from the Perlin function. The line

```
var mesh : Mesh = GetComponent(MeshFilter).mesh;
```

is the Unity method for getting the mesh of any object to which the script is attached. At the very bottom of the script is the option to recalculate the normal. The script will do this when the tick box

95

you selected before is ticked. This is the reason why one plane has updated shading and the other does not. The plane without the recalculated normal keeps the shading it started with on each polygon because as far as the rendering system is concerned, the angle between the light source and the normal has remained unchanged. It is possible to move vertices around and leave the normals where they were. In this case, the original normals are no longer orthogonal with their polygons. The line

```
mesh.RecalculateNormals();
```

ensures that all normals are recalculated and made orthogonal to their polygons after the polygons' vertices are moved. In this case, recalculating the normal is essential to getting the correct lighting effect on the surface.

2.4 Two-Dimensional Games in a 3D Game Engine

Although 3D game engines aren't often written to support 2D game creation, many developers use them for this purpose because (a) they are familiar with them, (b) they don't have to purchase software licenses for other development platforms, and (c) the engines provide support for multiple platforms and game types. As is the case with Unity, although it is not strictly a 2D game development environment, it can port to Android and iOS, making it attractive to developers. In addition, mechanics that are relevant in 3D games are equally so in 2D games.

To create a 2D game in a 3D environment, the one degree of freedom is removed. In the case of the following hands-on section, the *y* axis is all but ignored and the camera is placed into orthographic mode looking down on the scene as though it were playing out on the top of a table.

◉ Unity Hands On
A 2D Vector-Based Space Shoot 'em Up

Step 1. Download *Chapter Two/Basic2DGameStarter.zip* from the Web site, unzip, and open in Unity. In the Project, double-click on *basicgame* of the *Scenes* folder to open the scene. The Scene will appear with a planet and gun turret in the middle and a rocket ship to the lower left. The artwork used here is freely available from http://www.openclipart.org/.

Step 2. Press play. Nothing will happen, but you will notice that you can click on the Quit button and go back and forward between the game screen and the main menu. A fuller version of the game will be created as you proceed through this book.

Step 3. The objective in this hands-on session will be to get the rocket ship to attack the planet. To begin, create a new JavaScript file and call it *attack*. Attach the file to the Enemy game object in the Hierarchy. Open *attack.js* with the script editor. Add the script from Listing 2.2.

Listing 2.2 Script to Make One Game Object Face Another

```
private var target: GameObject;
function Start ()
{
      target = GameObject.Find("Base");
}
function Update ()
{
      this.transform.LookAt(target.transform.position);
}
```

Step 4. Save and play. The rocket ship will turn to face the planet. In *Update()*, the function *LookAt()* is used. It takes a target position and turns the game object to face it. In *Start()*, the target is set to the object called *base,* which is also the name given to the object. This object is called "Base." To see this in the Inspector, select the base in the hierarchy. The name of the planet object is shown in Figure 2.20.

FIG 2.20 The Inspector view of a game object's name.

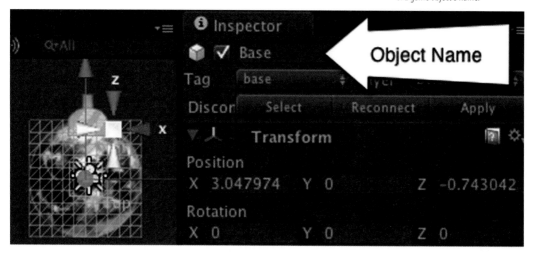

Listing 2.3 Moving an Object by a Small Amount Each Update

```
private var target: GameObject;
private var direction:Vector3;
function Start ()
{
     target = GameObject.Find("Base");
}
function Update ()
{
     this.transform.LookAt(target.transform.position);
     this.transform.Translate(Vector3.forward * 0.3);
}
```

Step 5. To make the rocket ship move toward the planet, modify the code to that listed in Listing 2.3.

Step 6. Save and play. The rocket ship will move toward the planet. However, when it gets to the planet it will stop moving and start flipping back and forth. Why? Each update, the rocket looks at the base and moves toward it. When it is on top of the base it looks at it and then moves forward. This moves it slightly away. The next update it flips around to look at the base again and moves a little toward it. infinitum.

Step 7. To make the rocket move away from the planet when it gets too close, we can test for the distance the rocket is from the planet and turn it back toward its starting position when it comes within a specific distance. To do this, modify your script to that in Listing 2.4.

Listing 2.4 Script to Make an Object Attack and Retreat from Another Object Based on the Distance between Them

```
private var target: GameObject;
private var direction:Vector3;
private var state = "ATTACK";
private var startingPosition:Vector3;
function Start ()
{
     target = GameObject.Find("Base");
     startingPosition = this.transform.position;
}
```

```
function Update ()
{
      direction = target.transform.position - transform.
                        position;

      //determine state
      if(direction.magnitude > 60)
      {
            state = "ATTACK";

      }
      else if (direction.magnitude < 10)
      {

            state = "RETREAT";
      }

      //act on state
      if(state == "ATTACK")
      {
            //look at and move toward planet
            this.transform.LookAt(target.transform.position);
            this.transform.Translate(Vector3.forward * 0.3);
      }
      else if (state == "RETREAT")
      {
                  //look at and move toward homebase
                  this.transform.LookAt(startingPosition);
                  this.transform.Translate(
                              Vector3.forward * 0.3);

      }
}
```

Step 8. Save and play. The rocket will move back and forth between the planet and its starting location. This is achieved by creating a new variable called *state* that stores the rocket's current objective or goal. This is a very simple version of a *finite state machine* used commonly in games for controlling AI. If the rocket is further than 60 away from the planet it will go into attack mode. If it gets closer than 10 it will retreat.

Step 9. So far we've created a rather unnaturally moving rocket ship. It will look better if it curves to turn rather than simply flipping on the spot. To achieve this, modify your code to that in Listing 2.5.

Listing 2.5 Adding a Slerp to the Movement for Smooth Turning

```
private var target: GameObject;
private var direction:Vector3;
private var state = "ATTACK";
private var rotationSpeed = 4.0;
```

```
private var attackDistance = 60;
private var retreatDistance = 10;
private var speed = 0.3;
function Start ()
{
      target = GameObject.Find("Base");
}
function Move()
{
      transform.rotation = Quaternion.Slerp(transform.
          rotation,
                        Quaternion.LookRotation(direction),
                        rotationSpeed * Time.deltaTime);

      this.transform.Translate(Vector3.forward * speed);
}
function Update ()
{
      direction = target.transform.position -transform.position;

      //determine state
      if(direction.magnitude > attackDistance)
      {
            state = "ATTACK";
      }
      else if (direction.magnitude < retreatDistance)
      {
            state = "RETREAT";
      }

      //act on state
      if(state == "ATTACK")
      {
            Move();
      }
      else if (state == "RETREAT")
      {
            direction *= -1;
            Move();
      }
}
```

Step 10. Save and play. The rocket will go toward the planet and when it gets too close will turn away. Once it reaches the bounds of the attack distance it will turn around and approach the planet again. Major changes to this code are the variables added to the top and the *Move()* function. The reason for creating variables for all the static values in the code is to make them easy for editing. If you want to play around with the values to see how it changes the behavior of the rocket, it can be done easily without trawling through the rest of the code. In addition, you can expose them by removing the *private* keyword and they will become editable in the Unity Editor's Inspector. The *Move()* function is more complex and needs further explanation before proceeding.

2.4.1 Quaternions

In 3D space there are three axes around which an object can rotate. These rotations are analogous with the rotational movements of an aircraft. As shown in Figure 2.21, a rotation about the *x* axis (b) creates *pitch*, a rotation about the *z* axis (c) creates *roll*, and a rotation about the *y* axis (d) develops *yaw*.

The angles used to specify how far to rotate objects around these axes are called *Euler angles*. Euler angles are often used in 3D software and game engines because they are intuitive to use. For example, if someone asked you to rotate around your vertical axis by 180° you would know this meant to turn around and look in the opposite direction.

However, there is a fundamental flaw in using Euler angles for rotations in software that can cause unexpected rotational effects. These angles are applied one after the other and therefore have a mathematical compounding effect. This consequence is seen in the mechanical devices used to stabilize aircraft, ships, and spacecraft—the gyroscope.

A simple gyroscope is illustrated in Figure 2.22. It consists of three discs attached to the outer structure of a vehicle (in this example a plane) and attached to each other at pivot points each representing rotations around the *x, y,* and *z* axes. These rotating discs are called gimbals. As the plane yaws, pitches, and rolls, the gyroscope responds to the forces with the rotating of the discs at their pivot points. The idea is that a plate attached to the central, third gimbal remains upright at all times. Navigational systems attached to the gyroscope monitor this plate to determine the orientation of the vehicle. For example, if the vehicle were on autopilot, the objective would be to keep it upright and level to the ground, and any change in the gyroscope's orientation assists with pitch, yaw, or roll corrections.

A situation can occur in which two of the gimbals become aligned, as shown in Figure 2.22d. This is called a *gimbal lock*. At this point, it can either be corrected with the right maneuver (e) or cause erratic behaviors. In Figure 2.22f, the third gimbal cannot rotate back such that the central plate is facing upward, as its pivot points won't allow it. In some circumstances, alignment of the first and second gimbals can also cause the third gimbal to flip upside down, even if the vehicle itself is not upside down. When this occurs, the navigational system becomes very confused as it attempts to realign the vehicle.

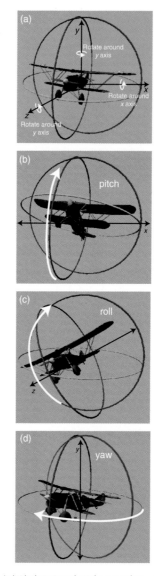

FIG 2.21 Individual rotations about the *x*, *y*, and *z* axes in 3D space.

While this is a simplistic examination of gimbals, the issue of gimbal lock is a reality. It is a mechanical reality that was experienced by the astronauts of the Apollo missions and it is a virtual reality when using Euler angles to rotate 3D objects. Just as the gyroscope compounds the rotations of the outer gimbal inward, multiplying *x*, *y*, and *z* angle rotations one after the other in software systems produces the same errors.

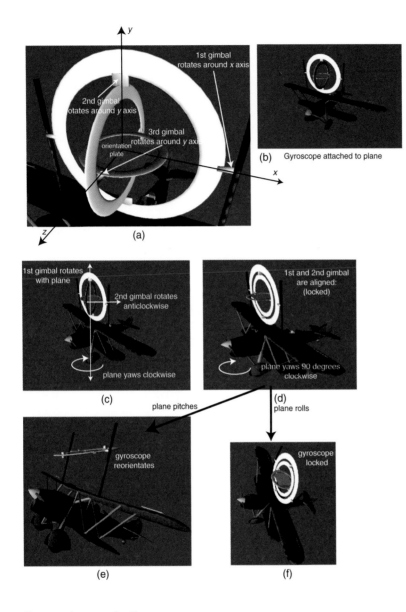

(b)   Gyroscope attached to plane

(a)

(c)

(d)

plane pitches

plane rolls

(e)

(f)

FIG 2.22 A simple gyroscope. (a) Gimbals and rotation points; (b) attaching the gyroscope to a plane; (c) a clockwise yaw of the plane forces the first gimbal to move with it, as it is attached and has no freedom of movement in that direction, while the second gimbal is free to move in response in the opposite direction; (d) a 90° yaw will cause the first and second gimbals to align, thereby entering a state of locked; and (e) after the first and second gimbals become locked, a pitch will retain the integrity of the third gimbal. (f) However, a roll can cause erratic behavior from gimbal 3.

Quaternions to the Rescue

Quaternions are mathematical constructs that allow for rotations around the three axes to be calculated all at once in contrast to Euler angles, which are calculated one after the other. A quaternion has x, y, and z components, as well as a rotation value.

In games using Euler angles, rotations can cause erratic orientations of objects. This is illustrated in Figure 2.23 where the rotations of two planes are compared. Each plane is rotated continually around the x, y, and z axes by

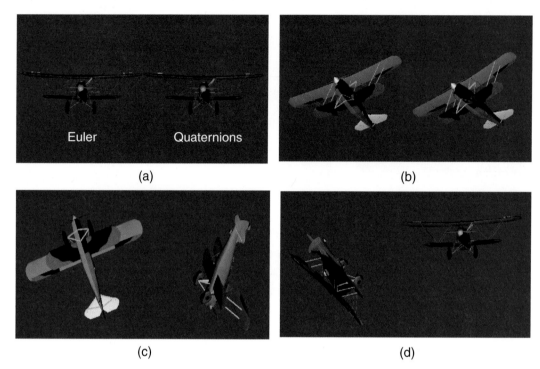

(a)

(b)

(c)

(d)

FIG 2.23 Two planes rotated 1° around each axis every frame. One uses the Euler angle to calculate the other quaternions. (a) Planes begin aligned, (b) planes remain aligned at first, (c) once the *x* angle becomes 90 for the Euler plane its rotations go off course with respect to the quaternion plane, and (d) even further in the simulation.

1°. The plane on the left in Figure 2.23 is rotated using Euler angles and the other uses quaternions. The movement of the quaternion plane is smoother.

Quaternions are used throughout modern game engines, including Unity, as they do not suffer from gimbal lock.

⊙ **For Research**
Quaternions
If you are interested in the complex inner workings of quaternions, check out *Visualizing Quaternions* by Andrew J. Hanson (2006, ISBN: 978-0120884001).

Although the rotation value for the transform component of GameObjects appears as Euler *x*, *y*, and *z* values in the inspector, Unity uses quaternions for storing orientations. The most used quaternion functions are *LookRotation()*, *Angle()*, and *Slerp()*.

LookRotation() given a vector will calculate the equivalent quaternion to turn an object to look alone the original vector. This means `this.transform .rotation = Quaternion.LookRotation(target.position - this .transform.position)` achieves the same result as `this.transform .LookAt(target.transform.position)`.

The *Angle()* function calculates the angle between two rotations. It might be used to determine if an enemy is facing directly toward or away from the player.

Slerp() takes a starting rotation and an ending rotation and cuts it up into small arcs. It is extremely effective in making rotating objects change from one direction to another in a smooth motion. Originally the previously created rocket ship was flipping back and forth as it changed direction. This occurs when the objects goes from the original-facing direction to the goal-facing direction in one frame. *Slerp()* breaks this rotation up so that small parts of it occur with each frame instead of all in one go.

Now that you have a little understanding of quaternions, we can continue examining the *Move()* function from Listing 2.5. It contains two quaternion functions: *LookRotation()* and *Slerp()*. *LookRotation()* takes a vector and turns it into a quaternion. It is being used here to convert the *direction* vector into a quaternion. This is required by the *Slerp()* function, which uses the rotation speed and the time between the drawing of frames (Time.deltaTime) to carve up the complete turn angle into smaller pieces, making the rocket ship turn around in a smooth motion.

◎ Unity Hands On
Quaternions

Step 1. To create bullets that come from the rocket, create a plane by selecting GameObject > Create Other > Plane from the main menu. If a small white plane does not appear in the Game or Scene, select the new Plane from the Hierarchy and set its position values to (0,0,0). It should appear somewhere near the planet.

Step 2. Create a red-colored material and add it to the plane.

Step 3. Set the scale *x*, *y*, and *z* values for the plane to (0.05,0.05, 0.05). It will now appear as a small red dot on the screen.

Step 4. Create a new JavaScript file and call it *moveBullet*. Enter the code shown in Listing 2.6 and attach it to the plane.

Listing 2.6 Script to Move an Object in Its Forward Direction at a Certain Speed

```
var speed = 1.0;
function Update ()
{
    this.transform.Translate(Vector3.forward * speed);
}
```

Step 5. Save and play. The plane will move upward and off the screen.

Step 6. From the Create menu in the Project, select Prefab. Change the name of the newly created prefab to *bullet*. A prefab is a game object in waiting. It's not in the game environment, but is ready to be called up at any time. The prefab is a template that can be used over and over again.

Step 7. Drag and drop the plane from the Hierarchy onto the bullet in the Project as shown in Figure 2.24. When you click on the bullet it will now have all the same properties as the plane. Ensure that the bullet has its transform position set to (0,0,0), its rotation to (0,0,0), and its scale to (0.05,0.05,0.05) in the Inspector. The bullet is going to be attached to the rocket. To ensure its relative position to the rocket, the bullet must be at the origin. Then when attached to the rocket it will be located at the rocket's position coordinates.

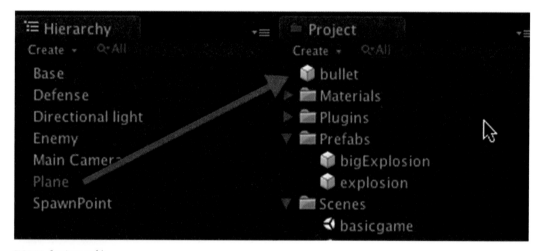

FIG 2.24 Creating a prefab.

Step 8. Delete the original plane from the Hierarchy. It will disappear from the Scene and Game but a template of it is now stored in the Project.

Step 9. Open *attack.js* in the script editor and modify the code as shown in Listing 2.7. Note that as the code is getting longer only snippets of the areas around the new code are shown. Anywhere "..." appears assume the code in this part remains unchanged.

The variable *aBullet* is exposed. Select Enemy and drop the bullet prefab from the Project onto the *aBullet* location in the attack script shown in the Inspector. This is illustrated in Figure 2.25. Because it is possible to drag the bullet prefab onto the script to set the variable, you can drag and drop any game object onto it, meaning that the rocket's bullets could be any game object.

Listing 2.7 Instantiating a New Game Object from a Prefab

```
var aBullet: GameObject;
private var target: GameObject;
private var direction:Vector3;
...
function Update ()
{
      direction=target.transform.position — transform.position;

      ...

      //act on state
      if(state == "ATTACK")
      {
          Move();
          Instantiate(aBullet, this.transform.position,
              this.transform.rotation);
      }
      else if (state == "RETREAT")

      ...

}
```

FIG 2.25 Setting a variable in a script to the value of an existing prefab.

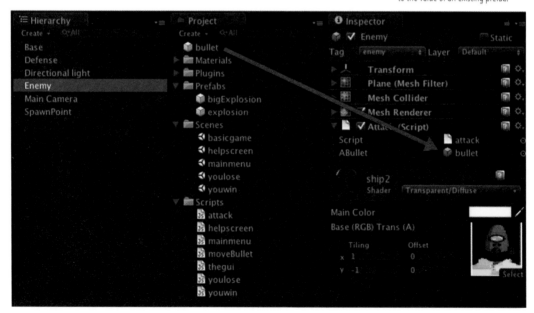

Step 10. Save and play. As the rocket moves in for the attack it starts creating bullets from the prefab. The bullet prefab has the *moveBullet* script attached to it that moves the bullet in a forward motion. However, because the bullet is created at the rocket's location and orientation, it travels forward relative to the rocket and therefore in the direction the rocket is facing.

Step 11. The current attack script will continue creating bullets as long as the program runs. Each bullet is a new game object. As the game runs you will see the Hierarchy fill up with bullet clones. This can become problematic as the game gets clogged up with game objects, many of which are off the screen and traveling toward infinity. They need to be destroyed. To do this, add the code shown in Listing 2.8 to the attack script.

Listing 2.8 Destroying a Game Object after 0.5 Seconds

```
function Update ()
{
    . . .
    if(state == "ATTACK")
    {
        Move();
        var newBullet:GameObject = Instantiate(aBullet,
                    this.transform.position,
                    this.transform.rotation);
        Destroy(newBullet,0.5);
    }
    . . .
}
```

Step 12. Save and play. The *Destroy()* function will delete the specified game object after the given amount of seconds (in this case 0.5 seconds). As the *Destroy()* function needs to know which object to destroy, a local variable is created to hold the instantiated game object. This is then passed to *Destroy()*.

Step 13. Instead of a continued stream of bullets it will look better if there is a delay between them. You can adjust the delay to whatever reloading speed you want. To add this functionality, modify the attack script to that in Listing 2.9.

Listing 2.9 Adding a Time Delay between Object Instantiation

```
. . .
private var state = "ATTACK";
private var rotationSpeed = 6.0;
private var attackDistance = 60;
private var retreatDistance = 10;
private var speed = 0.3;
private var reloadTime = 0.05;
private var lastShotTime = 0.0;
. . .
function Update ()
{
        . . .

        //act on state
        if(state == "ATTACK")
        {
                Move();
                if(lastShotTime + reloadTime < Time.fixedTime)
                {
                var newBullet:GameObject = Instantiate(aBullet,
                                        this.transform.position,
                                        this.transform.rotation);
                Destroy(newBullet,0.5);
                lastShotTime = Time.fixedTime;
                }
        }
        . . .
}
```

Step 14. Save and play. The *Time.fixedTime* value, stores the time since the game started playing. The variable *lastShotTime* records when the last bullet was shot, and *reloadTime* is the time allowed between shots. If a time interval of *reloadTime* has passed since the last shot, another bullet can be instantiated. Also, note that the *rotationSpeed* for the rocket has increased to give it more attack time.

Step 15. To test if the bullets are hitting the target, open and modify the code for the *moveBullet* script to that in Listing 2.10. The code tests the distance between a bullet and the base. If that distance is less than 5, a hit is registered. For now, the hit is only displayed in a print statement that shows up in the console.

Step 16. Save and play. When a bullet hits the base, the game will print out hit in the message bar and console (Figure 2.26). Double-clicking on the message bar text will open the console.

Listing 2.10 Testing the Distance between Objects

```
var speed = 0.5;
private var target:GameObject;
function Start ()
{
    target = GameObject.Find("Base");
}
function Update ()
{
    this.transform.Translate(Vector3.forward * speed);
    if(Vector3.Distance(target.transform.position,
                                    this.transform.position) < 5)
    {
        print("hit");
    }
}
```

FIG 2.26 Print messages showing up in the message bar and console.

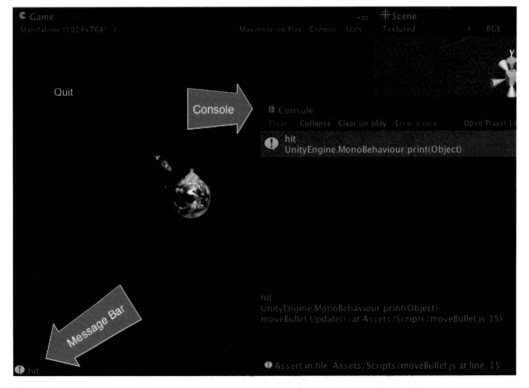

Step 17. To cause a small explosion when a bullet hits the base, modify *moveBullet* to instantiate an explosion game object when it hits, as shown in Listing 2.11.

Listing 2.11 Instantiating an Explosion

```
var speed = 2.0;
private var target:GameObject;
var explosion: GameObject;
function Start ()
{
      target = GameObject.Find("Base");
}
function Update ()
{
      this.transform.Translate(Vector3.forward * speed);
      if(Vector3.Distance(target.transform.position,
                    this.transform.position) < 5)
      {
            var exp:GameObject = Instantiate(explosion,
                        this.transform.position,
                        this.transform.rotation);
            Destroy(exp,1.0);
            Destroy(this);
      }
}
```

Step 18. Save. Before playing, select the *moveBullet* script from the Project and then locate the *explosion* Prefab and drag it onto the exposed variable *Explosion* in the Inspector window.

Step 19. Play. When a bullet hits the base, an explosion will occur instead of print. The explosion prefab is a particle system. You will learn more about these in later chapters. Just after the explosion is instantiated and set to be destroyed, the script also destroys the bullet game object. This will ensure that the bullet doesn't stay alive in the game environment after it has hit the base.

In this hands-on session you've learned some basic uses of vectors in a simple 2D game environment.

2.5 The Laws of Physics

Game players bring their own experience of the real world to a game environment. They understand that gravity makes things drop, acceleration changes the speed of an object, and when an object hits another object a reaction, such as bouncing or exploding, will occur based on the object's composition.

These expectations within game environments are essential to establishing the player's *suspension of disbelief*—a psychological state in which a player accepts the limitations of a medium in order to engage with the content. This can include anything from low-quality graphics to flying aliens. Anything that messes with the player's suspension of disbelief causes them to disengage and lose interest, such as being woken from a dream. A big part of ensuring a game environment is making the virtual world act and react like the real one.

The laws of physics are a set of complex rules that describe the physical nature of the universe. Adhering to these rules when creating a game is key to creating a believable environment in which the player interacts. Sometimes the laws are bent to suit narrative; however, they essentially remain static throughout. For example, players in a modern warfare game, taking place on earth, would expect gravity to react for their character as it does for them in the real world. In the case of science fiction, the effects of gravity may be altered to fit the story.

Physics is a fundamental element in games as it controls the way in which objects interact with the environment and how they move.

Although physics covers topics such as Einstein's theory of relativity and thermodynamics, the key ones used in game environments are Newton's three laws of motion and the law of gravity.

2.5.1 The Law of Gravity

Although it is a myth that an apple fell on Newton's head, he did devise his theory of gravity while watching an apple fall from a tree. In Newton's publication the *Principia*, the force of gravity is defined thus:

> *Every particle of matter in the universe attracts every other particle with a force that is directly proportional to the product of the masses of the particles and inversely proportional to the square of the distance between them.*

In short, this means the bigger an object, the more it attracts other objects and that this attraction gets stronger the closer it is. Kepler also used this law, a century later, to develop his laws of planetary motion.

In game environments, applying a downward velocity to an object simulates gravity. The *y* coordinate of the object's position is updated with each game loop to make it move in a downward direction. If you were to code this in Unity, the JavaScript would look something like this:

```
transform.position.y = transform.position.y - 1;        (2.4)
```

Unfortunately, the actual calculation for real gravity would be a little more complex than taking away one as the effect of earth's gravity is a downward acceleration of 9.8 meters per second.[2] This means the downward speed of an object gets faster by 9.8 meters per second with each second. An object starting with a speed of 0 after 1 second will be moving at 9.8 meters per second, after 2 seconds it will be moving at 19.6 meters per second, and after 3 seconds it will be moving at 29.4 meters per second.

In addition, a game loop may not take exactly 1 second to execute. This will throw out any calculations you attempt with each loop update on a second by second basis.

Fortunately, game engines take care of all the mathematics and allow you to set just one gravity value for your environment. Let's take a look at how Unity does it.

◁ Unity Specifics
Gravity

From the main menu, select Edit > Project Settings > Physics. The Physics properties will open in the Inspector as shown in Figure 2.27. The default setting is for a downward acceleration of 9.81 meters per second.[3]

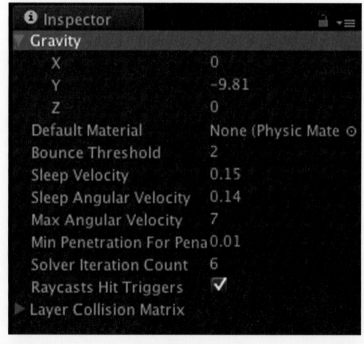

FIG 2.27 Unity's Physics properties.

Continued

---

[2]Earth's actual gravitational acceleration.
[3]This is acceleration due to gravity on earth.

As you can see, depending on your own game environment, gravity can be set in any direction, including upward and sideways.

⊙ **Unity Hands On**

Applying Gravity

Step 1. Start Unity and create a new project. Orient the Scene such that the *y* axis is pointing upward. Position the camera so that it has the same view as shown in the Scene. To do this, select the camera from the Hierarchy and then from the main menu GameObject > Align with View.

Step 2. Add a sphere to the Scene and position it at the top of the camera view. With the sphere selected in the Hierarchy, select from the main menu Component > Physics > Rigidbody. The result of this will be a new component added to the sphere in the Inspector, as shown in Figure 2.28. The Rigidbody component makes the sphere part of Unity's physics processing and as such gravity will be applied to it.

FIG 2.28 A Scene with a Sphere that has a Rigidbody attached.

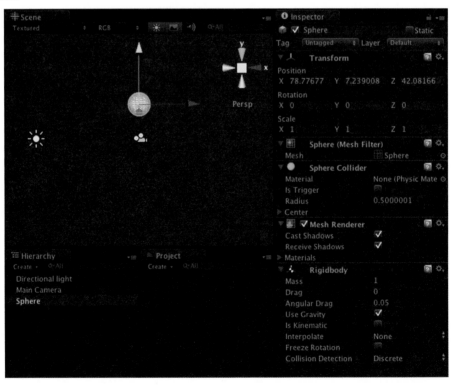

Step 3. Press play. The sphere will fall downward.

Step 4. Press stop and change the gravity via the main menu's Edit > Project Settings > Physics; in the Inspector click on Gravity to expand. You may want to set it to a positive *y* value or even have it go to the side with a change to the *x*. You choose.

Step 5. Press play to see the effect of the new gravity settings.

2.5.2 The First Law of Motion

Every body continues in its state of rest, or of uniform motion in a straight line, unless it is compelled to change that state by forces impressed upon it.

This means that an object will remain stationary and a moving object will keep moving in the same direction unless push or pulled. In the real world, a number of different forces act to move or slow objects. These include gravity and friction. In addition, objects colliding with each other will also act to change their movement.

◎ Unity Hands On
Newton's First

Step 1. Create a new Unity Project. Ensure that the *y* axis is pointing up and position the Main Camera to the same view.

Step 2. Select GameObject > Create Other > Plane from the main menu. Resize the plane to twice its original size to create a large ground area. You can do this by pressing "R" while the plane is selected or changing the scale *x*, *y*, and *z* values in the Inspector to 2. Add a directional light. Add a grass or dirt seamless texture to the plane.

Step 3. Select GameObject > Create Other > Cube from the main menu. Zoom in to center the cube in the Scene. Lift the cube so that it is slightly above the ground.

Step 4. With the cube selected in the Hierarchy, select Component > Physics > Rigidbody from the main menu to add physics processing to the cube.

Step 5. Press play. The cube will fall until it hits the ground and stops. Although the plane doesn't have a Rigidbody attached, it does have a Collider. Select plane in the Hierarchy and look for the Box Collider in the Inspector. This collider is used by the physics system. Although the ground plane is not affected by the cube hitting it, the cube, because it has a Rigidbody, is stopped by the collider of the plane.

Step 6. Lift the cube higher above the plane. Add a Rigidbody to the plane.

Step 7. Press play. Note that the plane and the cube both fall at the same rate.

Step 8. Select the plane from the Hierarchy and find its Rigidbody component in the Inspector. To add air friction, set the value of *Drag* to 10.

Step 9. Press play. The plane will fall away more slowly than the cube. When the cube hits the plane, the plane will speed up and possibly flip, depending on where you've placed the cube with respect to the plane.

Step 10. Remove the Rigidbody from the plane by selecting the small drop-down menu as shown in Figure 2.29.

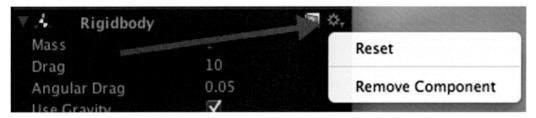

FIG 2.29 Removing a component from a GameObject.

Step 11. Select the cube in the Hierarchy, right-click on it, and select Duplicate as shown in Figure 2.30. Duplicating a GameObject after it has had components, such as a Rigidbody, attached to it will ensure that the duplicate has all the same attachments. Move the duplicate cube, which will be in the exact same location as the original.

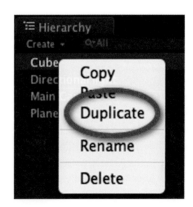

FIG 2.30 Duplicating a GameObject in the Inspector.

Step 12. Continue duplicating and moving to build a stack of cubes as shown in Figure 2.31.

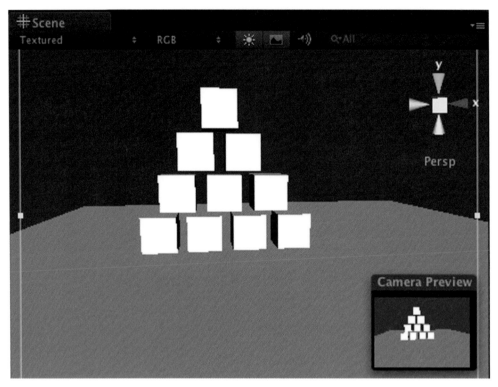

FIG 2.31 A stack of duplicated cubes, all with Rigidbodies.

Step 13. In the Project, create a new JavaScript file and call it *fire*. Open it in the script editor and enter the code in Listing 2.12. Save the script and attach it to the Main Camera.

Listing 2.12 Script to Create a Sphere as a Projectile on a Left Mouse Click

```
function Update ()
{
 if(Input.GetButtonDown("Fire1"))
 {
  var ray:Ray = Camera.main.ScreenPointToRay (Input.mousePosition);
  var sphere:GameObject =
                 GameObject.
                 CreatePrimitive(PrimitiveType.Sphere);
  sphere.transform.position = ray.origin;
  sphere.AddComponent ("Rigidbody");
  sphere.rigidbody.AddForce(ray.direction * 1000);
 }
}
```

Step 14. Save and play. A click in the Game will create a sphere at the click location and project it in the direction the camera is facing. Before a force is added to push the sphere, the *AddComponent()* function is used to add a Rigidbody component to the sphere as it is not attached by default. The *ScreenPointToRay()* takes the mouse click location and turns it into a vector (called a ray) that starts at the click location and continues in the direction the camera is facing. This direction is used as the push force on the sphere, propelling it forward.

Step 15. Gravity still affects the sphere. To see it in action, change the multiplier for the *AddForce()* function from 1000 to 100.

2.5.3 The Second Law of Motion

The acceleration produced by a particular force acting on a body is directly proportional to the magnitude of the force and inversely proportional to the mass of the body.

This means that a larger force is required to move a heavier object. In addition, a heavier object with the same acceleration as a lighter object will cause more destruction when it hits something as the force will be greater. Imagine throwing a bowling ball and a tennis ball at a wall with the same acceleration. Which one is going to leave a bigger hole?

◉ Unity Hands On
Newton's Second

Step 1. Begin by opening the Unity project from Section 2.5.2. Open the fire script and ensure that the *AddForce()* multiplier is set to 1000, for example, *AddForce(ray.direction * 1000)*.

Step 2. In the Hierarchy, select each cube in turn, locate the Rigidbody component in the Inspector, and set the *Mass* to 10.

Step 3. Press play. Note that the heavier cubes are now more difficult to knock over with the sphere.

Step 4. Edit *fire.js* to increase the mass of the sphere as shown in Listing 2.13. Save and play.

Listing 2.13 Script to Change the Mass of a Rigidbody

```
function Update ()
{
 if(Input.GetButtonDown("Fire1"))
 {
```

```
    var ray:Ray =
            Camera.main.ScreenPointToRay(Input.
                    mousePosition);
    var sphere : GameObject =
                    GameObject.CreatePrimitive
                            (PrimitiveType.Sphere);
    sphere.transform.position = ray.origin;
    sphere.AddComponent ("Rigidbody");
    sphere.rigidbody.mass = 10;
    sphere.rigidbody.AddForce(ray.direction * 1000);
    }
}
```

Step 5. Because the sphere has more mass, the added force has less effect. However, you may be able to get it to roll along the ground. The extra mass will be enough to knock over the cubes.

Step 6. Try setting the *AddForce()* multiplier to 10,000. Note that because the mass has increased 10-fold, the force required to move the sphere in the same way must also increase 10-fold.

2.5.4 The Third Law of Motion

To every action there is always opposed an equal reaction; or, the mutual actions of two bodies upon each other are always equal, and directed to contrary parts.

This can be rephrased to the well-known adage *for every action there is an equal and opposite reaction.* When a truck hits a car, energy from the movement of the truck is transferred to the car and it is propelled away from the truck. If a car hits another car of a similar size, some of the energy is transferred to the second car, while some goes back into the first car. If a car hits a brick wall, chances are most of the energy will go back into the car. This energy needs to go somewhere. In the case of cars, specially designed crumple zones absorb the energy. For a tennis ball, some of the energy is absorbed by the rubbery nature of the ball and the rest is used to propel the ball away. In other words, collisions occurring in the real world have an effect on the environment as well as the object.

The examples thus far examined in Unity see energy from an initial force transferred or totally absorbed by the objects. For a heavy sphere, cubes are knocked over easily, whereas a light sphere hits the cubes and drops straight to the ground. This rarely happens in the real world where things tend to *bounce*, to some degree. In Unity, adding a physics material to an object can simulate these extra effects.

◁ **Unity Specifics**

Physics Materials

In Unity, a physics material is created in the Project and then added to the object's Collider component. A physics material sets values for bounce and friction. The bounciness of an object can be set between 0 (no bounce) and 1 (full bounce) to simulate how much of a collision's force comes back to the object. For example, for a tennis ball, set bounce to 1. The friction value determines how well an object holds onto another surface when rubbed together. For example, rubber on concrete has a high friction value, whereas stone on ice has a low friction value. Friction is a force that slows down movement. Friction can be set to 0 (no friction) to an infinite number (total friction).

◉ **Unity Hands On**

Newton's Third

Step 1. Create a new Unity project with a sloping plane and cube as shown in Figure 2.32. Attach a Rigidbody to the cube. Press play and watch the cube drop down until it hits the plane and then rolls the rest of the way. Try to rotate the cube such that one side is parallel to the plane as shown.

Step 2. To create physics material, in Project select the Create menu and choose Physics Material, as shown in Figure 2.33. Rename the material box.

Step 3. Select the cube in the Hierarchy and locate its Box Collider in the Inspector. The first property will be Material. Click on the small circle to the very right of it and select the *box* physics material from the pop-up window. If you play the application at this point, there will be very little effect. Select box from the Project. The view of this physics material will appear in the Inspector as shown in Figure 2.34. Set the *Bounciness* value to 1. Press play to see the effect.

Step 4. To get a higher bounce, set the *Bounce Combine* value to *Maximum*. These combine values tell the physics engine how to work out the effect when two objects collide. When set to maximum it will apply the maximum bounce factor out of the two objects. If you set it to minimum the cube will not bounce, as the plane has no bounciness value.

Step 5. Now try setting *all* the box physics material values to 0 and the Friction Combine to minimum. Press play. With no bounce or friction, the box will fall to the plane and then slide down as if the surface was made of ice.

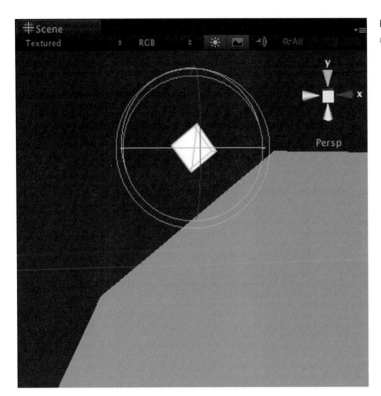

FIG 2.32 The initial scene required to demonstrate physics materials.

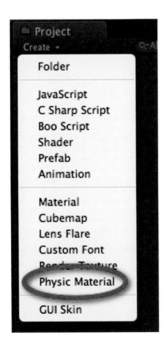

FIG 2.33 Creating physics material.

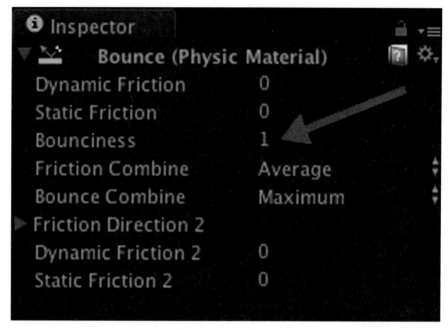

FIG 2.34 The Inspector view of physics material.

2.6 Physics and the Principles of Animation

In their book *The Illusion of Life*, Disney animators Ollie Johnston and Frank Thomas introduce 12 rules to be applied when creating animated films. These are

Squash and stretch:
> The deformation of objects in reaction to the laws of physics; for example, a tennis ball hitting a wall squashes on collision.

Anticipation:
> Presenting short actions or hints to a viewer of what is about to happen; for example, a person about to jump in the air will bend their knees first.

Staging:
> Presenting an idea such that no mistake can be made as to what is happening; for example, viewing an angry person's face gives a better impression of their mood than the back of their head.

Straight-ahead action and pose to pose:
> These are animation drawing methods. Straight-ahead action refers to drawing out a scene frame by frame. Pose to pose refers to drawing key frames or key moments in a scene and filling in the gaps later.

Follow-through and overlapping action:

> This is the way in which momentum acts on a moving object to cause extra motion even after the initial force has stopped; for example, a baseball pitcher's arm does not stop moving the moment the ball leaves his hand. In addition, his legs and body also move in response to the action. Overlapping action occurs when secondary objects move with the main object.

Slow in and out:

> Natural movement in which there is a change in direction decelerates into the change and accelerates out; for example, a car turning a corner slows into the corner and accelerates out. A person jumping will slow into the impact with the ground and speed up as he pushes off the ground with his legs.

Arcs:

> Motion in animals and humans occurs along curved paths. This includes the rotation of limbs and the rise and fall of a body when walking. The same curved movement is also found in the trajectory of thrown objects.

Secondary actions:

> These animations support the principal animation. They give a scene more realism; for example, a person walking along the street won't just be moving his legs. His arms might swing, he may be talking, and his hair could be flowing with the breeze.

Timing:

> This refers to the speed of actions. It is essential for establishing mood and realism; for example, a fast-moving character will appear to be in a hurry, whereas a slow-moving character portrays lethargy or disinterest. For realism, the correct timing of actions with motion and sound is critical. Slow animated walking characters can look like they are slipping across the ground if their forward movement and leg cycles are not matched.
>
> A delay between an action and a sound, such as a bomb exploding and the associated sound effect, adds to suspension of disbelief.

Exaggeration:

> Perfect imitations of the real world in animation can appear dull and static. Often it is necessary to make things bigger, faster, and brighter to present them in an acceptable manner to a viewer. Overexaggeration is also used in physical features of characters for the effects of physics; for example, in Warner Bros.' coyote and roadrunner films, when the coyote is about to fall from a great height, the time he spends in the air realizing his predicament is exaggerated far beyond what normal gravity would allow.

Solid drawing:

> This is the term given to an animator's ability to consider and draw a character with respect to anatomy, weight, balance, and shading in

a 3D context. A character must have a presence in the environment, and being able to establish volume and weight in an animation is crucial to believing the character is actually in and part of the environment.

Appeal:

This relates to an animator's ability to bring a character to life. It must be able to appeal to an audience through physical form, personality, and actions.

All but a couple of the preceding principles of animation can be conveyed in a game environment through the physics system. They are consequences of physics acting in the real world. We subconsciously see and experience them every day, albeit not with as much exaggeration as a game, and come to expect it in the virtual environment.

In the following hands-on sections you will get a chance to see how these principles can be applied in your own games.

2.6.1 Squash and Stretch

2D Boy's two-dimensional adventure *World of Goo* features many moving balls of Goo. Each time Goo accelerates it becomes elongated along the direction of movement, and it decelerates and squashes when it collides with another object. Such movement occurs in the real world and is explained by Newton's laws.

While game-based physics engines do allow for the creation of bouncy objects, typically they do not provide real-time squashing and stretching algorithms for the actual game object. The rigid body attached to a game object to simulate physics by very definition remains rigid even though its movement suggests otherwise. In most cases, it is too processor intensive in 3D environments to squash and stretch all objects, but just for fun this hands-on session will show you how to do it in Unity.

⦿ Unity Hands On
Squash and Stretch

Step 1. Download *Chapter Two/AnimPrinciples.zip* from the Web site, unzip, and open in Unity. In the Project, double-click on *squash* in the *Scenes* folder to open the scene. The warehouse scene from one of the Unity online resources will be visible.

Step 2. We want to be able to move around inside the warehouse and need to add a first person controller (FPC). Select Assets > Import Package from the main menu, and select the Character Controller package (Figure 2.35).

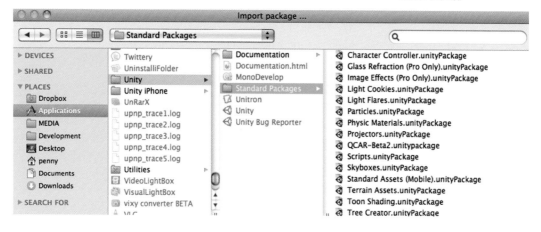

FIG 2.35 The Unity Packages folder location on a Mac.

Step 3. Unity will decompress the package and then show you the files it is about to add to your project. Select all and click on Import. A folder called Standard Assets will appear in the Project. Inside this folder locate the FPC and drag it into the Scene. A capsule-shaped object with a camera attached will show in the Scene, as illustrated in Figure 2.36.

FIG 2.36 Adding a First Person Controller to a scene.

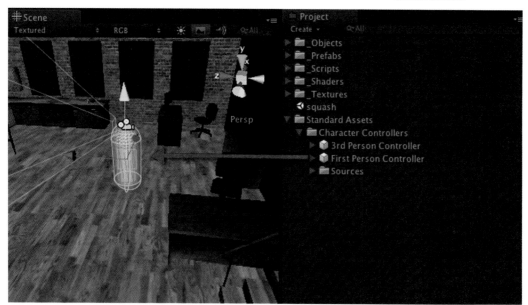

Step 4. Delete Main Camera from the Hierarchy. There is already a camera attached to the FPC and the Main Camera is no longer needed.

Step 5. Play. The FPC will fall straight through the floor. Why? The warehouse mesh does not have any colliders and therefore there is nothing to stop the FPC falling. Each surface of the mesh requires a mesh collider to be added.

Step 6. In the Hierarchy, select wareHouseFBX and expand it by clicking on the small triangle to the left of its name. This model is made up of a number of meshes. They are called polySurface88, polySurface89, and so on. Select polySurface88, scroll to the bottom of the list, and SHIFT select polySurface 1518. With all the surfaces selected, go to the main menu and select Component > Physics > Mesh Collider. Each surface will have a mesh collider added to it using its own mesh shape. Quickly scan through the polySurface meshes individually and note the new Mesh Collider component added and that the Mesh property of this is set to its own mesh.

Step 7. Play. The FPC will fall and hit the floor. You will be able to move around with the arrow or WASD keys and jump with the spacebar. If the FPC falls through the floor it will be because it either starts slightly merged with the floor or the floor does not have a mesh collider. Move the FPC up a little and check the floor mesh for a collider and try again.

Step 8. As you try and move around, you will find that the stairs pose a little challenge. To adjust the settings of the FPC to handle these, select the FPC in the Hierarchy and locate the Character Controller component in the Inspector. Change the value of Slope Limit to 80 and the Step Offset to 0.1. This will allow the FPC to go up slopes with up to an 80° incline and to move up stairs with a height of 0.1. Although the stairs are 90° for each vertical face, the small upward bounce the FPC experiences when it hits the stairs is enough to push it up to the next one with the Slope Limit set to 80. Try walking around with these new settings.

Step 9. Create a Sphere. Set its scale to (0.5,0.5,0.5) and position it at (0,0,0).

Step 10. Add a Rigidbody to the Sphere by selecting it in the Hierarchy and choosing Component > Physics > Rigidbody from the main menu.

Step 11. Create a JavaScript file and call it *blob*. Leave it empty.

Step 12. Attach *blob.js* to the Sphere.

Step 13. In Project, create a Prefab and call it *bullet*. Drag and drop Sphere from the Hierarchy and drop it onto the bullet prefab. Check that the prefab now has the properties of Sphere, including the *blob.js* script attached. Delete Sphere from the Hierarchy.

Step 14. Create a JavaScript file and call it *fire*. Add the script from Listing 2.14.

Listing 2.14 Instantiating a Game Object and Shooting It Forward Relative to the Creator

```
var bulletObject: GameObject;
function Update ()
{
      if(Input.GetButtonDown("Fire1"))
      {
      var newBullet: GameObject = Instantiate(bulletObject,
                        this.transform.position,
                        this.transform.rotation);
        newBullet.rigidbody.AddForce(this.transform.forward *
  500);
      }
}
```

Step 15. Save *fire.js* and attach it to the *Main Camera*, which is part of the FPC in the Hierarchy. Select the FPC Main Camera in the Hierarchy and drag and drop the bullet prefab from the Project onto the exposed bulletObject variable in the *fire.js* script as shown in Figure 2.37.

Step 16. Save and play. The right mouse button, called "Fire1" in the script, will instantiate copies of the bullet prefab and add a force with the same direction as the camera. To change the speed of the bullets, modify the force multiplier in *fire.js*.

● **Note**

If an object is moving too fast, Unity can sometimes miss the collision event and it will go through walls and floors. If this happens, try slowing the object down or making its collision component bigger. Also note that Unity will not register collisions between two complex mesh objects. If you have a mesh object that is not colliding, think of replacing its collider with a simple sphere or box collider. To do this, click on the object in the Hierarchy and select a new physics collider from the main menu.

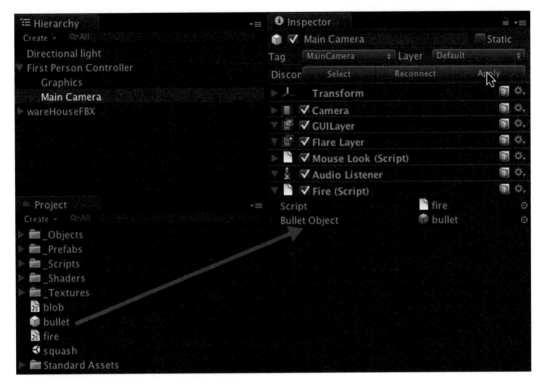

FIG 2.37 Setting a script variable to the value of a prefab object.

Step 17. We are now going to create sticky bullets. Open the *blob.js* file. Enter the script from Listing 2.15.

Listing 2.15 Turn off an Object's Physics on a Collision

```
function OnCollisionEnter(collision : Collision)
{
        if(collision.gameObject.name !=
            "First Person Controller")
        {
                rigidbody.isKinematic = true;
        }
}
function Update () {
}
```

Step 18. Save and play. You will have created sticky bullets that stop moving the instance they collide with something. The *isKinematic* setting in the script will turn off physics effects on the object when it is set to true. A test is performed to check if the object has hit the FPC before it turns off the physics. This is used to ensure that the bullets don't stick to the FPC.

Step 19. Finally, to make the bullet object squash when it hits the wall, modify your script to that in Listing 2.16.

Listing 2.16 Causing a Squash Effect by Changing an Object's Scale

```
function OnCollisionEnter(collision : Collision)
{
        if(collision.gameObject.name !=
            "First Person Controller")
        {
            rigidbody.isKinematic = true;
            Destroy (this.collider);

            var contact = collision.contacts[0];
            var rot = Quaternion.FromToRotation(Vector3.up,
                                    contact.normal);

            this.transform.position = contact.point;
            this.transform.rotation = rot;
            this.transform.localScale.x*=
                                collision.relativeVelocity.
                        magnitude/5.0;
            this.transform.localScale.y*= 0.2;
            this.transform.localScale.z*=
                                collision.relativeVelocity.
                        magnitude/5.0;
        }
}
function Update () {
}
```

Step 20. Save and play. The code now destroys the collider component to stop the FPC from hitting the stationary bullets. If you take this line out you will notice that the bullets create barriers the FPC collides with. Data are taken from the collision and used to rotate the object just as the *y* axis is aligned with the normal of the point of contact. This means that when the *y* axis is scaled down, the object presses flat to the object it collided with. The *x* and *z* scales can then be resized based on the collision velocity to create a bigger *splat*.

Step 21. Create a shiny black material for the bullet prefab, and take a walk around the warehouse, leaving blobs everywhere. Note that funny unaligned blobs will be caused by collisions with other complex meshes, such as chairs. This code works best with walls, floors, and other large flat areas.

Anticipation

A simple implementation of anticipation is seen in racing games. At the beginning of a race, a traffic light or countdown will display, giving the player a heads up to when the race is about to start. Another way to add anticipation is to have explosive devices with countdown timers. In *Splinter Cell*, for example, the lead character, Sam Fisher, may lay down explosive charges and then a countdown occurs before they explode.

⊙ Unity Hands On

Anticipation

Step 1. Open the project from the last hands-on session or download and open *Chapter Two/AnimPrinciplesA.zip*. We are now going to make the sticky bullets into timed explosive devices.

Step 2. Download *Chapter Two/Detonater.unityPackage* and import into your project, Assets > Import Package > Custom Package.

Step 3. Open *blob.js* and modify the code to that in Listing 2.17.

Listing 2.17 Creating a Timed Explosion

```
var explosion:GameObject;
var explosionLife:float = 5.0;
var detailLevel: float = 1.0; //seconds until explosion
var countdown: float = 5.0;
private var timeSet: float;
private var explosionActivated = false;
private var explosionDirection: Quaternion;
private var explosionLocation: Vector3;
function OnCollisionEnter(collision : Collision)
{
    if(collision.gameObject.name != "First Person Controller")
    {
    rigidbody.isKinematic = true;
    Destroy (this.collider);
    var contact = collision.contacts[0];
    var rot = Quaternion. FromToRotation(Vector3.up,
                                     contact.normal);
    explosionDirection = rot;
    var offsetSize = explosion. GetComponent("Detonator").
                                              size / 3;
    explosionLocation = contact.point + ((Vector3.Scale
                                     (contact.normal,
                    Vector3(offsetSize,offsetSize,
                    offsetSize))));

    //move object to exact point of contact
    this.transform.position = contact.point;
```

```
    //rotate so y axis is pointing outward from contact point
    this.transform.rotation = rot;
    this.transform.localScale.x*=
                        collision.relativeVelocity.
                        magnitude/5.0;
    this.transform.localScale.y*= 0.2;
    this.transform.localScale.z*=
                        collision.relativeVelocity.
                        magnitude/5.0;

    timeSet = Time.fixedTime + countdown;
    explosionActivated = true;
    }
}
function Explode()
{
    var exp : GameObject = Instantiate(explosion, explosion
                                                  Location,
                                explosionDirection);
    exp.GetComponent("Detonator").detail = detailLevel;
    Destroy(exp, explosionLife);
}
function Update ()
{
    if(Time.fixedTime >= timeSet && explosionActivated)
    {
        //set off explosion
        Explode();
        explosionActivated = false;
        //remove the explosive device from
        game environment
        Destroy(this.gameObject);
    }
}
```

Step 4. Click on the bullet prefab in the Project. Find the Explosion property of the blob script and set it to Detonator-Insanity. You can find this by clicking on the little circle next to the property field or drag and drop this prefab from the Project. It can be found in Standard Assets > Detonator > Prefab Examples.

Step 5. Save and play. Drop a sticky bullet somewhere and stand back and watch.

Follow-Through

Follow-through refers to actions occurring after and as a result of another action. For example, in racing games, a common follow-through is when one car clips another car and it goes spinning out of control. In most games where you have to blow something up there is bound to be a follow-through action that removes obstacles from the player's game progression.

◉ Unity Hands On

Follow-Through

Step 1. Open the project from the last hands-on session or download and open *Chapter Two/AnimPrinciplesB.zip*. We are now going to add a door that can be blown up with the timed explosive devices. Create a cube and modify its scale, rotation, and position as necessary to have it fit one of the doorways in the warehouse as shown in Figure 2.38. Rename the cube "Door."

FIG 2.38 A Cube used as a door.

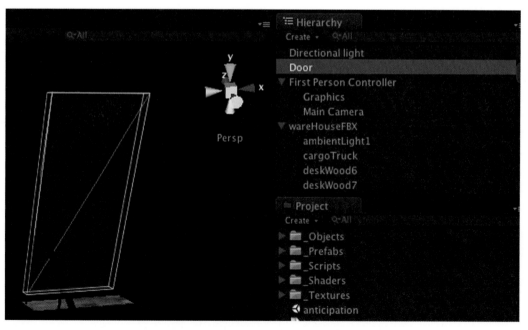

Step 2. Open *blob.js* and modify as shown in Listing 2.18.

Listing 2.18 Destroying Another Object in an Explosion

```
var explosion:GameObject;
var explosionLife:float = 5.0;
...
private var stuckOn: GameObject;
function OnCollisionEnter(collision : Collision)
{
        if(collision.gameObject.name != "First Person
Controller")
        {
                //record the object we are stuck on
                stuckOn = collision.gameObject;
                rigidbody.isKinematic = true;
                ...
}
function Explode()
{
        ...
        Destroy(exp, explosionLife);

        //if we are stuck on an object named Door //destroy it
        if(stuckOn && stuckOn.name == "Door")
        {
                Destroy(stuckOn);
        }
}
...
```

Step 3. Save and play. Position a sticky explosive on the door and watch as it gets destroyed.

Step 4. Create more cubes to fit in the other doorways. Ensure that they are named "Door" in the Hierarchy and any sticky explosive will destroy them. If you want to blow up anything the sticky bullet is stuck to, remove the if statement testing for just "Doors" (and the associated {})! Be careful though, you might fall through the floor if you destroy the wrong object.

Secondary Motion

Secondary motion brings the game environment to life. The simplest of movements can hint at a dynamic realistic environment with a life of its own. For example, a swaying tree or moving grass provides the illusion of a light breeze while also suggesting to the player that these are living things. How often have you been for a walk in a forest that doesn't move around you? Even in a still warehouse environment there is the opportunity to add secondary motion to add extra atmosphere to the scene.

⊙ Unity Hands On

Secondary Motion

Step 1. Open the project from the last hands-on session or download and open *Chapter Two/AnimPrinciplesC.zip*. We are going to add some curtains and wind effects reminiscent of morgue scenes from the original *Splinter Cell*.

Step 2. In the Scene, move your point of view such that you are looking into the room that has the truck in it. Add a cloth object by selecting GameObject > Cloth from the main menu.

Step 3. Rotate, resize, and position the cloth in the doorway as shown in Figure 2.39. Ensure that the cloth does not touch any sides or the top or bottom of the doorway. Rotate it with the normal facing outward (away from the truck). You will notice that the cloth object, just like a plane, only has one side. It will not be visible from inside the other room.

FIG 2.39 Positioning a cloth object in a doorway with attachments.

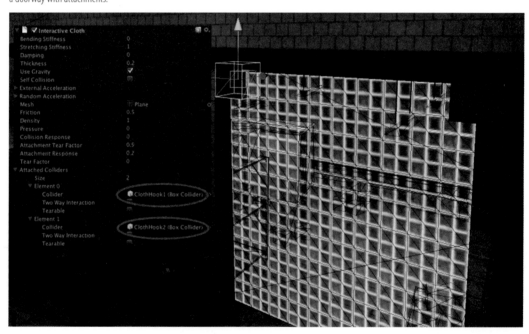

Step 4. Create a new material and add it to the cloth. Set the shader to Transparent/VertexLit. Make up your own Main Color (and set the alpha value to 80% for some transparency), Spec Color (this is the color that is reflected from the surface when lit),

and Emissive Color (this is the glow color). Select a texture. In this example, the innerWindow texture is used with the *x* and *y* tiling values set to 10 each.

Step 5. Create a cube. If you cannot see it, with the cube selected in the Hierarchy, select GameObject > Move to View from the main menu. The cube will move to the center of the Scene view.

Step 6. Position the cube at the top left of the cloth. The cloth must appear as though it is inserted into the side of the cube as shown in Figure 2.39. Create another cube and position it at the top right of the cloth. Rename the cubes, ClothHook1 and ClothHook2. It doesn't matter which one is which.

Step 7. Select the cloth in the Hierarchy and locate the Interactive Cloth component in the Inspector. Change the size for the Attached Colliders section to 2. Set the colliders for Element 0 to ClothHook1 and Element 1 to ClothHook2 as shown in Figure 2.39.

Step 8. Play. Note that the cloth becomes limp and hangs from the two cubes like a curtain. If the cloth falls to the ground or hangs from only one cube, it will be because the cubes do not intersect with the cloth in the corners.

Step 9. While still playing and watching in the Scene, select the cloth and locate the Interactive Cloth component in the Inspector. To add a blowing effect to the cloth, change the values of *x*, *y*, and *z* for the External Acceleration and Random Acceleration values. External Acceleration will add a constant fan like blowing force and Random Acceleration will randomly add puff like breezes to the cloth. It is a matter of playing around with these values to get the effect you want. Remember that while you are in play mode, any of the changes made to the cloth settings will revert when you stop. Note the values you would like to keep to reenter them once you are out of play mode.

Step 10. In the Hierarchy, drag and drop both ClothHook objects onto the InteractiveCloth object to make them child objects and attach them to the cloth.

Step 11. Press play and take your FPC through the cloth. Once inside the truck room, turn to look back at the cloth. It will not be visible because the normal is the other way around. The easiest way to fix this is to create another cloth object exactly the same and flip it around to face into the truck room.

Step 12. Right-click on the InteractiveCloth in the Hierarchy and select Duplicate. Two cloths will now appear in the Hierarchy. Rename them Cloth1 and Cloth2.

Step 13. Select Cloth2 and rotate it 90° such that its normal is pointing into the room with the truck.

Step 14. Play. This time you will be able to take the FPC back and forth between the rooms and see the cloth from both sides.

> ● **For Research**
> *Interactive Cloth*
> For more information on the settings for cloth, check out
>
> http://unity3d.com/support/documentation/Components/class-InteractiveCloth.html.

2.7 Two-Dimensional and 3D Tricks for Optimizing Game Space

The real world is a big place. The dream of many a game designer is to recreate the real world in all its detailed glory and vastness. Unfortunately, modeling everything down to the last nut and bolt and putting it into a game engine for real-time processing is not possible. However, many games do fake the vastness of the outside world very effectively, fooling the player into believing that the environment outside the game play area goes on forever.

A game requires a high frame rate to provide the player with a seamless game-playing experience. Between each frame, the computer must process all game object behavior, sound, physics, and player interactions. The number of game objects in view of the game has a large effect on the frame rate as they must be processed and re-rendered. Therefore, when designing a game level or environment it is critical to keep in mind how many things will need to be drawn in a scene and reduce this to an absolute minimum while keeping the quality high. Having said this, it might not necessarily be the number of objects in a scene that need to be reduced but reconsideration of how they are treated and drawn.

This section explores some common ways for optimizing 3D game worlds.

2.7.1 Reducing Polygons

Each polygon, being the smallest part of a mesh, adds to the processing of a scene. On high-end gaming machines the polycount must increase dramatically to affect the frame rate. However, on mobile devices, simply adding a couple of hundred polygons can bring a game to a halt. Here are some methods to reduce the polycount.

Use Only What You Need
When creating a model for a game, consider the number of superfluous polygons in the mesh and reduce. For example, the default plane object created by Unity is essentially a square. If you only ever use it as a square, such as for objects in the rocket ship game, this object is inefficient as it has many polygons. A simple square plane only requires two triangular polygons. In this case, create a square plane in Blender and import it instead.

Backface Culling

As discovered earlier, Unity does not show the reverse side of surfaces. This is called *backface culling* and is a common technique in computer graphics for not drawing the reverse side of a polygon. In some cases, however, as with the curtain in the warehouse example, it may be necessary to draw both sides. In the hands-on session we used two cloths, one for either side. This is an inefficient way as it immediately doubles the number of polygons used for the curtain. A better way is to turn backface culling off.

To do this in Unity requires the writing of a *shader*. A shader is a piece of code the game engine interprets as a texturing treatment for the surface of a polygon. When you set a material to *Diffuse* or *Transparent/Specular*, you are using a prewritten shader.

To write your own shader requires extensive knowledge of the shader language and complex computer graphics principles; however, numerous shaders are available on the Unity Web site for you to try, so here are the steps required to add a custom shader.

◉ Unity Hands On

Loading a Custom Shader

Step 1. Open Unity and create a simple scene with plane or other object to test the shader. If you prefer, you could add this to the curtain in the warehouse application.

Step 2. In the Project select Create > Shader. A new shader file will appear in the Project. Rename to backfaceOn. Double-click to open this file. Replace the existing code with that in Listing 2.19. This custom shader has been taken from http://unity3d.com/support/documentation/Components/SL-CullAndDepth.html.

Listing 2.19 A Custom Unity Shader to Remove Backface Culling

```
Shader "Backface On" {
  Properties {
    _Color ("Main Color", Color) = (1,1,1,0)
    _SpecColor ("Spec Color", Color) = (1,1,1,1)
    _Emission ("Emmisive Color", Color) = (0,0,0,0)
    _Shininess ("Shininess", Range (0.01, 1)) = 0.7
    _MainTex ("Base (RGB)", 2D) = "white" { }
  }
  SubShader {
    Material {
      Diffuse [_Color]
      Ambient [_Color]
      Shininess [_Shininess]
      Specular [_SpecColor]
      Emission [_Emission]
    }
```

```
      Lighting On
      SeparateSpecular On
      // Set up alpha blending
      Blend SrcAlpha OneMinusSrcAlpha
      // Render the back facing parts of the object.
      // If the object is convex, these will always be further away
      // than the front-faces.
      Pass {
        Cull Front
        SetTexture [_MainTex] {
          Combine Primary * Texture
        }
      }
      // Render the parts of the object facing us.
      // If the object is convex, these will be closer than the
      // back-faces.
      Pass {
        Cull Back
        SetTexture [_MainTex] {
        Combine Primary * Texture
      }
    }
  }
}
```

Step 3. Drag and drop the shader into Unity's Project view.
Step 4. Create a new material. In the shader drop-down selection box your new shader will be available as *Backface On*. You can now use the material like any other.

Level of Detail

Level of detail (LOD) is a technique for providing multiple models and textures for a single object with reducing levels of detail. For example, you may have a high polycount, high-resolution textured model, a medium polycount, medium-resolution textured model, and a low polycount, low-resolution texture model for a single character. The model that gets drawn by the renderer will depend on the distance the camera is away from the character. If the character is close, the highest quality version is used. If the character is far in the distance, the lowest quality version is used.

This method not only mimics human vision-making objects in the distance less defined, but also allows for the drawing of more objects in a scene as the ones farther away take up less memory.

◉ Unity Hands On
A Simple LOD Handler

Step 1. Download *Chapter Two/LOD.zip* from the Web site, unzip, and open in Unity. In the Project, double-click on *lodbuilding* of the *Scenes* folder to open the scene. The Scene will appear with a high-rise building and FPC.

Step 2. Play. Move around using the FPC controls.

Step 3. While playing, in the Game, click on the Stats button at the top right of the Game tab as shown in Figure 2.40. A window with game statistics will display as an overlay. In this window you can see how fast the application is running and how many triangles (a.k.a. polygons) are in the camera view.

FIG 2.40 The Stats button in the Game tab displays current game performance values.

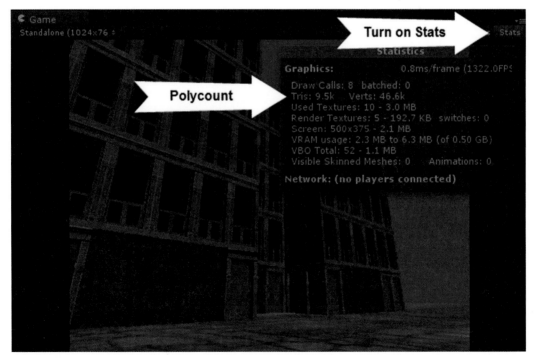

Step 4. Stop playing and create a new JavaScript file called *LODManager*. Add the code shown in Listing 2.20.

Listing 2.20 JavaScript to Manage Level of Detail (Inspired by Original Code Posted by Rich Hudson and "Leepo" on the Unity Forum)

```javascript
var lod1: Mesh;
var lod2: Mesh;
var lodDist1: float;
var lodDist2: float;
var updateInterval : float = 1.0;
var currentLOD : int = 1;
var meshFilter : MeshFilter;
var thisTransform : Transform;

function Awake()
{
    meshFilter = GetComponent(MeshFilter) as MeshFilter;
    thisTransform = transform;
    var startIn : float = Random.Range(0.0, updateInterval);
    InvokeRepeating("UpdateLOD",startIn,updateInterval);
}

function UpdateLOD()
{
    var distanceFromObject : float =
            Vector3.Distance(thisTransform.position,
                    Camera.main.transform.position);
    if (distanceFromObject < lodDist1)
    {
        if(currentLOD != 1)
        {
            currentLOD = 1;
            meshFilter.mesh = lod1;
        }
    }
    else if (distanceFromObject < lodDist2)
    {
        if(currentLOD != 2)
        {
            currentLOD = 2;
            meshFilter.mesh = lod2;
        }
    }
    else
    {
        currentLOD = 0;
        meshFilter.mesh = null;
    }
}
```

Step 5. Save the code. Attach it to the Building object in the Hierarchy. Select Building in the Hierarchy and locate the LOD Manager script component in the Inspector.

Step 6. Click on the small circle to select a mesh for the value of Lod 1. When the pop-up selector opens you will find two building meshes. Select the one with more detail.

Step 7. Set the value for Lod 2 the same way, except this time pick the less detailed building mesh.

Step 8. Set Lod Dist 1 to 80 and Lod Dist 2 to 120.

Step 9. Play. Turn around to face the building. Remain facing the building as you move backward by holding the down arrow key. When you get a distance of 80 away from the building the mesh will switch to the less detailed mesh. Move forward again and as you pass the 80 threshold it will become more detailed. Watch the Stats screen polycount change as you move back and forth. Now move even farther back. When you pass a distance of 120 the building will disappear because in the script it is set to "null" or not value after Lod Dist 2.

Step 10. Duplicate the Building object and move the copies around on the terrain to create a bigger city. Walk around it observing how the LOD snaps buildings in and out of different levels of detail.

What you have just experienced is a very simple implementation of LOD. It works well to reduce the polycount and yet keep many objects in the scene, giving a great depth to the environment. You may have experienced this snapping effect in games you have played.

2.7.2 Camera Viewing Volume

Previously in this chapter we examined the camera viewing volume and how it reduces the objects being drawn. To emphasize its effectiveness in association with LOD, we will run through a quick example.

⬤ **Unity Hands On**
Camera Viewing Volume and LOD

Step 1. Using the project from the previous hands-on session, create a prefab from the Building object and remove any others from the surface of the terrain.

Step 2. Create a new JavaScript file called *instantCity* and add the code in Listing 2.21.

Listing 2.21 A Quick and Easy Script to Create a Virtual City from One Building Object

```
var building:GameObject;
function Start()
{
    for(var i = 0; i < 20; i++)
    {
        for(var j = 0; j < 20; j++)
        {
            var newPos: Vector3 =
            new Vector3(
                i*Random.Range(100,200),0,
                j*Random.Range(100,200));
            var b:GameObject =
                Instantiate(building,newPos,Quaternion.identity);
        }
    }
}
function Update () {}
```

Step 3. Save the script and attach it to the First Person Controller. Click on the FPC and locate the script component in the Hierarchy. Drag and Drop the building prefab from the Project onto the building property of the script in the Inspector. In LOD Manager change the LOD Dist 1 to 500 and LOD Dist 2 to 1000.

Step 4. Play with both the Scene and the Game open. Orient your view in the Scene to be looking down on the terrain. When you first play the game note that all the buildings are created and positioned by the instantCity script. After this, buildings that are a certain distance from the FPC are removed. This is the LOD script in action. You can modify the distance values for the buildings LOD in the Inspector for the building prefab. In the Scene you will also see the FPC frustum. If it is larger than the range of the drawn buildings then it is too large.

Step 5. While playing, stand in one location and look around in the Game. How far can you see? If you can't see the buildings at the edge of the frustum, the far plane setting for the camera is too large. Try reducing it to see if it will have any effect on the environment. Remember, if you can't see a game object, there is no reason to try to draw it.

2.7.3 Fog

Another very (very) handy trick in reducing the visual size of a game environment is fog. In the previous examples when the FPC was at a far enough distance from the buildings they would slide behind the far plane of the camera or snap out of view because of the LOD. By adding fog, these other rather too obvious techniques can be hidden. A layer of fog can be added just before the far plane of the camera or the farthest distance of the LOD.

☯ Unity Hands On

Fog

Step 1. Open the project from the last hands-on session.

Step 2. Select Edit > Render Settings from the main menu.

Step 3. Tick the Fog box now available in the Inspector. Note that a gray fog covers the ground but not the sky in the Game.

Step 4. Play. Walk around the city. Buildings in the distance will be completely fogged out. As you move closer to a building the fog will lift.

Step 5. The thickness of the fog is modified in the Fog Density property of render settings. You will notice in the same place that you can change the color of the fog. The issue now faced is that the ground and buildings are fogged over, but the background color is not. This is a fact of life with using fog, as fog is only applied to game objects and not to the background. The best way to overcome this is to set the background color to the same color as the fog. This makes for a very convincing cloudy sky.

Step 6. Select the color picker for the fog and select a color. Note down the RGB and A values.

Step 7. In the Hierarchy, select the Main Camera attached to the FPC. Change the background color in the Inspector to the same color as the fog.

Step 8. Set the fog density to 0.005.

Step 9. Play. At this point it becomes a fine balance of testing if in the distance you can still see buildings disappearing instead of blurring into the fog. If so, try turning up the fog a little.

2.7.4 Textures

Fine-detailed, high-quality textures are the best defense against high polycounts. There is far more detail in a photorealistic image of a real-world item than could possibly fit into the polycount restrictions of any real-time game engine. Chapter One examined briefly the use of normal and specular maps to give extra texturing to game objects. Here we discuss two more popular tricks.

Moving Textures

When creating materials in Unity you may have seen properties for *x* and *y* offsets. These values are used to adjust the alignment and location of a texture on a polygon's surface. If these values are adjusted constantly with each game loop, the texture will appear animated. This is an effective way of creating an animation that doesn't involve modeling or extra polygons. It is often used in creating sky and water effects.

⦿ Unity Hands On

Animated Textures

Step 1. Create a new Unity project.

Step 2. In the Scene add a plane.

Step 3. Create a new material and add it to the plane.

Step 4. Find a seamless texture of your choosing from the Web.

Step 5. Drag and drop the new texture into the Project.

Step 6. Add the texture to the material. It should appear on the surface of the plane.

Step 7. Create a new JavaScript file called *animatedTexture*. Add the code in Listing 2.22.

Listing 2.22 JavaScript to Make a Texture Scroll over the Surface of an Object

```
var uvSpeed: Vector2 = new Vector2(0.0f, 1.0f );
var uvOffset: Vector2 = Vector2.zero;
function LateUpdate()
{
uvOffset += (uvSpeed * Time.deltaTime );
renderer.materials[0].SetTextureOffset("_MainTex", uvOffset);
}
```

Step 8. Attach the JavaScript to the plane.

Step 9. Play. The texture will move across the surface of the plane. To change the direction of the movement, modify the *x* and *y* values for the *uvSpeed* variable in the script. The *LateUpDate()* function is similar to the *Update()* function in that it executes for an object every game loop. However, with *LateUpDate()* it occurs as the very last function called for an object so that it can take into consideration any related processing occurring in the same game loop.

Step 10. Open the project with the warehouse. Create a new JavaScript file and enter the same code from Listing 2.22. Attach this script to polySurface437. This is the surface of the conveyor belt in the room where you placed the curtain. Play and watch the conveyor move!

Blob Shadows

Shadows give a scene an extra dimension of depth and add to visual realism. Generating shadows is processor intensive. Although shadows in game environments are covered in Chapter Seven, a quick and easy method for generating processor light shadows called Blob Shadows is introduced here.

Usually the game rendering system calculates shadows based on the position and intensity of lights and the position of game objects. When many real-time shadows need to be calculated, such as those of moving objects, such as characters, it can slow the frame rate considerably. This is a big problem for games on mobile devices where such shadowing is not practical.

◉ Unity Hands On
Blob Shadows

Step 1. Download *Chapter Two/BlobShadows.zip* from the Web site, unzip, and open in Unity. In the Project, double-click on *blobshadowexamples* of the *Scenes* folder to open the scene. The Scene will appear with a character standing on a plane.

Step 2. Select Assets > Import Package > Projectors from the main menu to import the projector package.

Step 3. Locate *Blob Shadow Projector* in the Project and drag and drop it onto the Male game object. A frustum object will appear under the Male model. This is the Blob Shadow Projector.

Step 4. Move the projector up until it is just above the top of the model's head. A black blob will appear on the ground. This is the blob shadow. The shadow is created using a material with the texture of the round black blob on it. When the projector intersects a plane, as it does here with the ground, the black texture is drawn inside the intersection area of the plane and the projector frustum.

Step 5. In its current state the Male model is also inside the projector frustum and therefore the shadow is drawn on it too. To fix this we place the model into another drawing layer. Select the Male object in the Hierarchy. In the Inspector at the very top to the right of Tag is a property called Layer. Click on the drop-down box next to Layer and select *Add Layer*.

Step 6. In the Tag Manager that opens in the Inspector, next to *User Layer 8*, type in *character*. This will create a new drawing layer called *character*.

Step 7. Select the Male object in the Hierarchy again. In the Inspector, set its Layer to character using the drop-down box.

Step 8. Select the Blob Shadow Projector in the Hierarchy. In the Inspector's Projector Component, set the *Ignore Layers* property to *character*. The projector will now ignore anything in the character layer, which in this case is the Male model, and draw the shadow object everywhere else it intersects.

This is a very effective way to add convincing shadows to objects without adding too much processing overhead.

2.7.5 Billboards

Billboarding is a technique that uses planes to fake a lot of background scenery. A billboard is a plane usually having a partially transparent texture applied to give it the appearance of being a shape other than a square. Common uses for billboards are grass, clouds, and distant trees.

To give the illusion that the billboard is viewable from all angles, the plane orientates itself constantly so that it is always facing the player.

◉ Unity Hands On
Billboards

Step 1. Open a new Unity project and add a ground plane and an FPC (for which you will need to import the Character Controller package).
Step 2. Download *Chapter Two/basicPlane.blend* and *grass.psd* from the Web site and add to your project.
Step 3. Add a Directional Light game object and rotate it down to give some shading to the ground plane.
Step 4. Add the basicPlane to the Scene and rotate it by −90° around the *x* axis to make it stand upright. If you can't see the surface after rotating, orient your view so that you are on the other side of the plane.
Step 5. Create a new material called grass. Set the shader to Transparent/Diffuse. Use the previously downloaded grass texture on it.
Step 6. Add this material to the basicPlane object. It will need to be dragged and dropped onto the Plane child object that is attached to basicPlane as this holds the mesh.
Step 7. Play. Walk around the scene with the FPC and examine the plane. From a distance it looks good. As you approach it and move around, it becomes apparent that the image is flat and not viewable from the underside.
Step 8. To update the plane so that it always faces the player, create a new JavaScript file called *billboard* and attach it to the basicPlane. Enter the code in Listing 2.23.

Listing 2.23 Script to Create a Billboard from a Plane

```
function Update()
{
        transform.LookAt(Camera.current.transform);
}
```

Step 9. Play. The plane will always face the player. If the grass texture appears upside down on the plane, set the *y* tiling value to −1 in the material.

Step 10. To see the full effect, duplicate the basicPlane object four or five times and move them around to create a bunch of grass. Play and walk around.

Step 11. When you walk over the top of the grass it will lay down flat. If the billboard were a tree you wouldn't want this to happen. Rather, rotating around the *x* axis should be turned off. That way the object will stay vertical and only turn around its *y* axis. To allow for this, modify *billboard.js* to the code in Listing 2.24.

Listing 2.24 Billboarding Script That Allows the *x* Rotation to Be Turned Off

```
var StayUpright = true;
function Update()
{
        transform.LookAt(Camera.current.transform);

        if(StayUpright)
                transform.eulerAngles.x = 0;
}
```

Step 12. Play. The grass will not bend over as the FPC approaches it. You can now turn this feature on and off using the tick box for *StayUpright* in the Inspector when *billboard.js* is attached to a game object.

More often than not, billboards are used on horizon lines and in the distance. Because they do not stand up under close scrutiny, you may want to use them on mass, but in areas of the game environment the player can't quite reach.

2.8 Summary

This chapter covered a variety of techniques for replicating real-world mechanics in a game environment. These have included movement with vectors and the physics system and optimization techniques that make the virtual world seem as extensive as the real world.

Most often satisfactory movement in a game environment can be achieved through knowledge of vector mathematics. Applying this first before jumping headlong into the physics system will optimize processing of the game environment. For example, in the rocket ship hands-on session, physics could have been employed to push the rocket ship around the planet. This would, however, have been overkill, as only a simple translation and slerping algorithm was required.

It is a common first-timer mistake when creating a game environment to make it detailed and vast without consideration for how game play will be affected as the frame rate drops. Many cannot understand how such top-quality AAA titles can run so fast with such intricate landscapes and mind-blowing special effects, and it is often the game engine that takes the blame. This is not the case, and this chapter has revealed some of the tricks employed by professionals to trick the player's perception of the environment.

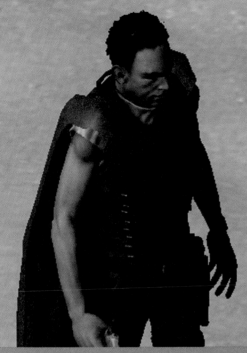

CHAPTER 3

Animation Mechanics

Animation is about creating the illusion of life. And you can't create it if you don't have one.

Brad Bird

3.1 Introduction

Animation is the underlying mechanic on which the visual aspect of computer games is built. It is the illusion of movement created through the display of a rapid succession of images, each slightly different from the other, creating the impression of motion. Animation is possible because of biological phenomena involving the human eye.

Originally, the perception of motion was explained by a theory known as *persistence of vision*, which refers to the afterimage that appears on the retina for approximately one-twenty-fifth of a second. You will notice this effect after staring at something and then closing your eyes. A negative type of imprint will be apparent. This effect is exaggerated if you look at a high-contrast image such as the shadowed side of a tree with the sun shining through from the other side. It was initially thought that humans saw animation when the afterimage from one still shot merged with the next. Although persistence of vision is a term still used to explain our ability to see movement when there is none in film and cinema, the theory was discredited as the main explanation by German Gestalt psychologist Max Wertheimer in 1912. Rather he proposed that the perception of motion was a psychological phenomenon called *phi*. Phi, in short, is the way in which the human brain automatically fills in the gaps between the images we see and therefore creates a perception of seamless motion.

The traditional technique for producing animation was to hand draw each image, known as a *frame*, and display them one after the other. Early Disney cartoons were produced in this manner. In order to provide smooth motion, the frames need to be shown at 24 frames per second. These frames are shot in twos such that each still image is displayed on two frames of film. This means that 12 drawings are required for 1 second of film.

For modern computer games, frame rates between 30 and 100 are acceptable. Of course, if there were no motion on the screen, a frame rate of 1 would be adequate. The frame rate in a computer game will differ depending on the background processing that is occurring during any given game loop. Ironically, fast action-paced games with lots of moving objects need to run at a higher frame rate in order for the player to take all the action in, although all the extra processing would be taxing on the processor and could lead to low frame rates.

Animation in the very first computer games was the result of using vector graphics to draw an object on the screen, clearing the screen, and redrawing the object at a slightly different location and rotation. Essentially, each frame was being drawn on the fly by an algorithm—the reason being that the computers of this time did not have memory available for storing art assets created by others; not to mention the absence of digital paint programs to produce them. For very simplistic graphics this worked effectively. The use of real-time drawing in one of the first computer games, *Spacewar!* (produced in 1962), is shown in Figure 3.1.

When read-only memory was introduced to arcade games in 1974, it allowed for the storage of predrawn graphics along with the game's program. The game could then load the various graphical assets and integrate them into the animation on the screen. These two-dimensional bitmaps were first referred to as *sprites*.

3.2 Sprites

Loading a 2D image onto the screen and redrawing it along a path will create a simple animation. This very principle is illustrated in the rocket ship workshop from Chapter Two in which the static rocket ship image is moved around the screen. The rocket ship and planet are sprites. In these examples,

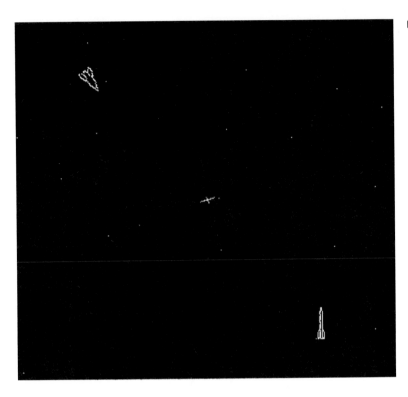

FIG 3.1 *Spacewar!*

sprites are dealt with by placing a texture representing the graphic element over a plane game object. The plane is then moved around the screen to create an animation. Both the rocket ship and the planet each have its own materials representing the different images.

The more materials used in a game, the less efficiently it will run. This is closely related to the way in which the power of two images is processed. In the case of Unity, each material adds extra load inside each game loop. This load is called a *draw call*. A draw call occurs when rendering commands are processed by the computer's graphics processor. Each material used equals one draw call. Therefore, if you have 100 materials it will cost you 100 draw calls.

⚙ Unity Hands On
Investigating Draw Calls

Step 1. Create a new Project in Unity.
Step 2. Add two planes to the Scene.
Step 3. Position the camera so that the planes are visible in the Game.
Step 4. Click the Stats button in the top right of the Game tab. Note that the number of draw calls is currently 1.

Step 5. Create two new materials in the Project called *Material 1* and *Material 2*. You don't need to give them any particular settings.

Step 6. Add *Material 1* to one plane and *Material 2* to the other. Now look at the number of draw calls. It will be equal to 2, the same as the number of materials.

Step 7. Right-click on one of the planes in the Hierarchy and select Duplicate. The number of draw calls will remain at 2 as there are still only two materials being used.

Step 8. Create another material and add it to the latest plane. The number of draw calls will increase to 3.

As the number of draw calls increases, the slower your game will run. Albeit a great number of draw calls would be required to make any noticeable difference on a high-performance gaming machine. However, if you port your application to a mobile device, a dramatic effect on performance is seen after around 15 draw calls.

Materials aren't the only things that will increase the number of draw calls. As the polycounts of the meshes in the game environment increase, so too will the draw calls. However, polycounts don't have a one-to-one relationship with performance as materials do. Therefore, it is essential to consider the way in which sprite materials are handled.

3.3 Texture Atlas

Considering that a single material made from a texture that is 512×512 will take the same number of draw calls as one that is 32×32, it seems a waste to use only a 32×32 texture. Therefore, if the 32×32 image were put into a 512×512 image, there would be plenty of space in that image for other small images. Combining images into one texture is a common technique in games and is called a *texture atlas*.

In a texture atlas, each smaller image has its own set of pixel coordinates and a width and height. To create such an atlas you can use a paint program such as Photoshop or Gimp to combine smaller images into a single larger one. Figure 3.2 shows an example texture map in Gimp. Each image is placed such that a bounding box around it does not overlap with any other image. This allows for easy extraction of single images from the texture map in the game engine. In this example, the bounding box for the small car starts at (0,0) pixels and ends at (40,40) pixels. Gimp is useful for creating texture atlases; the pixel location of the mouse cursor is shown in the lower left-hand corner of the window. This makes it easier to extract the bounding boxes for each image. In Gimp, however, (0,0) is in the upper left-hand corner of the image. If you were to use Adobe Illustrator, (0,0) is

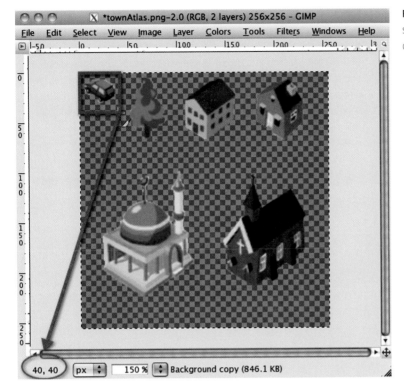

FIG 3.2 A texture atlas in Gimp showing the boundaries of a small car sprite image.

in the bottom-left corner. Keep this in mind when you are grabbing pixel coordinates. If your texture appears upside down, it could be because the y axis is inverted. This isn't a problem, just something that needs to be taken into consideration in your game scripts.

The coordinates of the bounding box are then used to manipulate the UV values of a mesh such that only the pixels inside the bounding box appear on the mesh as its texture. This requires a thorough understanding of vertices and UVs.

While the vertices of a mesh can have any value in 2D or 3D space, UVs are always specified between 0 and 1.

Unity Hands On
Modifying Mesh UVs for Sprite Mapping

Step 1. Download *Chapter Three/StaticSprites.zip* from the Web site. Unzip and open the project with Unity. Open the scene called *isostreet*. You will see an isometric view of a street scene with a number of smaller icons in the center. The camera is set to orthographic. As we are using only sprites and no true 3D objects, the perception of depth is not required. Play. Nothing will happen.

Step 2. In the Project create a new Shader. Edit the Shader by double-clicking to open and add the code given in Listing 3.1. Because sprites are two dimensional, usually you don't want them affected by a light in the game environment; so they don't look shaded and washed out, a special shader for them is a good idea.

Listing 3.1 Shader Code for an Unlit Texture with Transparency

```
Shader "Sprite"
{
   Properties
   {
      _Color ("Main Color", Color) = (1,1,1,1)
      _MainTex ("Base (RGB) Trans. (Alpha)", 2D) = "white" { }
   }
   Category
   {
      ZWrite On
      Alphatest Greater 0.5
      Cull Off
      SubShader
      {
         Pass
         {
            Lighting Off
            SetTexture [_MainTex]
            {
               constantColor [_Color]
               Combine texture * constant, texture * constant
            }
         }
      }
   }
}
```

Step 3. The groups of icons in the center of the Game are drawn on the SimplePlane object in the Hierarchy. Select it and note the texture atlas material. The objective is to isolate one of the icons and draw it on the plane when the game is run. To do this we need to modify the UV values with script. Create a new JavaScript file called setSprite and add the code in Listing 3.2.

Listing 3.2 Script to Modify the UVs of a Plane

```
//Texture Atlas Specifications
var startPixel:Vector2;
var endPixel:Vector2;
function Start()
{
    //get object mesh
    var mesh : Mesh = GetComponent(MeshFilter).mesh;
    //get existing uvs
    var uvs : Vector2[] = new Vector2[4];
    //get existing material
    var texture : Texture2D = renderer.material.mainTexture;
    //use Sprite shader
    renderer.material.shader = Shader.Find ( "Sprite" );
    //create new uvs from the start and end pixel values
    uvs[0] = new Vector2(startPixel.x/texture.width,
            (texture.height - endPixel.y)/texture.height);
    uvs[1] = new Vector2(startPixel.x/texture.width,
            (texture.height - startPixel.y)/texture.height);
    uvs[2] = new Vector2(endPixel.x/texture.width,
            (texture.height - startPixel.y)/texture.height);
    uvs[3] = new Vector2(endPixel.x/texture.width,
            (texture.height - endPixel.y)/texture.height);
    //reset the mesh uvs
    mesh.uv = uvs;
}
```

Step 4. The coordinates to be used are inverted in the *y* axis as specified in Gimp; therefore, the code turns them up the other way by subtracting all *y* values from the texture height. If you used pixel coordinates with (0,0) in the bottom-left corner then you would just leave out the `texture.height` part. Attach the new script to SimplePlane.

Step 5. Select SimplePlane in the Hierarchy and locate the attached script in the Inspector. Set the startPixel and endPixel values to (0,0) and (40,40), respectively, as shown in Figure 3.3.

Step 6. Play. The texture on SimplePlane will now become the little blue car. Because the code is focusing on a smaller part of a large image and stretching that part over the same sized surface, the final texture may look pixilated or too fuzzy. To fix this you will need to rescale the SimplePlane to suite. This can be done in the Inspector in the transform component by changing the *x* and *y* scale values.

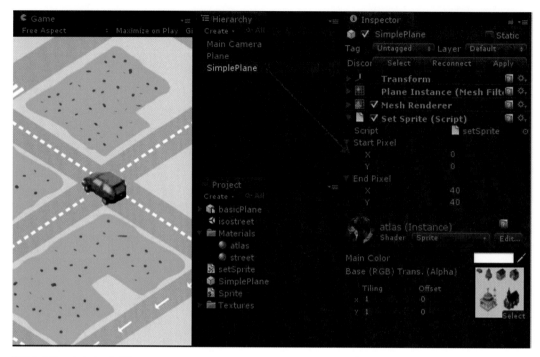

FIG 3.3 Setting pixel values for UV modification.

Step 7. To add more sprites to the scene, duplicate SimplePlane, and change its location and the start and end pixel values. Using the available icons in the texture map you will be able to make a nice street scene. SimplePlane can also be treated like the rocket ship from a previous workshop, and code can be added to move it around in the game.

> **⊙ Note**
>
> **Specifying UV Values**
>
> The listing in Listing 3.2 assumes that the pixel values for the sprite textures have the *y* values flipped. If you find that your sprite textures are upside down, change the code for all *y* values to `endPixel.y/texture.height`. This will turn the images up the other way.

3.4 Animated Sprites

Technically, any 2D image used as an object or character in a game is a sprite. However, the term is associated more often with a set of 2D animations representing specific movements of a game object. In this case, a sprite consists of a set of images that combine to animate specific gestures, such as walking, running, and jumping. The sprites are imported into a game engine and code is used to control how the frames are presented in the game environment to give the illusion of character movement.

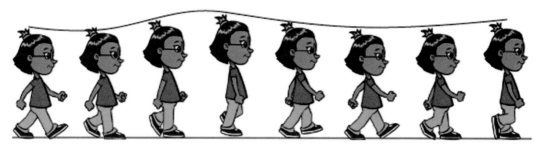

FIG 3.4 Half of a walk cycle where the other half would be a reversal of the arm and leg positions.

The animation images for a sprite are drawn based on the movement cycles originally developed for cartoon characters. Preston Blair, an acclaimed animator who worked for Disney, Warner Bros., and Hanna-Barbera, published many illustrations demonstrating various character poses through a series of movement cycles. Some of them can be found at http://www.animationarchive .org/pics/pbanimation26-big.jpg. The first of these cycles often referred to when teaching elementary animation is the *walk cycle* shown in Figure 3.4. Note in the walk cycle here, and the others by Preston Blair, the use of motion arcs for natural movement. The character rises and falls with each step.

Each of the images in Figure 3.4 becomes a single frame for the sprite. When these frames are cycled through in the game it gives the illusion of a walking character.

⊙ Unity Hands On
Creating a Texture Atlas with Code and Animated Sprite

> **Step 1.** Create a new Unity project.
> **Step 2.** Create a new Shader called *Sprite* and copy the code from Listing 3.1.
> **Step 3.** Add a plane into the Scene and orientate it such that the visible side faces the camera.
> **Step 4.** Download *Chapter Three/walkcycles.zip* from the Web site. Unzip the file and add all the images into the Project.
> **Step 5.** Create a new JavaScript file called *AnimatedSprite* and add the code shown in Listing 3.3.

Listing 3.3 Script to Build a Texture Atlas from a Series of Single Images

```
var textures: Texture2D[];
var atlas: Texture2D;
var framerate: float = 15.0;
private var currentFrame = 0;
private var totalWidth:float;
```

```
private var nextFrame: float = 0;
private var timeBetweenFrames;
function Start()
{
    totalWidth = textures[0].width * textures.length;

    //make texture atlas
    atlas = new Texture2D(totalWidth, textures[0].height);

    renderer.material.mainTexture = atlas;
    renderer.material.color = Color.white;
    renderer.material.shader = Shader.Find ( "Sprite" );

    for(var i: int = 0; i < textures.length; i++)
    {
        for (var y : int = 0;y < textures[i].height; y++)
        {
            for (var x : int = 0;x < textures[i].width; x++)
            {
                atlas.SetPixel (x +i*textures[i].width,y,
                        textures[i].GetPixel(x,y));
            }
        }
    }
    atlas.Apply();
}
```

Step 6. Attach *AnimatedSprite.js* to the plane.

Step 7. With the plane selected in the Hierarchy, locate the AnimatedSprite script component in the Inspector. Set the Size value for Textures to 16 and drag and drop all the walk cycle images onto the elements where Element 0 is walkcycle1, Element 1 is walkcycle2, and so on.

Step 8. Play. The texture atlas will be created and applied to the plane. In the game you will be able to see an image on the plane made up of the 16 walk cycle textures. The effect can be seen better if you stretch the plane out by modifying its *x* scale as shown in Figure 3.5.

Step 9. Ensure that the plane scale is (1,1,1). Now instead of all 16 images appearing on the plane at once we only want 1. To achieve this, the texture scale on the plane should be reduced to 1/16th of its size along the *x* axis. This can be done in the Inspector where the tiling and offset values for a material are set. However, because the atlas is being created dynamically (i.e., as the program runs), you'll want the code to set it to align with the number of frames in the walk cycle. To do this, modify *AnimatedSprite.js* as shown in Listing 3.4.

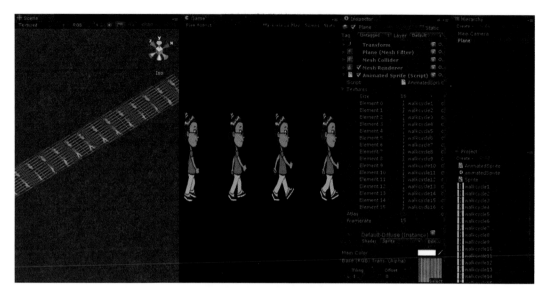

FIG 3.5 The created texture atlas.

Listing 3.4 Setting the Texture Offset and Scale to Display the First Frame from the Walk Cycle Atlas

```
var textures: Texture2D[];
var atlas: Texture2D;

...

function Start()
{
    totalWidth = textures[0].width *textures.length;

    ...

    for(var i: int = 0; i < textures.length; i++)
    {
        ...
    }
    atlas.Apply();
    renderer.material.mainTextureOffset = Vector2(0,0);
    renderer.material.mainTextureScale =
        Vector2 (1.0/textures.length,1);
}
```

Step 10. Play. The first frame will appear on the plane.

Step 11. Next, to animate the sprite, the frames need to change. Changing each Update() would be erratic and too fast as the time between Updates() is not fixed and depends on the processing occurring in the game. We therefore need to implement a timer that can switch the frames for us. Modify *AnimatedSprite.js* as shown in Listing 3.5.

Listing 3.5 Script to Swap Frames on a Texture Atlas According to a Set Frame Rate

```
var textures: Texture2D[];

...

function Start()
{
timeBetweenFrames = 1.0/framerate;

...

}
function LateUpdate ()
{
     if(Time.time > nextFrame)
     {
        renderer.material.mainTextureOffset =
            Vector2(currentFrame*textures[0].width/
                totalWidth,0);
        nextFrame = Time.time + timeBetweenFrames;
        currentFrame++;
        if(currentFrame > = textures.length)
        {
            currentFrame = 0;
        }
     }
}
```

Step 12. Play. The sprite will be animated.

Step 13. To change the speed at which the animation plays, select the plane in the Hierarchy and locate the Framerate variable of the AnimatedSprite component in the Inspector. This value controls the number of frames drawn per second. Change it to 100 to see the animation play faster and change it to 1 to see it run slower.

Step 14. Download *Chapter Three/background.psd* from the Web site. Add a new plane to the scene behind the sprite and put this new texture on it. It is a city background scene. Stretch the plane out to accommodate the texture. Set the material shader to Sprite to make it display correctly without lighting. If the image is upside down, rotate the plane by 180° around the *y* axis.

Step 15. Create a new JavaScript file named *scrollBackground*. Add the image scrolling code from Chapter Two, repeated here in Listing 3.6 for your convenience. Attach the JavaScript to the new plane.

Step 16. With this new plane selected, change the UVSpeed to (0.1,0) in the Inspector.

Step 17. Play. The background will scroll, making the character appear to walk along the street.

Listing 3.6 Code to Scroll a Texture over the Surface of a Mesh

```
var uvSpeed: Vector2 = new Vector2( 0.0f, 1.0f );
var uvOffset: Vector2 = Vector2.zero;
function LateUpdate()
{
   uvOffset + = ( uvSpeed * Time.deltaTime );
   renderer.materials[0].SetTextureOffset("_MainTex", uvOffset);
}
```

Step 18. To move the character itself with the arrow keys, create a new JavaScript called *walk.js*, add the code in Listing 3.7, and attach it to the character's plane.

Listing 3.7 Adding Forward, Backward and Idle Animations

```
var speed:float = 0.5;
function Update ()
{
      if(Input.GetKey("right"))
      {
            this.transform.position.x + = speed;
      }

      if(Input.GetKey("left"))
      {
            this.transform.position.x - = speed;
      }
}
```

Step 19. Play. The arrow keys will move the sprite back and forth in front of the background. Remove the scrolling script from the background to get a better idea of how the character is moving.

Step 20. With the walking speed set to 0.5 the character appears to slide across the ground. This is a common error made by beginner animators when creating walk cycles and placing the character into an environment whether it is in 2D or 3D. The idea is to get the walk cycle speed to match the motion speed so that each foot appears to be planted into the ground. For this character, a speed of about 0.06 is a close match for a frame rate of 15. Try this out.

Note

Making Your Own Sprite Frames

One of the easiest ways to create your own sprites, instead of drawing each frame by hand, is to use a software package that will do it for you. Adobe Flash has an export to image option that will allow you to create single frames from an animation and save them as a sequence of .png files.

Anime Studio Pro is a 2D animation software package that will take an image of a character and allow you to add your own bones (see Figure 3.6). You can then manipulate these bones to pose the character. After an animation has been created, *Anime Studio Pro* provides export features that will create a sequence of .jpg or .png files that can then be used on sprites in Unity.

FIG 3.6 Anime Studio Pro.

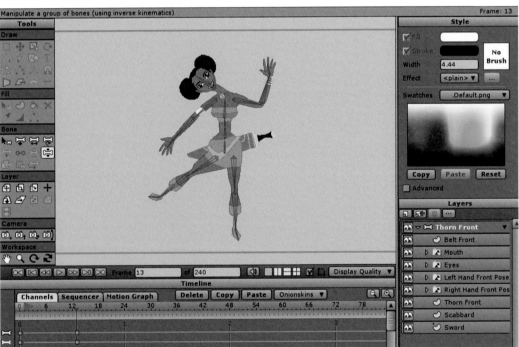

⊙ **On the Web**

More sprites: http://www.touchofdeathforums.com/resources.php

GIMP http://www.gimp.org

3.5 Baked 3D Animations

Calculating animations in real time through kinematics is a very processor-costly method for animating game characters. While this method can certainly produce spontaneous interactions with characters, far more artificially intelligent controls need to be programmed to make them feel real. If you examine game characters closely you will notice that they repeat the same actions in exactly the same way over and over. This is because it is less effort on the part of the animation to make; for example, why use five different walk animations when just one will suffice? It does not add anything more to a game having characters that can select from different walking styles as they see fit.

If you stop to observe ancillary characters in the crowd such as those in *Splinter Cell* or *Grand Theft Auto*, you will be able to spot their walk cycles and other repeated actions. Because the purpose of the game in these cases is not to eye the crowd, the same repeated walk cycle is not that important. You may also find a game hero climbs a drainpipe the same way he climbs a rope. Reusing animations is just a trick to get better performance out of a game and a way to keep the development budget down. In the end it is how these animations are used and how the game environment is designed around these limitations. For example, the animation for climbing a ladder could be used for scaling a building or a trellis if the objects are designed to have handholds and footholds in similar positions to a ladder.

When animations are fixed and not manipulated in real time by the program, they are called *baked*. This means that the entire animation sequence is calculated beforehand and that the program receives a set of model transformations for each frame.

Because the character modeler cannot possibly know at the time of animating how the player is going to direct and move the character, it is impossible to create a long strung out animation, for example, showing the character running up the road, jumping over a fence, and rolling through a window. If the player decides the character should not jump over the fence but rather hop on the nearest motorbike, a single long animation will not allow for visualization. Instead, animations are broken into short action segments that can later be put together in any order to facilitate fluid animation. Such segments might include walk, run, and jump cycles. Depending on how the player wants the character to move, he can then run, jump, run, and walk or walk, jump, jump, run, and walk seamlessly.

This means that each animation segment should start and end with the character in the same pose. When the next segment is added, there is no obvious gap in the sequence. As shown in Figure 3.7, the initial frame for the character's idle, run, walk, and shoot down animations has the character's feet and legs in exactly the same position. No matter what the sequence of

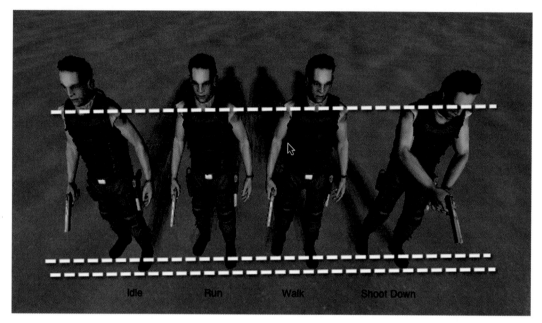

FIG 3.7 Starting frames for four different animations performed by the same character.

actions, the full movement of the character will appear fluid. In a situation where the animation switches to the shoot down, the arms and shoulders will move away from the initial poses of the others. If this is a very small movement, and given the legs don't move, the change in pose will appear as a simple frame change in any other segment.

If a situation arises where the character needs to go from a walking to a crawling action, two in-between sequences are required to stitch the animations together: one for getting down and one for standing up. Sometimes a single animation is reused for its reverse action. For example, getting down is reused for the standing up and walking forward is reused for walking backward. However, if you have a close look at both these examples, the results are usually very unconvincing and ruin the entire effect.

Baked animations can be made in software modeling and animation tools such as Autodesk's 3DS Max and Maya. The native format for animations in Unity is fbx, which can be created with both these applications. Once the fbx sequences have been imported into Unity, Script can be used to control how they play.

⊙ Unity Hands On
Controlling Character Animation

> **Step 1.** Download *Chapter Three/CharacterAnimation.zip* from the Web site. Unzip and open the project in Unity. Open the characterAnimation scene. In the Game you will see a character and simple terrain.

Note that in the Project, Character Models > Hero Artwork folder you will find a number of files named *Hero@****, where *** is an action such as *FireGun* or *IdleAnim*. Each one of these files is an fbx animated model. By naming them like this in the Project, when the original Hero model (the one at the very top of the list without the @***) is added to the Hierarchy, Unity will automatically be able to detect the other animation files that belong with Hero.

Step 2. Play. The current model in the scene is Hero@Idle. It will play, and the model will ever so slightly sway and then stop. What has occurred is that the animation played just once and then stopped. Animations will not loop automatically.

To access the full range of the Hero's animations, delete the Hero@Idle object from the Hierarchy. Locate the original Hero model (just called "Hero") in the Character Models > Hero Artwork folder in the Project and drag and drop it into the scene. The model will appear with both arms outstretched and two guns will appear floating next to it as shown in Figure 3.8. This position is called the bind pose, as the posture models are placed inside the animation software before their animations are bound to them.

FIG 3.8 The model and animations.

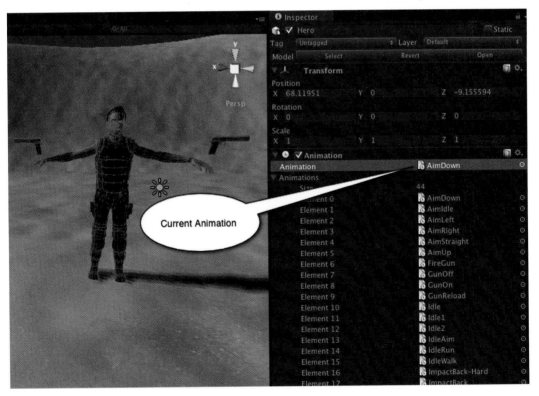

Step 3. When there are a series of animation files accompanying a model, as is the case here, Unity finds them all and adds them to the Animation component of the Inspector. As can be seen in Figure 3.8, this model has over 20 different animations. The animation set at the very top is the one that plays by default. It is the *current animation*. Change the current animation to WalkForward.

Step 4. Play. The character will take one step.

Step 5. To make the animation loop, create a new JavaScript file called *animationController* and add the code shown in Listing 3.8.

Listing 3.8 Script to Make the Current Animation Loop When the Game Object Is Created

```
function Awake()
{
        this.animation.wrapMode = WrapMode.Loop;
}
```

Step 6. Save and play. The model will walk on the spot. The WalkForward animation has a start and an end frame pose that matches. This allows the animation to play over and over again seamlessly. To see what an unmatched animation looks like, set the current animation to WalkIdle and run it again. You will notice a frame jump between the end of one loop and the start of the next.

Step 7. Add a rigidbody and a capsule collider to the model. As shown in Figure 3.9, position the capsule collider so that the model's feet appear to rest on the ground. For the rigidbody, freeze the *x*, *y*, and *z* axis rotation. This will stop the model from toppling over.

Step 8. Open the *animationController.js* script and modify as shown in Listing 3.9.

Listing 3.9 Adding Forward, Backward and Idle Animations

```
private var speed = 0.01;
function Awake()
{
        this.animation.wrapMode = WrapMode.Loop;
}
function Update ()
{
        if(Input.GetKey("up"))
        {
         this.transform.position — = this.transform.forward * speed;
        }
        else if(Input.GetKey("down"))
```

```
    {
        this.transform.position - = this.transform.forward * speed;
    }
}
```

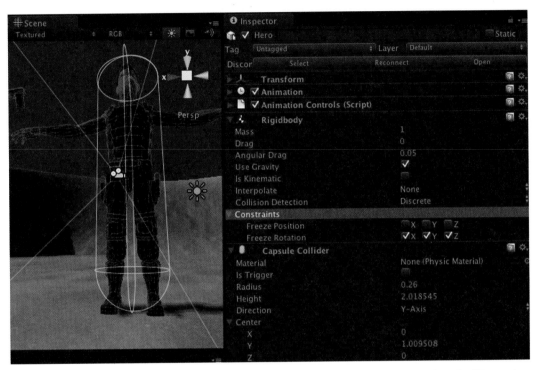

FIG 3.9 A capsule collider around an animated character.

Step 9. Play. The up and down arrow keys will move the character forward and backward. However, the backward animation will look strange as it is still applying the walking forward cycle. If the character seems to be skating across the ground, change the speed until it looks better. If the character is floating a little above the ground, move the capsule collider up a bit so that the feet of the model fall and touch the ground.

Step 10. To add in a forward, backward, and idle animation for the different states of the character, modify *animationControls.js* to the code in Listing 3.10.

Step 11. Play. The character will have a more natural movement when going backward and will stand still when the arrow keys are not pressed. The only problem now is that the start and end frames of the idle animation do not match well with the forward and backward start and end frames. To overcome this, the idle animation could be

167

Listing 3.10 Adding Forward, Backward and Idle Animations.

```
private var speed = 0.01;
function Awake()
{
 this.animation.wrapMode = WrapMode.Loop;
 this.animation.Play("Idle");
}
function Update ()
{
     if(Input.GetKey("up"))
     {
      this.animation.Play("WalkForward");
      this.transform.position += this.transform.forward * speed;
     }
     else if(Input.GetKey("down"))
     {
      this.animation.Play("WalkBackward");
      this.transform.position -= this.transform.forward * speed;
     }
     else if(Input.GetKeyUp("up") ||Input.GetKeyUp("down"))
     {
      this.animation.Play("Idle");
     }
}
```

recreated. This would prove quite laborious. A nice thing Unity lets you do is blend animations to give a more seamless transition.

Step 12. Change all the occurrences of **Play** in the Update function with the function name **CrossFade.**

Step 13. Play. The character will now transition smoothly between animation states.

Step 14. To make the camera follow the character, move the view around in the scene until you are looking at the character from behind in a position slightly up and to the right as shown in Figure 3.10. With the camera selected in the Hierarchy, select GameObject > Align With View from the main menu. Once you have the camera in a place you would like, drag and drop it in the Hierarchy onto the Hero game object. The camera will become a child object of the model and follow it wherever you move it.

Step 15. To add turning and running to the character, the same format as the existing code is used to test for the left and right arrow keys for turning and the right shift key for running. When turning, the model's transform is simply rotated. Modify *animationControls.js* to the code in Listing 3.11.

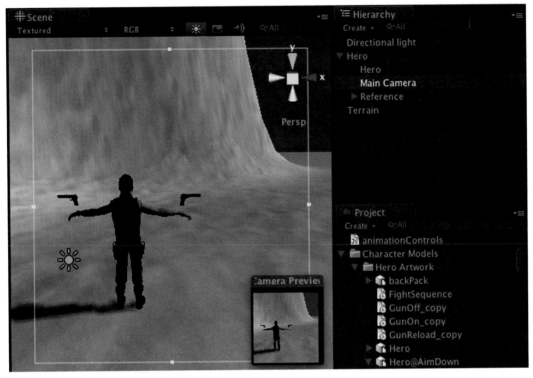

FIG 3.10 Positioning the camera for a third-person view.

Listing 3.11 Adding Running and Turning Controls to a Character

```
private var speed = 0.01;
private var runspeed = 0.1;
private var turnSpeed = 20.0;
function Awake()
{
     this.animation.wrapMode = WrapMode.Loop;
     this.animation.Play("Idle");
}
function Update ()
{
     if(Input.GetKey("up"))
     {
      this.animation.CrossFade("WalkForward");
      this.transform.position += this.transform.forward * speed;
     }
     else if(Input.GetKey("down"))
     {
```

```
    this.animation.CrossFade("WalkBackward");
    this.transform.position - = this.transform.forward
                            * speed;
}
else if(Input.GetKey("right shift"))
{
  this.animation.CrossFade("RunForward");
  this.transform.position + = this.transform.forward
                          * runspeed;
}
if(Input.GetKey("left"))
{
  transform.Rotate(-Vector3.up * Time.deltaTime *
                        turnSpeed);
}
else if(Input.GetKey("right"))
{
  transform.Rotate(Vector3.up * Time.deltaTime *
                        turnSpeed);
}

if(Input.GetKeyUp("up") ||
      Input.GetKeyUp("down") ||Input.
        GetKeyUp("right shift"))
{
      this.animation.CrossFade("Idle");
}
}
```

Step 16. Play. The right shift key will make the character run, and the left and right arrows will turn it. Many other animations come with the character. Try mapping these to keys in *animationControls.js* for yourself.

3.6 Biomechanics

Biomechanics is a field of study that examines the mechanical movement of biological systems such as humans, plants, and animals. It plays an important part in animation describing the way in which natural hierarchical systems such as the human skeleton move. The hierarchy for a skeleton begins at the skull and divides into a number of segments, including arms, legs, hands, and feet that connect to one another by joints. When higher level joints, such as the shoulder, move, any connected lower level segments, such as the hand, move too. In contrast, when a lower level joint or segment moves, such as a finger, any higher level segments, such as the skull, do not move. Aristotle first wrote about biomechanics in *De Motu Animalium* (*On the Movement of Animals*).

There are a number of ways a skeletal structure can be specified for animation. The Humanoid Animation Working Group (http://www.h-anim.org) is an international project with the goal of providing a standard profile for a humanoid skeleton so it can be used consistently across a number of applications. A partial view of the standard is illustrated in Figure 3.11. This makes the process of swapping characters in and out of games and virtual environments more streamlined. Imagine being able to take your favorite character from *Halo* and using it in *The Sims*. This of course would not work; however, if both games used the same rules of the H-Anim specification it would.

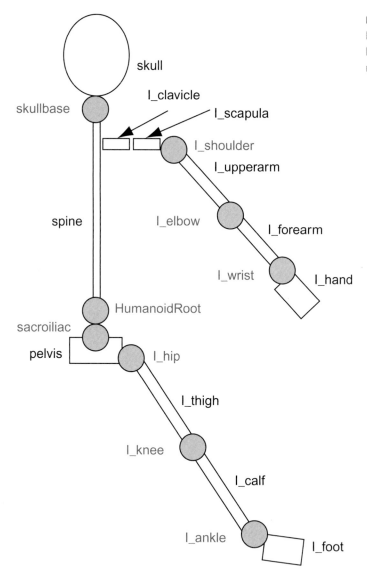

FIG 3.11 A partial view of the H.Anim project's specifications for a humanoid skeletal hierarchy showing minimal joints.

The premise behind H-Anim and any other skeletal representation is the connection of straight segments and rotatable joints. The way in which these structures move is analyzed by the applied mechanics discipline of kinematics.

Kinematics describes the motion of objects without consideration of the causes leading to the motion. It examines linear and rotational movement with respect to distance, direction, and velocity. These are the very same concepts developed in the previous chapter through the examination of vector mathematics. Kinematics can be examined from two points of view: forward and inverse.

Forward kinematics calculates the final position of the end of an articulated object given the angle and rotation of the joints and the length of the segments. To exemplify, forward kinematics can calculate the position of a character's hand given the rotation and angles of joints and the length of the bone segments. The hand in this case is what is known in kinematics as the end effector. To solve such a problem, simple vector mathematics is employed. Each bone has a length and direction that are specified as a vector. Adding all the vectors together will give the final destination. As illustrated in Figure 3.12, if the shoulder is positioned at (10,10) with the humerus (upper arm bone) making a vector of (3,−3), the radius and ulna (lower arm bones) making a vector of (2,2), and the hand with a vector of (1,0), the final position of the finger tips will be at (16,9).

Inverse kinematics is used in games to ensure that characters connect with the environment. For example, in *The Sims*, when a character interacts with an object, the game must ensure that the character is standing in the correct position to pick the object up. Although the bending over and picking up an object is a premade animation, the character still needs to be positioned in the correct location to perform

FIG 3.12 A forward kinematic example with an arm in 2D.

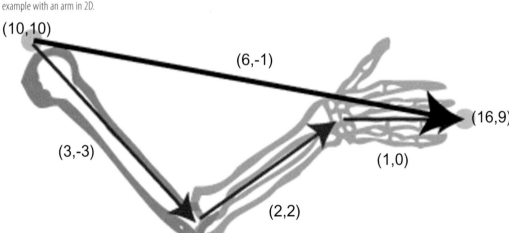

a convincing connection with the object. For that reason, if a Sim is required to pick up a guitar, the character will walk over to the item first and position itself such that when the pickup animation plays it looks as though the object is picked up.

Inverse kinematics is somewhat more complex than forward kinematics. It performs the reverse operation of forward kinematics, asking what the angles of the joints must be to position the end effector at a specific location. For example, if the shoulder is at (10,10), how should the bones in the arm be positioned to place the hand at (16,9)? This is not as simple as it might first appear because, when you think about it, the joints in the arm can make a variety of angles, as shown in Figure 3.13.

Try it for yourself. Grab hold of a doorknob and, keeping your shoulder at the same location in space, see how many different positions you can manipulate your arm into such that your hand stays touching the doorknob. These are just the movements for your arm, which consists of three basic joints and three principal segments. Imagine calculating inverse kinematics for something with 10 or more joints.

Although we consider the shoulder as a single joint, for the purposes of inverse kinematics, it is actually three. If you hold your arm straight out to the side you will be able to raise and lower it (like flapping to fly), move it

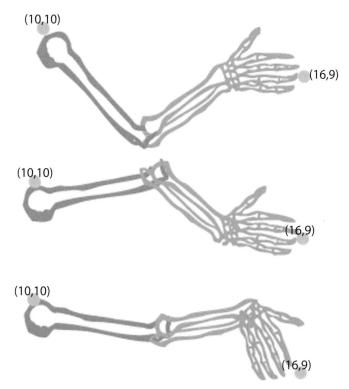

FIG 3.13 Three solutions to an inverse kinematic problem.

from side to side (like waving past traffic), and also rotate it (as though your outreached hand is turning a knob). Each distinct movement is called a degree of freedom (DOF). Therefore, the shoulder has three DOFs: two that translate the attached segment and one that rotates it.

● Unity Hands On
Inverse Kinematics

In this hands-on session you will learn how to implement simple inverse kinematic algorithms to control the angle and direction of a character's arms and weapon. In this workshop, the mouse will be used to position a target on the terrain. Inverse kinematics will be used to position the character to be aiming at the target.

Step 1. Download *Chapter Three/CharacterIK.zip* from the Web site. Unzip and open the project in Unity. The scene will contain the animated character from the last workshop.

Step 2. The first thing we are going to do is add something for the character to aim at on the terrain. To do this, the mouse will be used as a pointer. Where the mouse is clicked on the terrain, a target object will appear. This object will be a simple sphere. To achieve this, modify the animationControls script to that in Listing 3.12.

Listing 3.12 Script to Create a Target Object at the Mouse Location on the Terrain

```
private var speed = 0.01;
private var turnSpeed = 20.0;
private var aimPoint: GameObject;
function Awake()
{
    this.animation.wrapMode = WrapMode.Loop;
    this.animation.Play("Idle");
    aimPoint = GameObject.CreatePrimitive(PrimitiveType.
      Sphere);
    aimPoint.renderer.material.color = Color.magenta;
    //remove collider so sphere doesn'treact to physics
    Destroy(aimPoint.collider);
}
function Update ()
{
    if(Input.GetMouseButton(0))
    {
```

```
        //create a line from the mouse position into the screen
        var ray = Camera.main.ScreenPointToRay(Input.
                            mousePosition);
        var hit : RaycastHit;
        //determine where it hits something
        if (Physics.Raycast (ray, hit, 100))
        {
            //put the aiming object at that position
            aimPoint.transform.position = hit.point;
        }
    }
...
}
```

Step 3. Play. A red-colored sphere will appear on the terrain at the mouse location. It will appear to move around if you hold the left mouse button down and move the mouse. In this case the target is a primitive sphere; you could of course add any model you like by instantiating a game object.

Step 4. Next, the IK calculations need transformations of the bones and the end effector. Include these as variables at the top of the animationControls script as shown in Listing 3.13.

Listing 3.13 Adding Arm and End Effector Transformations for IK Calculations

```
private var speed = 0.01;
private var turnSpeed = 20.0;
private var aimPoint: GameObject;
//For IK----
//right arm bones
var armR: Transform;
var forearmR: Transform;
var handR: Transform;
//left arm bones
var armL: Transform;
var forearmL: Transform;
var handL: Transform;
var gun: Transform; //end effector
function Awake()
{
...
```

Step 5. Set each of the values for the transformations by locating the script attached to the Hero game object and dragging and dropping the appropriate child objects from the Hero onto the values in the Inspector as shown in Figure 3.14.

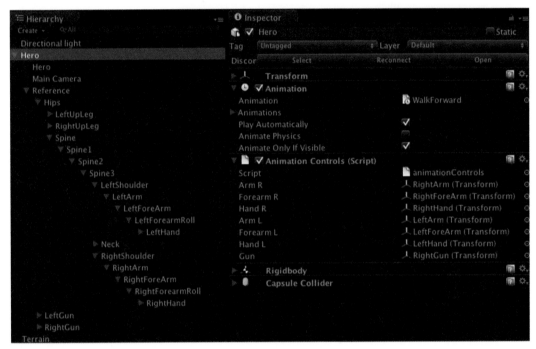

FIG 3.14 Attaching model bones to script variables.

Step 6. Before moving the arm bones into position, the end effector (gun) needs to be positioned. As it is going to point at the target, we can use the LookAt() function to change its orientation. The LookAt() function will rotate the object such that the positive *z* axis (the blue arrow) is pointing toward a target. If you click on the right gun in the Scene, you will notice that the blue axis is not aligned with the barrel of the gun. In this case, if you just use LookAt() it will orientate the side of the gun to face the target. This means after using LookAt() we have to make a 90° adjustment to get the barrel of the gun pointing at the target. To achieve this, add the new function in Listing 3.14 to the end of *animationControls.js*.

Listing 3.14 A Late Update Function to Change Orientation of a Game Object under Animation Control

```
private var speed = 0.01;

...

function Update()
```

```
{
...
}
function LateUpdate()
{
        //IK ----
        gun.LookAt(aimPoint.transform.position);
        gun.transform.Rotate(Vector3.up,90);
}
```

Step 7. Play. The gun in the character's hand will orientate to
always face the red sphere as the mouse moves it around the game
environment. Any manual modification to the character's animation,
such as inverse kinematics, must occur in the LateUpdate() function—
the reason being that normal animations for the character will still
be running and are assigned to the model before LateUpdate(). If
changes to the model occur before this, baked animations will simply
replace any changes that you make with code.

Step 8. Because the character's hands are grabbing the gun, it makes
sense that they move as the gun does. To do this, we need to record
the relative location of the hands before the gun moves and then use
this to line up the hands with the gun after the gun has moved. This
requires working with 4×4 matrices and quaternions. The following
changes you need to make to the animationControls script, shown
in Listing 3.15, have been designed to be as painless as possible.

**Listing 3.15 Storing the Relative Position between Hands and
Gun to Reset the Hand Position after the Gun Has Moved**

```
private var speed = 0.01;
private var turnSpeed = 20.0;
private var aimPoint: GameObject;
//For IK-----------------
//right arm bones
var armR: Transform;
var forearmR: Transform;
var handR: Transform;
var rightHandMat: Matrix4x4;
//left arm bones
var armL: Transform;
var forearmL: Transform;
var handL: Transform;
var leftHandMat: Matrix4x4;
var gun: Transform; //end effector
function ChangeCoordinateSystems(from: Transform, to: Transform):
Matrix4x4
```

```
{
        return to.worldToLocalMatrix *from.localToWorldMatrix;
}
function QuaternionFromMatrix(m: Matrix4x4):Quaternion
{
 var q: Quaternion;
 q.w = Mathf.Sqrt(Mathf.Max(0, 1 + m[0,0] + m[1,1] +
       m[2,2] ) ) / 2;
 q.x = Mathf.Sqrt(Mathf.Max(0, 1 + m[0,0] - m[1,1] -
       m[2,2] ) ) / 2;
 q.y = Mathf.Sqrt(Mathf.Max(0, 1 - m[0,0] + m[1,1] -
       m[2,2] ) ) / 2;
 q.z = Mathf.Sqrt(Mathf.Max(0, 1 - m[0,0] - m[1,1] +
       m[2,2] ) ) / 2;
 q.x * = Mathf.Sign(q.x * ( m[2,1] - m[1,2] ) );
 q.y * = Mathf.Sign(q.y * ( m[0,2] - m[2,0] ) );
 q.z * = Mathf.Sign(q.z * ( m[1,0] - m[0,1] ) );
 return q;
}
function Awake()
{
        this.animation.wrapMode = WrapMode.Loop;

        ...
        Destroy(aimPoint.collider);
        this.animation.Play("AimStraight");
}
function Update ()
{
...
        if(Input.GetKeyUp("up")||Input.GetKeyUp("down") ||
                        Input.GetKeyUp("right shift"))
        {
                this.animation.CrossFade("AimStraight");
        }
}
function LateUpdate()
{
        //IK ----
        //determine relative location between gun and hand
        //and store it.
        rightHandMat = ChangeCoordinateSystems(handR, gun);
        leftHandMat = ChangeCoordinateSystems(handL, gun);

        gun.LookAt(aimPoint.transform.position);
        gun.transform.Rotate(Vector3.up,90);
        //place hand back relative with gun using stored matrix
        handR.rotation = QuaternionFromMatrix(
```

```
                        gun.localToWorldMatrix *
                            rightHandMat);
    handL.rotation = QuaternionFromMatrix(
                        gun.localToWorldMatrix *
                            leftHandMat);
}
```

Step 9. Play. The hands will now orientate with the gun. They don't change position, just rotation, and therefore are a little inaccurate when the gun is in some orientations. So far we haven't used any inverse kinematic calculations. They start now. The objective will be to rotate the shoulder, elbow, and wrist joint to suit the gun orientation.

Step 10. Download *Chapter Three/IKplugins.zip* from the Web site. It contains two C# code files from the Locomotion project for calculating inverse kinematics. For more on this, see http://www.unity3d .com/support/resources/unity-extensions/locomotion-ik.html. Unzip these files. Create a folder in the Project called Plugins and place the *IK1JointAnalytic.cs* and *IKSolver.cs* in it.

Step 11. Now modify *animationController.js* to use the inverse kinematics code to rotate the shoulders, elbows, and wrists as shown in Listing 3.16.

Listing 3.16 Implementing an Inverse Kinematic Joint Rotation Solver

```
private var speed = 0.01;
...
var gun: Transform; //end effector
private var ikSolver:IK1JointAnalytic = new IK1JointAnalytic();
...
function LateUpdate()
{
 //IK ----
 rightHandMat = ChangeCoordinateSystems(handR, gun);
 leftHandMat = ChangeCoordinateSystems(handL, gun);

 gun.LookAt(aimPoint.transform.position);
 gun.transform.Rotate(Vector3.up,90);
 //Right arm
 var desiredRightWristPosition: Vector3 =
                (gun.localToWorldMatrix * rightHandMat).
                MultiplyPoint3x4 (Vector3.zero);
 var bonesR: Transform[] = new Transform[3];
 bonesR[0] = armR;
 bonesR[1] = forearmR;
 bonesR[2] = handR;
```

```
ikSolver.Solve( bonesR, desiredRightWristPosition );
handR.rotation = QuaternionFromMatrix(gun.
                   localToWorldMatrix * rightHandMat);

//Left arm
var desiredLeftWristPosition: Vector3 =  (gun.
                   localToWorldMatrix *  leftHandMat).
                   MultiplyPoint3x4 (Vector3.zero);
var bonesL: Transform[] = new Transform[3];
bonesL[0] = armL;
bonesL[1] = forearmL;
bonesL[2] = handL;
ikSolver.Solve( bonesL, desiredLeftWristPosition );
handL.rotation = QuaternionFromMatrix
           (gun.localToWorldMatrix * leftHandMat);
}
```

Step 12. Play. Drag the target sphere around in front of the character and note how the shoulders, elbows, and wrists bend to accommodate the orientation of the gun. The ikSolver.Solve() function does this by taking all the bones and the desired location of the end effector and calculating the best angles. Some angles are obviously undesirable, such as if the target goes behind the character. When this occurs, other techniques, such as turning the entire character around or changing her pose, are desirable.

Step 13. To end this workshop, we will add in some other animations based on the angle to the target such that when it is up high the AimUp animation will be used and when low the AimDown animation will be set. The character will also turn around automatically to face the target location. This requires a small change to the Update() function of animationController, as shown in Listing 3.17.

Listing 3.17 Adding More Appropriate Upper Body Poses to Match Arm Direction

```
function Update ()
{
 if(Input.GetMouseButton(0))
 {

    ...

 }
 //modify orientation and aim pose based on location of target
 var direction = aimPoint.transform.position -
                            this.transform.position;
```

```
var angleToTarget = Vector3.Angle(direction, this.
                            transform.up);
if(angleToTarget < 60 )
{
     this.animation.CrossFade("AimUp");
}
else if(angleToTarget < 80)
{
     this.animation.CrossFade("AimStraight");
}
else
{
     this.animation.CrossFade("AimDown");
}
direction.y = 0;
this.transform.rotation = Quaternion.Slerp (transform.
           rotation,
           Quaternion.LookRotation(direction), Time.
                       deltaTime);
if(Input.GetKey("up"))
{
...
```

Step 14. Play. Note how the character turns around and the animations change to better suit the height of the target.

> ⚙ **Research**
> *Inverse Kinematics*
>
> For further in-depth examination of inverse kinematic systems in Unity, download the locomotion project available from http://www.unity3d .com/support/resources/unity-extensions/locomotion-ik.html.

3.7 Animation Management

In the preceding examples of 3D animations, character action sequences were split into segments. In the case of 2D sprites, only one sequence was given (walking); in the 3D examples, each action was contained in its own separate file.

It's not always the case that animations come to game developers in this way. If you were to download a fully animated character from a site such as

TurboSquid, the character may come as a single file containing any number of animation sequences. In the case of 2D sprites, it is not uncommon to find all the action sequences for one character in a single texture atlas.

3.7.1 Single 2D Sprite Actions

As we've seen, a texture atlas is a convenient and optimizing way to keep sprites. More often than not, all the animations for a single character are kept in a texture atlas. This requires pixel management on the part of the programmer to ensure that the correct part of the texture is displayed at the right time. Figure 3.15 shows a texture atlas with several idle and walking animation frames. Although it is not strictly necessary to have the frames belonging to the same animation next to each other in the texture, it makes it monumentally easier to program if they are in sequence and packed together. It's also easier if each frame is the same size. In the image shown, each frame is 32 × 64.

Individual animations are specified with a starting frame and a number of frames; for example, the walk left animation starts at frame 3 and is three frames in length. By knowing the fixed width for a frame, the exact pixel value for the start of an animation sequence can be calculated. In this case, the walk left animation begins at frame 3, and therefore the starting x pixel location would be 3 × 32 = 96.

FIG 3.15 Joined frames for four separate animations. (Sprite art thanks to Dezire Soft at http://www .touchofdeathforums.com/smf/index .php/topic,26460.0.html.)

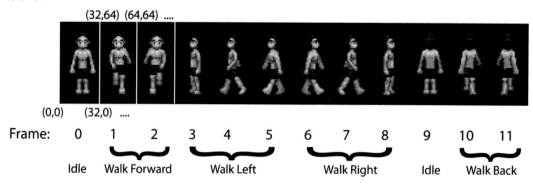

> **◁ Unity Specifics**
> If the sprite atlas does not have power of two dimensions, Unity will squash and stretch it to make it so. This will produce an undesirable effect with the frame locations. To correct this, select the texture in the Project and in the Inspector set the Texture Type to Advanced and the Non Power of 2 to None, as shown in Figure 3.16.

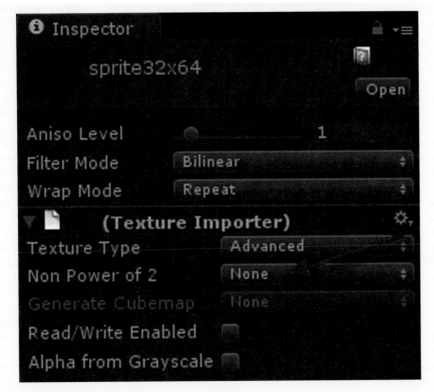

FIG 3.16

◉ **Unity Hands On**
Managing Animated Sprite Sequences

Step 1. Download *Chapter Three/SpriteManager.zip* from the Web
site. Open the project in Unity and open the spritemanage scene.
You will find a single basic plane with the *SpriteManagement.js* script
attached. The script will be empty. The plane will have a sprite texture
atlas on it.
Step 2. Open *SpriteManagement.js* in the script editor and add the
code in Listing 3.18.

Listing 3.18 Controlling Movement of a Sprite with Arrow Keys

```
private var nextFrame: float = 0;
private var timeBetweenFrames: float;
private var framerate: float = 5.0;
private var mesh : Mesh;
private var texture : Texture2D;
function Start()
```

```
{
    mesh = GetComponent(MeshFilter).mesh;
    texture = renderer.material.mainTexture;
    renderer.material.shader = Shader.Find( "Sprite" );
    timeBetweenFrames = 1.0/framerate;
}
function Update()
{
    if(Input.GetKey (KeyCode.UpArrow))
    {
        this.transform.position.z++;
    }
    else if(Input.GetKey (KeyCode.DownArrow))
    {
        this.transform.position.z--;
    }
    else if(Input.GetKey (KeyCode.LeftArrow))
    {
        this.transform.position.x--;
    }
    else if(Input.GetKey (KeyCode.RightArrow))
    {
        this.transform.position.x++;
    }
}
```

Step 3. Play. The sprite will be moveable with the arrow keys. The image on the sprite will be blurred, as it is not yet set up correctly.

Step 4. Next we need to create some simple data structures to store the frame size as well as the starting frames and length for each animation sequence. A neat way to do this is to create simple class structures to store the information. When named with meaningful variable names, the editor displays a nice way to edit the information. Modify *SpriteManagment.js* by adding the code in Listing 3.19 to the very top of the script.

Step 5. Select the Plane child object of basicPlane in the Hierarchy. In the Inspector, locate the attached SpriteManager script as shown in Figure 3.17. Note how the variables from the classes in the script are displayed in the Inspector. This makes them easy to recognize and edit. This could have been achieved easily using Vector2 data types; however, it would have been messier. Enter the values into the Inspector for the sprite dimensions and animation sequences as shown in Figure 3.17.

Listing 3.19 Creating Class Structures for Storing Values

```
class spriteDetails
{
      var pixelWidth: int;
      var pixelHeight: int;
}
class animFrame
{
      var startFrame: int;
      var numberOfFrames: int;
}
var singleSpriteDimensions: spriteDetails;
var idle: animFrame;
var walkleft: animFrame;
var walkright: animFrame;
var walkforward: animFrame;
var walkback: animFrame;
```

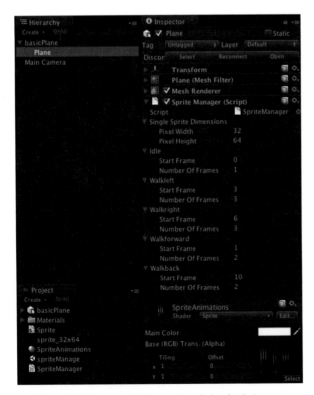

FIG 3.17 Variables contained in class structures displayed in the Inspector.

Step 6. Next you need to align the sprite walking direction with the animations and use the pixel values entered into the Inspector to display the correct animation sequence. To do this, a UV mapping code similar to that used in previous examples will be used. When a different arrow key is pressed, the animation sequence being displayed will change. Modify *SpriteManager.js* as shown in Listing 3.20.

Listing 3.20 Script to Manage Changing Animation States of a Sprite

```
class spriteDetails
{
      var pixelWidth: int;
      var pixelHeight: int;
}
...
var singleSpriteDimensions: spriteDetails;
var idle: animFrame;
var walkleft: animFrame;
var walkright: animFrame;
var walkforward: animFrame;
var walkback: animFrame;
var currentAnimation = "";
var currentFrame = 0;
var currentStartFrame = 0;
var totalFrames = 0;
...
function Start()
{
      ...
}
function SetAnimation(animName : String)
{
      if(currentAnimation == animName) return;
      currentAnimation = animName;
      if(currentAnimation == "WALK_LEFT")
      {
            currentFrame = walkleft.startFrame;
            currentStartFrame = walkleft.startFrame;
            totalFrames = walkleft.startFrame +
                          walkleft.numberOfFrames;
      }
      else if(currentAnimation == "WALK_RIGHT")
      {
            currentFrame = walkright.startFrame;
            currentStartFrame = walkright.startFrame;
            totalFrames = walkright.startFrame +
                          walkright.numberOfFrames;
```

```
        }
        else if(currentAnimation == "WALK_FORWARD")
        {
                currentFrame = walkforward.startFrame;
                currentStartFrame = walkforward.startFrame;
                totalFrames = walkforward.startFrame +
                                walkforward.numberOfFrames;
        }
        else if(currentAnimation == "WALK_BACK")
        {
                currentFrame = walkback.startFrame;
                currentStartFrame = walkback.startFrame;
                totalFrames = walkback.startFrame +
                                walkback.numberOfFrames;
        }
        else if(currentAnimation == "IDLE")
        {
                currentFrame = idle.startFrame;
                currentStartFrame = idle.startFrame;
                totalFrames = idle.startFrame +
                                idle.numberOfFrames;
        }

}
function UpdateSprite()
{
        var uvs : Vector2[] = new Vector2[4];
        var startPixel : Vector2;
        var endPixel : Vector2;

        startPixel.x = singleSpriteDimensions.pixelWidth *
                        currentFrame;
        startPixel.y = singleSpriteDimensions.pixelHeight *
                        currentFrame;

        endPixel.x = singleSpriteDimensions.pixelWidth *
                        (currentFrame + 1);
        endPixel.y = singleSpriteDimensions.pixelHeight *
                        (currentFrame + 1);

        uvs[0] = new Vector2(startPixel.x/texture.width,
                        (texture.height - endPixel.y)/texture.height);
        uvs[1] = new Vector2(startPixel.x/texture.width,
                        (texture.height - startPixel.y)/texture.height);
        uvs[2] = new Vector2(endPixel.x/texture.width,
                        (texture.height - startPixel.y)/texture.height);
        uvs[3] = new Vector2(endPixel.x/texture.width,
                        (texture.height - endPixel.y)/texture.height);
        mesh.uv = uvs;
```

```
        currentFrame++;
        if (currentFrame > = totalFrames)
        {
                currentFrame = currentStartFrame;
        }
}
function Update()
{
        if(Input.GetKey (KeyCode.UpArrow))
        {
                this.transform.position.z++;
                SetAnimation("WALK_BACK");

        }
        else if(Input.GetKey (KeyCode.DownArrow))
        {
                this.transform.position.z--;
                SetAnimation("WALK_FORWARD");
        }
        else if(Input.GetKey (KeyCode.LeftArrow))
        {
                this.transform.position.x--;
                SetAnimation("WALK_LEFT");
        }
        else if(Input.GetKey (KeyCode.RightArrow))
        {
                this.transform.position.x++;
                SetAnimation("WALK_RIGHT");
        }
        else
        {
                SetAnimation("IDLE");
        }
}
function LateUpdate ()
{
        if(Time.time > nextFrame)
        {
                nextFrame = Time.time + timeBetweenFrames;
                UpdateSprite();
        }
}
```

Step 7. Play. The sprite will now be animated with the correct sequence of frames depending on the direction it is moving.

3.7.2 Single-Filed 3D Animations

Original 3D FPS games such as *Quake 3 Arena* (Q3A) use a single track of 3D animation that defines many separate animations in the same way as an animated sprite texture atlas. Animations for a character in Q3A, a Quakebot, for example, are played from specified frames—some looped and some not. To create a series of animations for a Quake character, a number of different animations need to be specified and then glued together. For example, the running animation might go from frame 30 to frame 45, and the swimming animation might go from frame 46 to frame 57.

Animations in Q3A must be set up in a specific order. The order and length of the animations are displayed in Table 3.1.

TABLE 3.1 Order and frame size of animations used in Q3A[a]

Animation	Length (in frames)	Description
Category: Full body		
BOTH_DEATH1	~30	Full body animation
BOTH_DEAD1	~1	Death scenes and final
BOTH_DEATH2	~30	Death poses
BOTH_DEAD2	~1	
BOTH_DEATH3	~30	
BOTH_DEAD3	~1	
Category: Upper body		
TORSO_GESTURE	~45	e.g., taunting
TORSO_ATTACK	6*	Attack other player
TORSO_ATTACK2	6*	Attack other player
TORSO_DROP	5*	Drop arms as to change weapon
TORSO_RAISE	4*	Lift up new weapon
TORSO_STAND	1*	Idle pose for upper body
TORSO_STAND2	1*	Idle pose for upper body
Category: Lower body		
LEGS_WALKCR	~10	Crouched while walking forward
LEGS_WALK	~15	Walking forward
LEGS_RUN	~12	Running forward

Continued

TABLE 3.1 Order and frame size of animations used in Q3A—cont'd

Animation	Length (in frames)	Description
LEGS_BACK	~10	Back pedaling
LEGS_SWIM	~10	Swimming
LEGS_JUMP	~10	Jumping up forward
LEGS_LAND	~6	Landing after jump
LEGS_JUMPB	~10	Jumping up backward
LEGS_LANDB	~6	Landing after backward jump
LEGS_IDLE	~10	Idle pose for lower body
LEGS_IDLECR	~10	Crouched idle pose for lower body
LEGS_TURN	~8	Turning on the spot

[a]All animation lengths are approximations with the exception of those indicated by an asterisk, which need to be exact.

As shown in Table 3.1, upper and lower animations are separate with the exception of death scenes. Therefore, movement of the upper body is independent of the lower body. This allows for different animation effects by combining differing animation parts. However, this can be a slight problem when two unrelated animations are combined; for example, an upper TORSO_ATTACK combined with a LEGS_SWIM would look strange. Although this system of animation has the drawback of creating inappropriate movements, it does provide for an overall greater number of animations.

Because many of the animation sequences do not have a defined length, an animation configuration file needs to be generated for the QA3 game engine so that it can locate the correct animation progressions. The configuration file is called *animation.cfg* and is loaded into the QA3 engine with the appropriate model. The configuration file contains information on the first frame of the sequence, the length, in frames, of the sequence, the number of times to loop the animation, and how fast to play it. The file contains this information for each animation sequence in the order shown in Table 3.2.

TABLE 3.2 A partial animation configuration file

Animation	First frame	Number of frames	Times to loop	Frames per second
BOTH_DEATH1	0	30	0	25
BOTH_DEAD1	29	1	0	25
TORSO_GESTURE	90	40	0	15
TORSO_ATTACK	130	6	0	15

A model is defined as three separate parts: head, torso, and legs. Each part of the model is linked internally by what is known as a tag. Tags control the locations at which the parts of the model are connected. Because each part is dealt with separately, the tags essentially join them together. There are three principal tags in a QA3 model: tag_head (which joins the head to the torso), tag_torso (which joins the upper body to the lower body), and tag_weapon (which provides a location to attach the weapon model). For games such as QA3 that allow players to modify and create their own character models, having a standard format such as this is crucial in ensuring that the models are animated and rendered consistently.

◁ Unity Specifics
Single File, Multiple Animations
Unity supports model files that have all animations in the same file. Note that not all 3D model formats store animations; for example, .3ds do not, but .fbx do. When the model is imported into the Project, selecting it will bring up the import settings in the Inspector. An example is shown of the Lerpz character available from the Unity Web site in Figure 3.18.

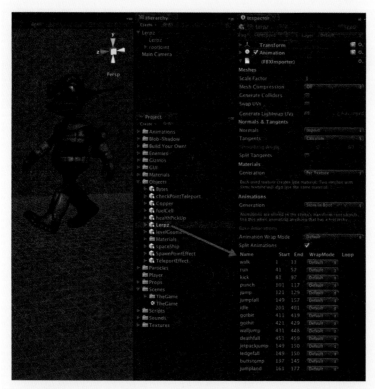

FIG 3.18 An animated FBX file in Unity with animation settings shown in the Inspector.

By specifying a name and the start and end frames for each specific animation sequence, Unity can divide a single file up for easy multiple animation use. For more details on settings in the Inspector, visit http://www.unity3d.com/support/documentation/Manual/Animations.html.

◉ Unity Hands On
Managing Multiple 3D Animations

Step 1. Download *Chapter Three/Sequenced3D.zip* from the Web site and open the *SingleAnimFile* scene. In it you will find the *Lerpz* model. If you play, at this point, the model will play through all the animations in the file as they have not been specified individually in the import settings.

Step 2. Select the *Lerpz* model in the Project. In the Inspector locate the individual animation section of the FBX Importer component.

Step 3. Add two animations as shown in Figure 3.19. Add a walk animation with starting frame 1 and ending frame 33 and a jump animation with starting frame 121 and ending frame 129. Click the Apply button at the bottom of the Inspector view.

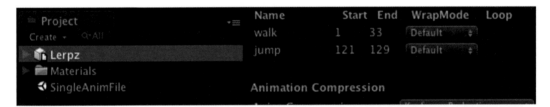

FIG 3.19 Adding two animations to the Lerpz character.

Step 4. Create a JavaScript file called *controls.js* and open with the script editor. Add the code shown in Listing 3.21.

Listing 3.21 Controlling Animations with Key Presses

```javascript
function Update ()
{
        if(Input.GetKeyDown("left"))
        {
                this.animation.Play("walk");
        }
        else if(Input.GetKeyDown("space"))
        {
                this.animation.Play("jump");
        }
}
```

Step 5. Play. The walk animation will play when the left arrow key is down, and the jump animation will play when the space is pressed. The issue now is that the animations only play once; for example, when the left arrow key is pressed the walk animation plays and then stops. To fix this, add the code in Listing 3.22 to the very top of the *controls.js* file.

Listing 3.22 Setting an Animation to Loop

```
function Start()
{
      this.animation["walk"].wrapMode = WrapMode.Loop;
}
```

Step 6. Play. The walk animation will now loop. It will only stop when the space bar is pressed for the jump animation.

Step 7. To make the model go into an idle mode when no key is pressed, you need to add an idle animation. To do this, select the model in Project and add an animation called idle with a start frame of 201 and an end frame of 401. Click the Apply button.

Step 8. The idle animation won't be added automatically to the model in the scene. Therefore, select the Lerpz object in the Hierarchy and locate the Animation component in the Inspector. Change the number of animations from 2 to 3. Set the third animation to *idle*.

Step 9. Edit *controls.js* to reflect the code in Listing 3.23.

Listing 3.23 Adding an Idle Animation to Play after Other Animations Are Finished

```
//REMOVE START FUNCTION
//function Start()
//{
      //this.animation["walk"].wrapMode = WrapMode.Loop;
//}
function Update ()
{
      if(Input.GetKey("right"))
      {
            this.animation.Play("walk");
      }
      else if(Input.GetKey("space"))
      {
            this.animation.Play("jump");
      }
      this.animation.CrossFadeQueued("idle", 0.5);
}
```

Step 10. Play. The CrossFadeQueued() function sets up an animation to play after currently playing animations finish. It also fades between animations, which, in this case, allows for a smooth transition between jump and idle.

3.7.3 Blending

While cross fading animations allows for one model posture to smoothly

Animation blending allows for different parts of different animations to be combined.

⊙ **Unity Hands On**

Animation Management

Step 1. Download *Chapter Three/CharacterAnimManager.zip* from the Web site. Unzip and open the project in Unity. Open the animationManagement scene and play. The WASD and arrow keys can be used to move the character around the environment.

Step 2. Open the *AnimationManager.js* file in the script editor.

Step 3. Note the use of the Input.GetAxis() function. It is a clean way to get the character movement from typical game control mappings. For example, using Input.GetKeyDown() for all the different keys to move forward and backward would be many more lines of code than the two given here.

Listing 3.24 Script to Play FireGun Animation When Space Is Pressed

```
private var speed = 0.03;
...
function Update ()
{
    ...
    else
    {
        this.animation.Play("Idle");

    }
    if(Input.GetKeyDown("space"))
    {
        print("Firing");
        this.animation.Play("ShootStraight");
    }

    this.transform.Translate (0, 0, translation);
    this.transform.Rotate (0, rotation, 0);
}
```

Step 4. The current version of the code allows the character to walk around the environment. Let's add some code to fire the character's gun. Add the lines shown in Listing 3.24.

Step 5. Play. It appears as though nothing happens when the space bar is pressed. However, note that "Firing" is being printed in the console, which proves that the if statement is being executed. If you press the space bar a bunch of times and watch the character closely you may see it flinch. So what is happening? The ShootStraight animation starts to run, but before many or any frames play, the Update() function runs again; if the character is not moving, the animation gets set to Idle before ShootStraight has finished playing. This is a common issue in managing animations.

Step 6. To fix this issue in the past, a programmer would have to write code to test if one animation has finished playing before another starts. This can still be done; however, in this case, Unity provides a very neat way for giving priority to animations—layers. Each animation can be assigned a layer. Animations in higher level layers have a higher priority, and lower level animations cannot interrupt their frames. Modify the Start() function of animationManagement script to that shown in Listing 3.25.

Listing 3.25 Placing All Animations Except Shooting into a Lower Layer

```
function Start()
{
    //loop all animations unless otherwise set
    this.animation.wrapMode = WrapMode.Loop;
    this.animation["Idle"].layer = -1;
    this.animation["WalkForward"].layer = -1;
    this.animation["WalkBackward"].layer = -1;
    //don't loop shooting animation
    this.animation["ShootStraight"].wrapMode =
                            WrapMode.Clamp;
    this.animation.Stop();
}
```

Step 7. This new code will place the idle and walking animations in layer −1. By default, all animations are in layer 0. This means the shooting animation will remain in 0 and be given priority over those in −1. In addition, animations in layer −1 are cyclic and therefore set to loop. We don't want the shooting animation to loop; therefore, it is set to clamp, which plays it once and stops. Because the shooting animation is in a higher layer, when it is set to play, it becomes visible on the screen while the other animations take a back seat. When the shooting animation reaches the end and stops (because it is not set to loop), animations in the next lower layer can play. In this case it will be the idle and walk cycles. Press play to see this in action.

Step 8. Note that when now shooting, the entire shoot animation plays; however, it ends abruptly as the shoot animation finishes and the character jumps back into the idle animation. This can be fixed by blending the animations together to give a smoother transition. Instead of using the Play() function, CrossFade() is used to blend the current animation with a new one. Modify your code with the changes in Listing 3.26.

Listing 3.26 Blending Animation for Smooth Transitions

```
private var speed = 0.03;
...

function Update ()
{

    ...
    if(translation > 0)
    {
        this.animation.CrossFade("WalkForward");
    }
    else if (translation < 0)
    {
        this.animation.CrossFade("WalkBackward");
    }
    else
    {
        this.animation.CrossFade("Idle");
    }

    if(Input.GetKeyDown("space"))
    {
        this.animation.CrossFade("ShootStraight");
    }
    ...
}
```

Step 9. Play. Note how the transition between animation states is smoother.

Step 10. The last issue to take care of is the shooting while moving. Currently, if the character is moving and the space bar is pressed, the character will play the shoot animation and slide along the ground. You can deal with this in two ways. Stop the character moving and shooting at the same time or include an animation in which the character is moving and shooting simultaneously. Instead of creating an entirely new animation, you can blend the top of the shooting animation with the bottom of the walking animation with code. Add the code in Listing 3.27 to your script.

Listing 3.27 Creating a Blended Animation

```
private var speed = 0.03;
private var rotationSpeed = 0.5;
private var currentAnimation = "";

function Start()
{
    ...
    this.animation["ShootStraight"].wrapMode = WrapMode.
                                              Clamp;

    //create a blended animation
    this.animation.AddClip(animation["ShootStraight"].
            clip, "ShootUpperBody");
    this.animation["ShootUpperBody"].AddMixingTransform(
            this.transform.Find("Reference/RightGun"));
    this.animation["ShootUpperBody"].AddMixingTransform(
            this.transform.Find("Reference/Hips/Spine"));
    this.animation["ShootUpperBody"].wrapMode =
            WrapMode.Clamp;

    this.animation.Stop();
}

function Update ()
{
    currentAnimation = "idle";
    ...
    if(translation > 0)
    {
        this.animation.CrossFade("WalkForward");
        currentAnimation = "walk";
    }
    ...

    if(Input.GetKeyDown("space"))
    {
        if(currentAnimation == "walk")
        {
            this.animation.CrossFade("ShootUpperBody");
        }
        else
        {
```

```
                         this.animation.CrossFade("ShootStraight");
              }
         }
         ...
   }
```

Step 11. Play. A new animation clip will be created that uses the ShootStraight animation as a basis and mixes the transformations for the gun and spine animations from any other animation playing in another layer at the same time. In this case it is restricted to WalkForward.

3.8 Secondary Animation

Secondary animation refers to movement that occurs as a result of primary animation. For example, when a character walks, in response to the movement, his hair might move and his muscles ripple. If a character shoots a weapon you'd expect a recoil action. Secondary animation is caused by the law of physics, which dictates that every action has an equal and opposite reaction. Without the extra animation a character can appear static and unrealistic.

Depending on the level of secondary animation, it can be processor intensive and not feasible in a real-time game environment. The avatars used in *Quake Arena* and *Unreal Tournament* are very simple with tight-fitting clothing and close-cut hair. This is not because the artist couldn't be bothered or at the time didn't have the technology to create highly realistic models—it is simply because animating all the extra elements with secondary animation was not feasible on the hardware available at the time these games were released. Even today, hair and cloth in 3D real-time environments are limited. A very nice example of the secondary animation of cloth can be seen in *Assassin's Creed*. The cloak and ropes of the main character move in response to the character's movements and the wind.

As hardware capabilities increase so will the quantity and quality of secondary animation.

Other animations that could also be considered secondary to the main character are those that bring the environment to life, for example, trees swaying in the breeze, water running in a river, other characters walking down the street, or even the main character's own clothing, such as a cape.

◉ Unity Hands On
Adding Secondary Animations

Step 1. Download *Chapter Three/SecondaryAnimation.zip* from the Web site. Unzip and open with Unity. Open the secondaryAnim scene. The scene is the final product from the previous workshop. Double-click on Hero in the Hierarchy to center the scene on the character.

Step 2. From the main menu, select GameObject > Create Other > Cloth. A large plane will be added to the scene. Drag the Interactive Cloth object in the Hierarchy onto the top-level Hero object. The Interactive Cloth will become a child object of Hero.

Step 3. Download *Chapter Three/Cape.blend* from the Web site and drag and drop the file into the Project.

Step 4. Locate the cape model in the Project and click on the small arrow next to it to expand. Next, select the Interactive Cloth from the Hierarchy and locate the Interactive Cloth component in the Inspector. Drag the Cape New mesh in the Project onto the Mesh variable in the Inspector as shown in Figure 3.20.

FIG 3.20 Creating a cape using a 3D cape model and an interactive cloth object.

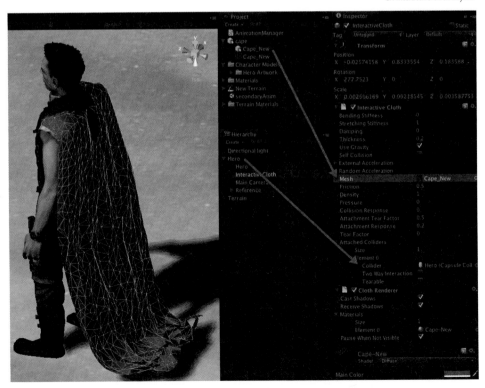

Step 5. At this point the cloth cape object will be immensely huge. Double-click on the Interactive Cloth object in the Hierarchy to position the camera in the scene on its location. You will now need to scale, rotate, and transform the cape such that it is in the same position relative to the character shown in Figure 3.20. If you haven't moved the character, the correct cape transforms are also shown in Figure 3.20.

Step 6. With the cape in position, select the Interactive Cloth and add one Attached Collider in the Inspector. Drag the main Hero object from the Hierarchy onto the Collider variable as shown in Figure 3.20. The cape must intersect with the character's collider in order for it to stick to it. This is the same principle used for hanging up the curtain in the warehouse of Chapter Two.

Step 7. Play. The cape will be attached to the character's shoulders and move when he moves.

Step 8. A final touch would be to add a shader with backface culling turned off so that the cape is visible from both sides. The code for this is similar to that used for the curtain in Chapter Two. However, one small detail needs to be added to ensure that the cape casts a shadow. Create a new shader in the Project and call it BackfaceOn. Open the file in script editor by double-clicking on it and replace the code with ALL of that in Listing 3.28. The part shown in bold is the line needed for shadows that would have been missing from the curtain shader in Chapter Two.

Listing 3.28 A Backface on Shader, Which Casts Shadows

```
Shader "Backface On" {
    Properties {
        _Color ("Main Color", Color) = (1,1,1,0)
        _SpecColor ("Spec Color", Color) = (1,1,1,1)
        _Emission ("Emmisive Color", Color) = (0,0,0,0)
        _Shininess ("Shininess", Range (0.01, 1)) = 0.7
        _MainTex ("Base (RGB)", 2D) = "white" { }
    }

    SubShader {
        Material {
            Diffuse [_Color]
            Ambient [_Color]
            Shininess [_Shininess]
            Specular [_SpecColor]
            Emission [_Emission]
        }
        Lighting On
        SeparateSpecular On
```

```
   // Set up alpha blending
   Blend SrcAlpha OneMinusSrcAlpha
   // Render the back facing parts of the object.
   // If the object is convex, these will always
   // be further away
   // than the front-faces.
   Pass {
      Cull Front
      SetTexture [_MainTex] {
         Combine Primary * Texture
      }
   }
   // Render the parts of the object facing us.
   // If the object is convex, these will be
   // closer than the
   // back-faces.
   Pass {
      Cull Back
      SetTexture [_MainTex] {
         Combine Primary * Texture
      }
   }

   }
   FallBack "Diffuse"
}
```

Step 9. Play. The character now has a fully fledged flowing cape complete with secondary animation. The final character is shown in Figure 3.21.

⬤ **Note**

The cape model used in the previous workshop was a freely available model from Turbosquid. The original file had too many polygons to be used for cloth rendering. It slowed down the processor such that the application ran at a snail's pace. To reduce the polycount, the cape model was opened with Blender, and with the object selected and placed in Edit mode, the Poly Reducer was used as shown in Figure 3.22. Running this script several times reduced the cape down to fewer than 2000 polygons.

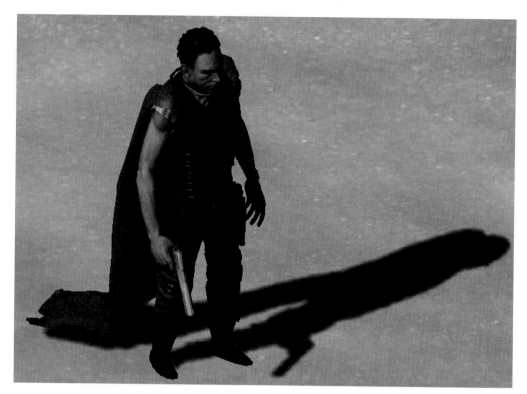

FIG 3.21 The character complete with cloth cape.

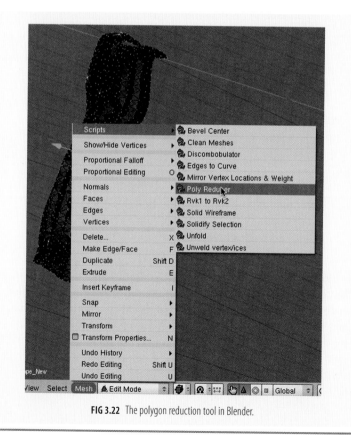

FIG 3.22 The polygon reduction tool in Blender.

3.9 Summary

This chapter examined 2D and 3D animation principles and techniques. As moving and animated objects are key elements in games, understanding how a game engine manages and manipulates these assets is key to including them effectively in games.

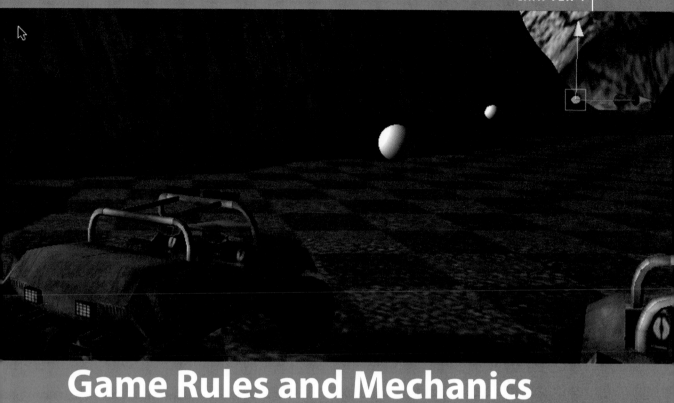

CHAPTER 4

Game Rules and Mechanics

But how can we speak of mere play, when we know that it is precisely play and play alone, which of all man's states and conditions is the one which makes him whole and unfolds both sides of his nature at once?

Friedrick von Shiller

4.1 Introduction

Games for recreational use are as old as known civilization. The oldest complete board game set thought to be the precursor of backgammon, the *Royal Game of Ur* (played with seven markers and three tetrahedral dice), dates back to 3000 BC. Other such games include *Wei-qi,* otherwise known as *Go,* played in China as far back as 2000 BC, and the Egyptian *Dogs and Jackals* (1800 BC).

The underlying activity in games is *play.* Play can be found in all human cultures and most animal populations. At the most instinctual level, play provides teaching and learning opportunities. For example, young children will play to assist them in practicing life skills. This is also evident in the animal kingdom through observing the young of cats, dogs, and other mammals; for example, puppies play fight with each other and practice pouncing on inanimate objects in preparation for the grown-up world. The key element of play is the cause-and-effect nature that reinforces certain behaviors. To practice is to attempt to get better at some skill set. Without feedback on one's actions, knowing how to improve is impossible.

When play becomes structured and goals, rules, and actions are applied they turn into games. In the playground, simple play involving chasing other children turns into a game of *Tiggy* or *Brandy* when one child becomes "it" and the objective is to tag another child in order to make him or her "it."

These fundamental actions of human behavior found in the play and games of children are found at the very heart of computer games and make up the set of core game mechanics presented herein.

4.2 Game Mechanics

If play is the practice of core human "mechanical" behavior, then a game mechanic should define and constrain this behavior in a system with rules and rewards; for example, a child playing at stacking blocks will be learning how to position them correctly to build a stable tower. Once goals and/or restrictions are placed on the activity it becomes a game; for example, build a stack of blocks to 1 meter or build a stack of blocks to 1 meter in 30 seconds. In this example, there is the play action (stacking), a goal (1 meter in 30 seconds), feedback (if the blocks are placed incorrectly they will fall over), and rules (use only these blocks).

The theme throughout this book plays on the word *mechanic* to refer to the actions taking place in games from the internal workings of animation and programming to the interactions between the environment and the player. However, the term *game mechanic*, in game studies, is used to refer to designed game/player relationships that facilitate and define the game's challenges. They are complex systems that include a set of possible player actions, motivations, goals, and feedback. Understanding that a game mechanic is much more than just an action and what other elements may be applied with that action opens up a plethora of almost infinite ideas for games by mixing and matching actions, goals, and rules. The cycle is illustrated in Figure 4.1. The player is presented with a challenge. To complete this challenge they have tools they can use to perform actions and rules that define the scope of these actions. The tools include peripheral computing objects such as keyboards and game controllers, as well as virtual in-game tools such as vehicles, weapons, and keys. The rules dictate how the player can act in the environment. In a board game, rules are written in an instruction booklet and monitored by players. In a computer game, the player is made aware of the rules and the game's programming code ensures that the player follows them. The program also provides feedback to players based on their actions to assist them in learning how to better play the game and achieve the challenge. Part of the feedback mechanism is to also inform players when they succeed or fail.

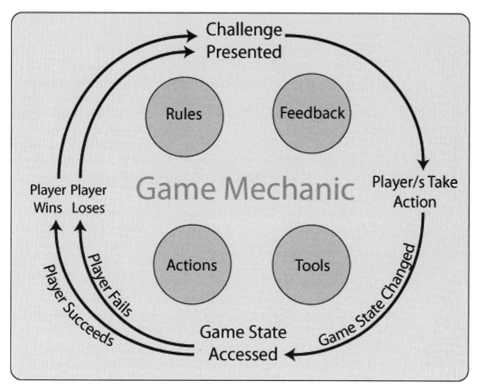

FIG 4.1 The game mechanic cycle.

One of the developers of the original *Halo*, the game that launched Microsoft's Xbox, described the game as 5 minutes of fun over and over again. This first person shooter (FPS) game, in a visually rich 3D environment, employs numerous game mechanics that revolve around shooting and blowing things up. As a whole the game is represented by the ultimate game mechanic that challenges the player to uncover the secrets of a ring-shaped planet named Halo while battling a variety of aliens. This umbrella mechanic is broken down into a number of smaller mechanics that see players performing the same tasks over and over again in order to complete their objectives, with the key mechanics being *kill or be killed*, typically found in FPS games. As such you could say each of these tasks is a minigame in itself, although not as compelling to a player as automatons as they are put together and embedded within an engaging narrative. However, in order to understand how to design a game like *Halo* it is necessary to examine the most fundamental of game mechanics.

Consider the game of paper–rock–scissors in which two players simultaneously count to three and then present their hands gesturing for rock, paper, or scissors. If one person has paper and the other rock, paper wins because it can wrap rock. If one person has scissors and the other paper, scissors wins because scissors cut paper. If one person has rock and the other scissors, rock wins because rock blunts scissors. If both players show the same gesture the game is tied. One game of paper–rock–scissors completes one of the game mechanic cycles. The challenge is to show a hand gesture that is superior to your opponent on the count of three, the player action is to make a hand gesture, and the rules determine whose gesture wins.

This chapter introduces common generic game mechanic actions such as matching, sorting, searching, and hitting. Examples of how each of these is represented visually in a game and the programming that controls them are explained in depth. Common algorithms and data structures used for each mechanic will be worked through with the reader integrating where appropriate the key art assets.

4.3 Primary Mechanics

All primary game mechanics sit at the very heart of natural human behavior and ability. Humans have evolved to perform them instinctually. Abilities that have evolved over millions of years out of the need to survive now find themselves as repetitive actions in games. Why?

Humans are a pattern-seeking species. Our brains have evolved to deal with the plethora of sensations and information they deal with every day by symbolizing our knowledge internally. All decision-making activities therefore involve a prediction of risks and rewards as we can never have enough time to do to a rational atomic analysis of a situation. We are good at developing intuitive understandings of situations and internally develop our own understandings whether right or wrong, by which we then make future decisions. So reliable have our brains become on being able to process information in this way that we receive neurochemical rewards of dopamine when we make sense out of complete chaos. For this reason we believe that we can see patterns where there are none. How often have you heard something like "that cloud looks like an elephant"? The greater the randomness and the more we make sense of it and have that judgment justified, the greater the neurochemical reward.

As Raph Koster points out in his book *A Theory of Fun for Game Design*, the thing that make games fun is their ability to engage the human mind. They do this by presenting the brain with challenges that it is best designed to achieve. In short, this involves repetition and lots of pattern matching. The following sections outline many primary game action mechanics that all in some form require pattern matching and involve primitive human ability. One or more of these actions can be found in all games.

4.3.1 Searching

Searching is a basic human cognitive process that involves perception and scanning of an environment. Whether one is searching for car keys, looking through a telephone directory, or trying to find a friend in a crowd, the process requires the human brain to take snapshots of the environment and scan it quickly for items matching their internal symbolization.

In computer games, this ability is leveraged to make the player look for a specific piece of information, item, location, or character in an environment. The objective of the player's search may be to find an item needed to proceed in the game, for example, a key to open a door, or to navigate a maze to get from one place to another.

Searching for the mineral resource titanium in an asteroid field in *EVE Online* is one primary mechanics employed in the game play. In order to begin making money to buy anything and progress in the game, mining minerals is the first action rookie players must learn. Part of the mining process is searching for minerals in mine fields and finding asteroids that have enough of the type you are looking for.

Looking for ammunition clips and medical packs has a long tradition in FPS games such as in *Quake*. This action will either see a player who is low on fire power or health searching the game level madly for any of these items or trying to remember where he saw the last one and returning to that location. Often with this action, if the player does not need ammunition or health, the item cannot be picked up or used and therefore remains in the same location until it is needed.

4.3.2 Matching

Matching is an activity that is part of the searching process. For the human brain, identifying one object as being similar to another is a simple thing. To be searching for something is to be able to identify when the mental image you have of the thing you are looking for is the same thing you are looking at; that is, they match. Many day-to-day activities involve matching, such as finding a pair of socks to putting the right PIN into an ATM.

In a game, matching is used to get players to put one or more things together because they are smaller pieces of a whole or are the same color or shape or have other similar characteristics. This common action may find players putting together parts of a machine to make it work as a whole or placing the same colored items next to each other on a grid.

Guitar Hero uses matching superbly. The entire game is focused around the player's ability to match the guitar string on the screen with the button on the peripheral device. Not only must the player match the right note at the right time, but his rhythm of button pressing is also evaluated.

4.3.3 Sorting

Attempting to make order out of chaos is a common human behavior. People with very extreme cases of requiring everything to be in its place may suffer from compulsive obsessive disorder. However, in many cases when things are sorted, life is much easier. When things are in order and we can rely on them being in order, it lifts some of the cognitive load off doing other tasks. For example, if money is sorted correctly in a shop's till, it makes the task of giving a customer change easier. Imagine trying to do grocery shopping in a place where none of the items was sorted on the shelves.

Games use this sorting desire to motivate players to arrange two or more items according to their characteristics, such as size, color, species, age, or name. Sorting can also be employed in activities where performing tasks in order is necessary to complete a challenge.

For example, in the 2D puzzle game *Machinarium*, players must make their way through levels by having their character, a little robot, make machines work in certain orders to accomplish particular tasks. In one level, the robot must wire a circuit panel one way to perform the first task and then rewire it in another to get the second one done. In *The Sims*, the player can sort the activities their Sim must do in order to satisfy their most immediate needs.

At a simpler level, games such as *Bejewelled* use matching with sorting to get the player to sort through randomly placed colored jewels to sort like ones into lines.

4.3.4 Chancing

Chance devices such as die and the drawing of straws for purposes of sorting, selecting, and division are common among many cultures, and the practice is referenced in classical Greek literature as early as the Trojan wars and beforehand in Egyptian artifacts.

Using chance in decision making is referred to as risk. Research has shown that the types of risks people take today stem back to situations encountered by our ancestors, including competition with other individuals, competition with other cultures, mating, resource allocation, and environment. For example, chasing a bear away from one's food could pose certain risk, as would going to war with another tribe.

Chance in games is used to determine the probability to future outcomes. This is one of the oldest actions used in games involving the use of dice: rolling or coin tossing to determine an outcome based on chance. Without some element of probability in which players knew what the outcome of their actions would be before they did them, there would not be any need to take a risk. Research has shown the greater the risk, the higher the neurochemical reward.

The most obvious and earliest use of probability in adventure games came when the board game of *Dungeons and Dragons* was computerized. The board game involves the rolling of dice to determine the character's ability levels, for example, how strong they are or how likely they are to shake off a magical spell. Probability also comes into play when characters face off against each other. If players knew for sure which character would win, there would be no enjoyment in a battle, nor reason for one. However, the game uses die rolls, which, in combination with their ability levels, are used to calculate success or failure. The computer game does the same thing. This mechanism has flowed through into almost all games to give an element of chance in situations and to make the outcome unknown.

4.3.5 Mixing

Mixing actions involves the combining of objects or actions to produce an outcome unachievable otherwise. In day-to-day life, people mix ingredients to make food, paint pigments to make new colors, and multitask actions to get jobs completed more quickly.

In computer games, actions can be combined to allow characters to perform tasks they couldn't do with single actions, for example, jumping while running to leap across a crevasse in the game world or combining multiple keystrokes to perform special moves such as those available to characters in the fighting game *Super Smash Brothers*.

Combining game objects to produce other game objects is also an example of mixing. For example, in *Doodle God*, players begin with the four elements (fire, wind, earth, and water) that they must combine in different combinations to discover other objects such as coal, turtles, and plasma. In *The Sims Medieval*, the wizard character has the ability to mix herbs and minerals to make potions.

4.3.6 Timing

Human society is run by time. Even before the advent of mechanical time-keeping devices, the earth's revolution around the sun meant humans were constantly on a time schedule.

The use of time in a computer game can be applied to as a game mechanic. It could involve completing a task within an allotted time, timing an action, or waiting for some event to occur. This mechanism is used to instigate urgency in situations such as racing, whether it be against the clock or an opponent or to generate anticipation when waiting for something to occur or forcing patience upon a player who has to wait for the game environment to change.

Time is a blatant obvious mechanism in racing games. It is used in *Project Gotham*, for example, to determine how long it takes a player to get around a track. This time is then converted into points. If the time is better than another set time, it may unlock another track or racing car.

In *EVE Online*, time is used to add respect to the long process of training one's character with new skills. In the only massively multiplayer role-playing game, players may fly larger and faster ships only when they have trained for long enough. Training tends to take many hours and sometimes days in real time. As the player's character can continue to train when the player is not logged in, it is also a clever mechanism to keep players attached to their character and to keep them logging back in to check on their progress and start new training regimes.

4.3.7 Progressing

Life is about progressing, whether it be growing from a baby to an adult, getting a university degree, or getting a job promotion. Humans, in general, experience stages in their lives that correlate with their age and achievements.

Games employ a progression scheme in which the player begins as a *noob* and progresses to the level of *expert* at the end. Along this journey, progression schemes are put in place that give players a feeling of achievement for their efforts. For example, in *EVE Online*, the longer you play the game, the higher the training level you can achieve. In *StarCraft*, the more you play, the more money you can make to spend on upgrading your equipment. In *The Sims*, one of the game goals is to progress the job of your Sim until it reaches its lifetime achievement.

Progression will occur naturally in any game as a player becomes more familiar and skilled at the game play. However, as can be seen from the preceding examples, it can also be built in as a reward system and a way to progress the player through game levels or narrative.

4.3.8 Capturing

To capture is to take something that belongs to someone else through force or your own efforts. Throughout history there is a long list of tribes capturing members of other tribes, armies capturing cities, and pirates taking ships.

Some games embed this mechanic as the primary objective of the game. For example, *Civilization* requires players to take over others cities and countries. The Dutch East India Company challenges players to take cities along the spice route in order to be able to build a more profitable trading company between European and east Asian cities.

Capturing can also be used in a game in not such a literal sense. For example, it could involve knocking out another game character in order to steal his weapon or stealing a car to make a quick getaway.

4.3.9 Conquering

In a similar vein to capturing is the action of conquering. Whereas capturing is more likened to stealing, conquering is about outdoing or annihilating the competition. Like capturing, human races have a long history of conquering.

For example, the Spanish conquered and wiped out the Aztec Empire in the region now known as Mexico beginning in August 1519 and declaring final victory on August 13, 1521.

Outdoing an opponent is a classic game play goal. For example, in *chess*, the aim is to get your opponent into checkmate while taking pieces along the way or make them surrender. In the online *StarCraft* one-on-one games, this too is the objective. In *Black & White*, the player who takes the part of a god must gather more loyal worshippers than the other gods in order to drive the other gods away and rule over an island.

Again, this mechanic need not be so literal. The conquering of another opponent in a game environment might mean you own a bigger house, have more money, or have a better car. This is the clichéd need to "outdo the Joneses" and can be a direct goal in the game environment or could evolve as an interpersonal consequence of players comparing their individual game play success and status with each other.

4.3.10 Avoidance

One key to human survival is the avoidance of disliked and harmful things. This includes not eating poisonous substances, not sitting on a fire, and getting out of the way of large moving objects.

Numerous games require the player to avoid items and situations that are harmful to their character. *Space Invaders* requires players to move their ship so that it doesn't get hit by alien fire, and FPS games require the player to avoid enemy fire. *Jojo's Fashion Show*, a game in which the player must dress models according to particular themes, even requires the player to avoid wearing the wrong clothes.

Instead of telling players what they can do, avoidance is all about showing them what they can't. The inability to avoid whatever it is they should be avoiding penalizes players through reduced points or health given the situation.

Avoidance places constraints on the actions of players such that they must keep in mind what they can't do while trying to progress through the game environment.

4.3.11 Collecting

Collecting is another natural human behavior. At the extreme, someone who cannot control collecting items is classified as a *compulsive hoarder*. In a game environment, however, items are there to be collected for a purpose.

Some items can be collected and placed in an inventory to be used at a later time. When used, these might disappear or go back into the inventory. The collecting mechanic is often used with searching. In Disney's *Princesses* game, children are required to walk through the virtual kingdom searching for and collecting magical items to help the princesses.

Other collection activities can happen almost by mistake. In the 2D platformer versions of *Super Mario Brothers*, collecting coins, stars, and other items happens just as the player moves the character through the levels, as the items are unavoidable. They are not challenging to pick up, and the number found collected is a record of progression through the level rather than achievement.

The original *Doom* and *Wolfenstein* 3D games introduced the concept of collecting points for finding secret rooms, killing all the guards and or monsters, and finding extra damage power-ups and the like. A count at the end of each level reveals how many have been found. A lack of finding them does not stop the player from progressing, but can give some incentive to replay that level to find all the added extras.

⊕ For Research

This is by no means an exhaustive list of game action mechanics. If you are interested in learning more, visit the links:

- http://lostgarden.com/2006/10/what-are-game-mechanics.html
- http://gamification.org/wiki/Game_Mechanics
- http://gamestudies.org/0802/articles/sicart

4.4 Developing with Some Simple Game Mechanics

This section revisits a number of the primary game action mechanics with some practical implementations in Unity. Note that more than one mechanic is required in order to make a playable game prototype or to make an interactive application slightly game-like. For example, matching marbles of the same color is not a game. It's just matching. But matching as many marbles as you can, of the same color in 2 minutes, instantly provides the player with a challenge, a goal, and a reward.

4.4.1 Matching and Sorting

Matching is a simple yet compelling game mechanic that sees the player scanning a number of items to find ones that are similar. This mechanic occurs in games such as *Bejeweled*, in which the player swaps adjacent gemstones arranged in a grid to make horizontal or vertical sets of three or more of the same colored gem. When a line is created, it disappears from the grid and the player gets some points. The matching mechanic is found across a wide range of popular games such as *solitaire*, where card suits are matched, *monopoly*, in which property colors are matched, *memory*, where images must be matched, to even *kinect* games, where body poses are matched.

Sorting is a game mechanic that is usually found with matching. It entails moving objects around to position them in a specific order or to match them. The game of memory does not including sorting, but solitaire does as the player sorts through the deck of cards to arrange them into suits.

For either mechanic there must be visual clues as to how the player should be sorting or matching game objects. For example, in *Dr. Mario 64,* the good doctor throws colored vitamins shaped like pills into a jar full of viruses. When four or more viruses and vitamins line up, they disappear. For this level of simplistic matching and sorting, iconic art is used throughout. For example, in *Dr. Mario 64*, the vitamin pills look like capsules and the viruses are small colored squares with sick and angry looking faces.

It is important to engage the player in these games with logical icons. If items need to be matched or sorted, they should look similar in appearance or have very clear shared characteristics that make them part of a particular group. If leaving a player to guess what matches with what or what goes where is not the objective of your game, don't make it one.

⊙ Unity Hands On
Matching and Sorting

In this hands-on session you are going to create a game that involves matching and sorting. Balls of different colors will fall down the screen. At the bottom of the screen will be four different-colored containers. The player will be required to use the mouse to sort the balls horizontally so that they eventually land in the container that matches their color. Halfway down the screen a bar will appear. The player will only be able to change the horizontal position of the balls while they are above the bar. Points are accrued for each correctly sorted ball.

> **Step 1.** Download *Chapter Four/Matching.zip* from the Web site. Unzip and open the project in Unity. Open the scene called *maingame*. Play it and you will see a Score area and a quit button. The quit button will take you back to the main menu where you can press the play button to get back to the main game screen.
>
> **Step 2.** Download *Chapter Four/Beaker.blend* from the Web site. Add it to the project.
>
> **Step 3.** Add the beaker to the Scene. Position it at (0,0,10) where it will become visible in the Game.
>
> **Step 4.** Add a GameObject > Create Other > Directional Light to the scene.
>
> **Step 5.** Create a new Material to the Project. Set its shader to Transparent/Diffuse. Set the main color to red and give it an alpha value of 100.
>
> **Step 6.** Put the red material on the beaker.
>
> **Step 7.** Add three other beakers to the Scene and give them the colors green, blue, and yellow.

Step 8. Move each of the beakers so that they make a line across the bottom of the camera's view as shown in Figure 4.2.

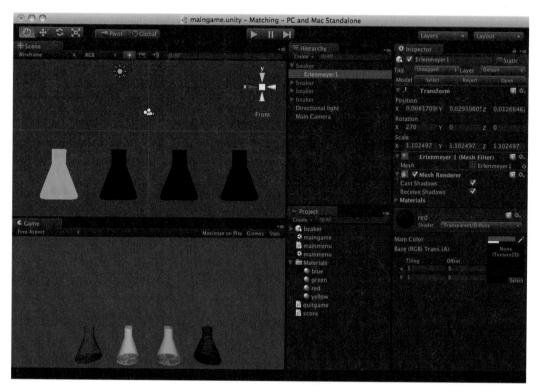

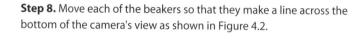

FIG 4.2 The initial setup for a matching and sorting game.

Step 9. Add a cube to the scene. Position it at (0,2,0) and give it a scale of (20,0.2,1) as shown in Figure 4.3. Tick the *Is Trigger* box of the Box Collider and set the z size to 10. The cube will appear as a white strip across the game with a large box collider. Ticking the *Is Trigger* box for the Box Collider will enable triggering an event when another object collides with it; however, it will not cause any physics events. This will allow objects to fall through it, but we can detect when this is happening programmatically.

Step 10. Create a sphere. Position it at (0,0,0) and scale it to (0.5,0.5,0.5). Attach a Rigidbody and set the drag to 10. In the Rigidbody settings for Constraints, tick the Z value of Freeze Position. This will keep the sphere always at its initial z value (in this case 0) even after a physics event.

Step 11. Turn the sphere into a prefab object called ball. Delete the original sphere object from the Hierarchy.

Step 12. Create a new JavaScript file called *destroyWhenGone.js*. Enter the code shown in Listing 4.1.

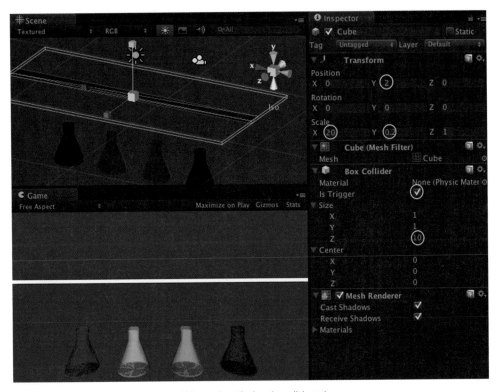

FIG 4.3 Adding a cube with a large box collider to the scene.

Listing 4.1 Code to Destroy an Object When It Moves out of the Camera's View

```
function OnBecameInvisible()
{
    Destroy(this.gameObject);
}
```

Step 13. Attach *destroyWhenGone* to the ball prefab. This code will destroy the object when it goes outside the area visible on the screen—the reason being that soon we will create code to spawn balls continually. When balls move outside the screen, they will be outside the game play area. In this case, they are no longer needed; instead of the physics system processing their location constantly and the game engine performing any other behaviors with them, it makes more sense to just get rid of them completely.

Step 14. Create a new JavaScript file called *spawn.js*. Enter the code shown in Listing 4.2.

Listing 4.2 Spawning Objects at Random Intervals

```
var ball:GameObject;
function Update ()
{
     if(Random.Range(0,200) < 1)
     {
      var sphere : GameObject =
          Instantiate(ball, Vector3(0,5,0),
                        Quaternion.identity);
     }
}
```

Step 15. Attach this script to the camera. With the camera selected in the Hierarchy, locate the script in the Inspector and set the value for ball to the ball prefab created previously.

Step 16. Play. At random intervals a ball will be created and fall down the screen. When it goes out of view it is destroyed. A ball is created according to a generated random number between 0 and 200. If this number is less than 1, a ball is instantiated. To increase the interval between balls, increase the upper range. To have them appear more quickly, lower the upper range.

Step 17. To have the balls spawn at locations across the entire screen, modify the *spawn.js* code to that in Listing 4.3.

Listing 4.3 Setting a Random Value for the Position of Game Objects

```
var ball:GameObject;
function Update ()
{
     if(Random.Range(0,200) < 1)
     {
      var ballStartPosition = new Vector3(Random.Range
        (-6,6),8,0);
      var sphere : GameObject =
        Instantiate(ball,ballStartPosition, Quaternion.
        identity);
     }
}
```

Step 18. Play. Because the starting *x* value for each ball is taken randomly from the range −6,6, balls will appear across the width of the screen, as this is the range of *x* values for the beakers. You may have placed your beakers at different distances depending on the screen resolution. In this case, increase or decrease the random range to suit. The starting *y* position is set to 8. If this is not beyond the top of your screen, you may want to increase it a little. The balls should spawn just beyond the player's view.

Step 19. At this stage, balls will fall straight through the beakers. To add collisions, find the "Erlenmeyer1" meshes for each beaker object and attach a Component > Physics > Mesh Collider to each one. Ensure that the Mesh setting for this collider is set to "Erlenmeyer1" as shown in Figure 4.4.

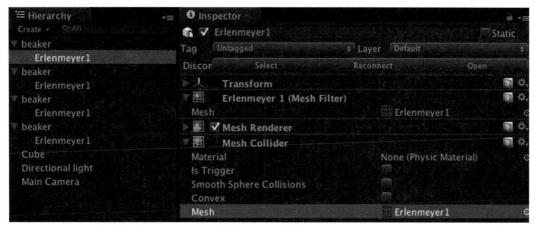

FIG 4.4 Attaching a Mesh Collider to the Mesh renderer of an object.

Step 20. Play. The balls will now collide with the beakers. If you want the balls to fall faster, lower their drag value in the ball prefab. However, as the game play starts to take shape you'll be glad that they are falling more slowly.

Step 21. Modify *spawn.js* to that shown in Listing 4.4. This will add an array of materials to the script so that each ball spawned can be assigned a random color. The shader for the material is changed to Diffuse, as we will be using the existing transparent-colored materials on the beakers, but we don't want the balls to be transparent.

Listing 4.4 Coloring a Game Object Using an Array of Materials

```
var ball:GameObject;
var materialArray: Material[];
function Update ()
{
     if(Random.Range(0,200) < 1)
     {
      var ballStartPosition = new Vector3(
        Random.Range(-6,6),8,0);
      var sphere : GameObject =
          Instantiate(ball, ballStartPosition,
            Quaternion.identity);
```

```
        sphere.renderer.material =
             materialArray[Random.Range(0,materialArray.
                length)];
        sphere.renderer.material.shader = Shader.
          Find("Diffuse");
      }
   }
```

Step 22. With the main camera selected in the Hierarchy, locate the spawn script. Click on the small triangle next to Material Array to expose the array values. Set the Size to 4. For each of the elements that appear, drag and drop the blue, green, red, and yellow materials into the locations as shown in Figure 4.5.

FIG 4.5 Adding materials to an array in a script.

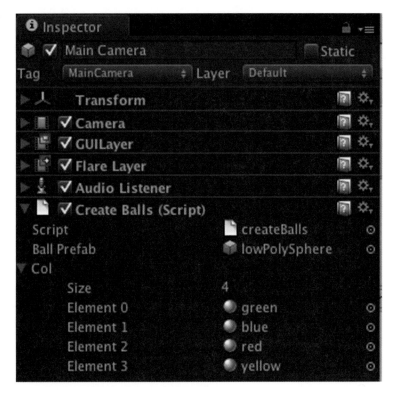

Step 23. Play. Each ball that falls will be assigned a random color. The colors are picked out of the array using the same Random.Range() function used for the spawn timing.

The next step involves moving balls with the mouse. The coding for this is not as simple as it might sound. Therefore, this hands-on session will be placed on hold to provide you with some essential background knowledge.

The Screen and the World
Most games, especially those on a computer with mouse control, require calculations that transform the mouse position on the screen in 2D to game environment coordinates in 3D. This is necessary when you need to program for the player clicking on and interacting with objects in the 3D world. They are not actually clicking on the game world; they are, in fact, clicking on an imaginary transparent flat plane through which the game is being viewed.

The screen coordinates are usually set most commonly with (0,0) in either the upper or lower left corner or right in the center. The mouse position is either counted in pixels or screen size proportions. For example, if the screen resolution was 640 pixels wide and 480 pixels high with (0,0) being in the lower left corner, the mouse coordinates when exactly in the center of the screen would be (320,240). When screen coordinates are proportional, values range from 0 to 1 in both the x and y directions no matter the resolution. For example, if (0,0) were in the top left corner, (1,1) would be in the lower right. The mouse position when the pointer is in the center of the screen would be (0.5,0.5).

If the different formats for the 2D screen space weren't complicated enough, the 3D game world coordinates will be affected by rotation, perspective, or orthographic views and scaling. The nature of the problem is illustrated in Figure 4.6.

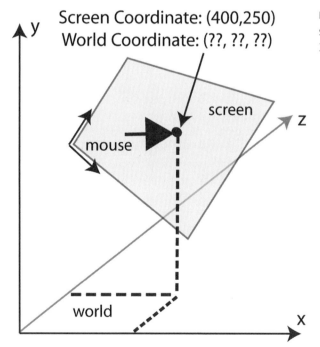

Screen Coordinate: (400,250)
World Coordinate: (??, ??, ??)

FIG 4.6 The difference between 2D screen coordinates and the 3D world.

◁ Unity Specifics

Screen, Viewport, and World Vectors

Unity, as with all 3D graphics systems, has three coordinate systems: screen space, viewport, and world. The screen and the viewport are 2D systems, and the world is 3D. The screen coordinates by default range from (0,0) to (screen width in pixels, screen height in pixels). The viewport coordinates are proportional, going from (0,0) to (1,1), and the world coordinates are infinite. Having said that, the coordinates (−10,−50) in screen space and (−0.5,−1) in the viewport are legitimate. They just don't appear in the visible range of the camera, just like 3D coordinates outside the camera frustum.

Unity has a number of useful functions for converting all these coordinate systems among each other. They can all be found in the script reference by searching for "Camera." To try them out, create a new Unity Project with the script in Listing 4.5. Attach the script to the camera, and the converted coordinates will be displayed in the console.

Listing 4.5 Code to Convert the Mouse Position on the Screen to Viewport and World Coordinates

```
function Update ()
{
    print("Screen to Viewport" +
        camera.ScreenToViewportPoint(Input.mousePosition));
    print("Screen to World" +
        camera.ScreenToWorldPoint(Input.mousePosition));
}
```

At first the coordinates may not change when you move the mouse over the screen. This will occur if the camera is in perspective mode and the near plane distance is very small—the reason being that the closer the near plane is to the camera, the more the frustum becomes a pyramid with the screen space representing the apex. Therefore, the screen is almost a single point in 3D space and essentially you are moving the mouse around on this point as far as the 3D coordinate system is concerned. Changing the camera to orthographic will give a square view volume and provide more screen space area with respect to the 3D world. You can also move the near plane farther away from the camera if you want the mouse position changes to register.

There are also functions called ViewportToScreenPoint(), ViewportToWorldPoint(), WorldToScreenPoint(), and WorldToViewportPoint().

Step 24. Select the ball prefab in the Project. At the very top of the Inspector click on Tag. Select Add Tag from the pop-up menu. The Inspector will change to a different view. Select the triangle next to Tags at the very top of the Inspector and type ball into Element 0. Reselect the ball prefab in the Project, click on Tag again, and find the newly added ball tag in the pop-up menu. Select it. This process is illustrated in Figure 4.7.

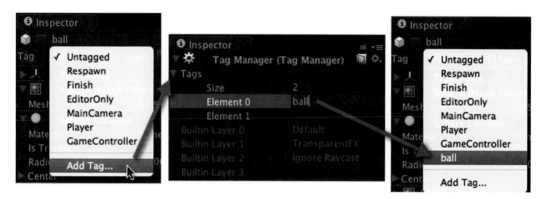

FIG 4.7 Adding a new tag.

◉ Unity Hands On
Matching and Sorting—Continued

Step 1. Create a new JavaScript file called *clickndrag*, add the code in Listing 4.6, and attach it to the ball prefab.

Listing 4.6 Script Allowing Mouse Selection and Dragging of Game Object

```
private var focusObj: GameObject = null;
private var lastMousePosition: Vector3;
private var deltaMousePosition: Vector3;
var mouseSensitivity = 40.0;
function Update ()
{
    //when fire button is pressed
    if( Input.GetButtonDown("Fire1"))
    {
        focusObj = null;
        //cast a ray
        var ray = Camera.main.ScreenPointToRay (Input.
                mousePosition);
        var hit : RaycastHit;
```

```
                //if the ray hits an object and that
                //object is a ball
                if(Physics.Raycast (ray, hit, 100) &&
                        hit.transform.gameObject.tag == "ball")
                {
                        //take hold of it with the focusObj variable
                        focusObj = hit.transform.gameObject;

                        //remember the location of the mouse
                        lastMousePosition = Input.mousePosition;

                }
        }
        //if the fire button is down
        if(focusObj && Input.GetButton("Fire1"))
        {
         //calculate how far the the mouse has moved across
         //the screen
         deltaMousePosition = Input.mousePosition -
                                lastMousePosition;

            //use this value to set the position of the object
            focusObj.transform.position.x + =
                        deltaMousePosition.x/mouseSensitivity;

            //remember the location of the mouse
            lastMousePosition = Input.mousePosition;
        }

        //if the fire button is released
        if(focusObj && Input.GetButtonUp("Fire1"))
        {
            //forget about the object that was clicked on
            focusObj = null;
        }
}
```

Step 2. Play. You will now be able to move the balls horizontally to line them up with the same colored beakers by clicking on them and dragging the mouse. To change the mouse sensitivity, modify the related variable at the top of the script. Note that it is exposed so that you can change it easily in the Inspector.

Step 3. The ability to move the ball once it has gone below the white line (fashioned from the cube added at the beginning) needs to be added next. The easiest way to do this is to change the ball's tag as it passes through the trigger collider of the cube. To achieve this, create a new JavaScript file called *stopBalls* and add the code in Listing 4.7. Attach this script to the cube.

Listing 4.7 Script to Register a Collision on a Triggering Collider

```
function OnTriggerEnter (obj : Collider)
{
     obj.gameObject.tag = "Untagged";
}
```

Step 4. Play. When the balls go through the cube collider it causes the OnTriggerEnter() function to run. When a collider is set to be a trigger only, it does not cause any collisions in the physics engine and therefore the OnCollisionEnter() and similar functions do not work. For each collision function there is an equivalent set of trigger functions. When the balls are below the white line they will no longer be moveable by the mouse.

Step 5. To complete this game we need to add a scoring mechanism. We will use a trigger collider at the entrance to each beaker to count the balls falling into them. Add four spheres to the Scene and resize and position them like corks in the top of each beaker as shown in Figure 4.8.

FIG 4.8 Plugging the top of a container with colliders.

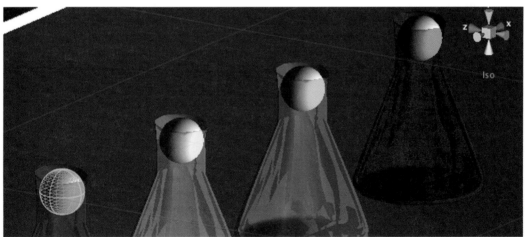

Step 6. For each sphere, remove the Mesh Filter and Mesh components, as we only require the Sphere Colliders. For each ensure that the Is Trigger value is ticked.

Step 7. Create new JavaScript called *countBalls* and add the code shown in Listing 4.08.

Listing 4.8 Code to Test the Color of a Game Object Against a Variable Value

```
var colorMatch:Material;
var score: int = 0;
function OnTriggerEnter (obj : Collider)
{
    if(obj.gameObject.renderer.material.color ==
        colorMatch.color)
    {
        score = score + 1;
    }
}
```

Step 8. Attach *countBalls.js* to each of the spheres in the tops of the beakers.

Step 9. For each sphere, select it in the Hierarchy and set the value of Color Match by dragging the corresponding material from the Project onto the script component.

Step 10. Because the code is attached to each sphere, each sphere will keep a tally of the correctly colored balls. These four values need to be added together to determine the total score. Open the *score.js* script in the script editor and modify the existing code to that in Listing 4.9. The GetComponent() function gains access to the *countBalls* script, which is attached to the sphere objects and pulls out the score by referring to the variable by name.

Listing 4.9 Totalling a Score from Multiple Sub-Scores

```
var score = 0;
var scoreStyle: GUIStyle;
//create an array to hold all scoring objects
var scoringObjects: GameObject[];
function OnGUI ()
{
    //reset the score value being displayed on the screen
    score = 0;
    //loop through each score object
    for(var i = 0; i < scoringObjects.length; i++)
    {
        //extract the score from the object and tally
        score + =
        scoringObjects[i].GetComponent("countBalls").score;
    }

    GUI.BeginGroup (Rect (Screen.width - 85, 5, 80, 80));
```

```
        GUI.Box (Rect (0,0,80,60), "Score");
        GUI.Label (Rect (0, 20, 80, 30), String.Format("{0:0}",
                                         score),scoreStyle);

        GUI.EndGroup ();
}
```

Step 11. Save and select the main camera in the Hierarchy. Locate the score script component in the Inspector and, at the very bottom set under scoringObjects, set size to 4 and assign the values for the array of beaker spheres by dragging and dropping each one in place as shown in Figure 4.9.

FIG 4.9 Adding game objects to an array in another script.

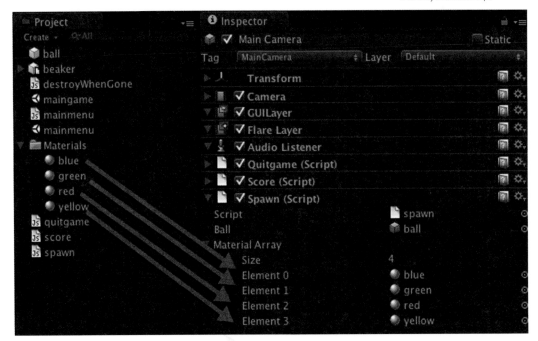

Step 12. Save and play. Your game now keeps score.
Step 13. Save the scene (File Save Scene) and double-click on the *mainmenu* Scene in the Project.
Step 14. Open *mainmenu.js* in the script editor. This script is attached to the main camera and displays a small menu with a play button. Play to see this appear on the screen. Click on the play button and it will take you to the *maingame* Scene. To swap scenes,

227

the function Application.LoadLevel() is used. The name you give to this function is the name you gave the scene when it was saved. You can't reference another scene, however, if it is not included in the build. To include a scene, when the scene is open, select File Build Settings from the main menu. The window that opens has an area at the top where all included scenes are listed. Press the Add Scene button to put the scene into the list. The scene at the top of the list is the one that will open first when your game is run as an application. Drag and drop the scenes in the list to change the order. Press the Build button at the bottom of the window to create a stand-alone application. This includes an app for the Mac and an exe for Windows. These are the files that you can then distribute to others for playing.

Step 15. Modify the code in *mainmenu.js* to that in Listing 4.10.

Listing 4.10 Setting Player Preferences with Menu Selection

```
function OnGUI ()
{
        GUI.BeginGroup (Rect (Screen.width / 2 - 50,
                              Screen.height / 2 - 60, 100, 120));
        GUI.Box (Rect (0,0,100,120), "Main Menu");

        if(GUI.Button (Rect (10,40,80,30), "Play Level 1"))
        {
                PlayerPrefs.SetInt("Level", 1);
                Application.LoadLevel("maingame");
        }

        if(GUI.Button (Rect (10,80,80,30), "Play Level 2"))
        {
                PlayerPrefs.SetInt("Level", 2);
                Application.LoadLevel("maingame");
        }
        GUI.EndGroup ();
}
```

Step 16. The PlayerPrefs.SetInt() functions allow a system level setting of a variable. In this case it is called *Level* and it is set to 1 or 2 depending on the button pressed. This makes the variable available to be picked up by the *maingame* Scene when it opens. You can also use PlayerPrefs to store highest scores and other player details that can be used when the game is played the next time. To get the player's level preference before the game starts, open *spawn.js* and modify the code as shown in Listing 4.11.

Listing 4.11 A Start Function That Loads Player Preference and Uses It to Set the Difficulty of the Game

```
var ball:GameObject;
var materialArray: Material[];
function Start()
{
     var playerlevel = PlayerPrefs.GetInt("Level");
     if(playerlevel == 1)
     {
          GameObject.Find("Cube").transform.position.y = 0;
     }
     else if(playerlevel == 2)
     {
          GameObject.Find("Cube").transform.position.y = 2;
     }
}
function Update ()
{
     ...
}
```

Step 17. Before playing, check that the white line cube you have used is called Cube in the Hierarchy. If it is not, change the name in the script by replacing the text "Cube" with the name you used. Play. The main menu buttons now set the level of difficulty that changes the height of the white line. The higher it is, the harder the game becomes.

Step 18. Finally, we want to add an end game scenario. To make it simple, we will have the game end after 20 balls have been caught. First, create a new scene with File > New Scene. After the scene opens select File > Save Scene and call it *gameover*. A scene icon with this name will appear in the Project.

Step 19. Download *Chapter Four/gameover.png* from the Web site and add it to the Project.

Step 20. Create a new JavaScript file called *showScore.js* and add the code in Listing 4.12.

Listing 4.12 Displaying a Gameover Screen with the Score

```
var goImage: Texture2D;
function OnGUI ()
{
     var scoreText = "You Scored " +
     PlayerPrefs.GetInt("LastScore");
```

```
GUI.BeginGroup (Rect (Screen.width / 2 - 100,
                           Screen.height / 2 - 100, 200, 200));
GUI.Box (Rect (0,0,200,200), goImage);
GUI.Label (Rect (55, 15, 100, 30), scoreText);
if(GUI.Button (Rect (25,165,150,30), "Back to Menu"))
{
        Application.LoadLevel("mainmenu");
}
GUI.EndGroup ();
}
```

Step 21. Attach *showScore.js* to the Main Camera. Select the camera in the Hierarchy and locate the script in the Inspector. Drag and drop the gameover texture from the Project onto the goImage variable in the script component.

Step 22. Play to check that it displays correctly.

Step 23. From the main menu, select File > Build Settings and click on Add Current to add the gameover scene to the game build.

Step 24. Open *score.js* and change the code to check for a gameover situation and to save the score before switching to the gameover scene. This is given in Listing 4.13.

Listing 4.13 Code to Gather a Total Count of Balls in Each Beaker

```
var score = 0;
var scoreStyle: GUIStyle;
var scoringObjects: GameObject[];
private var maxBalls:int = 20;
function OnGUI ()
{
    score = 0;
    for(var i = 0; i  scoringObjects.length; i++)
    {
            score + =
                    scoringObjects[i].
                        GetComponent("countBalls").
                            score;
    }

    GUI.BeginGroup (Rect (Screen.width - 85, 5, 80, 80));
    GUI.Box (Rect (0,0,80,60), "Score");
    GUI.Label (Rect (0, 20, 80, 30),
                String.Format("{0:0}", score),scoreStyle);
    GUI.EndGroup ();
```

```
var totalBalls =
    scoringObjects[0].GetComponent("countBalls").
        totalBalls +
    scoringObjects[1].GetComponent("countBalls").
        totalBalls +
    scoringObjects[2].GetComponent("countBalls").
        totalBalls +

scoringObjects[3].GetComponent ("countBalls").
    totalBalls;
if(totalBalls >= maxBalls)
{
    PlayerPrefs.SetInt("LastScore",score);
    Application.LoadLevel("gameover");
}
}
```

Step 25. The aforementioned code adds together the balls in each beaker. However, each beaker does not currently keep its own count. To fix this, open *countBalls.js* and update as shown in Listing 4.14.

Listing 4.14 Code to Make Each Beaker Keep a Count of Balls That Have Entered

```
var colorMatch:Material;
var score: int = 0;
var totalBalls: int = 0;
function OnTriggerEnter (obj : Collider)
{
    if(obj.gameObject.renderer.material.color == colorMatch.
                                                        color)
    {
        score = score + 1;
    }
    totalBalls++;
}
```

Step 26. If you don't want to wait until you've caught 20 balls to check your handiwork, change the value of 20 in *score.js* to a lower value.

Step 27. Open the *mainmenu* scene and test out your game.

4.4.2 Shooting, Hitting, Bouncing, and Stacking

The shooting, hitting, bouncing, and stacking mechanics used in computer games are synonymous with similar mechanics that make real-world games with a ball so popular. In order to play, players must understand the laws of physics and how they can achieve their goals by using the physical properties of the game environment to their best ability. For example, 10-pin bowling requires the player to toss a ball down an alleyway constructed of polished timber with gutters on each side in order to mow over as many pins as possible. Players must take into consideration the weight of the ball, the speed as with they throw, the angle at which they throw with respect to the length of the alley, and the mass of the pins. Players adapt succeeding attempts at knocking the pins over based on past performance. For example, if players find that they tend to always land the ball in the right gutter, they might decide to release it closer to the left or try to spin the ball in the opposite direction.

Many computer games implement these trial-and-error environmental impact practices. For example, the highly successful mobile game *Angry Birds* sees the player attempting to use a slingshot to hurl birds at stacked objects in order to knock them over. The Xbox Kinect game *Kinectimals* also presents the player with the same knock-over-the-stack minigames. Each time players take a shot at something they gather feedback from their attempt based on the number of items knocked over or the direction in which the ball (or bird) went and how fast they were flung. Players then use this knowledge to improve their next try.

Game engines that include physics systems such as Unity take much of the work out of creating these types of games as developers can rely heavily on the physics calculations doing most of the work for them. For example, the old PC game *Gorillas* that saw gorillas throwing bananas across the screen in an attempt to hit each other using a variety of trajectories had to have the mathematics programmed directly into its base code. Today, the task is simpler because the player can just throw an object and let the physics system take care of the rest—well almost.

◉ Unity Hands On
Shooting

In this hands-on session you will create a simple cannon to fire cannonballs at a stacked structure on the other side of a terrain.

Step 1. Download *Chapter Four/Shooting.zip* from the Web site. Unzip and open the project in Unity. Open the scene called *scorchedEarth2011*. In the game you will see a terrain and a cannon.

Step 2. Create a new JavaScript file called *aim.js*. Enter the code shown in Listing 4.15. This script provides rotation to a game object

Listing 4.15 Rotating a Game Object Around Its Axes with the Arrow Keys

```
function Update ()
{
    if (Input.GetKey ("up")) //if up key is pressed
    {
        //rotate upward around the side axis
        this.transform.RotateAround (this.transform.
            position,
            this.transform.right, 20 * Time.deltaTime);
    }
    if (Input.GetKey ("down"))
    {
        //rotate downward around the side axis
        this.transform.RotateAround (this.transform.
            position,
            this.transform.right, -20 * Time.deltaTime);
    }
    if (Input.GetKey ("right"))
    {
        this.transform.RotateAround (this.transform.
            position,
            this.transform.forward, -20 * Time.deltaTime);
    }
    if (Input.GetKey ("left"))
    {
        this.transform.RotateAround (this.transform.
            position,
            this.transform.forward, 20 * Time.deltaTime);
    }
}
```

when the arrow keys are pressed. The rotation occurs around the object's position and axes at a rate proportional to *Time.deltaTime*, which is the time passed since the last frame update. This creates a nice smooth rotational movement.

Step 3. Save and attach the script to the cannon2 object in the Hierarchy.

Step 4. Play. Use the arrow keys to rotate the cannon.

Step 5. Next we want the cannon to shoot when the mouse is clicked. Create a new prefab from a sphere and add a rigidbody to it. Name this prefab cannonball.

Step 6. Change *aim.js* as shown in Listing 4.16 to add shooting capability.

Listing 4.16 Code to Instantiate an Object and Shoot It from Another Game Object

```
var cannonball:GameObject;
function Update ()
{

    ...
    if (Input.GetKey ("left"))
    {
            this.transform.RotateAround (this.transform.position,
                this.transform.forward, 20 * Time.deltaTime);
    }

    if(Input.GetKeyDown ("space"))
    {
            var cannonball:GameObject = Instantiate(cannonball,
                this.transform.position, this.transform.
                    rotation);
            cannonball.rigidbody.AddForce(this.transform.
                up * 10000);
    }
}
```

Step 7. Save the code. Select Cannon in the Hierarchy; in the Inspector, set the aim script component's Cannonball variable to the prefab just created.

Step 8. Play. Press the space bar to shoot cannonballs from the cannon. Modify the value of 10000 in the *aim.js* script if you want to see the effects of adding more or less force to the balls.

Step 9. On the terrain opposite the cannon is a flat area. Create a cube and place it on the flat area. Ensure that you switch between top and side views to get it in the correct location. Coordinates near (1758,134,953) are good.

Step 10. Add a rigidbody to the cube.

Step 11. Right-click on the cube in the Hierarchy and select Duplicate. Use the arrow keys in the Scene to move the duplicate cube next to the original.

Step 12. Continue this process to create your own castle of cubes. Copy and Paste will have the same effect as Duplicate and make the building process quicker.

Step 13. Play. Attempt to knock over the cubes with the cannonballs by changing the direction of the cannon. If the cannon seems too far away for you, drag and drop the cannon object onto the Main Camera in the Hierarchy. It will become attached to it. Move the camera to the desired location in the Scene. The cannon will move with it.

Step 14. To add some impact explosions, import the detonator package (*Detonator.unitypackage*) used in Chapter Two.

Step 15. Create a JavaScript file called *explode* and enter the code shown in Listing 4.17. This is the same code used for the flattening sphere bombs in Chapter Two but with the flattening part removed.

Listing 4.17 Creating an Explosion on Impact

```
var explosion:GameObject;
var explosionLife:float = 5.0;
var detailLevel: float = 1.0;
var countdown: float = 5.0;
private var explosionDirection: Quaternion;
private var explosionLocation: Vector3;
function OnCollisionEnter(collision : Collision)
{
 rigidbody.isKinematic = true;
 Destroy (this.collider);
 var contact = collision.contacts[0];
 var rot = Quaternion.FromToRotation(Vector3.up, contact.
normal);
 explosionDirection = rot;
 var offsetSize = explosion.GetComponent("Detonator").
size / 3;
 explosionLocation = contact.point + ((Vector3.Scale(contact.
normal,
                 Vector3(offsetSize,offsetSize,offsetSize))));

 timeSet = Time.fixedTime + countdown;
 explosionActivated = true;

 if(collision.gameObject.name ! = "Terrain")
 {
          Destroy(collision.gameObject,1);
 }
 Explode();
 Destroy(this.gameObject);
}
function Explode()
{
     var exp : GameObject = Instantiate (explosion,
explosionLocation,
                                    explosionDirection);
     exp.GetComponent("Detonator").detail = detailLevel;
     Destroy(exp, explosionLife);
}
```

Step 16. Save this code and attach it to the cannonball prefab.

Step 17. In the Standard Assets > Detonator > Prefab Examples folder in the Project, select a detonator prefab and drag and drop it onto the Explosion variable of the explode script attached to the cannonball.

Step 18. Play. The cannonballs will now explode when they impact.

Step 19. To allow the player to set the strength of the cannonball shot, we will add a meter. The shot strength will build up while the space is held down and the cannonball will be released when the space is released. Create a new JavaScript file called *strengthMeter.js* and add the code in Listing 4.18.

Listing 4.18 Creating a Visual Meter for Setting Cannon Strength

```
var shotStrength : float;
function OnGUI () {
     GUI.Box (Rect (0,0,220,40), "Force");
     shotStrength = Slider (Rect (10,20,200,30), shotStrength);
}
function Slider (screenRect : Rect, strength : float) : float
{
     strength = GUI.HorizontalSlider (screenRect,
strength, 0.0, 1.0);
     return strength;
}
```

Step 20. Attach this new script to the Main Camera.

Step 21. Edit *aim.js* to reflect the changes shown in Listing 4.19.

Listing 4.19 Script to Build up Firing Strength When Space Is Down and to Fire When Space Is Released

```
var cannonball:GameObject;
function Update ()
{

     ...
     if (Input.GetKey ("left"))
     {
          this.transform.RotateAround (this.transform.
               position,
               this.transform.forward, 20 * Time.
                    deltaTime);
     }
```

```
if(Input.GetKey("space"))
{
        //each loop the space is down increase the strength
        Camera.main.GetComponent("strengthMeter").
            shotStrength =
        Camera.main.GetComponent("strengthMeter").
            shotStrength + 0.01;
}

if(Input.GetKeyUp ("space"))
{
        var cannonball:GameObject = Instantiate(cannonball,
            this.transform.position, this.transform.
                rotation);
        //use built up strength to influence the shot
        var strength = Camera.main.
            GetComponent("strengthMeter").
                shotStrength * 10000;
        cannonball.rigidbody.AddForce(this.transform.
                up * strength);
        //set strength back to 0 after a shot
        Camera.main.
            GetComponent("strengthMeter").
                shotStrength = 0;
}
}
```

Step 22. Play. This time when firing, hold down the space bar to build up the strength and then release when you think it is enough. Slider bars used in the GUI only allow values between 0 and 1, which is why the final strength is multiplied with the maximum allowed strength in order to create a larger force for the cannon.

4.4.3 Racing

Racing involves one or more players attempting to get from one location to another in order to beat the clock or beat one another. Racing is a common sport found involving unaided human participants (in many Olympic events), motor vehicles (such as formula 1 or drag racing), and animals (including horses, dogs, and, on Australia Day in Australia, cockroaches!).

Many computer games include racing in a variety of forms. *Project Gotham* sees players racing around the streets of the world's cities in production cars, *Grand Theft Auto* requires the player to race away from authorities or to locations, and *Kinect Sports* allows players to race in track and field events.

Racing need not involve people or vehicles moving around a track. Performing a task within a certain time is *racing against the clock*. In *The Sims*, for example, a player's Sims can be given packages to deliver downtown or tasks to perform within a specified time period. If the job gets done, the Sim is rewarded.

◎ Unity Hands On
Racing

In this hands-on session you will create a simple racing game.

> **Step 1.** Download *Chapter Four/Racing.zip* from the Web site. Unzip and open the project in Unity. Open the scene called *racing*. In the game you will see a terrain and a car.
>
> **Step 2.** Play. The car can be driven with the arrow keys. The Main Camera is attached to the car prefab, such that when the car moves, the camera automatically moves too.
>
> **Step 3.** Select the car prefab in the Hierarchy. Right-click on it and select Duplicate. Call the duplicate *Player2*. Select Player2 and in the Scene move it so the cars sit side by side.
>
> **Step 4.** Select Player2 in the Hierarchy and delete the Car script component in the Inspector. Also delete the Main Camera object attached to Player2. This isn't needed as the original car already has a camera.
>
> **Step 5.** Add a sphere to the Scene. Select it in the Hierarchy and delete the Sphere Collider component. Position the sphere in front of Player2 raised slightly above the ground. We are going to use a series of spheres as points to specify a path for Player2 to follow. This is a common technique used in games to direct the movement of nonplayer characters (NPCs). Each sphere acts as a waypoint.
>
> **Step 6.** Number and duplicate the sphere; place the duplicate farther down the road as shown in Figure 4.10 (you may want to increment the sphere number). Each waypoint should be in line of sight of the other. Because the NPC is traveling in a straight line between each waypoint, if they are on the other side of the terrain, the NPC will travel through the terrain mesh. This won't look real or be very fair to the human player.
>
> **Step 7.** Continue duplicating and positioning spheres until the whole track is covered.

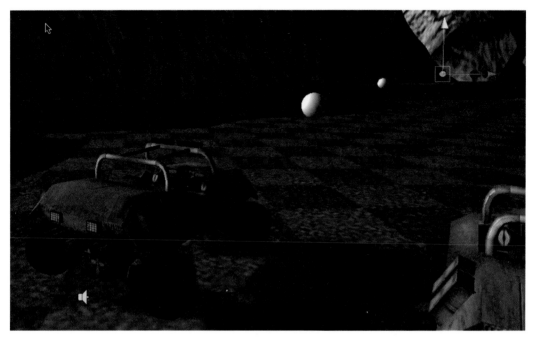

FIG 4.10 Adding and positioning waypoints.

Step 8. Attach the script *waypoints.js* from the Project onto Player2. Select Player2 in the Hierarchy and locate the waypoint script in the Inspector. Add each sphere to the script under the Waypoints variable, as shown in Figure 4.11. Ensure that the spheres are added in the order you would like the Player2 car to move around the track, with the first sphere in front of the car being assigned to Element 0.

Step 9. Play. The NPC car will start moving off following the waypoints. In the Inspector you can change the speed, rotation speed, and accuracy values of the waypoint script to modify the car's behavior. When following a path and moving, sometimes objects don't land in the exact location of a waypoint. We need to give a *close enough is good enough* value. This is the value called *accuracy*. Rotation speed will cause the car to make tighter turns the higher the value.

Step 10. At this point, Player2 may appear to sink into the road when moving. This is because the collider does not include the wheels. The player's car does not sink because of the Car script. As Player2 no longer has this script, select the chassis collider element under Player2 in the Hierarchy and modify the size and position of the Box Collider to include the wheels. Now Player2 will not sink.

Step 11. Now experiment with the speed of Player2 by racing against it.

Step 12. To create a finish line, add a cube to the scene. Resize it to stretch across the road. Remove its Mesh Filter and Mesh Renderer components. Leave the Box Collider and tick the Is Trigger box. The remaining box collider for the cube should be big enough to trigger an event when the NPC or player drives through it.

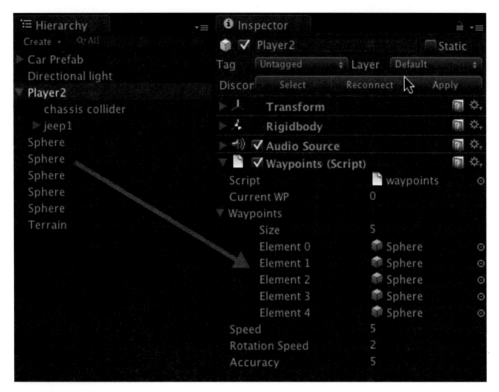

FIG 4.11 Adding spheres as waypoints to the waypoint script.

Step 13. Create a new JavaScript file called *finishline.js* and attach it to the new cube. Enter the code in Listing 4.20. This will cause a Game Over screen to pop open when either car collides with the cube.

Listing 4.20 Call a Game Over screen

```
private var winner = "";
private var playerLocation: Vector3;
private var npcLocation: Vector3;
function Start()
{
     //remember location and orientation of both cars at
     //the start
     playerLocation = GameObject.Find("Car Prefab").
                          transform.position;
     npcLocation = GameObject.Find("Player2").
                        transform.position;
}
function OnTriggerEnter(collision: Collider)
{
     //if there is no winner yet
     if(winner == "")
```

```
        {
                //make this one the winner
                winner = collision.gameObject.name;
        }
}
function OnGUI ()
{
        if(winner ! = "")
        {
                GUI.BeginGroup (Rect (Screen.width / 2 - 100,
                            Screen.height / 2 - 100, 200, 200));
                GUI.Box (Rect (0,0,200,200), "Game Over");
                GUI.Label(Rect (20,20,200,100), "Winner: " + winner);
                if(GUI.Button (Rect (50,60,100,30), "Play Again"))
                {
                        //reset the game
                        winner = "";
                        GameObject.Find("Car Prefab").transform.
                                    position = playerLocation;
                        GameObject.Find("Player2").transform.
                                    position = npcLocation;

                        GameObject.Find("Player2").
                                    GetComponent("waypoints").
                                    currentWP = 0;
                }
                GUI.EndGroup ();
        }
}
function Update () {
}
```

Step 14. The preceding script uses the name of the colliding object to display the winner on the screen. Currently, both the Car Prefab and the Player2's elements are named the same. Select each chassis collider in the Hierarchy and give them different names in the Inspector.

Step 15. Play. But be ready for a quick restart when you click on Play Again.

We will leave this hands-on session at this point. When artificial intelligence is introduced later in the book, we will return to look at modifying the behavior of the NPC.

4.4.4 Avoidance and Collecting

Avoidance is a game action that involves players having to go out of their way not to interact with another game object or to make an effort not to perform some action. In the original *Donkey Kong*, the player had to get to the top of a set of scaffolding while avoiding rolling barrels. In all FPS games the player has to avoid being shot. In *Snakes and Ladders* the player must avoid landing on the head of a snake, and in *Mine Sweeper* the player has to avoid mines.

Collecting is the opposite action to avoidance. The player must make all attempts to gather items. In *Mario Brothers*, players can collect coins and other items to improve their abilities and score. In *Dungeons and Dragons*, players collect magic potions and experience points and weapons. In *EVE Online*, players collect minerals.

Parts of these mechanisms are their visual cues. Items to be avoided should look like they should be avoided. For example, the lava flows in *Doom* obviously looked menacing and hot because they were red and bubbling. In nature, humans are attuned to the warnings of red colors. Red represents hot. Fire is hot, the sun is hot, and lava is hot. The game player already has a built-in instinct for avoidance. The same goes for sharp prickly objects. From cactus to underwater mines, the spikes relay a message of "keep away." As a game designer, if you can leverage human instinct and assume much about how someone will play your game, a lot of the work explaining how the game works is already done for you.

The same principle works for collecting. Why do you think so many games have little gold coins for the player to pick up?

◉ Unity Hands On
Avoiding and Collecting

In this hands-on session you will reuse the starting project from the previous workshop and add items to the map—some that you have to run over to collect and some that must be avoided. The objective will be to collect as many rubber ducks as possible in 2 minutes and get them to the finish line.

> **Step 1.** Download *Chapter Four/DuckRacing.zip* from the Web site. Unzip and open the Project in Unity. Open the scene called *racing*. In the game you will see a terrain and car.
> **Step 2.** Drag the cone prefab into the Scene to create a traffic cone object. This needs to have a collider attached to it in order to make it interact with the car. With cone selected in the Hierarchy, select Component > Physics > Box Collider from the menu. As shown in Figure 4.12, modify the box collider values to position it around the traffic cone.

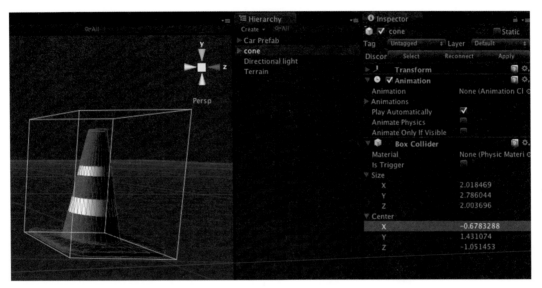

FIG 4.12 Positioning a box collider around an existing mesh.

Step 3. Drag and drop the cone from the Hierarchy onto the cone prefab in the Project to replace it with a new copy that includes a collider. Remove the existing cone from the Hierarchy.

Step 4. Using the new cone prefab, add several cones into the Scene on the road in front of the car.

Step 5. Play. Try to run over the cones. They won't budge because they do not have a rigidbody attached.

Step 6. Because all the new cones are linked to the prefab, to add rigidbodies to them all, just add a single rigidbody to the cone prefab in the Project. Select it and then Components > Physics > Rigidbody from the main menu.

Step 7. Play. The cones will now move out of the road when hit with the car. If your cones seem to fall through the ground, check that their starting position in the scene has the rigidbody above the terrain. If there is any overlap, gravity will cause the cones to fall through the ground.

Step 8. Create a prefab call *Duck*, attach the *RubberDucky* model, and then add a rigidbody and a box collider. Add the *Duck* prefab to the scene.

Step 9. Create a new cube. Make it about twice the size of the car and position it behind the car. Embed it in the ground so that only a small part of the top appears out. It should be low enough to drive the car up onto. Offset the box collider so that it is above the ground, as shown in Figure 4.13. Tick the Is Trigger box for the collider.

243

FIG 4.13 A cube used as a platform.

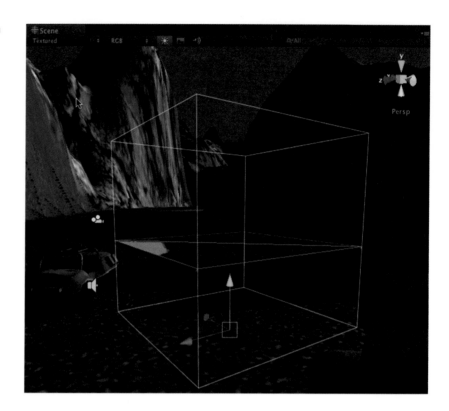

Step 10. Create a new JavaScript file called *releaseDuck.js*. Add the code in Listing 4.21.

Listing 4.21 Script to Make a Game Object Appear after Collision with Another

```
var duckObj: GameObject;
function OnTriggerEnter(collision: Collider)
{
    print(collision.gameObject.name);
    if(collision.gameObject.name == "chassis collider")
    {
     var newDuck = Instantiate(duckObj, this.transform.
       position, Quaternion.identity);
     //start duck up above the ground
     newDuck.transform.position.y = 10;
    }
}
```

Step 11. Attach the code to the large cube. Select the cube in the Hierarchy; in the Inspector, set the duckObj variable of the releaseDuck script to the duck prefab. Now when the car drives up onto the platform, a new duck will be released. Note that the collision in the script is checked that the car is the one doing the colliding, as otherwise each time a duck is created it would cause the collision to create another duck, ad infinitum. The name of the collision object is "chassis collider," as this is the name of the child object of the car prefab that has the collider attached.

Step 12. As with the previous game, create another large box collider for a finish line. Ensure that the Is Trigger box is selected.

Step 13. Assign the tag duck for the duck prefab. All created ducks will have this tag.

Step 14. Create a JavaScript file called *finish.js*. This script will be attached to the finish line collider and count the number of ducks going through it. Use the code in Listing 4.22 to register the duck count.

Listing 4.22 Counting Ducks That Pass Through a Collider

```
var duckCount = 0;
function OnTriggerEnter(collision: Collider)
{
    if(collision.gameObject.tag == "duck")
    {
        duckCount++;
        Destroy(collision.gameObject);
    }
}
```

Step 15. Attach *finish.js* to the finish line. Note that after a duck is counted it is destroyed. This will ensure that the player can't keep pushing the duck back and forth over the finish line to get extra points.

Step 16. Next, download *Chapter Four/corfont.ttf* from the Web site. This is the font used to display the time and score. Add the font to the Project. Select it and give it a size of 32 in the Inspector, as shown in Figure 4.14. Press the Apply button. Note that once you have changed the size of this font, it will stay this size for all the places you use it. If you want to use the same font with a different size in the same game, rename the font file, drag it into the Project for another copy, and change the size of the new one.

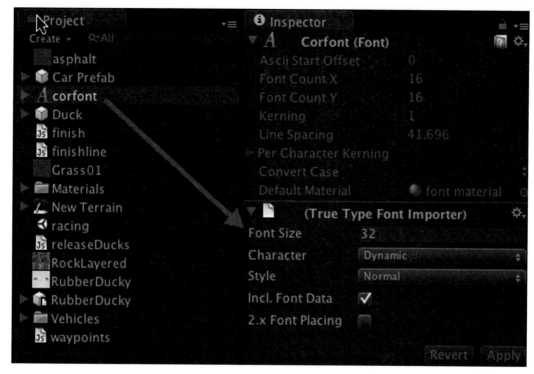

FIG 4.14 Changing the size of a font.

Step 17. Modify *finish.js* to include some code to display a GUI as shown in Listing 4.23.

Listing 4.23 Displaying a Simple GUI with a Score

```
var duckCount = 0;
var myStyle: GUIStyle;
function OnGUI ()
{
    GUI.BeginGroup (Rect (Screen.width / 2 - 100, 10, 250, 70));
    GUI.Box (Rect (0,0,250,70), "Duck Herding");
    GUI.Label (Rect (10,10,250,70),"Score", myStyle);
    GUI.EndGroup ();
}
function OnTriggerEnter(collision: Collider)
{
    ...
}
```

Step 18. Unlike the previous GUIs we've used before, this one includes a variable called myStyle. This will allow you to set font, size, colors, backgrounds, and more for a GUI element. After modifying *finish.js,* select the finish line object in the Hierarchy and look for the finish script in the Inspector. As shown in Figure 4.15, once a script uses the GUIStyle on an object (such as the score label in *finish.js*), the Inspector allows you to set a whole lot of properties relating to the GUI. In this case, the previously added font, its color, and alignment have been changed. Change these in your game and press play to see the GUI come up on the screen.

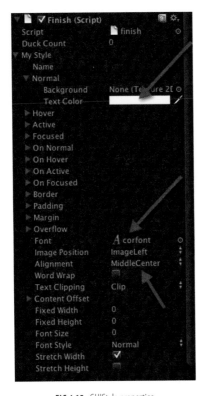

FIG 4.15 GUIStyle properties.

● For Rsearch

Unity GUI System

The entire Unity GUI system is explained in the manual at http://unity3d .com/support/documentation/Components/GUI%20Scripting%20Guide .html.

Step 19. To print out the score and the time since the game started, modify *finish.js* to reflect Listing 4.24.

Listing 4.24 Using a GUI.Label to Print the Score to the Screen

```
var duckCount = 0;
var myStyle: GUIStyle;
function OnGUI () {
      GUI.BeginGroup (Rect (Screen.width / 2 - 100, 10,
          250, 70));
      GUI.Box (Rect (0,0,250,70), "Duck Herding");
      GUI.Label (Rect (10,10,250,70),"Score: " +
duckCount + " Time: " +
                                     Time.fixedTime, myStyle);
      GUI.EndGroup ();
}
function OnTriggerEnter(collision: Collider)
{

      ...

}
```

Step 20. Save and play. Note how the score and time value changes in size. This is because as the time changes, so do the numbers being displayed. Because the font being used is not a fixed width, the entire text length can grow and shrink depending on what is written. To fix this, instead of putting the score in the middle, set the alignment to MiddleLeft in the Inspector view of myStyle.

Step 21. Play. You may want to play around with the positioning of the GUI later, but for now try out some duck herding.

Step 22. Finally, to make the game run out after 2 minutes, we will add a timer. Edit the *finish.js* script to reflect the changes in Listing 4.25.

Listing 4.25 Adding a Game Over Event Timer

```
var duckCount = 0;
var myStyle: GUIStyle;
var levelLength = 120; //seconds
private var gameOver = false;
function OnGUI ()
{
      GUI.BeginGroup (Rect (Screen.width / 2 - 100, 10,
          250, 70));

      if(gameOver)
      {
```

```
            GUI.Box (Rect (0,0,250,70), "Game Over");
            if(GUI.Button (Rect (75,30,100,30), "Play Again"))
            {
                    Application.LoadLevel("racing");
            }
    }
    else
    {
            GUI.Box (Rect (0,0,250,70), "Duck Herding");
            GUI.Label (Rect (10,10,250,70),"Score: " + duckCount +
                " Time: " + Time.fixedTime, myStyle);
        }
        GUI.EndGroup ();
    }
function OnTriggerEnter(collision: Collider)
{
        if(collision.gameObject.tag == "duck")
        {
                duckCount++;
                Destroy(collision.gameObject);
        }
}
function Update ()
{
        if(Time.timeSinceLevelLoad > levelLength)
        {
                gameOver = true;
        }
}
```

Step 23. Play. Once the game reaches 2 minutes, the game over screen will come up and you can choose to play again. Unlike the previous workshop, where the position of the players was reset with the play again button, this one reloads the entire level. This saves a lot of work remembering the locations of players and ensuring that any stray ducks are removed from the environment. A clean reload will put the game back in its starting state.

4.4.5 Searching

Searching is common human activity. Whether it is for food (in combination with collecting—hunting and gathering), car keys, or Russian Ultra-nationalists in Tom Clancy's *Ghost Recon*, the human brain is attuned to quickly examining environments and looking for icons and patterns. Naturally, the searching mechanism goes hand in hand with matching.

The ways in which searching is implemented as a game mechanic are as varied as game genre. In *Doom,* the player has to find colored keys to unlock the same colored security doors; in *Full Throttle,* the player must locate and use objects to help him in his quest to find a murderer in a cross-country road trip; and in *Manhunter: New York,* the player is entrusted with the task of hunting down resistance fighters. Searching can be performed by moving the mouse around a scene to find and pick up objects. This is the mechanism employed in the original *Myst.* It can also involve moving the main character around a game level, such as looking for medkits in *Quake.*

◎ Unity Hands On
A HUD Radar for Searching

In this hands-on session we are going to create a game environment with a number of items scattered over a large map that players must seek out. To assist them on their quest, a heads-up display (HUD) radar system will be deployed to give them some basic location details for the items.

> **Step 1.** Download *Chapter Four/RadarSearching.zip* from the Web site. Open the project with Unity. Open the *hudRadar* scene. This is the finished project from the Chapter Three character animation workshop.
>
> **Step 2.** Create a new JavaScript file named *radar.js* and add the code given in Listing 4.26.

Listing 4.26 Creating a HUD Radar to Track Game Objects with the Tag orb

```
var orbspot : Texture;
var playerPos : Transform;
private var mapScale = 0.1;
private var radarSpotX: float;
private var radarSpotY: float;
private var radarWidth = 100;
private var radarHeight = 100;
function OnGUI ()
{
   GUI.BeginGroup (Rect (10, Screen.height - radarHeight - 10,
                              radarWidth, radarHeight));
        GUI.Box (Rect (0, 0, radarWidth, radarHeight), "Radar");
        DrawSpotsForOrbs();
   GUI.EndGroup();
}
function DrawRadarBlip(go, spotTexture)
{
   var gameObjPos = go.transform.position;
```

```
    //find distance between object and player
    var dist = Vector3.Distance(playerPos.position, gameObjPos);

    //find the horizontal distances along the
    //x and z between player and object
    var dx = playerPos.position.x - gameObjPos.x;
    var dz = playerPos.position.z - gameObjPos.z;

    //determine the angle of rotation between the
    //direction the player is facing and the location
    //of the object
    deltay = Mathf.Atan2(dx, dz) * Mathf.Rad2Deg - 270 -
                              playerPos.eulerAngles.y;
    //orient the object on the radar according to the
    //direction the player is facing
    radarSpotX = dist * Mathf.Cos(deltay * Mathf.Deg2Rad) *
        mapScale;
    radarSpotY = dist * Mathf.Sin(deltay * Mathf.Deg2Rad) *
        mapScale;

    //draw a spot on the radar
    GUI.DrawTexture(Rect(radarWidth/2.0 + radarSpotX,
                    radarHeight/2.0 + radarSpotY, 2, 2),
                    spotTexture);
}
function DrawSpotsForOrbs()
{
    var gos : GameObject[];
    //look for all objects with a tag of orb
    gos = GameObject.FindGameObjectsWithTag("orb");
    var distance = Mathf.Infinity;
    var position = transform.position;
    for (var go : GameObject in gos)
    {
        DrawRadarBlip(go,orbspot);
    }
}
```

Step 3. Attach the script to the Main Camera, which is a child object of the Hero game object.
Step 4. Locate the OrbPrefab in the Orb folder in the Project. Create a tag for this prefab and call it *orb*. Ensure that after creating the tag it is assigned to the OrbPrefab in the Inspector.
Step 5. In order to draw radar blips on the HUD, you will need to create a texture. This need only be a very small texture of a single color as it will only take up one pixel on the screen. Create a .png

image that is 8 × 8 pixels and color it red. Call the file *spot.png* and add it to the Project.

Step 6. Select Main Camera in the Hierarchy and locate the Radar script in the Inspector. Drag and drop the spot texture from the Project for the value of *Orbspot*. Drag and drop thr Hero child object of Hero (yes there is one inside the other) from the Hierarchy onto the Player Pos value for the Radar script. This will be used as the center and orientation for the radar.

Step 7. Play. The radar HUD will appear on the screen without any red blips.

Step 8. Locate the OrbPrefab in the Project. Drag and drop as many orbs as you like onto the terrain in the Scene at any location you like. Put some near the player.

Step 9. Play. The radar will be populated with red spots indicating the location of the orbs. As the player turns and moves, the radar will reorientate to show objects in the forward-facing direction at the top of the radar screen.

Step 10. The radar will not encompass the entire map. Orbs will only come into view as the player moves within a certain distance of them. To fit more of the environment map onto the radar, change the value of *mapScale* at the top of *radar.js* to a smaller value. If you want less of the environment map visible, make the value larger.

4.5 Rewards and Penalties

Let's face it; we play games for the rewards—whether they be in the form of points, unlocked levels, kudos, virtual clothing, virtual food, virtual health, more votes, more friends, or more money. It's the rewards that provide players with motivation to perform any of the actions listed in this chapter. In some texts, rewards are listed as a mechanic themselves; however, they are really the motivation or reason for performing the mechanic in the first place.

Rewards aren't just given at the end of the game but throughout to influence the player's behavior. They teach the player how to play and how to play better by providing continued feedback from the game environment. Sometimes this feedback can also be perceived negatively by the player as a penalty for incorrect game play.

Feedback can both be positive or negative and involve the addition or subtraction of something to/from the game environment. The feedback can be given for player actions to indicate success or failure. Together with action without feedback and feedback without action, this makes for six distinct categories, as shown in Figure 4.16.

With the exception of *confusion*, these classifications come from the domain of behavior management called *operant conditioning*. They are applicable in games, as operant conditioning is a behavioral management technique used

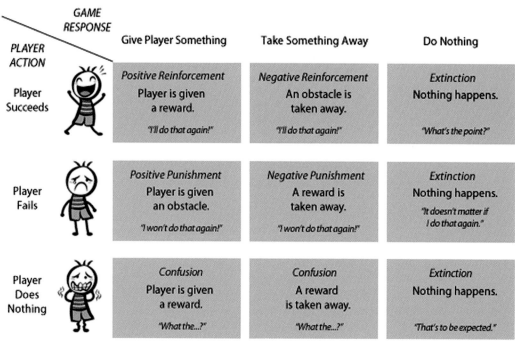

FIG 4.16 Player action versus game response matrix.

for teaching the most relevant behaviors to participants under voluntary circumstances; that is, people wanting to be conditioned are open to behavior management techniques that will teach them to behave in the most appropriate way to succeed. These techniques include the following.

Positive Reinforcement

This is a situation in which positive behavior is followed by positive consequences. For example, when players complete a challenge successfully they are rewarded with something that influences their future game play progress in a good way. This could be in the form of gaining new powers or abilities, getting money to spend in the game environment to better their status, or simply getting points. This type of reward keeps players motivated to continue playing for more reward.

Negative Reinforcement

This occurs when positive behavior is followed by the elimination of negative consequences. For example, if a player is in harm's way and can do something to get out of the situation, the removal of the continued harm is a reward. Such a situation will happen when a player being fired upon in a FPS stops being fired upon when he takes cover. This reinforces to the player that hiding and ducking is a desirable behavior to keep the character alive.

Positive Punishment

This occurs when negative behavior is followed by the addition of a negative consequence. In a game, this is a situation in which a handicap is placed on the player's progress after he has done something wrong or performed inadequately. This type of punishment occurs in *The Sims* when the player makes the Sim eat rotten food. The Sim gets sick and is then in a bad mood for an allocated period of time.

Negative Punishment

This is the condition where negative behavior is followed by the removal of positive consequences. It is like taking away a child's toy when she is naughty. In the multiplayer version of the original *Halo* in sniper mode, the more frequently a player gets killed, the longer before the character will spawn again. In this example, the negative punishment is taking away the game world.

Extinction

This occurs when neither positive nor negative behavior attracts any feedback. This could happen when a player shoots at a tree or picks up a rock and tosses it in the ocean. As far as the game environment and the player's progress through the game are concerned, the action performed requires no feedback as it neither interrupts nor enhances the game play.

Confusion

Confusion is not a technique in operant conditioning. In fact, it has the exact opposite effect as it provides feedback when no action has occurred. When this occurs in a game, the player becomes confused as to the reason behind any reward or penalty.

There is a fine line in game play between reinforcement and punishment. For example, in the *Black & White* series where the player is essentially a god, he can pick up and throw rocks at villages. In the real world, morally, this would be considered negative behavior and something that should be punishable. However, in the case of *Black & White*, the player is rewarded with more faith and worshipping from the villagers. This game play should be considered in the category positive reinforcement because it reinforces behavior in the player that the game designer wanted. Punishment in a game is therefore a feedback mechanism that should stop the player from doing something for which the game wasn't designed. One example comes from *Colin McRae Rally*, a rally driving simulation game. If a player goes off the road or drives in the wrong direction for too long the game resets the player's position on the road. It stops the player from performing the behavior and also slows down his time.

Some rewards and penalties inherently exist in a game environment without the need for onscreen advice or information. In the case of 3D environments, designers can force players in certain directions by physically restricting their access to out-of-bound areas of a level map. For example, the map levels in *Halo* may seem infinitely large; however, although the player can move freely around the map by foot or vehicle, the terrain and physics system prevents him from going to parts of the map that don't exist. Any attempt to walk or drive up steep mountain edges just results in the player sliding down the side.

When using feedback to mould a player's behavior, the effectiveness of the feedback will be increased and decreased according to a variety of factors.

Saturation

The more a player is rewarded with or receives the same feedback, the less he will be motivated by it. For example, if a player receives a gold star for some activity, the highest award for a particular game, the less likely he will be motivated to try it again. Of course in order for this strategy to be effective, the game must be sufficiently difficult that the first time he plays he is more likely to get a bronze star and get better with time.

Immediacy

The time between the player's action and the feedback is critical. Rewarding a player minutes after he has performed a task successfully will make it difficult for the player to attribute the reward with the action. It's like punishing a puppy an hour after it has chewed up your shoe. There is no association. Haptic feedback mechanisms in games such as vibrating controllers would not make sense if the actions in the game didn't meet exactly with the vibrations. The same applies to sound effects.

Consistency

The feedback given to players needs to align with their beliefs about the environment and how consistently it reacts to their interaction. In an FPS, players would expect to get killed 100% of the time they step on a land mine. However, if this does not turn out to be the case, and instead they only die 20% of the time, the feedback will not become an effective way to curb player behavior.

Cost Versus Benefit

Players will evaluate the effort they need to spend on an action based on the reward. This fits with *the greater the risk, the greater the reward* philosophy. The evaluation will differ from person to person based on their attitudes toward risk aversion. For example, in *EVE Online*, mining and trading in the more dangerous zones of the universe can make greater amounts of money. Because there is a bigger chance a pirate will blow up your ship in these areas, the designer has to provide extra incentive for the player to go there in the first place.

4.6 Summary

This chapter examined how games *play* the human brain by providing it with the tasks for which it was designed. These fundamental game interaction patterns are known as game mechanics. An understanding of what makes these mechanics so compelling and how they can be manifest in a game environment is critical to designing a playable game. It is these very primary mechanics that define what the player does when engaged in playing your game. For example, in defining *Bejeweled*, one could say it is a game where the player sorts and matches jewels. It's laughable how obviously simple these mechanics are when you think about it, but it takes some ingenuity to put them together in the right context to make a truly exceptional game to stand for all time.

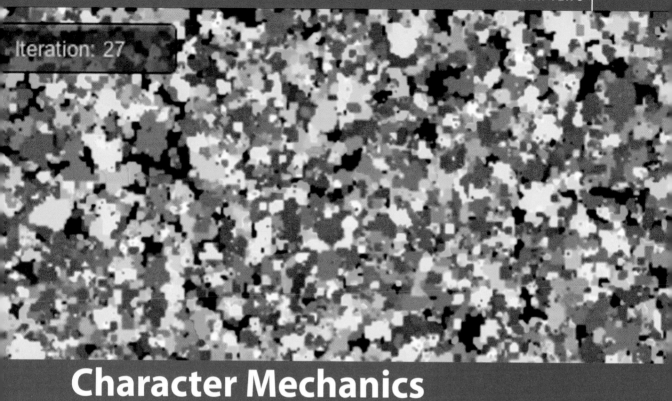

CHAPTER 5

Iteration: 27

Character Mechanics

We are builders of our own characters. We have different positions, spheres, capacities, privileges, different work to do in the world, different temporal fabrics to raise; but we are all alike in this,—all are architects of fate.

John Fothergill Waterhouse Ware

5.1 Introduction

It seems appropriate to have a chapter about Artificial Intelligence (AI) that follows one on elementary game mechanics as these are the very same mechanics that drive the AI domain. In the field, researchers and developers create algorithms that can search, sort, and match their way through tasks as complex as pattern matching in face and voice recognition systems and reasoning and decision making in expert systems and vehicle control. It makes sense that algorithms used for making artificial brains are modeled on the same ones that compel fundamental human behavior and make game playing so much fun.

Of all the forms and applications of AI, games use a very small subset, the majority of which to develop the behavior of nonplayer characters (NPCs).

AI is used primarily for decision making in NPCs that allow them to find their way around maps and interact intelligently with other players. Occasionally, novel uses such as machine learning are employed to create characters that can learn from the game environment and the player, such as the creatures in *Black & White*.

Artificial intelligence algorithms require a lot of computational processing. In the past, after all the animation and special effects were placed in a game, only about 10% of the computer's processing capabilities remained for AI. This has stunted the development of AI in games for quite a while. However, with advances in technology, more and more AI is creeping in.

Some examples of AI in games include:

- *F.E.A.R.* A first person shooter (FPS) in which the player must outsmart supernatural beings. It uses planning algorithms that allow characters to use the game environment in a smart way, such as hiding behind objects or tipping them over. Squad tactics are also used to present formidable enemies that can lay down suppression fire and perform flanking maneuvers.
- *Halo.* An FPS in which the player must explore an extraterrestrial environment while holding back aliens. The aliens can duck for cover and employ suppression fire and grenades. Group tactics also cause enemy troops to retreat when their leader is killed.
- *The Sims.* A god view game in which the player controls a household of virtual people called Sims. This game introduced the concept of smart objects that allowed inanimate objects in the environment to provide information to the characters on how they should be used. The Sims themselves are driven by a series of basic desires that tell them when they are hungry, bored, tired, and so on.
- *Black & White.* This god view game has the player in the role of an actual god overseeing villages of little people while trying to dominate the villages of other gods. The player is given a creature in the form of a gigantic animal such as a tiger. This creature is programmed with an AI technique called belief–desire–intention, which makes the character act based on what it might need or want at any particular time.

Artificial intelligence is a theoretically intensive field grounded in applied mathematics, numerical computing, and psychology. This chapter provides but a scrapping of what the domain has to offer games. It is a gentle introduction designed to give you an appreciation for the field and to fuel your desire to experiment with its use in your own games.

5.2 Line of Sight

The simplest method for programming an NPC to follow the player and thus provide it with modest believable behavior is using the line of sight. Put simply, the NPC sees the player, turns to face the player, and travels in a straight line forward until it reaches the player. This straightforward approach can make the player feel under attack and that the NPC is a threat and has bad intentions. In fact, the NPC has no intentions whatsoever. It is just a computer algorithm. This illustrates how the simplest of programming feats can create a believable character. Although you will examine numerous techniques in this chapter to program *intelligence*, sometimes complex AI systems are not required just to achieve the behavior you want in your artificial characters.

In an open game environment, the easiest way to determine if an NPC has seen the player is to use simple vector calculations. As shown in Figure 5.1, a field of vision is defined for an NPC based on the direction it is facing, its position, visible range, and the angle of its vision (α).

If a player is inside this range the NPC can be said to have detected the presence of the player (see player 1); if not, the player is still hidden (as is the case with player 2). The problem is very similar to that in Chapter One where vectors were being calculated for the pirate to follow to the treasure. Instead

FIG 5.1 Vectors between an NPC and players used to determine line of sight.

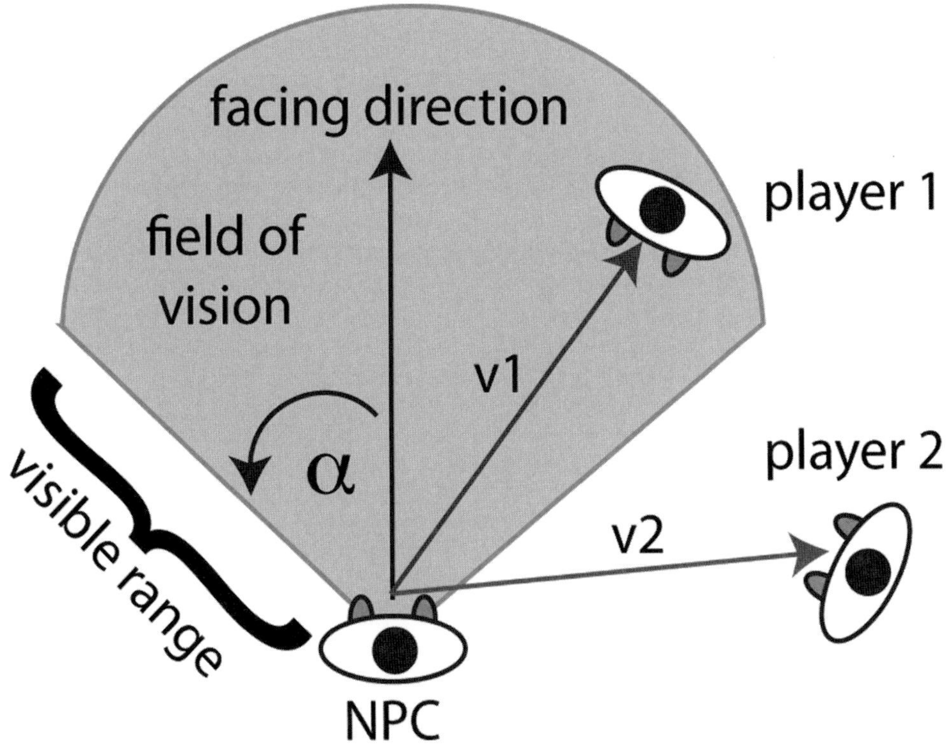

of treasure, the goal location is a moving player. The NPC detects the player within its field of vision using the vector between its position and the players. This is calculated as

$$\text{direction} = \text{player.position} - \text{NPC.position};$$

The magnitude (length) of the direction vector represents the distance the player is from the NPC. If the angle between the facing vector and direction vector is less than the angle of vision and the magnitude of the direction vector is less than the visible range, then the player will be detected by the NPC.

The next workshop will demonstrate this in Unity.

◉ Unity Hands On
Line of Sight AI

Step 1. Download *Chapter Five/ChasingAI.zip* from the Web site. Open the chasingAI scene. In it you will find a large terrain and a solitary robot.

Step 2. Open the AI script with the script editor and add the code shown in Listing 5.1.

Listing 5.1 Basic Line of Sight Script

```
var target : Transform;          //the enemy
private var seeRange = 100.0;    //maximum attack distance -
                                 //will attack if closer than
                                 //this to the enemy
private var shootRange = 20.0;
private var keepDistance = 10.0; //closest distance to get to enemy
private var rotationSpeed = 5.0;
private var speed = 0.01;
private var state = "PATROL";
function Start()
{

        Patrol();
        this.animation["shoot"].wrapMode = WrapMode.Loop;
        this.animation["run"].wrapMode = WrapMode.Loop;
        this.animation["idle"].wrapMode = WrapMode.Loop;

}
function Update ()
{
        if (CanSeeTarget ())
        {
                if(CanShoot())
```

```
            {
                    state = "SHOOTING";
                    animation.CrossFade("shoot");
                    speed = 0.00;
                    Shoot();
            }
            else
            {
                    state = "PURSUE";
                    animation.CrossFade("run");
                    speed = 0.08;
                    Pursue();
            }
     }
     else
     {
            state = "PATROL";
            if (!animation.IsPlaying("idle"))
            {
                    animation.Play ("idle");
                    speed = 0.00;
            }
            Patrol();
     }
}
function Patrol ()
{
     //stand around
}
function CanSeeTarget () : boolean
{
     if (Vector3.Distance(transform.position, target.
                position) > seeRange)
          return false;

     return true;
}
function CanShoot(): boolean
{
     if (Vector3.Distance(transform.position, target.
                position) > shootRange)
           return false;

     return true;
}
function Pursue()
{
```

```
        var position = target.position;
        var direction = position - transform.position;
        direction.y = 0;

        // Rotate towards the target
        transform.rotation = Quaternion.Slerp (
            transform.rotation, Quaternion.
            LookRotation(direction),
            rotationSpeed * Time.deltaTime);

        transform.eulerAngles = Vector3(0,transform.
            eulerAngles.y, 0);
        // Move the character
        if(direction.magnitude > keepDistance)
        {

            direction = direction.normalized * speed;
            transform.position += direction;

        }
}
function Shoot()
{
        var position = target.position;
        var direction = position - transform.position;
        direction.y = 0;

        // Rotate towards the target
        transform.rotation = Quaternion.Slerp(transform.rotation,
            Quaternion.LookRotation(direction),
            rotationSpeed * Time.deltaTime);
        transform.eulerAngles = Vector3(0, transform.
            eulerAngles.y, 0);
}
```

Step 3. Locate the AI script in the Inspector attached to the robot object in the Hierarchy. Drag and drop the First Person Controller from the Hierarchy onto the exposed *target* variable. This sets the object that the NPC will consider its enemy.

Step 4. Play. The CanSeeTarget() and CanShoot() functions use the variables seeRange and shootRange, respectively, to determine when the player is close enough to pursue and close enough to shoot. If you run away from the NPC backward as fast as possible you'll notice the point at which it gives up chasing you.

Step 5. The current code does not take into consideration the direction the NPC is facing. If you approach it from behind, it will still sense your presence when you are close enough. For it to use a field of vision angle, modify the AI script as shown in Listing 5.2.

Listing 5.2 Restricting the Field of Vision of an NPC to an Area in Front of It

```
var target : Transform;          //the enemy
...
private var keepDistance = 10.0; //closest distance to get to enemy
private var rotationSpeed = 5.0;
private var sightAngle = 30;
private var speed = 0.01;
private var state = "PATROL";
function Start()
...
function CanSeeTarget () : boolean
{

    var directionToTarget = target.position − transform.
        position;
    var angle =
          Vector3.Angle(directionToTarget, this.
            transform.forward);
    if (Vector3.Distance(transform.position, target.position) >
          seeRange || angle > sightAngle)
          return false;

    return true;
}
```

Step 6. Play. You will now be able to sneak up behind the NPC without it noticing you.

5.3 Graph Theory

It would be impossible to begin talking about the ins and outs of AI without a brief background in graph theory. Almost all AI techniques used in games rely on the programmers having an understanding of graphs. A graph in this context refers to a collection of nodes and edges. Nodes are represented graphically as circles, and edges are the lines that connect them. A graph can be visualized as nodes representing locations and edges as paths connecting them. A graph can be undirected, which means that the paths between nodes can be traversed in both directions or directed, in which case the paths are one way. Think of this as the difference between two-way streets and one-way streets. Graphs are drawn with nodes represented as circles and edges as lines as shown in Figure 5.2. Nodes and edges can be drawn where nodes represent coordinates such as those on a flight plan or as symbolic states where the physical location in the graph is meaningless. For example, the state diagram in Figure 5.2 could be drawn with nodes in any position and any distance from one another. Some directed graphs allow bidirectional traversal from one node to another in the same way as undirected graphs. However, if arrows are already being used in a directed graph to show some one-way-only paths, they should also appear on bidirectional edges for consistency.

Both nodes and edges can have associated values. These values could be the distance between nodes, such as those representing distances in the flight plan of Figure 5.2, or the time it takes to complete an action, such as nodes in the action plan of Figure 5.2.

The ways in which graphs are useful in games AI will become evident as we progress through the chapter.

FIG 5.2 Undirected and directed graph representations and some examples.

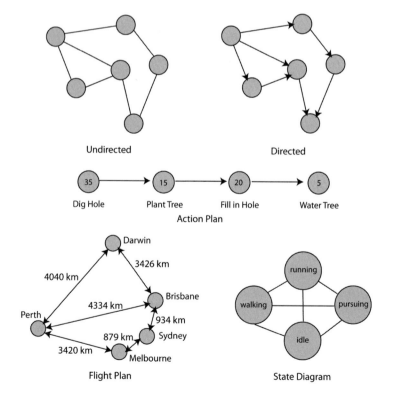

5.4 Waypoints

The concept of waypoints was introduced in Chapter Four as a means of marking a route on a map that NPCs can follow. In the workshop we developed a very simple algorithm to cycle through the waypoints and have an NPC follow them continuously.

A waypoint is simply a remembered location on a map. Waypoints are placed in a circuit over the map's surface and are connected by straight line paths. Paths and waypoints are connected in such a way that an NPC moving along the paths is assured not to collide with any fixed obstacles. Waypoints and their connecting paths create a graph. Moving from waypoint to waypoint along a path requires an algorithm to search through and find all the nodes and how they are connected to each other. An example maze and a set of waypoints are illustrated as a graph in Figure 5.3. The graph does not necessarily need to reflect the physical layout of the maze when drawn. This example only shows which nodes connect to other nodes, not the location of the nodes or the distances between them.

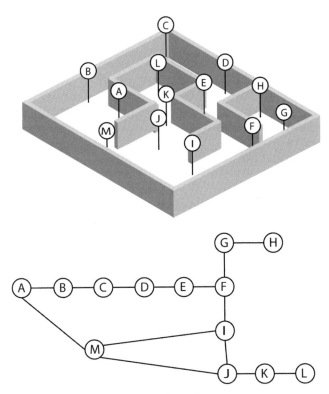

FIG 5.3 A maze with a set of waypoints.

In the graph of Figure 5.3, an NPC wanting to move from waypoint A to waypoint L could not simply plot a straight line between the two waypoints as they are not connected directly by an edge. The NPC then has the choice of navigating from waypoint A to waypoint L with the following sequences: A,M,J,K,L or A,B,C,D,E,F,I,J,K,L or A,M,I,J,K,L. The second sequence is obviously longer than the others, although all are legitimate paths. So how do you determine the best path from one waypoint to another?

Usually you will want an NPC to move from one waypoint to another via the shortest path. Often the meaning of shortest refers to the Euclidian distance between points, but not always. In real-time strategy (RTS) games where maps are divided up into grids of differing terrain, the shortest path from one point to another may not be based on the actual distance, but on the time taken to traverse each location; for example, the shortest Euclidean distance from point C2 to point A2 of Figure 5.4 will take an NPC through a river. Moving through the river may take the NPC twice as long as if it were to go the longer distance across the bridge. The definition of shortest is therefore left up to a matter of utility. The term *utility* originates in classical game theory and refers to the preferences of game players. If time is more important to an NPC than distance,

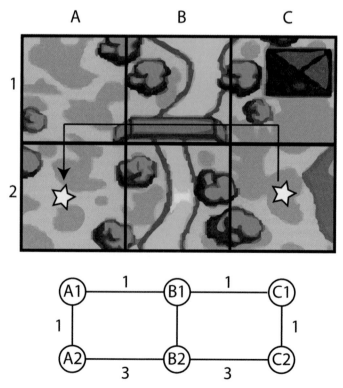

FIG 5.4 An example tiled strategy game map showing different terrain and a graph with utilities.

then the NPC will place a higher utility on time, thus avoiding the river. Utility values can be represented on a graph as weights on the edges, as shown in Figure 5.4. In this example, to travel from waypoint C2 to A2 directly via B2 will cost the NPC 3+3 = 6 points. Assuming a high number means less desirable, we might attribute these weights with travel time and say this route will take the NPC 6 hours. Further examination of the graph shows that it will only cost 4 hours to travel from waypoint C2 to A2 via points C1, B1, and A1.

In order to implement waypoints effectively in a game there needs to be an efficient way to search through them to find the most appropriate paths.

5.4.1 Searching Through Waypoints

There are High methods to find the shortest path from one node to another in a graph. These include algorithms such as breadth-first search (BFS) and depth-first search (DFS).

The BFS takes the given starting node and examines all adjacent nodes. Nodes that are adjacent to a starting node are ones that are connected directly to the starting node by an edge. In turn, from each of the adjacent nodes, nodes adjacent to these are examined. This process continues until the end node is found or the search for adjacent nodes has been exhausted. The algorithm can be written as Listing 5.3.

Listing 5.3 A Breadth-First Search Algorithm

1. Let i = 1.
2. Label starting node as i.
3. Find all unlabeled nodes adjacent to at least one node with label i. If there are no adjacent nodes, stop because we have run out of nodes. If the ending node is found, stop because we have found a path.
4. Label all nodes found in step 3 with i + 1.
5. Let i = i + 1, go to step 3.

This algorithm will always find the shortest path (Euclidean distance) from the start to the end vertices, assuming that each vertex is the same distance apart. For example, in a maze game where the environment is represented by a grid of squares of equal size, each square represents a node for the purposes of the algorithm. As shown in Figure 5.5, the starting square is labeled with a 1. Radiating out from this square, all adjacent squares are labeled with a 2. All squares adjacent to the 2 squares not already labeled with a 1 or a 2 are labeled with a 3. This process continues until the destination square is found. This can be quite a long way of searching, as almost all squares in the grid will be examined. This algorithm can be

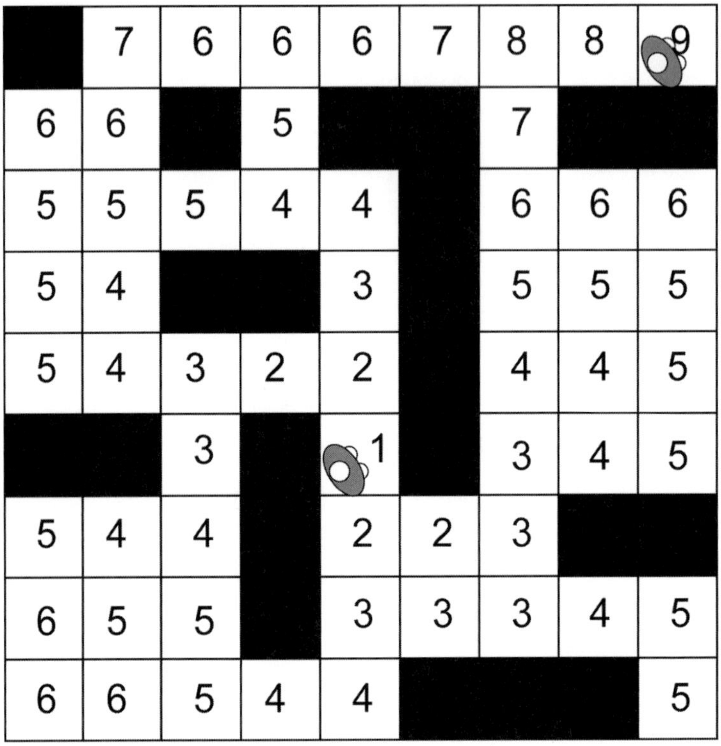

FIG 5.5 Environment map for a maze with path found using BFS.

modified to take into consideration other costs such as terrain type and traversal times in addition to or instead of distance by keeping track of all possible paths to the destination and adding up the costs. The path with the least cost can then be selected.

The DFS is simpler than the BFS and hence less effective. Instead of radiating out from the starting node, this algorithm simply follows one adjacent node to the next until it reaches the end of a path. Recursion works well for this algorithm and can be written as Listing 5.4.

Listing 5.4 A Depth-First Search Algorithm

DFS(a, vertex)
1. Let i = a;
2. Label node as i
3. For each adjacent node, *n*, to i, if n is labeled skip it; if n is the end node then stop the search; else if n is not labeled run this algorithm with DFS(a+1, *n*).

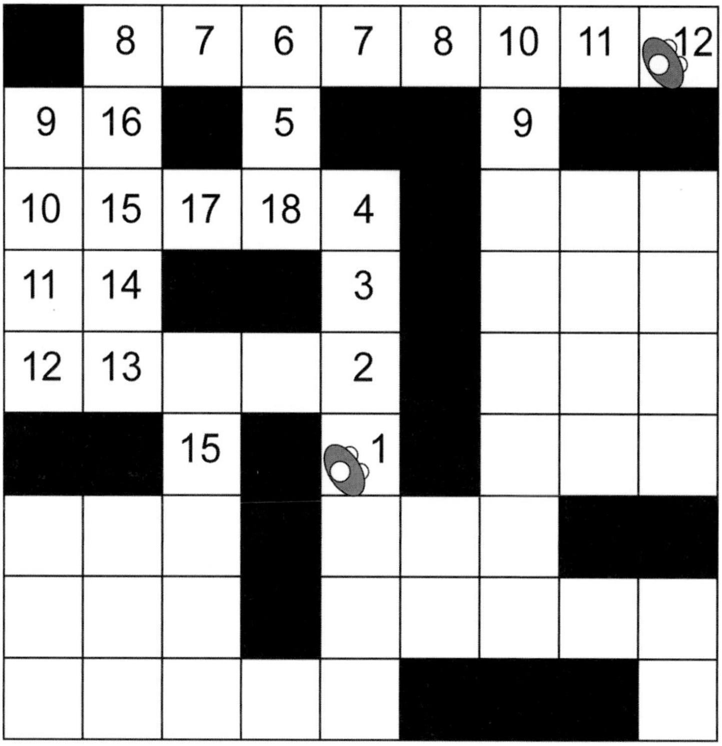

FIG 5.6 Environment map for a maze with path found using DFS.

An implementation of this algorithm is shown in Figure 5.6. Note that the algorithm does not find the shortest path to the destination, just a path. The success of finding the destination in a reasonable time is left to the luck of which adjacent node is selected first. In Figure 5.6, nodes are selected in an anticlockwise order beginning with the one immediately above the current node. If a clockwise order had been chosen the path would be different. Of course, this algorithm could also be modified to perform an exhaustive search to find all paths to the destination; by finding the path with a minimum cost the best could be selected. However, it is an ineffective way of finding the shortest path.

The most popular algorithm used in games, for searching graphs, is called A* (pronounced A-Star). What makes A* more efficient than BFS or DFS is that instead of picking the next adjacent node blindly, the algorithm looks for one that appears to be the most promising. From the starting node, the projected cost of all adjacent nodes is calculated, and the best node is chosen to be the next on the path. From this next node the same calculations occur again and the next best node is chosen. This algorithm ensures that all the best nodes are examined first. If one path of nodes does not work out, the algorithm can return to the next best in line and continue the search down a different path.

The algorithm determines the projected cost of taking paths based on the cost of getting to the next node and an estimate of getting from that node to the goal. The estimation is performed by a heuristic function. The term *heuristic* seems to be one of those funny words in AI that is difficult to define. Alan Newell first defined it in 1963 as a computation that performs the opposite function to that of an algorithm. A more useful definition of its meaning is given by Russell and Norvig in *Artificial Intelligence* published in 1995. They define a heuristic as any technique that can be used to improve the average performance of solving a problem that may not necessarily improve the worse performance. In the case of path finding, if the heuristic offers a perfect prediction, that is, it can calculate the cost from the current node to the destination accurately, then the best path will be found. However, in reality, the heuristic is very rarely perfect and can only offer an approximation.

◉ Unity Hands On

Pathfinding with A*

Step 1. Download *Chapter Five/Waypoints.zip* from the Web site. Open the project and the scene *patrolling*. Programming the A* algorithm is beyond the scope of this book and has therefore been provided with this project. If you are interested in the code, it can be found in the Project in the Plugins folder.

Step 2. Locate the robot model in the Robot Artwork > FBX folder in the Project. Drag the model into the Scene as shown in Figure 5.7. For the terrain and building models already in the scene, the robot will need to be scaled by 400 to match. If the textures are missing, find the material called *robot-robot1*, which is on the *roothandle* submesh of the robot; set it to *Bumped Diffuse*; and add the appropriate textures for *Base* and *Normalmap*. The texture files will be in the Project. The model may also have a cube on its head. Make this invisible by finding the *headhandle* subobject of the robot in the Hierarchy and unticking its Mesh Renderer.

Step 3. Waypoints can be added to the scene in the same way as they were in Chapter Three. Any GameObject can act as a waypoint. Create 9 spheres and arrange them in a circuit around the building. Add a 10th sphere out the front and an 11th sphere in the driveway as shown in Figure 5.8. Name the spheres Sphere1, Sphere2, etc.

Step 4. Create a new JavaScript file called *patrol* and open it in the script editor. Add the code shown in Listing 5.5.

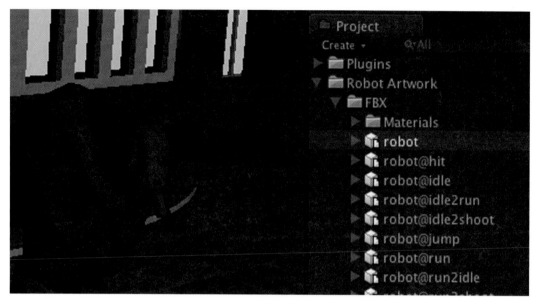

FIG 5.7 A robot model added to the scene and scaled by 400.

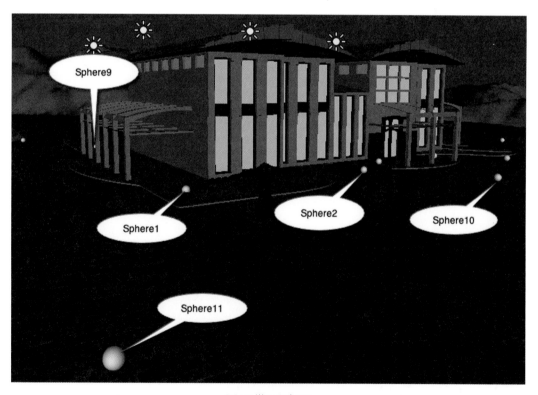

FIG 5.8 Waypoint layout.

Listing 5.5 Initializing Waypoints in a Graph Object

```
var waypoints: GameObject[];
//create a new graph to process waypoints
var graph: Graph = new Graph();
var currentWP: int = 0;
private var speed: int = 8;
private var rotationSpeed: int = 5;
private var accuracy: Number = 1.0;
function Start ()
{
    if(waypoints.length > 0)
    {
        // add all the waypoints to the graph
        for(var i = 0; i < waypoints.length; i++)
        {
            graph.AddNode(waypoints[i], true, true);
        }

        //create edges between the waypoints
        graph.AddEdge(waypoints[0], waypoints[1]);
        graph.AddEdge(waypoints[1], waypoints[2]);
        graph.AddEdge(waypoints[2], waypoints[3]);
        graph.AddEdge(waypoints[3], waypoints[4]);
        graph.AddEdge(waypoints[4], waypoints[5]);
        graph.AddEdge(waypoints[5], waypoints[6]);
        graph.AddEdge(waypoints[6], waypoints[7]);
        graph.AddEdge(waypoints[7], waypoints[8]);
        graph.AddEdge(waypoints[8], waypoints[0]);
    }
}
function Update()
{
    //draw the paths in the scene view of the editor
    //while playing
    graph.debugDraw();
}
```

Step 5. Attach the *patrol* script to the *robot* in the Hierarchy. Add the waypoints in order to the Waypoints array of the patrol script as shown in Figure 5.9.

Step 6. Play. While playing, switch to the Scene. The code in the Update function will draw lines along the edges. The blue tip indicates the

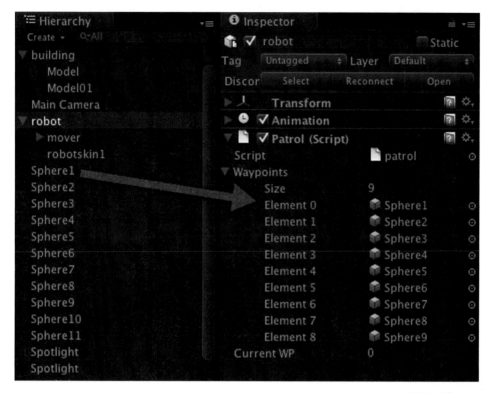

FIG 5.9 Adding waypoints
to the patrol script.

direction of the path. If you have all the waypoints collected correctly,
there should be a circuit around the building.

Step 7. To get the robot guard to patrol around the building,
modify the patrol code as shown in Listing 5.6.

Listing 5.6 Ordering Guard to Traverse Waypoints

```
var waypoints: GameObject[];
...
function OnGUI ()
{
     GUI.Box (Rect (10,10,100,90), "Guard's Orders");
     if (GUI.Button (Rect (20,40,80,20), "Patrol"))
```

```
        {
                graph.AStar(waypoints[0],waypoints[8]);
                this.animation.Play("run");
                this.animation["run"].wrapMode = WrapMode.Loop;
        }
}
function Start ()
{

    ...

}
function Update()
{
 //draw the paths in the scene view of the editor while playing
 graph.debugDraw();

 //if there is no path or at the end don't do anything
 if(graph.getPathLength()==0 || currentWP == graph.
   getPathLength())
 {
        this.animation.Play("idle");
        return;
 }
 //if we are close enough to the current waypoint move to next
 if(Vector3.Distance(
        graph.getPathPoint (currentWP).transform.position,
            transform.position) < accuracy)
 {
        currentWP++;
 }

 //if we are not at the end of the path
 if(currentWP < graph.getPathLength())
 {
        //keep on movin'
        var direction =
                graph.getPathPoint(currentWP).transform.position -
                                                transform.position;
                transform.rotation =
                        Quaternion.Slerp(transform.rotation,
                                Quaternion.LookRotation(direction),
                                        rotationSpeed * Time.deltaTime);
                transform.Translate(0, 0, Time.deltaTime
                        * speed);
 }
}
```

Step 8. Play. When the Patrol button is pressed the A* algorithm will calculate a path between the first and last waypoint and the guard will start running around it.

● Note

The character in this instance will move between the positions of waypoints. If you have placed your spheres on the ground, the character will sink into the ground as it is aiming its (0,0,0) position, which is in the center of the model, to the (0,0,0) of the sphere. To make the character appear to be moving on the terrain, move the spheres up to the right height. You can do this collectively by selecting all spheres in the Hierarchy by holding down shift while clicking on them and then dragging them up in the Scene.

In addition, if a character ever gets to a waypoint and starts circling it unexpectedly, it will be the accuracy setting. You may have it set to small; if the character can never get close enough to a waypoint it will just keep trying. In this case, set the accuracy value to something higher.

Step 9. Using the A* algorithm to calculate a circuit is a little bit of overkill, as a circuit can be performed simply using the code from Chapter Three. So now we will put it through its paces by adding some more button commands to get the character to move about the building. Modify the patrol code to that in Listing 5.7.

Listing 5.7 Testing A* Pathfinding by Giving Movement Commands to a Character

```
var waypoints: GameObject[];
var graph: Graph = new Graph();
var currentWP: int = 0;
private var currentNode: GameObject;
private var speed: int = 8;
private var rotationSpeed: int = 5;
private var accuracy: Number = 1;
function OnGUI ()
{
    GUI.Box (Rect (10,10,100,140), "Guard's Orders");
    if (GUI.Button (Rect (20,40,80,20), "Patrol"))
    {
        graph.AStar(waypoints[0],waypoints[4]);
        this.animation.Play("run");
        this.animation["run"].wrapMode = WrapMode.Loop;
    }
    if (GUI.Button (Rect (20,65,80,20), "Front Door"))
    {
        graph.AStar(currentNode,waypoints[2]);
        currentWP = 0;
```

```
                this.animation.Play("run");
                this.animation["run"].wrapMode = WrapMode.Loop;
        }
        if (GUI.Button (Rect (20,90,80,20), "Driveway"))
        {
                graph.AStar(currentNode,waypoints[10]);
                currentWP = 0;

                this.animation.Play("run");
                this.animation["run"].wrapMode = WrapMode.Loop;
        }
        if (GUI.Button (Rect (20,115,80,20), "Front"))
        {
                graph.AStar(currentNode,waypoints[9]);
                currentWP = 0;

                this.animation.Play("run");
                this.animation["run"].wrapMode = WrapMode.Loop;
        }
}
function Start ()
{
        if(waypoints.length > 0)
        {
                ...

                //create edges between the waypoints
                graph.AddEdge(waypoints[0], waypoints[1]);
                graph.AddEdge(waypoints[1], waypoints[2]);
                graph.AddEdge(waypoints[2], waypoints[3]);
                graph.AddEdge(waypoints[3], waypoints[4]);
                graph.AddEdge(waypoints[4], waypoints[5]);
                graph.AddEdge(waypoints[5], waypoints[6]);
                graph.AddEdge(waypoints[6], waypoints[7]);
                graph.AddEdge(waypoints[7], waypoints[8]);
                graph.AddEdge(waypoints[8], waypoints[0]);

                //and back the other way
                graph.AddEdge(waypoints[1], waypoints[0]);
                graph.AddEdge(waypoints[2], waypoints[1]);
                graph.AddEdge(waypoints[3], waypoints[2]);
                graph.AddEdge(waypoints[4], waypoints[3]);
                graph.AddEdge(waypoints[5], waypoints[4]);
                graph.AddEdge(waypoints[6], waypoints[5]);
                graph.AddEdge(waypoints[7], waypoints[6]);
                graph.AddEdge(waypoints[8], waypoints[7]);
                graph.AddEdge(waypoints[0], waypoints[8]);

                //create edges to extra to waypoints
                graph.AddEdge(waypoints[0], waypoints[9]);
                graph.AddEdge(waypoints[0], waypoints[10]);
                graph.AddEdge(waypoints[9], waypoints[10]);
```

```
            graph.AddEdge(waypoints[5], waypoints[9]);
            //and back again
            graph.AddEdge(waypoints[9], waypoints[0]);
            graph.AddEdge(waypoints[10], waypoints[0]);
            graph.AddEdge(waypoints[10], waypoints[9]);
            graph.AddEdge(waypoints[9], waypoints[5]);
        }
        currentNode = waypoints[0];
}
function Update()
{

        //draw the paths in the scene view of the editor
        //while playing
        graph.debugDraw();

        ...
        if(graph.getPathLength()==0||currentWP==graph.
          getPathLength())
        {
            this.animation.Play("idle");
            return;
        }

        //the node we are closest to at this moment
        currentNode = graph.getPathPoint(currentWP);

        ...
}
```

Step 10. The preceding code adds extra paths between the original circuit waypoints to point back the other way. This makes it possible to travel in any direction between points. Extra paths are also added between points in the driveway and out the front of the building. Play and switch to the Scene to see the red lines connecting the points (illustrated in Figure 5.10).

A new variable called currentNode has also been added to keep track of the waypoint the character last visited. This enables the algorithm to plot out paths based on the character's current position to the destination node.

This waypoint system is used in the next workshop after the development of a self-motivated character is explained.

5.5 Finite State Machines

The most popular form of AI in games and NPCs is *nondeterministic automata*, or what is more commonly known as *finite state machines* (FSM). An FSM can be represented by a directed graph (digraph) where the nodes symbolize states and the directed connecting edges correspond to state transitions. States

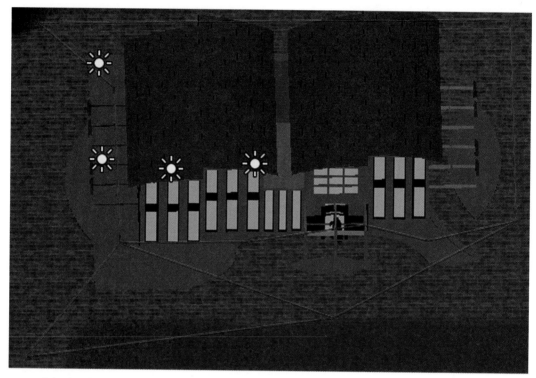

FIG 5.10 Debug lines showing paths in a waypoint graph.

represent an NPC's current behavior or state of mind. Formally, an FSM consists of a set of states, S, and a set of state transitions, T. For example, an FSM might be defined as *S = {WANDER, ATTACK, PURSUE}* and *T={out of sight, sighted, out of range, in range, dead}* as shown in Table 5.1.

In short, the state transitions define how to get from one state to another. For example, in Table 5.1, if the NPC is in state WANDER and it sights its opponent, then the state transitions to PURSUE. The state is used to determine elements of the NPC's behavior, for example, when the NPC is in state ATTACK the appropriate attacking animation should be used.

TABLE 5.1 State transition for an FSM

	Transitions (*opponent is...*)				
State	*out of sight*	*sighted*	*out of range*	*in range*	*dead*
WANDER	*WANDER*	*PURSUE*	-	-	-
PURSUE	*WANDER*	-	*PURSUE*	*ATTACK*	-
ATTACK	-	-	*PURSUE*	*ATTACK*	*WANDER*

Programming an FSM is a case of providing an NPC with a *state* value that represents its current behavior. Each state is accompanied by an *event* value representing the status of that state. The event tells us if the NPC has just entered that state, has been in the state for a while, or is exiting the state. Keeping track of this is critical for coordinating NPC movements around the environment and its animations. The FSM runs each game loop; therefore, knowing where the NPC is within a state is important for updating its status, the status of other game characters, and the environment.

For example, consider a Sim whose state changes to "take bath." Before it can take a bath, it needs to make its way to the bathroom, run the bath, get undressed, and hop in the bath. This would happen on entering the state. The state would then enter update mode where the Sim is sitting in the bath washing itself, singing, blowing, bubbles, and so on. Once the Sim is clean, the state transitions to the exit phase in which it gets out of the bath and redresses. In pseudocode, the code might look something like that in Listing 5.8.

Listing 5.8 Code for Simple Finite State Machine

```
function FSM()
{
  if( state == "BATH")
  {
    if (event == "ENTER")
        {
                walkToBath();
                runBath();
                getUndressed();
                hopInBath();
                event = "UPDATE";
        }
    else if (event == UPDATE)
            {
                while(!clean)
                {
                        wash();
                }
                event = "EXIT";
            }
            else if (event == "EXIT")
            {
                getOutOfBath();
                getDressed();
                state = "IDLE";
                event = "ENTER";
            }
     }
}
```

The FSM works by entering a state and then transitioning from enter, through update to exit. At the end of each event, the event is updated such that the next loop the FSM runs the code goes into the next event. On exiting a state, the state value is changed to something else and the event is set to enter.

● Unity Hands On
Implementing an FSM

In this workshop you will learn how to implement an FSM in conjunction with a waypoint system and the A* algorithm to program a guard character that patrols a warehouse and pursues intruders.

> **Step 1.** Download *Chapter Five/FSM.zip* from the Web site and open the scene warehousePatrol. In the Scene you will see the warehouse model, the robot from the last workshop, and a waypoint system of spheres.
>
> **Step 2.** Create a new tag named *waypoint* and set it for the tag of each sphere.
>
> **Step 3.** Create a new JavaScript file called *patrol* and open with the script editor. Enter the code in Listing 5.9 and attach it to the robot.

Listing 5.9 Setting up a Waypoint System with Automatic Waypoint Collection

```
private var graph: Graph = new Graph();
private var currentWP: int = 0;
private var currentNode: GameObject;
private var speed: int = 8;
private var rotationSpeed: int = 5;
private var accuracy: Number = 1;
function CreateBiPath(a: String, b: String)
{
        var w1 = GameObject.Find(a);
        var w2 = GameObject.Find(b);

        if(w1 && w2) //if both objects exist
        {
                //create edges between the waypoints
                //in both directions
                graph.AddEdge(w1, w2);
                graph.AddEdge(w2, w1);
        }
}
function Start ()
{
        //automatically find all game objects with tag waypoint
        //and add to the graph
        var gos : GameObject[];
```

```
        gos = GameObject.FindGameObjectsWithTag ("waypoint");

        for (var go : GameObject in gos)
        {
            graph.AddNode(go, true, true);
        }

        CreateBiPath("Sphere3","Sphere2");
        CreateBiPath("Sphere2","Sphere1");
        CreateBiPath("Sphere1","Sphere4");
        CreateBiPath("Sphere3","Sphere4");
        CreateBiPath("Sphere4","Sphere5");
        CreateBiPath("Sphere5","Sphere6");
        CreateBiPath("Sphere6","Sphere7");
        CreateBiPath("Sphere7","Sphere8");
        CreateBiPath("Sphere8","Sphere9");
        CreateBiPath("Sphere9","Sphere10");
        CreateBiPath("Sphere10","Sphere11");
        CreateBiPath("Sphere11","Sphere12");
        CreateBiPath("Sphere12","Sphere13");
        CreateBiPath("Sphere13","Sphere14");
        CreateBiPath("Sphere14","Sphere15");
        CreateBiPath("Sphere15","Sphere17");

        currentNode = GameObject.Find("Sphere2");
}
function Update()
{
        //draw the paths in the scene view of the editor
        //while playing
        graph.debugDraw();
}
```

Step 4. Play. Go into the Scene view and have a look at the paths that have been created. In this code, a function has been written to help take away part of the laborious job of programming which points connect by creating bidirectional paths. This code also populates the waypoint graph automatically by looking for all the spheres that were tagged with *waypoint* in the Start() function.

Step 5. Locate Sphere2 and place the guard model near it as it has been set as the initial value for currentNode and will be used as the starting location of guard. Alternatively, you could add code such as `this.transform.position = currentNode.transform.position` to the end of the Start() function to have the code place the model.

Step 6. Modify the patrol script to that in Listing 5.10.

Listing 5.10 Adding an FSM Function

```
private var graph: Graph = new Graph();
...
private var state = "idle";
private var event = "enter";
private var goalLocation: GameObject;
function CreateBiPath(a: String, b: String)
{
    ...
}
function Start ()
{
    ...
}
function FSM()
{
    if(state == "patrol")
    {
        if(event == "enter")
        {
            graph.AStar(currentNode,goalLocation);
            currentWP = 0;

            this.animation.Play("run");
            this.animation["run"].wrapMode =
                WrapMode.Loop;
            event = "update";
        }
        else if (event == "update")
        {
            //if there is no path or we are at the
            //end of the path don't do anything
            if(graph.getPathLength() == 0 ||
                currentWP == graph.getPathLength())
            {
                state = "idle";
                event = "enter";
                return;
            }

            //the node we are closest to at this moment
            currentNode = graph.getPathPoint(currentWP);

            //if we are close enough to the current
            //waypoint start moving toward the next

            if(Vector3.Distance(
             graph.getPathPoint(currentWP).
                    transform.position,
                    transform.position) < accuracy)
```

```
                {
                        currentWP++;
                }

                //if we are not at the end of the path
                if(currentWP < graph.getPathLength())
                {
                        //keep on movin'
                        var direction =
                graph.getPathPoint(currentWP).transform.
                        position —
                        transform.position;
                        transform.rotation =
                                Quaternion.Slerp(transform.
                                        rotation,
                                        Quaternion.
LookRotation(direction), rotationSpeed * Time.deltaTime);
                        transform.Translate(0, 0,
                                Time.deltaTime * speed);
                }
        }
        else if (event == "exit")
        {

        }
    }
    else if(state == "idle")
    {

        this.animation.Play("idle");
        event = "update";

        if(event == "update")
        {
                //just remain idle most of the time
                if(Random.Range(0,1000) < 1)
                {
                        state = "patrol";
                        event = "enter";
                        if(currentNode ==
                                GameObject.Find("Sphere17"))
                                goalLocation =
                                        GameObject.
                                                Find("Sphere2");
                        else
                                goalLocation =
                                        GameObject.
                                                Find("Sphere17");
                }
        }
    }
}
```

```
}
function Update()
{
    //draw the paths in the scene view of the editor
    //while playing
    graph.debugDraw();

    FSM();
}
```

Step 7. Play. With the 1 in 1000 chance of the guard going into patrol mode, if you watch it for a while it will start moving from its current location to the last waypoint. When it gets there it will go into idle mode again, until after another 1 in 1000 chance it will start to patrol back in the other direction. Note that as with the waypoints in the previous workshop, the spheres may need to be moved up so that the guard model doesn't sink into the floor.

Step 8. Select Assets > Import Package > Character Controller from the main menu to add the First Person Controller prefab to the Project.

Step 9. Drag the First Person Controller prefab from the Project into the Hierarchy. Delete the existing main camera, as the First Person Controller has its own camera.

Step 10. Move the First Person Controller into the same room as the guard so you can watch it moving.

Step 11. In the Hierarchy, shift-select all the *polySurface* submeshes of the warehouse model and select Components > Physics > Mesh Collider to add colliders to the warehouse. Without the colliders, the First Person Controller will fall through the floor.

Step 12. Play. You will now be able to watch the guard patrolling from the first person view.

Step 13. The guard model will seem dark as there is no directional light so add one to the scene.

Step 14. Next we are going to add code to make the guard shoot and chase the player. To do this, add pursue and attack states as shown in Listing 5.11.

Listing 5.11 Extending an FSM with More States

```
private var graph: Graph = new Graph();
...
private var prevState = "";
private var state = "idle";
private var event = "enter";
private var goalLocation: GameObject;
var target:Transform;
```

```
private var seeRange = 10;
private var shootRange = 5;
private var keepDistance = 1;
private var heightOffset:float = 0.3;
function CreateBiPath(a: String, b: String)
{
      ...
}
function CanSeeTarget () : boolean
{
      if (Vector3.Distance(transform.position,target.
           position) > seeRange)
                  return false;
      return true;
}
function CanShootTarget(): boolean
{
      if(!CanSeeTarget()) return false;
      if (Vector3.Distance(transform.position, target.
           position) > shootRange)
                  return false;
      return true;
}
function Start ()
{
      ...
}
function FSM()
{
      var direction: Vector3;
      var position: Vector3;

      if(state == "patrol")
      {
           if(prevState != state)
           {
                graph.AStar(currentNode,goalLocation);
                currentWP = 0;
                this.animation.Play("run");
                this.animation["run"].wrapMode = WrapMode.
                   Loop;
                event = "update";
           }
           else if (event == "update")
           {
                ...
           }
           else if (event == "exit")
           {
```

```
            }
    }
    else if(state == "attack")
    {
        if(prevState != state)
        {
            this.animation.CrossFade("shoot");
            this.animation["shoot"].wrapMode =
                WrapMode.Loop;
            event = "update";
        }
        else if(event == "update")
        {
            position = target.position;
            direction = position - transform.
                position;
            direction.y = 0;
            // Rotate towards the target
            transform.rotation =
                    Quaternion.Slerp(transform.
                                            rotation,
                    Quaternion.LookRotation(direction),
                    rotationSpeed * Time.deltaTime);
            transform.position.y = target.position.y +
                                    heightOffset;
        }
    }
    else if(state == "pursue")
    {
        if(prevState != state)
        {
            this.animation.CrossFade("run");
            this.animation["run"].wrapMode =
                WrapMode.Loop;
            event = "update";
        }
        else if(event == "update")
        {
            position = target.position;
            direction = position - transform.
                position;
            direction.y = 0;
            // Rotate towards the target
            transform.rotation =
                    Quaternion.Slerp(transform.rotation,
                    Quaternion.LookRotation(direction),
                    rotationSpeed * Time.deltaTime);

            // Move the character
            if(direction.magnitude > keepDistance)
```

```
                {
                        transform.Translate(0,0,Time.deltaTime *
                          speed);
                }
                transform.position.y = target.position.y +
                                                heightOffset;
            }
        }
        else if(state == "idle")
        {
                this.animation.Play("idle");
                event = "update";

                if(event == "update")
                {
                        ...
                }
        }
}
function Update()
{
        //draw the paths in the scene view of the editor
        //while playing
        graph.debugDraw();

        if(CanShootTarget())
        {
                prevState = state;
                state = "attack";
        }
        else if(CanSeeTarget())
        {
                prevState = state;
                state = "pursue";
        }
        else
        {
                prevState = state;
                state = "idle";
        }

        FSM();
}
```

Step 15. The preceding code now controls the shooting and pursuing actions of the guard. Setting the state's event to enter has also been replaced. If the NPC's previous state was different from the current state, it runs the original `event` = "enter" code—the same as initializing a state. The distance the NPC shoots and pursues is controlled by variables at the

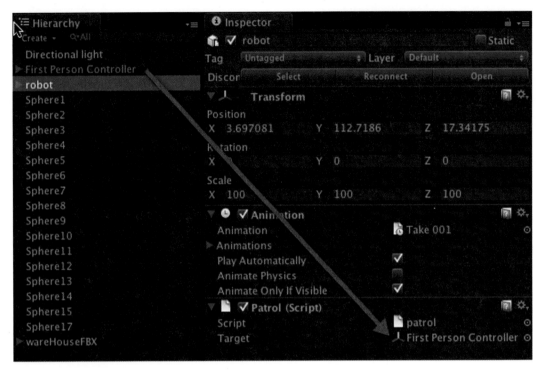

FIG 5.11 Setting the first person controller as the target for an NPC.

top of the code. Before playing, locate the patrol script attached to the robot model in the Hierarchy and set the *target* variable to the *First Person Controller* as shown in Figure 5.11.

When the NPC is pursuing and attacking the player, its position is made relative to the player. Because the model sizes of the player and the robot mesh are different sizes and the center points differ with respect to their *y* position, without some kind of height offset for the robot, it will either sink into the ground or float above it. This is the same issue the NPC has when following the waypoints and the reason why spheres are lifted above the ground. To fix this, the *heightOffset* variable has been added.
To get the best offset value usually the game needs to be played a number of times and the NPC observed. If you know the exact height of the model's mesh and its center position, it could be calculated.

Step 16. Play. The guard will chase and shoot at the player, but move up the stairs into another room and see what happens. The guard will follow the player but take shortcuts through the walls of the warehouse.
Step 17. This presents another problem to solve. We could make the NPC stick to the waypoints and paths while trying to follow the player, but what if the player goes somewhere there are no waypoints? You could

also spend a lot of time placing waypoints all over the map as a solution. However, a simpler solution is to place temporary waypoints down on the map that draw out the path the player is walking and have the NPC follow them instead. This is another common technique used in games called *breadcrumb pathfinding*. To develop a simple breadcrumb script, create a new JavaScript file called *breadcrumbs* and add the code in Listing 5.12.

Listing 5.12 Recording Player Movement with Breadcrumbs

```
var breadcrumbs:Array = new Array();
private var lastPos:Vector3;
function RemoveBreadCrumb()
{
    Destroy(breadcrumbs[0]);
    breadcrumbs.RemoveAt(0);
}
function Update ()
{
    if(lastPos != this.transform.position)
    {
        var bc =
            GameObject.
                CreatePrimitive(PrimitiveType.Sphere);
            bc.transform.position = this.transform.
                position;
            Destroy(bc.collider);
            bc.transform.localScale = Vector3(0.5,0.5,0.5);
            bc.renderer.material.color = Color.green;
            breadcrumbs.Add(bc);
    }
    lastPos = this.transform.position;

    if(breadcrumbs.length > 100)
    {
        RemoveBreadCrumb();
    }
}
```

Step 18. Attach this script to the First Person Controller.
Step 19. Play. Walk backward and look at the green spheres being added to the map. These are your breadcrumbs. They mark the last 100 locations your First Person Controller was on the map. Of course, in a real game you wouldn't see these but they are added here for illustrative purposes.
Step 20. To get the NPC to follow these breadcrumbs when it is in pursuit, modify the patrol script as shown in Listing 5.13.

Listing 5.13 Adding Breadcrumb Following Code to the NPC

```
...
else if(state == "pursue")
{
    if(prevState != state)
    {
        ...
    }
    else if(event == "update")
    {
        position =
            target.gameObject.
            GetComponent("breadcrumbs").
                breadcrumbs[0].
            transform.position;

        if(Vector3.Distance(position,this.transform.
            position)< 2)
        {
            target.gameObject.
              GetComponent("breadcrumbs").
                RemoveBreadCrumb();
        }
        direction = position - transform.position;
        direction.y = 0;

    ...

}
...
```

Step 21. Play. When the NPC is in pursuit of the player it will follow the breadcrumb trail. As it reaches a breadcrumb it deletes it from the player's breadcrumb array.

Step 22. Last but not least, we want the NPC to continue patrolling when the player manages to move beyond its range. To do this we need to set the state to idle and also find the NPC its closest waypoint. That way the A* algorithm can work to set the NPC back on its patrol path. To do this, modify the patrol script to that in Listing 5.14.

Listing 5.14 Finding the Closest Waypoint to Set NPC Back to Patrol

```
private var graph: Graph = new Graph();
...
function CanShootTarget(): boolean
{
    ...
}
```

```
function findClosestWP()
{
      var gos : GameObject[];
      gos = GameObject.FindGameObjectsWithTag("waypoint");
      var closest:GameObject = gos[0];

      for (var go : GameObject in gos)
      {
            if(Vector3.Distance (
            closest.transform.position, this.transform.
              position) >
            Vector3.Distance (
                  go.transform.position,this.transform.
                    position))
            {
                  closest = go;
            }
      }
      return closest;
}
...
function FSM()
{
      var direction: Vector3;
      var position: Vector3;

      if(state == "patrol")
      {
            if(prevState != state)
            {
                  graph.AStar(currentNode,goalLocation);
                  graph.printPath();
                  currentWP = 0;

                  this.animation.Play("run");
                  this.animation["run"].wrapMode =
                    WrapMode.Loop;
                  event = "update";
                  prevState = state;
            }
      ...
      else if(state == "idle")
      {
            this.animation.Play("idle");
            event = "update";
            prevState = state;

            if(event == "update")
            {
```

```
                         //just remain idle
                         if(Random.Range(0,1000) < 1)
                         {
                                 state = "patrol";
                                 event = "enter";
                                 currentNode = findClosestWP();
                                 ...
                         }
                 }
         }
}
function Update()
{
        //draw the paths in the scene view of the editor
        //while playing
        graph.debugDraw();

        if(CanShootTarget())
        {
                prevState = state;
                state = "attack";
        }
        else if(CanSeeTarget())
        {
                prevState = state;
                state = "pursue";
        }
        else if(state != "patrol")
        {
                prevState = state;
                state = "idle";
        }
        FSM();
}
```

Step 23. Play. If you can manage to outrun the NPC, you will find that it goes into idle mode and then resumes its patrolling path.

5.6 Flocking

When you observe the movement of crowds or groups of animals their motions appear aligned and coordinated; for example, a flock of birds flying across the sky appears synchronized, staying together as a group, moving toward a common goal, and yet not all following the exact same path.

Applying flocking principles to NPCs in a game can add extra realism to the environment as secondary animations. If the game is set in a jungle setting, having a flock of birds fly across the sky looks far better than random birds flying in random directions.

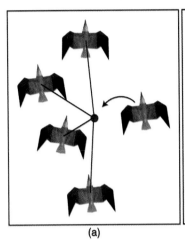
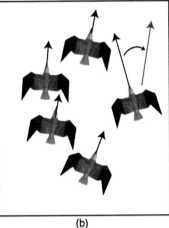
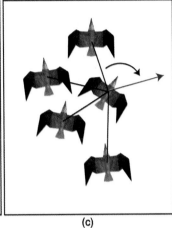

(a)   (b)   (c)

In 1986, Craig Reynolds developed an unparalleled simple algorithm for producing flocking behavior in groups of computer characters. Through the application of three rules, Reynolds developed coordinated motions such as that seen in flocks of birds and schools of fish. The rules are applied to each individual character in a group with the result of very convincing flocking behavior. These rules (illustrated in Figure 5.12) include

FIG 5.12 Flocking rules: (a) move toward average group position, (b) align heading with average group heading, and (c) avoid others.

1. moving toward the average position of the group
2. aligning with the average heading of the group
3. avoid crowding other group members

Flocking creates a moving group with no actual leader. The rules can be increased to take into consideration moving toward a goal position or the effect of wind. These rules are used to create a flock of birds in the following workshop.

⊙ **Unity Hands On**

Flocking

Step 1. Download *Chapter Five/flocking.zip* from the Web site and open the *testFlock* scene. Play. You will see a radar showing the position of seagulls created with the globalFlock script attached to the camera. To move the camera, use the arrow keys. This will allow you to look at parts of the flock. Currently the seagulls do not move. In the globalFlock script 100 seagulls are being created. If you want more, change the value of 100. If your computer starts to slow you may need to reduce the flock size.

Step 2. Open the flock script and add the code in Listing 5.15.

Step 3. Attach the flock script to the *SeagullPrefab* in the Project.

Step 4. Play. Each seagull will have a random speed setting and be flying in a straight line. You can use the arrow keys to follow the birds.

Step 5. Let's apply the first flocking rule to the population. Modify the flock script as shown in Listing 5.16.

Listing 5.15 Starting Script for Flocking

```
var speed: float = 0.001;
private var rotationSpeed: float = 5.0;
var averageHeading: Vector3;
var averagePosition: Vector3;
private var neighbourDistance = 2.0;
function Start()
{
     speed = Random.Range(0.1,1);
}
function Update ()
{
     transform.Translate(0, 0, Time.deltaTime * speed);
}
```

Listing 5.16 Script to Make Seagulls Move to the Average Location of Their Neighbors

```
var speed: float = 0.001;
...
function Update ()
{
     if(Random.Range(0,5) < 1)
          ApplyRules();

     transform.Translate(0, 0, Time.deltaTime * speed);
}
function ApplyRules()
{
     var gos : GameObject[];
     gos = GameObject.FindGameObjectsWithTag("Seagull");

     var vcentre: Vector3;
     var vavoid: Vector3;
     var gSpeed: float;

     //var wind: Vector3 = new Vector3(1,0,1);
     //var goalPos:Vector3 = new Vector3(10,0,10);

     var dist: float;
     var groupSize: int = 0;
     for (var go : GameObject in gos)
     {
          if(go != this.gameObject)
          {
               dist =
                    Vector3.Distance(go.transform.
                    position,
```

```
                           this.transform.position);
                    if(dist <= neighbourDistance)
                    {
                           vcentre += go.transform.position;
                           groupSize++;

                    }

           }
      }
      if(groupSize)
      {
           vcentre = vcentre/groupSize;

           var direction = vcentre - transform.position;
           if(direction != Vector3.zero)
                 transform.rotation =
                       Quaternion.Slerp(transform.rotation,
                           Quaternion.
                                 LookRotation(direction),
                           rotationSpeed * Time.
                                           deltaTime);

      }
}
```

Step 6. Play. Small flocks will form in the population. In the script, Random.Range is used to apply the rules about one in five game loops. This ensures that not all the birds have the rules that run each game loop. If this happens, the application runs very slowly and gets slower the more birds you have. Note that the average position is also only determined for neighboring birds, not the whole population. This is determined by the `neighbourDistance` variable. If you make this value larger, you will get one big flock.

Step 7. Currently, because the birds have random speeds, birds will eventually break away from their flocks because they can't keep up or are going too fast. To keep them together, the second rule is applied. Birds in the flock match the average speed. To achieve this, modify the flock script to that in Listing 5.17.

Listing 5.17 Applying an Average Speed to a Flock

```
function ApplyRules()
{
     ...
     for (var go : GameObject in gos)
     {
```

```
             if(go != this.gameObject)
             {
                  dist =
                            Vector3.Distance(go.transform.
                                                    position,
                        this.transform.position);
                  if(dist <= neighbourDistance)
                  {
                    vcentre += go.transform.position;
                    groupSize++;
                    gSpeed = gSpeed +
                      go.GetComponent("flock").speed;
                  }
             }
        }

     if(groupSize)
     {
             vcentre = vcentre/groupSize;
             speed = gSpeed/groupSize;

             ...

     }
}
```

Step 8. Play. Averaging of the speed will help keep the formed flocks together.

Step 9. Finally, adding the third rule will enable the birds to keep out of each other's way. Before changing the code, observe the current flocking movement. Once a bird is flying in a circular pattern within the flock it stays with that pattern. Now change the flock script to that in Listing 5.18.

Listing 5.18 Adding Avoiding Behavior to Flocking Script

```
function ApplyRules()
{
     ...
     for (var go : GameObject in gos)
     {
             if(go != this.gameObject)
             {
             dist = Vector3.Distance(go.transform.position +
             this.transform.position);
             if(dist <= neighbourDistance)
             {
               vcentre += go.transform.position;
               groupSize++;
```

```
            if(dist < 0.5)
            {
            vavoid = vavoid + (this.transform.position -
                    go.transform.position);
            }

            gSpeed = gSpeed + go.GetComponent("flock").
                    speed;
            }
        }
    }

    if(groupSize)
    {
        vcentre = vcentre/groupSize;
        speed = gSpeed/groupSize;

        var direction = (vcentre + vavoid) - transform.
            position;
        ...
    }
}
```

Step 10. Play. Take a close look at the birds' behavior. You will notice they now dart out of the way in a similar movement to what is observed in real flocking birds.

So far, the flocks created are reminiscent of crows or vultures circling in the sky around their next meal. This could be used for a dramatic effect in a game to point out the position of something sinister in the game environment. More often than not, flocks used for ambience tend to be traveling across the scene. To achieve this type of flocking, more rules can be added.

Step 11. To make the birds move across an endless sky, we can add a *wind* value. This is a vector indicating the direction of travel. Modify the flock script to that in Listing 5.19.

Listing 5.19 Directing Flock to Fly in a Set Direction

```
function ApplyRules()
{
    ...
    var wind: Vector3 = new Vector3(1,0,1);

    var dist: float;
    var groupSize: int = 0;
    for (var go : GameObject in gos)
```

```
    {
        ...
    }

    if(groupSize)
    {
        vcentre = vcentre/groupSize + wind;
        speed = gSpeed/groupSize;

        ...
    }
}
```

Step 12. Play. The added wind vector will cause the birds to fly along the same course. The birds will still flock together, but instead of circling they will form close-streamed groups.

Step 13. If you want the birds to fly across the screen to a particular location, a goal position can also be added to the rules. Modify the flock script to that in Listing 5.20.

Listing 5.20 Directing Flock to Fly to a Specific Location

```
function ApplyRules()
{
    ...
    var wind: Vector3 = new Vector3(1,0,1);
    var goalPos:Vector3 = new Vector3(10,0,10);

    var dist: float;
    var groupSize: int = 0;
    for (var go : GameObject in gos)
    {
        ...
    }
    if(groupSize)
    {
        vcentre = vcentre/groupSize +
                        wind + (goalPos - this.transform.
        position);
        speed = gSpeed/groupSize;

        ...
    }
}
```

Step 14. Play. The birds will form into groups flying toward a single goal location.

These very flocking rules have been used in movies to create flocking characters. They were used in *Batman Returns* to create realistic swarms of bats and in *The Lion King* for a herd of wildebeest.

The rules can also be modified in games to develop intelligent group enemy behavior and optimize processing speeds. For example, in the workshop that introduced breadcrumb path finding, if there were hundreds of enemies, having them all process the breadcrumbs could prove computationally costly. Furthermore, if each one even had to run the A* algorithm, it could certainly slow down performance. However, if just one *leader* followed the breadcrumbs, the rest could flock and follow that leader.

5.7 Decision Trees

Decision trees are a hierarchical graph that structure complex Boolean functions and use them to reason about situations. A decision tree is constructed from a set of properties that describe the situation being reasoned about. Each node in the tree represents a single Boolean decision along a path of decision that leads to the terminal or *leaf* nodes of the tree.

A decision tree is constructed from a list of previously made decisions. These could be from experts, other players, or AI game experience. They are used in *Black & White* to determine the behavior of the creature. For example, a decision tree based on how tasty the creature finds an object determines what it will eat. How tasty it finds an object is gathered from past experience where the creature was made to eat an object by the player.

To illustrate the creation of a decision tree for an NPC, we will examine some sample data on decisions made about eating certain items in the environment. The decision we want made is a yes or no about eating given the characteristics or *attributes* about the eating situation. Table 5.2 displays some past eating examples.

Given the attributes of a situation (hungry, food, and taste), a decision tree can be built that reflects whether the food in question should be eaten. As you can see from aforementioned data, it is not easy to construct a Boolean expression to make a decision about eating. For example, sometimes it does matter if the NPC is hungry and other times it does not; sometimes it matters if the food is tasty and sometimes it does not.

To construct a decision tree from some given data, each attribute must be examined to determine which one is the most influential. To do this, we examine which attributes split the final decision most evenly. Table 5.3 is a count of the influences of the given attributes.

TABLE 5.2 Examples for making an eating decision[a]

Example	Attributes			Eat?
	Hungry	**Food**	**Taste**	
1	Yes	Rock	0	No
2	Yes	Grass	0	Yes
3	Yes	Tree	2	Yes
4	Yes	Cow	2	Yes
5	No	Cow	2	Yes
6	No	Grass	2	Yes
7	No	Rock	1	No
8	No	Tree	0	No
9	Yes	Tree	0	Yes
10	Yes	Grass	1	Yes

[a]Values for the attribute taste are 0 for awful, 1 for ok, and 2 for tasty.

TABLE 5.3 Attribute influence over the final eat decision

Attribute	Eat = yes	Eat = no	Total influences
Hungry			
Yes	5	1	
No	2	2	
Total exclusive 0s	*0*	*0*	*0*
Food			
Rock	0	2	
Grass	3	0	
Tree	2	1	
Cow	2	0	
Total exclusive 0s	*1*	*2*	*3*
Taste			
0	2	2	
1	1	1	
2	4	0	
Total exclusive 0s	*0*	*1*	*1*

To decide which attribute splits the eat decision, we look for examples where an attribute's value definitively determines if Eat is yes or no. In this case, when Food equals Rock, every instance of Eat is no. This means that we could confidently write a Boolean expression such as

```
if food = rock
then eat = no
```

without having to consider any of the other attributes. The total number of exclusive 0s counted in a column determines the attribute with the best split. By exclusive we mean that the value of the attribute must be 0 in one column and greater than 0 in another. If both columns were 0, then the value would have no effect at all over the decision. In the cases of Rock, Grass, and Cow, the final value for Eat is already known and thus these values can be used to create instant leaf nodes off the root node as shown in Figure 5.13. However, in the case of Tree, the decision is unclear, as sometimes Eat is yes and sometimes it is no.

To find the next best splitting attribute, outcome decisions involving the Tree value are combined with the remaining attributes to give the values shown in Table 5.4.

In this case, the second best attribute is Hungry. Hungry can now be added to the decision tree under the Tree node to give the graph shown in Figure 5.14. Note that the yes and no choices for Hungry provide definitive answers for Eat, and therefore the nodes do not need to be classified further with any other attributes. The decision tree in Figure 5.14 is the complete decision tree for data from Table 5.2. You could say in this case that the taste of the food is irrelevant.

FIG 5.13 Partial decision tree for data from Table 5.3.

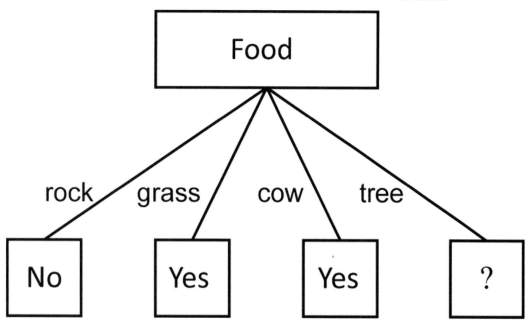

TABLE 5.4 Attribute influence over the final eat decision with Food = Tree

Attribute	Eat = yes	Eat = no	Total influences
Food = Tree and Hungry			
Yes	2	0	
No	0	1	
Total exclusive 0s	*1*	*1*	*2*
Food = Tree and Taste			
0	1	1	
1	0	0	
2	1	0	
Total exclusive 0s	*0*	*1*	*1*

FIG 5.14 Complete decision tree for eating objects.

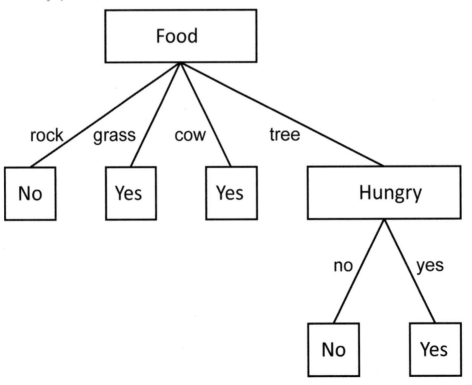

A famous algorithm used for creating decision trees from examples (and that used in *Black & White*) is ID3 developed by computer scientist J.R. Quinlan in 1979.

◉ Unity Hands On
Decision Trees

In this workshop we create a very simple decision tree for an RTS AI game opponent that will decide on its strategy based on the map layout. The decision being made is about whether or not to give priority to mining for minerals and gas instead of building defenses or attacking the enemy. Based on the amounts of nearby minerals and gases, the ease of entry by which the enemy can access the base, and the overall distance to the enemy, a table with all combinations of the values for each decision variable (the attributes) is drawn up. Data for decision making are shown in Table 5.5.

In this case, data are fictitious; however, they could be gathered from other human players or experience from previous games.

TABLE 5.5 Data for RTS AI build decisions

Rule	Number of mineral resources nearby	Number of gas resources	Easy enemy access to base	Distance to enemy	Give priority to mining
1	Low	High	No	Far	Yes
4	Low	High	Yes	Far	Yes
7	Low	Low	No	Far	No
10	Low	Low	Yes	Far	No
13	High	High	No	Far	Yes
16	High	High	Yes	Far	Yes
19	High	Low	No	Far	Yes
22	High	Low	Yes	Far	Yes
25	Low	High	No	Close	Yes
28	Low	High	Yes	Close	No
31	Low	Low	No	Close	No
34	Low	Low	Yes	Close	No
37	High	High	No	Close	Yes
40	High	High	Yes	Close	Yes
43	High	Low	No	Close	Yes
46	High	Low	Yes	Close	No

Step 1. Download *Chapter Five/DecisionTrees.zip* from the Web site and open the *decisionTree* scene in Unity. Play to see the decision tree constructed from data in Table 5.5. This tree is illustrated in Figure 5.15.

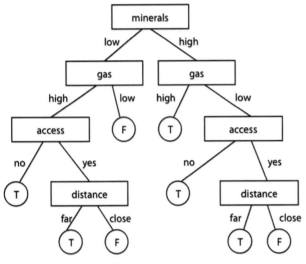

```
|num_minerals|
  <High> |num_gas|
    <High>      |True|
    <Low>       |access|
      <No>          |True|
      <Yes>         |distance|
        <Close>         |False|
        <Far>           |True|
  <Low> |num_gas|
    <High>      |access|
      <No>          |True|
      <Yes>         |distance|
        <Close>         |False|
        <Far>           |True|
    <Low>       |False|
```

Unity Demo Output

FIG 5.15 A tree graph produced from data in Table 5.5.

Note that the full code for decision tree construction using the ID3 algorithm is contained in the Plugins > ID3.cs file in the Project. The original code can be found at http://codeproject.com/KB/recipes/id3.aspx. Data have been changed to reflect the values in Table 5.5. Although we are not focusing on C# in this book, the complexities of most AI algorithms lend themselves to being written in more robust language than JavaScript. The objective here is not to teach you C# but rather to point out parts of the code you could experiment with changing should you want to create your own decision tree.

Step 2. Open *ID3.cs* in the script editor. Scroll to the very bottom of the code to find the createDataTable() function.
Step 3. First the attributes are defined. For each of these are a set of values. Data are then laid out in a table. The name of each column is the attribute name followed by a final decision column, in this case named *strategy*. Following this, each row from data is added to the table. If you want to create your own decision tree you can add as many attribute columns as you wish by following the same coding format. Just ensure that there is an associated column for each item in data. The last column, denoting a decision, is a Boolean value.

Decision trees provide a simple and compact representation of complex Boolean functions. Once constructed, a decision tree can also be decomposed into a set of rules. The beauty of the decision tree is that the Boolean functions are learned from a set of complex data that could take some time for a programmer to deconstruct manually into rules. In addition, a decision tree can be updated as the program runs to incorporate newly learned information that may enhance the NPC's behavior.

5.8 Fuzzy Logic

Fuzzy logic provides a way to make a decision based on vague, ambiguous, inaccurate, and incomplete information. For example, properties such as temperature, height, and speed are often described with terms such as *too hot*, *very tall*, or *really slow*, respectively. On a daily basis we use these terms to make decisions with the unspoken agreement as to the interpretation of such vague statements. If you order a hot coffee, for example, you and the barista have an idea for a range of temperatures that are considered hot (for coffee).

Computers, however, only understand exact values. When you set the temperature on an oven to cook a pie you give it an exact temperature—you can't tell it you want the pie just *hot*. There is, however, a type of computational logic system that interprets vague terminology by managing the underlying exactness of the computer. It is called fuzzy logic. It is based on the concept that properties can be described on a sliding scale.

Fuzzy logic works by applying the theory of sets to describe the range of values that exist in vague terminologies. Classical set theory from mathematics provides a way of specifying whether some entity is a member of a set or not. For example, given the temperatures $a = 36$ and $b = 34$ and the set called *Hot*, which includes all numerical values greater than 35, we could say that a is a member of the set *Hot* and b is not.

Classical set theory draws lines between categories to produce distinct true and false answers; for example, $b = Hot$ would equate to false. Fuzzy logic blurs the borderlines between sets (or makes them fuzzy!). Instead of a value being a member of a set, fuzzy set theory allows for a degree of membership.

To illustrate this, Figure 5.16 conceptualizes the difference between classical and fuzzy sets—the difference being that values in fuzzy sets overlap. In this example, the lower ranges of warm values are also members of the cold set. Values in fuzzy sets are given a *degree of membership* value that allows them to be partially in one set and partially in another. For example, the temperature value 34 could be 20% in the cold set and 80% in the warm set.

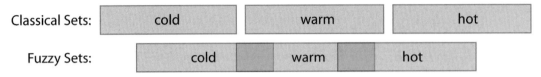

Classical Sets:	cold	warm	hot

Fuzzy Sets:	cold	warm	hot

FIG 5.16 Classical sets have distinct boundaries. Fuzzy sets do not.

A fuzzy rule can be written as

```
if   x is A
then y is B
```

where *x* and *y*, known as *linguistic variables*, represent the characteristics being measured (temperature, speed, height, etc.) and *A* and *B*, known as *linguistic values*, are the fuzzy categories (hot, fast, tall, etc.). A fuzzy rule can also include *AND* and *OR* statements similar to those in Boolean algebra. The following are examples of fuzzy rules:

```
if    temperature is hot
or    UV_index is high
then  sunburn is likely
if    temperature is warm
and   humidity is low
then  drying_time will be quick
```

Given a set of fuzzy rules and a number of inputs, an output value can be deduced using fuzzy inferencing. There are two common ways to inference on fuzzy rules: Mamdani style and Sugeno style, both named after their creators. The Mamdani style is widely accepted for capturing human knowledge and uses a more intuitive form of expressing rules.

The Mamdani style consists of four steps: fuzzification, rule evaluation, aggregation, and defuzzification. Consider the following rules by which an NPC may operate:

```
Rule 1:    if    health is good
           and   shield is adequate
           then  mood is happy

Rule 2:    if    health is bad
           or    shield is moderate
           then  mood is indifferent

Rule 3:    if    health is bad
           and   shield is inadequate
           then  mood is angry
```

Fuzzification takes inputs in the form of discrete values for the NPC's health and shield strength and fuzzifies them. To fuzzify them, we simply pass them through the respective fuzzy sets and obtain their degrees of membership.

Rule evaluation involves substituting the degrees of membership into the rules given. For example, if the value for *health is good* was 17% and the value for *shield is adequate* was 25%, Rule 1 would become:

if 17% and 25% *then mood is (17%) happy*

Only the part of the rule in the *if statement* (shown in bold) has the fuzzy values substituted. If the values are connected by an AND, the smallest degree of membership is assigned to the *then* part. If the values are connected by an OR, the larger degree of membership is assigned. Assuming *health is bad* is 50% and *shield is moderate* is 25%, Rule 2 would become:

if 50% or 25% *then mood is (50%) indifferent*

These values are then used to *clip* the fuzzy sets for happy and indifferent pertaining to mood. In brief, 17% of the happy set and 50% of the indifferent set are merged to create a new fuzzy set as shown in Figure 5.17. This is the third step of Rule Aggregation.

The final step is defuzzification. This takes the final aggregated fuzzy set and converts it into a single value that will be the fuzzy output. The final fuzzy set contains the value; all that is needed is to extract it. The simplest method for doing this is called the *centroid* technique, which finds the mathematical center of gravity of the set. This involves multiplying all the values in the set with their degree of membership, adding them together, and dividing by the sum of all the degrees of membership in the set. This gives a percentage value, in this case, pertaining to the *mood* value. For example, the result might be a 40% mood that would result in the mood being *indifferent*.

Developing a fuzzy logic engine requires a great deal of understanding in programming and mathematics. There is certainly not enough room in this chapter to provide a full example. Therefore, the next workshop uses an Open Source fuzzy logic engine called DotFuzzy (available from http://havana7.com/dotfuzzy/) written in C#.

FIG 5.17 Merged fuzzy sets.

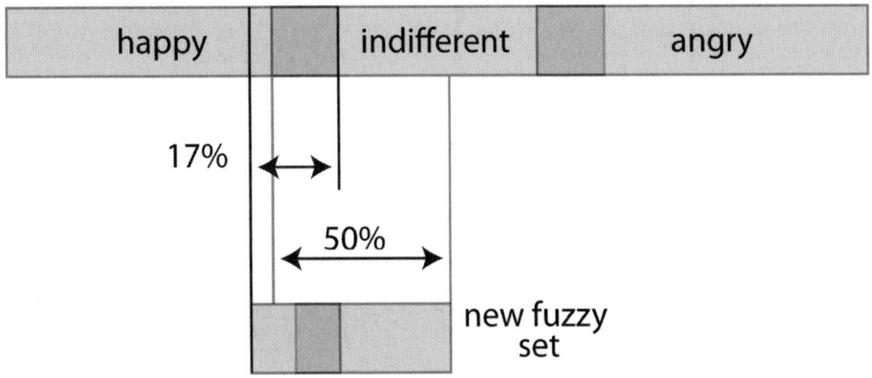

⊙ Unity Hands On

Fuzzy Logic

This hands-on session uses the DotFuzzy engine to create behavior rules for an NPC. The NPC's health and shield strength will be used to calculate its mood. Depending on its mood, it will decide to chase, attack, or ignore the player who is able to shoot at it.

Step 1. Download *Chapter Five/FuzzyLogic.zip* from the Web site and open the fuzzyAI scene. Play. You can walk around the scene and shoot spheres from the large gun being held by the player. In the middle of the environment you will find a robot. This robot has similar code to that used in the Line of Sight workshop; however, it will not attack you. The robot's health and shield strengths are displayed on the screen. If you shoot at the robot with the left mouse button, its health and shield strength will go down. If you leave the robot alone, it will recover after some time.

The DotFuzzy engine has been loaded and is in the Project Plugins folder.

Step 2. Open the fuzzyBrain JavaScript file with the script editor. The linguistic variables for the engine are defined at the top. Add the code as shown in Listing 5.21.

Listing 5.21 Implementing a Fuzzy Logic Engine in Unity

```
import DotFuzzy;
var moodValue: float = 100;
var explode: GameObject;
var health: LinguisticVariable;
var shield: LinguisticVariable;
var mood: LinguisticVariable;
var fuzzyEngine: FuzzyEngine;
var botHealth: int = 100;
var botShield: int = 100;
private var updateTime = 2; //seconds
private var lastUpdate = 0;
function OnCollisionEnter(obj: Collision)
{
    print("hit");
    var e = Instantiate(explode,
        this.transform.position, Quaternion.identity);
    Destroy(e.gameObject,2);
    Destroy(obj.collider.gameObject);
    botShield -= 10;
```

```
        botHealth -= (10 + (100 - botShield)/5.0);
        if(botHealth < 0) botHealth = 0;
        if(botShield < 0) botShield = 0;

        health.InputValue = botHealth;
        shield.InputValue = botShield;

        //set alpha color of shield relative to shield strength
        GameObject.Find("Shield").renderer.material.color =
                              Color(1,0,0,botShield/200.0);
}
function UpdateStatus()
{
        if(botHealth == 100 && botShield == 100) return;
                                    //don't bother updating
        if(botHealth > 100) botHealth = 100;
        if(botShield > 100) botShield = 100;

        if(Time.fixedTime > lastUpdate + updateTime)
        {
                if(botHealth < 100)
                      botHealth += 5;
                if(botShield < 100)
                      botShield += 10;

                GameObject.Find("Shield").renderer.material.color =
                                  Color(1,0,0,botShield/200.0);

                health.InputValue = botHealth;
                shield.InputValue = botShield;
                moodValue = fuzzyEngine.Defuzzify();
                lastUpdate = Time.fixedTime;
        }

}
function Start()
{
        health = new LinguisticVariable("Health");
        health.MembershipFunctionCollection.Add(
                new MembershipFunction("Bad", 0, 0, 20, 40));
        health.MembershipFunctionCollection.Add(
                new MembershipFunction("Moderate", 30, 50, 60, 80));
        health.MembershipFunctionCollection.Add(
                new MembershipFunction("Good", 70, 90, 100, 100));
        shield = new LinguisticVariable("Shield");
        shield.MembershipFunctionCollection.Add(
                new MembershipFunction("Low", 0, 0, 10, 50));
        shield.MembershipFunctionCollection.Add(
                new MembershipFunction("Medium", 20, 50, 60, 80));
        shield.MembershipFunctionCollection.Add(
                new MembershipFunction("High", 40, 80, 100, 100));
```

```
        mood = new LinguisticVariable("Mood");
        mood.MembershipFunctionCollection.Add(
            new MembershipFunction("Angry", 0, 0, 20, 40));
        mood.MembershipFunctionCollection.Add(
            new MembershipFunction("Indifferent", 30, 50,
                50, 80));
        mood.MembershipFunctionCollection.Add(
            new MembershipFunction("Happy", 60, 90, 100, 100));

        fuzzyEngine = new FuzzyEngine();
        fuzzyEngine.LinguisticVariableCollection.Add(health);
        fuzzyEngine.LinguisticVariableCollection.Add(shield);
        fuzzyEngine.LinguisticVariableCollection.Add(mood);
        fuzzyEngine.Consequent = "Mood";

        fuzzyEngine.FuzzyRuleCollection.Add(new FuzzyRule(
"IF (Health IS Good) AND (Shield IS High) THEN Mood IS
    Happy"));
        fuzzyEngine.FuzzyRuleCollection.Add(new FuzzyRule(
"IF (Health IS Bad) OR (Shield IS Low) THEN Mood IS Angry"));
        fuzzyEngine.FuzzyRuleCollection.Add(new FuzzyRule(
"IF (Health IS Moderate) AND (Shield IS High) THEN Mood IS
    Indifferent"));
        fuzzyEngine.FuzzyRuleCollection.Add(new FuzzyRule(
"IF (Health IS Moderate) OR (Shield IS Medium) THEN Mood IS
    Indifferent"));
        fuzzyEngine.FuzzyRuleCollection.Add(new FuzzyRule(
"IF (Health IS Bad) AND (Shield IS High) THEN Mood IS
    Indifferent"));
}
function Update ()
{

}
```

● **Note**

Defining Fuzzy Sets

Fuzzy sets are defined by four values representing the degrees of
membership of values at each quarter. These four values can be seen
in the MembershipFunction()s of Listing 5.21. Sets are drawn from four
values given such that each value represents the x coordinate on a
quadrilateral and the respective y values are 0, 100, 100, 0. The x values
will vary among sets, but the y values are always the same. Figure 5.18
illustrates the sets associated with the linguistic variable Health.

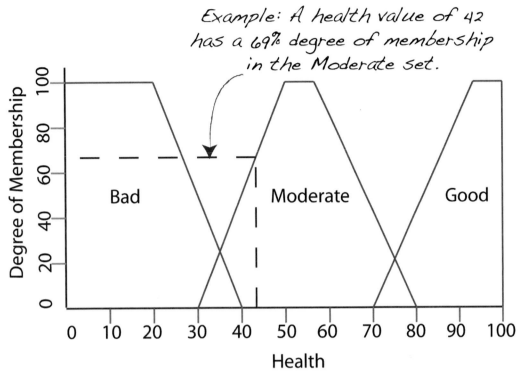

FIG 5.18 Visualizing a fuzzy set.

Step 3. Note in *fuzzyBrain.js* how the fuzzy rules are written out in an English-type manner. This allows you to write out your own fuzzy rules to suit the purposes of your NPC. Using fuzzy rules creates NPCs that are less predictable, as not even the programmer can be sure what they will do under specific conditions.

Step 4. Play. When you shoot at the robot, it will ignore you until its health and shield strength become reasonably low. When it is almost dead it will run away and wait for its strength to return. The robot model doesn't have a death animation and therefore when its health and shield reach 0 they stay at zero. You will not be able to kill it.

This workshop has provided a very brief overview of including fuzzy logic in a game environment. It demonstrates how to link the DotFuzzy engine into Unity. From this point you will be able to create your own rules and define fuzzy behaviors for other NPCs.

5.9 Genetic Algorithms

Evolutionary computing examines intelligence through environmental adaptation and survival. It attempts to simulate the process of natural evolution by implementing concepts such as selection, reproduction, and mutation. In short, it endeavors to replicate the genetic process involved in biological evolution computationally.

Genetics, or the study of heredity, concentrates on the transmission of traits from parents to offspring. It not only examines how physical characteristics such as hair and eye color are passed to the next generation, but it also observes the transmission of behavioral traits such as temperament and intelligence. All cells in all living beings, with the exception of some viruses, store these traits in *chromosomes*. Chromosomes are strands of deoxyribonucleic acid (DNA) molecules present in the nuclei of the cells. A chromosome is divided up into a number of subparts called *genes*. Genes are encoded with specific traits such as hair color, height, and intellect. Each specific gene (such as that for blood type) is located in the same location on associated chromosomes in other beings of the same species. Small variations in a gene are called *alleles*. An allele will flavor a gene to create a slight variation of a specific characteristic. A gene that specifies the blood group A in different people may present as an allele for A+ and in another person an allele for A−. Chromosomes come in pairs, and each cell in the human body contains 23 of these pairs (46 chromosomes total) with the exception of sperm and ova, which only contain half as much. The first 22 pairs of human chromosomes are the same for both males and females, and the 23rd pair determines a person's sex. At conception, when a sperm and ova meet, each containing half of its parent's chromosomes, a new organism is created. The meeting chromosomes merge to create new pairs. There are 8,388,608 possible recombinations of the 23 pairs of chromosomes with 70,368,744,000,000 gene combinations.

Evolutionary computing simulates the combining of chromosomes through reproduction to produce offspring. Each gene in a digital chromosome represents a binary value or basic functional process. A population is created with anywhere between 100 and many thousands of individual organisms where each individual is represented usually by a single chromosome. The number of genes in the organism will depend on its application. The population is put through its paces in a testing environment in which the organism must perform. At the end of the test each organism is evaluated on how well it performed. The level of performance is measured by a fitness test. This test might be based on how fast the organism completed a certain task, how many weapons it has accumulated, or how many human players it has defeated in a game. The test can be whatever the programmer deems is a best judgment of a fit organism. Once the test is complete, the failures get killed off and the best organisms remain.

These organisms are then bred to create new organisms, which make up a new second-generation population. Once breeding is complete, first-generation organisms are discarded and the new generation is put through its paces before being tested and bred. The process continues until an optimal population has been bred.

A chromosome in a genetic algorithm is represented by a string of numbers. Each chromosome is divided into a number of genes made up of one or more of the numbers. The numbers are usually binary; however, they need not be restricted to such.

Steps involved in a genetic algorithm are:

Create a population and determine the fitness

A genetic algorithm begins by specifying the length of a chromosome and the size of the population. A 4-bit chromosome would look like 1100. Each individual in the population is given a random 4-bit sequence. The population is then allocated some task. How each individual performs determines its fitness. For example, if the task is to walk away from a starting location, then individuals who walk the farthest are the fittest.

Mate the fittest individuals

The population is sorted according to fitness and the top proportions of the group are mated. This involves crossing their chromosomes to create new individuals. The process of crossover involves slicing the chromosomes and mixing and matching. For example, parents with chromosomes 0011 and 1100 with their chromosomes sliced half-way will produce offspring with chromosomes 0000 and 1111.

In nature, a rare event occurs in breeding called *mutation*. Here, an apparently random gene change occurs. This may lead to improved fitness or, unfortunately, a dramatically handicapped offspring. In evolutionary computing, mutation can reintroduce possibly advantageous gene sequences that may have been lost through population culling. Introducing new randomly generated chromosomes into the population or taking new offspring and flipping a gene or two randomly can achieve mutation. For example, an individual with a chromosome 0101 could be mutated by flipping the third gene. This would result in 0111.

Introducing the new population

The final step is to introduce the new population to the task at hand. Before this occurs, the previous population is killed off. Once the new population's fitness has been determined, they are again sorted and mated.

The process is a cycle that continues creating and testing new populations until the fitness values converge at an optimal value. You can tell when this has occurred as there will be very little change in the fitness values from population to population.

An example of a working genetic algorithm can be found in the Unity project available from the Web site as a download from *Chapter Five/GeneticAlgorithms .zip*. In this project, NPCs are programmed to navigate a maze based on genetic algorithms. Each generation has 60 seconds to explore as much of the maze as possible. The ones that explore the most are bred for the next generation.

Each NPC does not know what the maze looks like. It only has information on its current surrounding area. This information is coded into a binary sequence. From the NPC's location what is to the left, front, and right of it are recorded. Take, for example, the layout in Figure 5.19. To the left is a wall, to the front is a wall, and to the right is free space. This is coded with a 1 for a wall and a 0 for a space. In this example, the code would be 110 (wall to left, wall in front, and space to right).

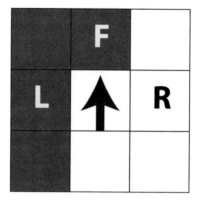

FIG 5.19 An example maze layout.

The NPC has four actions available to it: move forward, turn left and move forward, turn right and move forward, and turn around and move forward. These are coded into the NPC's chromosome as 1, 2, 3, and 4 for each action, respectively.

Returning to the maze layout, at any position the NPC could be faced with one of six layouts. These being:

1. [0,0,0], no walls
2. [0,0,1], a wall to the right
3. [0,1,1], walls to the front and right
4. [1,1,1], walls left, front, and right
5. [1,0,0], a wall to the left
6. [1,0,1], walls to the left and right

For each possible maze configuration, the NPC has an associated action. In this case, the NPC's DNA is six chromosomes long. An example is shown in Figure 5.20.

In Figure 5.20, if the NPC encounters a wall to the right only, its associated action is 2, meaning turn left and move forward. In the case of a wall to the

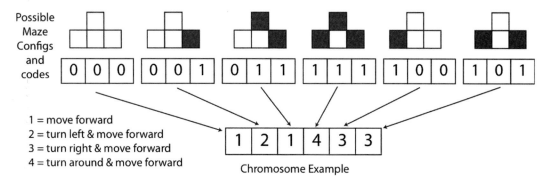

1 = move forward
2 = turn left & move forward
3 = turn right & move forward
4 = turn around & move forward

Chromosome Example

FIG 5.20 All possible maze configurations and an example NPC DNA string.

front and right, the action tells the NPC to move forward. This is obviously a bad choice, but nonetheless, the NPC has nothing to go on but the actions provided in its DNA. The fewer times an NPC's DNA leads it into a wall, the farther it will get exploring the maze.

In the beginning, 100 NPCs are created each with random DNA setting. The NPCs are allowed to explore the maze. The ones that get the farthest will have DNA sequences that allow them to move farther. These are the ones kept for breeding. Now and then mutations are thrown in to create DNA sequences that may not occur from the natural selection process. Results from 10 generations of this program are shown in Figure 5.21. Feel free to download the code and play around with it for yourself.

5.10 Cellular Automata

Many strategy and simulation games are played out on a grid. The best example is *SimCity*. The AI running beneath *SimCity* is a cellular automata. In short, a cellular automata is a grid of cells with associated values where each value is updated constantly by the value in neighboring cells. *SimCity* uses this mechanism to decide what happens in associated cells based on what the player is doing. For example, if the player puts a nuclear power plant in a particular location, any mansions in surrounding cells become worthless and soon the occupants will move out. Cells between an apartment block and the bus stop will affect the distance the occupants must travel to work and also the occupancy rate. Such a simple AI mechanic can create some very complex-looking relationships.

One of the most famous cellular automata is the *Game of Life* developed by researcher John Conway in 1970. It is an infinite 2D grid of cells. Each cell can be in one of two states: dead or alive. The state of the cell is based on

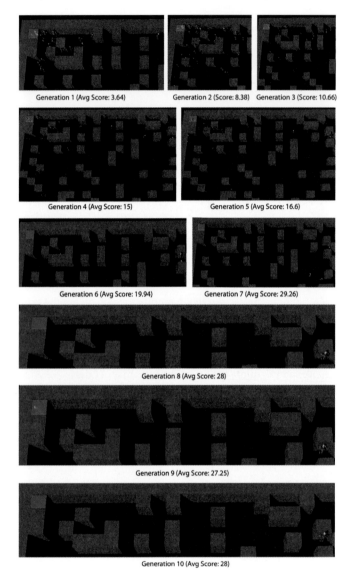

Generation 1 (Avg Score: 3.64) Generation 2 (Score: 8.38) Generation 3 (Score: 10.66)

Generation 4 (Avg Score: 15) Generation 5 (Avg Score: 16.6)

Generation 6 (Avg Score: 19.94) Generation 7 (Avg Score: 29.26)

Generation 8 (Avg Score: 28)

Generation 9 (Avg Score: 27.25)

Generation 10 (Avg Score: 28)

FIG 5.21 A maze exploring genetic algorithms over 10 generations.

the states of its closest eight neighbors. Each update, the status of the cell is calculated using four rules. These are:

1. If the cell is alive but has less than two alive neighbors, it dies
2. If the cell is alive and has two or three alive neighbors, it remains alive
3. If the cell is alive but has more than three alive neighbors, it dies
4. If the cell is dead but has exactly three alive neighbors, it becomes alive

In the same way that the simple flocking rules create complex behaviors, so too does the *Game of Life*. An example run of the *Game of Life* is shown in

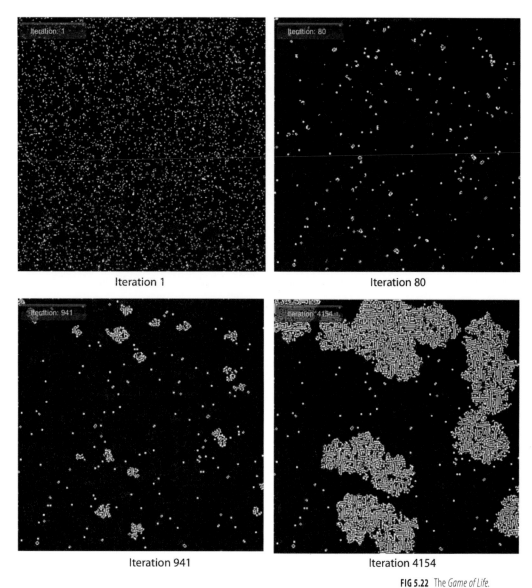

Iteration 1

Iteration 80

Iteration 941

Iteration 4154

FIG 5.22 The *Game of Life*.

Figure 5.22. The Unity project for this can be downloaded from *Chapter Five/CellularAutomata.zip*.

5.11 Summary

This chapter has given a broad but brief introduction to some of the AI techniques used in games. There are numerous other AI techniques, such as neural networks and Bayesian networks, that have not been covered. Many of the topics are complex mathematically; if you require a deeper understanding of the domain, there are many good books available dedicated to the topic.

● On the Web

If you are interested in checking out some more uses of AI in games, the author highly recommends these Web sites:

- http://aigamedev.com/
- http://aiwisdom.com/

For now though, it is hoped that you've come to appreciate the beauty of AI in the examples contained herein and opened up a new realm of possibilities for implementation of these mechanics in your own games.

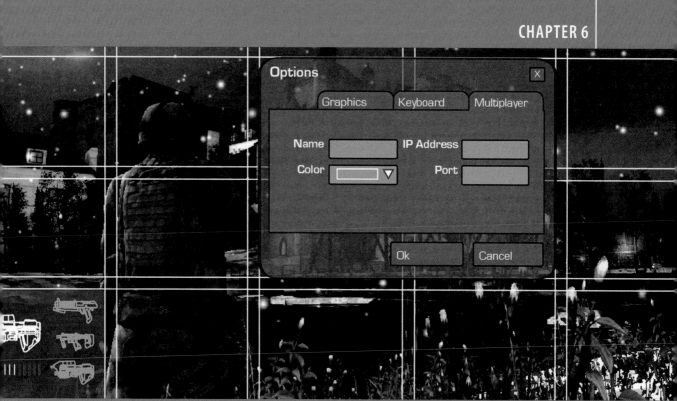

CHAPTER 6

Player Mechanics

You have to learn the rules of the game. And then you have to play better than anyone else.

Albert Einstein

6.1 Introduction

We've already examined numerous ways for the player to interact with the game environment. One of the easiest methods is to let the physics engine do all the work for determining how the player's avatar collides and moves game objects. Before physics engines, this was probably one of the more difficult and laborious jobs in programming the player mechanics.

Players require feedback from the game in order to determine their status and progress. This could be in the form of a heads-up display (HUD) that informs them of their health, money, enemy location, and much more. One of the first classic HUDs that comes to mind is that from *Wolfenstein*. The bottom of the screen shows the player's health, the weapon they are carrying, the weapons they have in their possession, and a comical image of the player's face. The face changes from a determined *bring-it-on* expression through various phases until bloody and exhausted. The facial expression is synchronized with the player's health value, giving a visual representation to a numerical value.

A visual representation of the player's status is a common way to relay information from the game to the player. For example, hovering the mouse over a unit in *Starcraft* presents a small health bar from which the player can immediately determine the viability of the unit. Instead of giving the player a health value, the visual health bar gives an almost fuzzy representation of the unit's status. It can also change from green to red when the unit's health becomes critical.

The player's status bar can be as simple as a health bar or more complex such as the dials used in *Crysis* and *Halo*. These dials allow for more complex information to be relayed to the player than just a health value. For example, in both aforementioned games, the dials provide health and shield information. A nice addition to these advanced interfaces was introduced in the original *Splinter Cell* with a meter showing how visible the player's avatar was in the environment based on its position in the shadows.

There are all sorts of numeric values stored in the game code for keeping track of the player's status. This chapter examines some of the ways of making these values accessible and user-friendly for the player.

6.2 Game Structure

It's common in software development to design flowcharts that outline the structure of software. Flowcharts can be created at many differing levels depending on the level of detail required. For example, one flowchart can show the menu and scene structure illustrating the menu items and where they go when a player selects them. At another level a flowchart can specify how the player interacts with the environment and what happens to him when he performs different actions.

Flowcharts assist in the formalization of ideas about the game and help communicate these ideas among game development team members. If you are the sole developer, a flowchart can outline the game structure and support your design process, ensuring that all menu selections go somewhere and the player is able to get from each game screen to another. You wouldn't want a player to enter a particular section of the game and then not have any way to get back!

Although there are all manner of standards used to create flowcharts, often they are made up with square and diamond shapes connected by arrows. The squares contain information or screen mockups, and the diamonds represent decisions that allow the program flow to change based on the

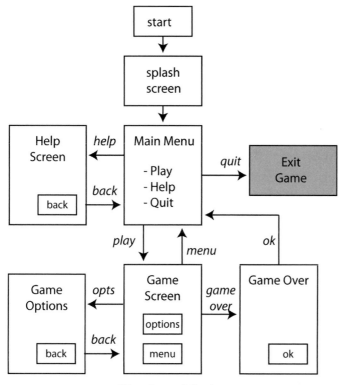

FIG 6.1 An example flowchart.

player's choices. The arrows indicate the path the player will take to get from one screen to another. A flowchart can take any form that meets your needs (Figure 6.1).

More often than not, once you've decided on the basic game and mocked up some prototypes, chances are you won't yet have created or thought about the main menu, splash screen, game over screen, etc. This is when it is best to create a flowchart to ensure that you've thought about all the game elements and possible situations that could be encountered by the player.

◁ **Unity Specifics**

Graphical User Interface (GUI) Objects

Unity has an extensive built-in set of GUI objects. You will have already experienced a number of them in previous workshops. They appear in the OnGUI() functions. For more details about these objects, have a look at the Unity documentation available at http://unity3d .com/support/documentation/Manual/Game%20Interface%20 Elements.html.

○ **Hands On**
Application Structure
In this workshop you will learn how to turn a flowchart, such as the one in the previous section, into a skeleton for a game. Each box with menu options in the flowchart becomes a scene in Unity and the scenes are linked to each other with buttons.

Step 1. Open Unity and create a new project.
Step 2. The first screen a player sees is the splash screen. This usually contains some artwork with the name of the game and/or your company logo. Unity takes care of this initial scene for you. All you need to do is supply the artwork as a single image file. If you are building for PC or Mac, Unity supplies the player with a dialog box for setting screen resolution and other preferences. For other platforms the startup will be different, for example, for iOS and Android applications, the dialog box doesn't appear, just the splash screen. If you are using Unity Indie, your splash image is replaced with the Unity logo.
Step 3. Using Photoshop or a drawing package of your choosing, create a quick splash image. Make it 256 × 256 in size.
Step 4. Drag the image into the Project in Unity.
Step 5. Select File > Build Settings from the main menu.
Step 6. On the Build Settings window, click on the Player Settings button at the very bottom of the screen. These settings will appear in the Inspector as shown in Figure 6.2.

FIG 6.2 Unity Build Settings and Player Settings.

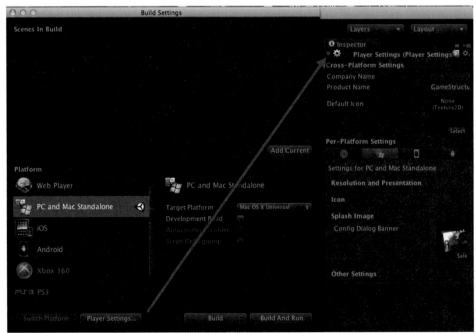

Step 7. The Build Settings window also allows you to change the target platform; for now we are building for Mac or PC. Click on Build and Run. Give the application a name and location when asked. When the application runs you will see a dialog box with your splash image, such as the one in Figure 6.3. In this part of the Inspector you can also give your application an icon image.

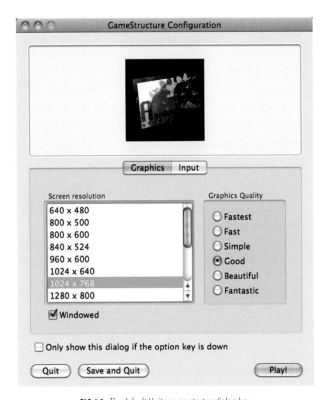

FIG 6.3 The default Unity game startup dialog box.

Step 8. This dialog box can be turned off in the Player Settings of the Inspector under Resolution and Presentation > Display Resolution Dialog.

Step 9. You've already experienced the use of scenes in Unity, but haven't created your own and linked them yet. So, to begin, let's make the current scene the main menu. Although there is nothing in the scene, save it with File > Save Scene As and call it *mainmenu*. This scene name will appear in the Project.

Step 10. Create a new JavaScript file and name it *mainmenu*. Open it in the script editor. Add the code shown in Listing 6.1.

Listing 6.1 Script to Create a Three-Buttoned Main Menu in the Center of the Display

```
function OnGUI ()
{
     GUI.BeginGroup (
        Rect (Screen.width / 2 - 50, Screen.height / 2 - 50,
        100, 150));
   GUI.Box (Rect (0,0,100,150), "Main Menu");
   GUI.Button (Rect (10,40,80,30), "Play");
   GUI.Button (Rect (10,70,80,30), "Help");
   GUI.Button (Rect (10,100,80,30), "Quit");
   GUI.EndGroup ();
}
```

Step 11. Attach the script to the Main Camera. Play. Note the menu with the buttons. Currently the buttons do not do anything. Values in the Rect() function inside each of the GUI items define the *x, y* positions of the item and then the width and height, respectively. For detailed definitions on all GUI items, see the Unity Manual at http://unity3d.com/support/documentation/Manual/Game%20 Interface%20Elements.html.

Step 12. Before we can link the buttons to other scenes, we need to create these scenes. From the main menu select File > New Scene. Then select File > Save Scene and call it *game*. In the Project you will now see two scenes (they have little unity icons next to them): *game* and *mainmenu*. Whatever assets are in Project are available for all scenes. The objects in each individual scene show up in the Hierarchy. Now you are in the *game* scene; note that the *mainmenu* code is no longer attached to the Main Camera. This is because it is a different Main Camera. This one is in the *game* scene.

Step 13. Create a new JavaScript file called *gamescenemenu* and add the code in Listing 6.2. Attach the script to the Main Camera.

Listing 6.2 Script to Set a Button to Load Another Level

```
function OnGUI()
{
     if( GUI.Button(Rect(10, 10, 80, 30), "Back"))
   {
        Application.LoadLevel("mainmenu");
   }
}
```

Step 14. The if statement around the button checks for when it is pressed. Application.LoadLevel causes another scene to be loaded. The name given to this function MUST be exactly the same as the name of the scene as it appears in the Project.

Step 15. Before testing the code, the scenes need to be linked in the build settings. Select File > Build Settings. At the top of the window is a large area called Scenes in Build. Any scenes that will be in the final game must be added to this area. You can do this by dragging the scenes from the Project into the space, as shown in Figure 6.4.

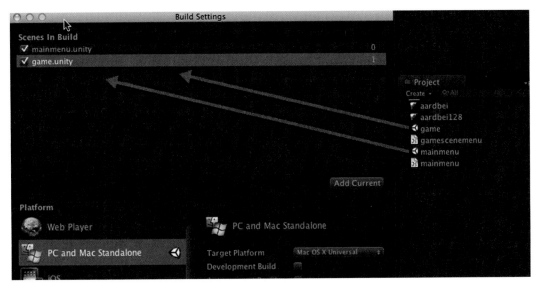

FIG 6.4 Add scenes to the game build.

Step 16. The scene at the very top is the one that will open first when the application is built and run. However, if you are in the Unity Editor, the scene currently open will be the one run. That way you don't need to navigate through the scenes each time you want to test something in the current open scene.

Step 17. With the game scene open, press Play. A Back Button will appear in the top left corner. Press the button. It will take you back to the main menu scene. Buttons on the main menu will not take you anywhere as they are not programmed to do so.

Step 18. Create another scene for the help screen and add a back button to it. Link up all menus in all scenes such that you can navigate around the game environment. The function for the quit button is Application.Quit(). It won't work in the Editor or Web player versions, but can be tested with the other platform versions.

Step 19. To modify the look of the GUI components, a style can be added. This allows you to set the color, font, and highlighting preferences for GUI elements. To explore this, open the mainmenu scene. Open *mainmenu.js* in the script editor. To the very top of the script add `var myStyle: GUIStyle;`

Step 20. Select the Main Camera in the Hierarchy and locate the attached mainmenu script in the Inspector. It will now have a style component added as shown in Figure 6.5.

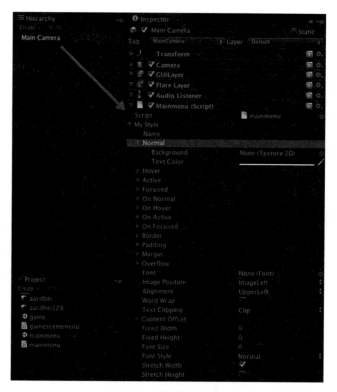

FIG 6.5 The GUI Style component.

Step 21. In the Inspector you can set all the values pertaining to the look and feel of your GUI element. For detailed information on what all these settings do, see http://unity3d.com/support/documentation/Components/class-GUIStyle.html.

Step 22. To change the font on a button, visit http://1001freefonts.com/ and download a font to use. Unzip the file and place the .ttf font file into the Project. When selected in the Project, the Inspector displays font details, including the size. This is where you can change the size as required. Ensure that you click on the apply button at the bottom if you change these settings.

If you require the same font at different sizes, drag multiple copies of the .ttf file into the Project and give them different names, such as myFontSmall or myFontBig, and set their individual sizes.

Step 23. Select the Main Camera; in the Inspector, set the Font value of *My Style* to the font just added.

Step 24. Open *mainmenu.js*. Modify as shown in Listing 6.3.

Listing 6.3 Applying a Style to a GUI Object

```
var myStyle: GUIStyle;
function OnGUI () {
     GUI.BeginGroup (
         Rect (Screen.width / 2 - 50, Screen.height / 2 - 50,
         100, 150));
   GUI.Box (Rect (0,0,100,150), "Main Menu", myStyle);
   GUI.Button (Rect (10,40,80,30), "Play", myStyle);
   GUI.Button (Rect (10,70,80,30), "Help", myStyle);
   GUI.Button (Rect (10,100,80,30), "Quit", myStyle);
   GUI.EndGroup ();
}
```

Step 25. Play. The menu will have the new font applied.

Step 26. Note that the buttons are now just text. When you apply a style, all the other stylings disappear. It's now up to you to set the background images for the buttons and other GUI objects. The default background and color are set in the Normal value of the style. Create a test image to use as the background. For now this can just be a plain black or white .jpg file. Add it to the Project and then set the Background value for Normal to this image. Play. The button now has a font and color.

Step 27. The button can be made to change when hovered over, pressed, and so on. This is done by setting the values of the other style attributes appearing below Normal in the Inspector. Note that you cannot just set the font color for these. You must set a background texture and a color, as otherwise they do not activate. Try setting the Hover values. Play.

Step 28. In the last step, creating values for button hovering will also have set them for the entire menu box. This may be an undesirable effect. You can create multiple GUIStyles and add them to whatever elements you see fit. In this case, create a separate style for the main menu GUI.Box and change it so the Hover values do not activate.

6.3 Principles of Game Interface Design

For the the most part, HUDs are displayed as 2D screen overlays whether the game is 2D or 3D. Sometimes extra essential information is displayed directly on or near a character in the game environment. For example, in *Dead Space*, a third person space game, the player's health and air values are displayed as colored bars and circles directly on the avatar's space suit.

The best-designed HUDs are ones that show the most amount of information without cluttering the screen or distracting the player from the game itself. A great majority of HUDs are designed with critical information across the bottom of the screen, synonymous with the original *Wolfenstein* and *Doom* HUDs. Extra information such as a radar appears on the left-hand side.

So where do you start when designing an interface? How do those people who design good game interfaces know how to do it? It's the same as for animation. As there are principles of animation so too are there principles for interface design. The research domain known as *graphical user interface design* has, for as many years as there have been computer screens, endeavored to analyze the interactions between human and computer and classify and categorize best practice.

The following builds on an examination of the principles of user interface design compiled by Talin at http://sylvantech.com/~talin/projects/ui_design.html and information at http://en.wikibooks.org/wiki/GUI_Design_Principles. For our purposes, this general list relating to all software applications is reworked to focus on best practice for computer games.

6.3.1 User Profiling

Before designing a HUD you need to know for whom you are designing. You should consider the player's existing skills and experience, goals, and needs.

If you are creating a serious game, chances are the players will be nongamers. In this case the interface needs to be ultraintuitive to the point of holding the player's hand through every step in the initial game play. If you are developing an Xbox game that is a sequel to an existing franchise, for example, *Assassins Creed VII*, you'd keep the interface similar to the other versions as you might expect a great deal of the players to be hard-core gamers who've grown up playing the previous six versions.

The objective of the game will also be central to your design considerations. The player's goals and needs should be clearly visible. For example, in *The Sims*, the character's needs, such as sleep and food, are clearly displayed in the bottom center of the screen, as ensuring these needs are satisfied is the main objective of the game. If the player is on a mission, these mission objectives need to be visible in addition to how close the player is to achieving them.

For example, in *Majesty 2*, a role-playing game in which the player is the ruler of the land, a single mission is split into subgoals displayed as a list in the bottom left corner of the screen. As these goals are achieved, the subgoals are visibly ticked off.

6.3.2 Metaphor

As we've already established, the human brain loves to work with patterns. Metaphors are the perfect example of how we love to liken one thing to another and how we make sense of new imagery from our experiences. The perfect example of this with respect to game mechanics and interfaces is the *play button* first appearing on original analogue sound-playing devices. The little triangle with its right-facing apex is a universally understood icon—so much so that it is used in games to indicate *play* with the meaning of either starting the game or, if in the game, unpausing it to make game time run forward. Play and its counterparts (stop, pause, rewind, and fast forward) appear in all manner of games from *Project Gotham*, *SimCity*, and *The Sims*. This recognition of well-known icons extends to other imagery in your interface. For example, a small floppy disk is often used to represent *Save* (although nowadays younger players will not have even seen a real one).

Two popular metaphors that have arisen purely within the game domain are the *space bar* for jump and holding down the *shift key* to run. Although they are not visual metaphors they are still part of the user interface and clearly illustrate how metaphors can be leveraged. Any seasoned desktop computing gamer will expect that these exist in any new FPS game without even reading the manual.

Metaphors also extend to any menu systems in the game. Since the Mac OS and Windows 3.1 moved to the menu strip across the top of applications, all desktop users, even gamers, expect to find *save* and *open* functionality under the *File* menu option.

Colors are also metaphoric. The use of the correct color immediately conveys messages to the player without words or other imagery: for example, red represents something bad, such as an error, low health, or danger; yellow represents a warning or that caution is needed; and green is good. Although the interpretation of some colors is culturally dependent,[1] these three colors are consistent globally thanks to the UNESCO Vienna Convention on Road Signs and Signals that defines the traffic light colors worldwide.

Your use of color in a game interface can represent the state of a player, object, or character. It also assists in the differentiation of game elements; for example,

---

[1] In Western culture the color white is associated with weddings and the color black with funerals. In Japanese cultural heritage, this is the opposite, with black being considered to bring good luck at weddings.

enemy characters may have different colored uniforms. Color coding will also group items, making it easier for the player to distinguish among them. An obvious example of this is *Bejewelled* in which the player must match jewels. The jewels not only have the same shape but also the same color.

Although designing an extremely new and unique interface may seem appealing, if you don't stick with well-used and-known metaphors you will just end up frustrating the player. The interface is not something you want to get in the players' way and stop them from your ultimate objective—having them play it! Navigating the interface should not be the game.

6.3.3 Feature Exposure

Unless you are developing a very simple game, displaying all player options, statuses, and inventory items on the screen at the same time is impossible. However, such information and commands should not be buried to the point that it becomes frustrating to find. Remember, the interface is not the game.

Another common metaphor linked to feature exposure is the *ESC key*. Many FPS games have this linked to the display of the main menu, making feature exposure one key press away.

In games that have toolbars that are commonly used, they always appear on the screen: for example, *Starcraft*, *SimCity*, *Civilization*, and the majority of other city building or strategy/simulation games where the player must access the toolbar constantly. However, sometimes not all features can be exposed at the top toolbar level as there may be too many and the interface would be overcomplicated. In this case the toolbar is given a hierarchical structure in which one option clicked opens up a second lot of options. For example, in *Starcraft*, selecting the build option for a space construction vehicle opens up a submenu for categories of buildings, being normal or advanced, and these provide a further submenu of the exact buildings that are available.

How you decide to expose information and options to the player should be based on what the player needs to know and do, followed by various depths of what the player may want to know and do. What the player needs to know and do will be directly related to the objectives of the game. For example, the primary objective in all FPS games is *not to die* and therefore you will always find a health indicator present on the screen.

The following game interface elements should be considered for exposure depth:

- Primary player data, including health, money, armor level, current remaining ammunition, and current weapon, should always appear on the screen.

- Primary player actions, including building, moving units, pickup item, drop item, and swap guns, should always appear on the screen.
- The toolbar (if any) should always appear on the screen. It may have a roll-out feature that extends it into a bigger toolbar.
- The main menu should be one click, key press, or button press away. In some cases, it can appear inconspicuously across the top of the game window as a fully exposed feature.
- Submenu items should be one click, key press, or button press away from their associated main menu item.
- Dialog boxes are only for displaying or gathering information as it becomes available or is required. They involve textual exchange with the player and are best kept hidden until required.
- The help screen should be accessible directly from the main screen via the use of a metaphoric button with a "?" or one click away from the main menu.

6.3.4 Coherence

Elements of your interface design should fit together both functionally and visually. For example, submenu colors and fonts should fit with the main menu colors and fonts. In addition, the game interface should match the functionality of the platform for which it has been built. For example, Xbox *Kinect* games all allow the players to stand up straight with their left arm out at 45° to call up the main menu.

Artwork, borders, colors and fonts of toolbars, menus, buttons, and other interface items should follow a common theme. For example, *The Sims* interface is instantly recognizable by its blue-on-blue color theme with round-edged windows.

Functionality should be coherent in that the same commands in different areas of the game perform the same actions. If you can click an X in the top right of a window to close it, all windows should allow for it. Any buttons that do the same thing should be named the same. For example, another metaphoric example in interfaces is the "Ok" button. If you are using an "Ok" button, don't change the capitalization on some occurrences such that it is "Ok" in one window and "OK" in another and don't change it to be "Yes" somewhere else.

An example of bad coherence in game interface design is exposed by Marcus Andrews in his Gamasutra article *Game UI Discoveries: What Players Want* (http://gamasutra.com/view/feature/4286/game_ui_discoveries_what_players_.php). *Far Cry 2* has a very elegant and embedded interface. Player status and information are built into displays in the 3D environment. For example, a radar system is built into the player's weapon, the player's hand can be revealed holding a compass, and bullets can be dug out of the player's arm as he recovers (all in 3D). Where the coherence fails is in the 2D messages that appear on the screen to give player status updates.

While the 3D part of *Far Cry 2* nicely immerses players into the 3D environment where for a while they are brought back to the reality that they are looking through a 2D screen, it is not practical for all elements.

While we are on the subject of 2D versus 3D, it has been cool in the past to create 3D menus. In reality, these just do not add anything. They become difficult to read and skew any images placed on the surface.

6.3.5 State Visualization

For players, being able to see their status clearly is paramount, which is why player health for FPS games is the largest item shown in the screen, money is always visible in RTS, and the player's position and lap times are highlighted on the screen in racing games.

In addition to primary information, the interface should act like other software interfaces in that it shows players their current choice. For example, if they have selected a particular building in an RTS its information is shown somewhere on the screen, including its name, units it can produce, its health, and other functions. In addition, the selected item is accompanied by a highlighted square around it or it changes color to indicate that it is currently selected.

For functionality that is in the game, but not necessarily available at the time, grayed out images or buttons should be used. These can be accompanied by a comment about why they are grayed out to assist the player. For example, in *EVE Online*, players may not be able to buy a particular ship because they don't have the training to fly it. In such a case, ways to acquire the relevant training are given to the player.

6.3.6 Shortcuts

Learning keyboard shortcuts is synonymous with learning what the buttons on a game controller control. These shortcuts allow players to get to regularly used functionality or to information embedded in the menu system or toolbar and usually require some clicking action to achieve. Players will use shortcuts to perform game actions more quickly.

In regular software applications, shortcut keystrokes reflect their name and location in the menu system; for example, in Windows, ALT + F opens the File menu and CTRL + S saves the current document.

If possible, shortcuts should meet with any metaphors already in the space: for example, ESC for the main menu.[2]

---

[2] *Starcraft* uses F10 for the main menu!

6.3.7 Layout

The display of the player interface on the screen should follow graphic design principles. This assists the player develop a spatial sense of the layout, which enhances his performance. Things to consider in your design include the presentation of key information in prominent locations, using sizing and contrast to distinguish elements, grouping related actions and data, and using fixed locations for certain types of information and actions. In addition, the layout should be well organized. Graphic designers use a grid system of evenly spaced horizontal and vertical lines to group and align related components.

This key principle is known as CRAP (contrast, repetition, alignment, and proximity). Contrast makes some elements more dominant than others and more important items easier to find on the screen. Repetition refers to the repeated use of design elements, such as using the same font, sizing, and colors. This creates unity and consistencies, making the interface appear whole. Alignment connects the elements and creates a visual flow for the eye to follow. Proximity refers to grouping similar and related elements of the interface in the same place on the screen.

Furthermore, to add with alignment, the screen is ruled into equal-sized parts with smaller gutters dividing each area. How many sections you need on the screen is entirely up to you. If the smallest area holds your smallest screen object, then larger objects can span multiple areas.

An example screen layout illustrating the CRAP rule with ruled sections is shown in Figure 6.6. Contrast is achieved through the use of a white and gray color scheme. It is sometimes difficult in FPS environments to display information on the screen without a background color as the text can get lost in the 3D scene behind it. In this case, a partially transparent gray is used to define the edge of the HUD and also give more definition to the white text. Never use black text on a HUD without a background, as it is almost impossible to see. Buttons and textboxes also have contrast between the fill color and the outline. In addition, contrast is used in the weapon selection area to distinguish between the current weapon and other weapon choices. Repetition occurs in the reuse of the same font for all the text, the same color for items, the shape of items, and the graphical bar used to represent the health and armor strength. Alignment is achieved through the use of ruled lines. These lines make it clear where things are placed on the screen, taking away any guesswork. The text and input boxes on the Options window are also aligned. Textboxes should all be the same size and text labels left aligned to meet the box. In other designs you may find the text label above the box. Finally, proximity is achieved by grouping related elements. Information important to the player, that being their health and armor strength, is positioned together with weapon selection nearby.

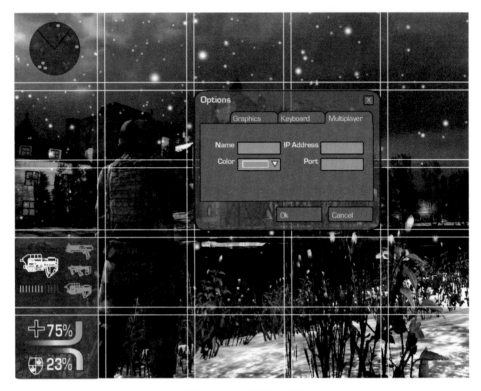

FIG 6.6 An example HUD for an FPS.

6.3.8 Focus

The HUD displays the player status and other information but should also draw the eye to any critical changes made to the interface. Color changes and animations work best for attracting the player's attention. The interface in Figure 6.6 uses global colors for danger, caution, and good to represent the player's health and armor strength. In addition, red is used to display spent ammunition cartridges. As the player's health becomes critical, the health value or bar could blink on and off to further attract the attention of the player.

A blatant way to attract the player's attention is to present a pop-up window, which stops him from playing. A well-known example of this is the Xbox's "Saving. Do not turn off your console" warning.

6.3.9 Help

It goes without saying that a game should present the user with help on how to play. In her book *The Art of Human Computer Interface Design*, Brenda Laurel lists five basic help needs an interface should be able to provide the user: goal oriented, descriptive, procedural, interpretive, and navigational.

With respect to a game, you should attempt to fulfill these needs [in order] to translate to the following player questions.

1. What is the goal of this game? What is my immediate goal? What should I be doing right now? The goal of the game should be immediately clear from the beginning. Most games provide a backstory video clip, whereas others have tutorial levels that step the player through the game. For example, *Halo* provides a video scene explaining some of the game goals up to the point when the Master Chief is first thrown from the helicopter, whereas *SimCity* holds the player's hand through a step-by-step tutorial.

2. What are these options and what do they do? Not all icons used in the HUD will be metaphor related, and therefore players may not know what will happen if they click on certain buttons in a toolbar. To assist players, most games, especially RTS that have numerous toolbars and even layered toolbars, include mouse over tooltips. They don't appear straight away, but are timed for when players hover too long over a button or some element of the game environment.

Some tutorials ease players into options by making them available one at a time after each is explained and used. In other games, making new options and game actions available is part of the game. In *Alice Greenfingers*, a market gardening game, the player starts out only being able to dig, plant seeds, water, and pick the crop. As players gain more experience, they are given more types of seeds to plant and different farming implements to use. Each time one is introduced it is explained.

3. How do I perform certain actions in the game? Answering this with your interface requires some intuition and mind reading on the part of your game. If it is a very complex environment it could be impossible to know what the player wants to achieve. In a puzzle game, however, where there are limited options on what the player's next move will be, the game can provide hints on the next best move by monitoring the player's progress. In the iPad game *Fishdom*, the player can raise money to put fish in their virtual aquarium by playing a *Bejewelled*-type puzzle game. When players stop interacting with the puzzle game, they are presented with the next best move after a short period.

4. Why did that happen? The feedback mechanisms within the game environment should always endeavor to explain anything that has occurred in the game environment. This can occur passively; for example, if a player steps on a mine and gets blown up, resulting in his health value going down, it is obvious what happened.

Continued

However, if the player's status changes without any environmental feedback or visual clues, more active explanations are required. For example, in the RTS kingdom building game *Stronghold*, the player's economic status is linked to the population of the kingdom. If people leave the kingdom, something not necessarily observed by the player, they start to lose money. As villages start to leave, the game displays information on the screen informing the player that his population is dropping and he needs to act fast to increase it again. The game also gives hints on how this might be achieved.

SimCity also does this through the team of virtual mayoral advisers. On first starting a city, Mr. Neil Fairbanks pops up asking the player if he wants some help. Later in the game, as pollution and power become issues, other advisers come along to help. Instead of anticipating what the player is trying to do, they give advice on the state of the player's city.

5. Where am I? This question needs to be answered on two levels. First the player might be lost in the game environment itself or might be lost in the toolbar or menu system. To address the first, minimaps, compasses, or a zooming in and out capability can be added to the game to assist the player to navigate. Sometimes the actual navigation can be the goal of the game, in which case, this type of help should not be supplied.

For the latter, menu and toolbar navigational aids are rare in games. Unlike software such as Microsoft Word or Adobe Photoshop where the help search will provide a set of instructions and illustrations as to where to locate certain commands and actions, games do not tend to do this—at least not in the game environment itself. This type of information is usually supplied in the paper manual accompanying the physical purchase of the game or in digital format online. While this type of information is not part of the HUD or game interface, it is indeed something that should be considered as ancillary information to accompany your game.

◁ **On the Web**
You can check out some really good HUD designs online at http://feedgrids.com/originals/ post/a_look_through_14_beautiful_video_game_hud_designs.

6.4 Inventories

Inventories are a game mechanic that spans numerous game genres. Basically they are a list of items players have in their possession. In *The Sims*, each Sim has an inventory of items such as books, food, and other objects they can take with them to different locations. If a Sim is required to deliver a parcel, it is added to their inventory. When they arrive at the parcel's destination, it is removed. In *Splinter Cell*, the player's character Sam Fischer carries quite an arsenal around with him.

Inventories can be a fixed size, allowing only a finite number of items or infinite items. In the *Dungeons and Dragons* classic title *Eye of the Beholder*, characters could only carry several items. In order to take on another item, the player had to decide which item to discard to make way for the new one. This inventory size restriction adds a new mechanic all of its own where players must preference the items they have. In *Doom*, the player could have up to six weapons (each switchable with the keys 2–7 on the keyboard), whereas in *Halo*, if Master Chief picks up a weapon, the current weapon is thrown away (with the exception that sometimes he can brandish a gun in each hand).

One example of a very complex inventory is the one players have in *EVE Online*. Players can have multitudes of ships, minerals, ship parts, and blueprints in their possession. And these aren't all in the same location. Minerals and parts can be on ships and ships can be docked on different planets. It is quite a feat of logistics to manage the location of items and ships to facilitate the most efficient game play.

In the following workshop you will create a *Doom*-like scenario with a user interface and fixed size inventory in which the player collects colored keys to open the same color doors.

☉ Hands On

Step 1. Download and open *Chapter Six/Inventory.zip*. Open the file in Unity and open the scene called *maze*. Play. The Unity default third person avatar will appear in front of a large red door. This door is the entry to the maze. The player will need a red key to open the door.

Step 2. There is a key model in the Project. Add it to the hierarchy and position it on the ground somewhere near the avatar but far enough away that the player will have to walk over to it. Change the material color to make the key red. Change the name of the key instance in the Hierarcy to *RedKey*.

Step 3. Create a new tag called *key*. Give RedKey this tag.

Step 4. Add a box collider to the RedKey.

Step 5. Create a new JavaScript file called *pickup*. Add the code shown in Listing 6.4.

Listing 6.4 Picking up a Collided-with Object

```
var attachPoint: GameObject;
function OnControllerColliderHit (hit : Controller
  ColliderHit)
{
    if(hit.gameObject.tag == "key")
  {
            Destroy(hit.gameObject.collider);
            hit.gameObject.transform.parent =
            attachPoint.transform;

  }
}
function Update () {
}
```

Attach this script to the 3rd Person Controller in the Hierarchy. The OnControllerColliderHit() function works in the same way as OnCollisionEnter(). It is a specific collider function for the Character Controller component that is part of the 3rd Person Controller.

Step 6. With the 3rd Person Controller selected, locate the script in the Inspector. You will see the exposed value for attachPoint. This is being used in the script as the transform to which the key will be attached. Essentially, the avatar will pick up the key and it will appear to be attached in the same location as the current wrench. If you look through the hierarchy of the 3rd Person Controller you will see that the wrench model is attached to *Bip001 R Hand*. Therefore, we want this to be the parent of the key after the player has walked over the key. As shown in Figure 6.7, set the *Bip001 R Hand* object to the attachPoint variable by dragging it from the Hierarchy onto the value in the Inspector.

Step 7. Note that the key's collider is destroyed to stop it interfering with the character's collider after it is picked up.

Step 8. Play. Walk the avatar over the key. It will be picked up—sort of. It will be attached to the avatar and move in time with the wrench in the avatar's hand. It just won't be aligned so nicely.

Step 9. To fix the alignment of the key, play the game and walk the avatar over to pick up the key. Press pause. Switch to the Scene view. Change the view around to zoom in on the key. Now translate, rotate, and scale the key until it fits neatly in the avatar's hand, as shown in Figure 6.8. Write down the values for the RedKey transform in the Inspector. Stop playing.

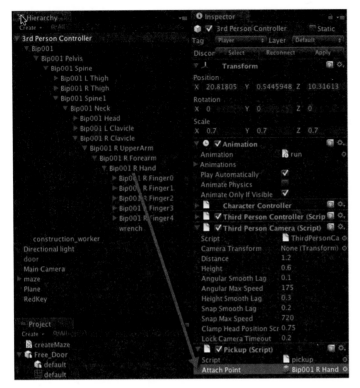

FIG 6.7 Setting an attach point for an object.

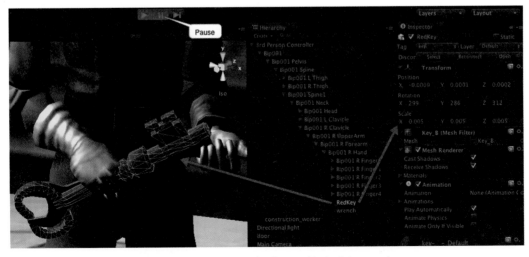

FIG 6.8 Determining positioning values for game objecting during game play.

Step 10. Using the values you wrote down, hard code the new positioning information into the key pickup code as shown in Listing 6.5. These values set the local transform of the key. It will still move with its parent, the right hand.

Listing 6.5 Setting the Local Transform for a Child Game Object

```
var attachPoint: GameObject;

function OnControllerColliderHit (hit :
  ControllerColliderHit)
{
     if(hit.gameObject.tag == "key")
   {
              Destroy(hit.gameObject.collider);

              hit.gameObject.transform.parent
                 =attachPoint.transform;
              hit.gameObject.transform.localPosition =
Vector3(-0.0009,0.0001,0.0002);
              hit.gameObject.transform.localScale =
                              Vector3(0.005,0.005,0.005);
              hit.transform.localEulerAngles =
                 Vector3(299,286,312);

   }

}
```

Step 11. Play. The avatar will now pick up the key and hold it correctly.

Step 12. Because the avatar is already holding the wrench object it seems logical that it should drop it after picking up the key. You'll then want to be able to pick it up again. The first step in achieving this is to select the wrench in the Hierarchy and set its tag to "key."

Step 13. Play. Pause the game and take note of the transform values for the wrench as you did for the key. These will be used to reset the wrench's position when it is picked up again.

Step 14. Now modify the *pickup.js* script to that shown in Listing 6.6. The code keeps a record of the currently held object with the currentObj variable. This is used to attach and drop the object.

Listing 6.6 Setting Transform Positions for Multiple Picked-up Objects

```
var attachPoint: GameObject;
private var currentObj: GameObject;
function Start()
{
     //first held object
     currentObj = GameObject.Find("wrench");
}
function OnControllerColliderHit (hit :
   ControllerColliderHit)
{
     if(hit.gameObject.tag == "key")
     {
          Destroy(hit.gameObject.collider);

          hit.gameObject.transform.parent = attachPoint.
            transform;

          if(hit.gameObject.name == "wrench")
          {
               hit.gameObject.transform.localPosition =
                    Vector3(-0.001,0.0003,0.0005);
               hit.gameObject.transform.localScale =
                    Vector3(1,1,1);
               hit.transform.localEulerAngles =
                    Vector3(13.6,332,319.1);
          }
          else
          {
               hit.gameObject.transform.localPosition =
                    Vector3(-0.0009,0.0001,0.0002);
               hit.gameObject.transform.localScale =
                    Vector3(0.005,0.005,0.005);
               hit.transform.localEulerAngles =
                    Vector3(299,286,312);
          }

          //release the previously held game object
          currentObj.transform.parent = null;
          currentObj.AddComponent(BoxCollider);

          //set currentObj to the new object - just picked up
          currentObj = hit.gameObject;
     }
}
```

Step 15. Now that the player can pick up a key, we want to make it possible for the key to open the red door. To do this, create a new JavaScript file called opendoor and open it in the script editor. Add the code shown in Listing 6.7.

Listing 6.7 Script to Slide a Game Object in the *x* Direction

```
var open = false;
function Update ()
{
      if(open)
      {
            this.transform.position.x+=Time.time * 0.01;
            if(this.transform.position.x > 21.8)
                  open = false;
      }
}
```

Step 16. Attach this script to the door object and then add the tag door.

Step 17. The script will activate when the open variable is set to true. This will cause the door to slide along its *x* axis. The open variable needs to be set to true when the 3rd Person Character walks into the door while holding the RedKey object. To make this happen, modify the pickup script to that in Listing 6.8.

Listing 6.8 Script to Activate a Game Object's Code When Collision Conditions Are Met

```
var attachPoint: GameObject;
private var currentObj: GameObject;
function Start()
{
      //first held object
      currentObj = GameObject.Find("wrench");
}
function OnControllerColliderHit (hit : ControllerColliderHit)
{
      if(hit.gameObject.tag == "door")
      {
            if(currentObj.gameObject.name == "RedKey")
                  hit.gameObject.GetComponent ("opendoor").
                  open =
                                    true;
      }
      else if(hit.gameObject.tag == "key")
```

```
    {
            Destroy(hit.gameObject.collider);

            hit.gameObject.transform.parent = attachPoint.
                transform;
...
```

Step 18. Play. The door will only open when the player walks up to it holding the RedKey object.

At the moment it is obvious which object the character is holding because it is visible in its hand. However, should the character be able to carry multiple objects, they won't all be visible in the 3D environment all of the time. Therefore, a graphical interface will be created to indicate which items the character has picked up.

Step 19. Create a new JavaScript file called *gui* and add the code shown in Listing 6.9.

Listing 6.9 A Simple GUI Indicating Inventory Items

```
var redkey : Texture2D;
var bluekey : Texture2D;
var yellowkey : Texture2D;
var greenkey : Texture2D;
var greykey : Texture2D;
var theRedKey: GameObject;
var theBlueKey: GameObject;
var theYellowKey: GameObject;
var theGreenKey: GameObject;
var theWrench: GameObject;
function OnGUI ()
{
        GUI.BeginGroup (Rect (Screen.width/2.0 - 120,
                        Screen.height - 80, Screen.width,
                        240));
        GUI.Box (Rect (0,0,240,80), "");
        GUI.Box (Rect (3,3,75,75),"Health");
        GUI.Box (Rect (83,3,75,75),"Pic");

        //keys in inventory
        if(theRedKey)
            GUI.Box (Rect (160,3,35,35), redkey);
        else
            GUI.Box (Rect (160,3,35,35), greykey);

        if(theBlueKey)
            GUI.Box (Rect (200,3,35,35), bluekey);
        else
            GUI.Box (Rect (200,3,35,35), greykey);
```

```
        if(theYellowKey)
                GUI.Box (Rect (160,42,35,35), yellowkey);
        else
                GUI.Box (Rect (160,42,35,35), greykey);

        if(theGreenKey)
                GUI.Box (Rect (200,42,35,35), greenkey);
        else
                GUI.Box (Rect (200,42,35,35), greykey);

        GUI.EndGroup ();
}
```

Step 20. Attach this script to the Main Camera.

Step 21. Select the Main Camera in the Hierarchy and locate the script in the Inspector. The script requires five images to be added for the values of the colored keys. A file called *Chapter Six/keys.zip* with the images for these can be downloaded from the Web site or you can create your own. Place the key images in the Project and drag each over to the Inspector to match the places in the script as shown in Figure 6.9. This script allows for an inventory of four keys.

FIG 6.9 Adding images for the keys into the GUI.

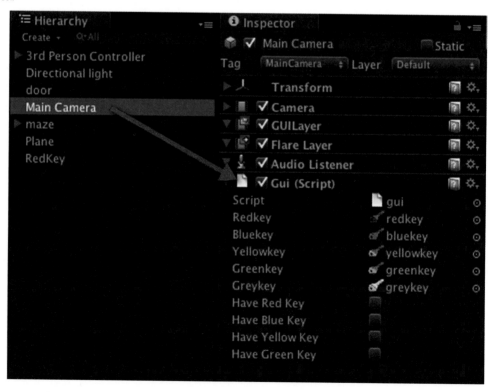

Step 22. There are also five pickup objects at the top of the script, which will hold onto the wrench and keys that have been picked up. When a game object exists, the associated colored key icon will appear in the GUI.

Step 23. Open *pickup.js* and edit the code as shown in Listing 6.10 to cause the red key icon to turn on when the character picks up the red key.

Step 24. The new script will set the haveRedKey Boolean value in the *gui.js* script to a value of true when the RedKey is picked up. This will cause the GUI to display the red key icon in place of the grayed out one. Play to test it.

Listing 6.10 Setting a Boolean Value for the Inventory

```
var attachPoint: GameObject;
private var currentObj: GameObject;
...
function OnControllerColliderHit (hit : ControllerColliderHit)
{
 if(hit.gameObject.tag == "door")
 {
     ...
 }
 else if(hit.gameObject.tag == "key")
 {
     ...

  if(hit.gameObject.name == "wrench")
  {
      ...
   else
   {
   hit.gameObject.transform.localPosition =
       Vector3(-0.0009,0.0001,0.0002);
   hit.gameObject.transform.localScale =
       Vector3(0.005,0.005,0.005);
   hit.transform.localEulerAngles =
       Vector3(299,286,312);

   if(hit.gameObject.name == "RedKey")
   {
   Camera.main.GetComponent("gui").theRedKey =
                                   hit.gameObject;
}
...
```

Step 25. To test out another key, duplicate the RedKey in the Hierarchy. Move its position in the environment. Rename the key *GreenKey.*

Step 26. Create a green-colored material and place this on the GreenKey object so that it appears green.

Step 27. Modify *pickup.js,* just below the previous change, to register the GreenKey being picked up as shown in Listing 6.11.

Listing 6.11 Picking up Another Inventory Item

```
. . .
else
{

    hit.gameObject.transform.localPosition =
        Vector3(-0.0009,0.0001,0.0002);
    hit.gameObject.transform.localScale =
        Vector3(0.005,0.005,0.005);
    hit.transform.localEulerAngles =
        Vector3(299,286,312);

    if(hit.gameObject.name == "RedKey")
    {
      Camera.main.GetComponent("gui").theRedKey = hit.
        gameObject;
    }
    else if(hit.gameObject.name == "GreenKey")
    {
      Camera.main.GetComponent("gui").theGreenKey = hit.
        gameObject;

    }
}
. . .
```

Step 28. Play. The red and green keys are not recorded as having been picked up by the character. There is now only one problem. Currently the picked-up item is being thrown away when another is picked up. We want the character to keep hold of the key. To fix this, modify *pickup.js* as shown in Listing 6.12.

Step 29. The code in Listing 6.12 will now cause any previously held object to become invisible. It will still be in possession of the character but just not seen in the game environment. Only the last picked-up item is visible.

Listing 6.12 Making a Previously Held Game Object Invisible after Picking up Another Item

```
...
if(hit.gameObject.name == "RedKey")
{
Camera.main.GetComponent("gui").theRedKey = hit.gameObject;
}
else if(hit.gameObject.name == "GreenKey")
{
Camera.main.GetComponent("gui").theGreenKey = hit.gameObject;
}
}

//---REMOVE OR COMMENT OUT LINES BELOW TO KEEP HOLD OF
//OBJECT

//release the previously held game object
//currentObj.transform.parent = null;
//currentObj.AddComponent(BoxCollider);

//make object invisible
currentObj.renderer.enabled = false;

//set currentObj to the new object — just picked up
currentObj = hit.gameObject;
...
```

Step 30. We need to provide a way for the player to cycle through held items. Using *Doom* as a model, we will use the keyboard keys 1 through 5. Modify *gui.js* to accept player input as shown in Listing 6.13.

Listing 6.13 Script to Make Inventory Items Visible When Associated Keys Are Pressed

```
var redkey : Texture2D;
...
function OnGUI ()
{
    ...
}
function ResetKeys()
{
```

```
        if(theRedKey)
                theRedKey.renderer.enabled = false;
        if(theBlueKey)
                theBlueKey.renderer.enabled = false;
        if(theYellowKey)
                theYellowKey.renderer.enabled = false;
        if(theGreenKey)
                theGreenKey.renderer.enabled = false;
        if(theWrench)
                theWrench.renderer.enabled = false;
}
function Update()
{
        if(Input.GetKeyDown("1") && theRedKey)
        {
                ResetKeys();
                theRedKey.renderer.enabled = true;
        }
        else if (Input.GetKeyDown("2") && theBlueKey)
        {
                ResetKeys();
                theBlueKey.renderer.enabled = true;
        }
        else if (Input.GetKeyDown("3") && theYellowKey)
        {
                ResetKeys();
                theYellowKey.renderer.enabled = true;
        }
        else if (Input.GetKeyDown("4") && theGreenKey)
        {
                ResetKeys();
                theGreenKey.renderer.enabled = true;
        }
        else if (Input.GetKeyDown("5") && theWrench)
        {
                ResetKeys();
                theWrench.renderer.enabled = true;
        }
}
```

Step 31. In the preceding code, note how the objects must be tested to exist before they can be made visible or invisible. Trying to make a null game object invisible will throw an error. Before testing, you will need to assign the wrench object to the script as shown in Figure 6.10, as this object is never picked up. It is the default held object. If you wanted other inventory items to be present at the start of the game you could of course add them in the Hierarchy as well.

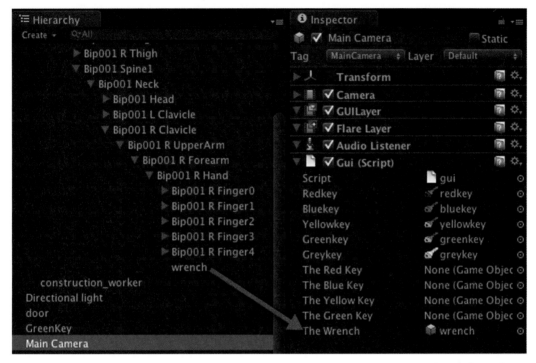

FIG 6.10 Assigning the wrench as a default inventory item.

Step 32. Key 1 for the red key, key 4 for the green key, and key 5 for the wrench will now swap the currently held game object, but only if you have the items in your inventory.

Step 33. Previous changes to the script will have disabled the red key opening the red door. Before we fix this, let's add a couple of green doors for the matching green key. Rename the existing door in the Hierarchy to RedDoor. Duplicate the RedDoor and name the resulting door GreenDoor. Use the green material from the green key to make the GreenDoor green. Duplicate the GreenDoor so that there are two. Keep their names the same. Locate the doors in the maze as shown in Figure 6.11.

Step 34. Modify *pickup.js* to test the door being collided with and the current visible key as shown in Listing 6.14.

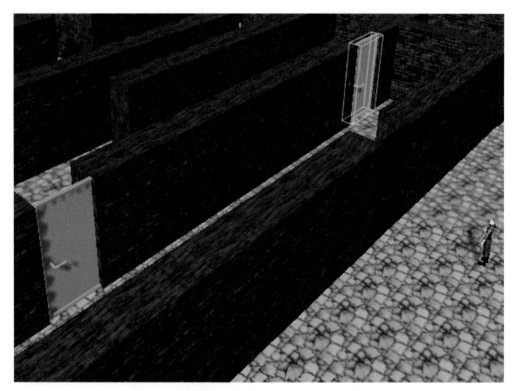

FIG 6.11 Adding green doors to the maze.

Listing 6.14 Matching the Door with the Key in Order to Open It

```
...
function OnControllerColliderHit (hit : Controller
  ColliderHit)
{
  if(hit.gameObject.tag == "door")
  {
      if(hit.gameObject.name == "RedDoor"
      && Camera.main.GetComponent("gui").theRedKey &&
      Camera.main.GetComponent("gui").theRedKey.renderer.
      enabled)
      {
          hit.gameObject.GetComponent("opendoor").
          open = true;
      }
      else if(hit.gameObject.name == "GreenDoor" &&
      Camera.main.GetComponent("gui").theGreenKey &&
      Camera.main.GetComponent("gui").theGreenKey.
      renderer.enabled)
```

```
            {
                  hit.gameObject.GetComponent("opendoor").
                  open = true;
            }
}
else if(hit.gameObject.tag == "key")
{
...
```

Step 35. Now all the code is in place for adding the yellow and blue keys; create your own yellow and blue doors and add the necessary code to complete the scenario.

To complete the GUI, the player's health and head shots are required. You can create your own head shot portraits or download ones from the Web site at *Chapter Six/health.zip.*

Step 36. Open *gui.js* and modify as per Listing 6.15.

Listing 6.15 Adding Health Portraits to the GUI

```
...
var greykey : Texture2D;
var healthOk: Texture2D;
var healthBad: Texture2D;
var healthAwful: Texture2D;
var healthDead: Texture2D;
var theRedKey: GameObject;
var theBlueKey: GameObject;
var theYellowKey: GameObject;
var theGreenKey: GameObject;
var theWrench: GameObject;
var health: int = 100;
function OnGUI ()
{
      ...
      GUI.Box (Rect (3,3,75,75),"Health");

      if(health > 75)
            GUI.Box (Rect (83,3,75,75),healthOk);
      else if(health > 30)
            GUI.Box (Rect (83,3,75,75),healthBad);
      else if(health > 0)
            GUI.Box (Rect (83,3,75,75),healthAwful);
```

```
        else
              GUI.Box (Rect (83,3,75,75),healthDead);

        //keys in inventory
        if(theRedKey)
...
```

Step 37. Select the Main Camera in the Hierarchy and locate the gui script in the Inspector. Set the values for each of the new health textures as shown in Figure 6.12.

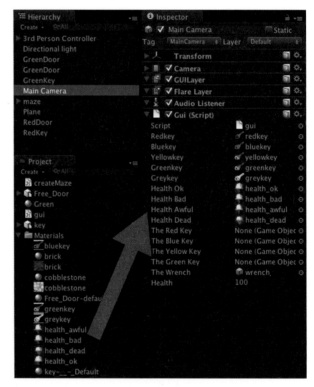

FIG 6.12 Adding character health status images to the gui script.

Step 38. Play. Because the current value of the health variable in the gui script is 100, the picture representing good health of the character will display in the GUI.
Step 39. To add the health value into the GUI, modify gui.js as shown in Listing 6.16.

Listing 6.16 Adding a Health Value to the GUI

```
. . .
var theWrench: GameObject;
var health: int = 100;
var healthStyle: GUIStyle;
function OnGUI ()
{
    . . .

    GUI.Box (Rect (3,3,75,75),"Health");
    GUI.Label (Rect (3,10,75,75),health.ToString(),
        healthStyle);

    if(health > 75)
            GUI.Box (Rect (83,3,75,75),healthOk);
    else if(health > 30)
. . .
```

Step 40. Note that the health value is using its own custom GUIStyle. This style sets the font, font color, and font alignment. Settings for healthStyle can be modified in the Inspector view for the Main Camera as shown in Figure 6.13.

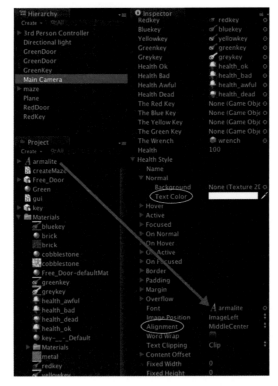

FIG 6.13 Setting custom GUI item font, color, and alignment.

Step 41. Now you will need something to reduce the health of the player in order to see the changing effect in the GUI. Select Assets > Import Package > Particles from the main menu.

Step 42. In the Project, locate the Fire1 prefab in the Standard Assets > Particles > Fire folder and drag it into the Scene as shown in Figure 6.14.

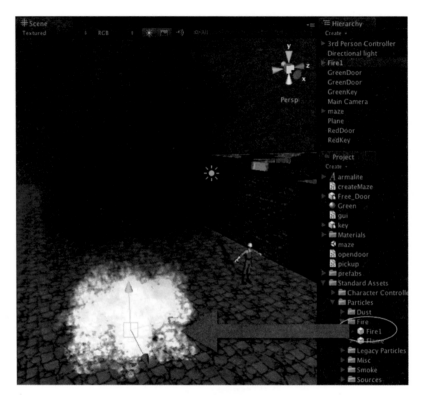

FIG 6.14 Adding a fire particle system to a scene.

Step 43. While Fire1 is selected in the Hierarchy the fire will be animated in the Scene. Because Unity will activate any particle system when selected, you can see how it changes as its properties are modified. We will examine particle systems in depth in the next chapter.

Step 44. With Fire1 selected in the Hierarchy, select Component > Physics > Box Collider from the main menu to add a collider to the fire. Modify the collider's values as shown in Figure 6.15 to enclose the fire with the box. This box will be used to determine if the player has walked into the fire.

Step 45. Check the fire's box collider IsTrigger box. This will allow the player to walk into the fire and also trigger a collision message.

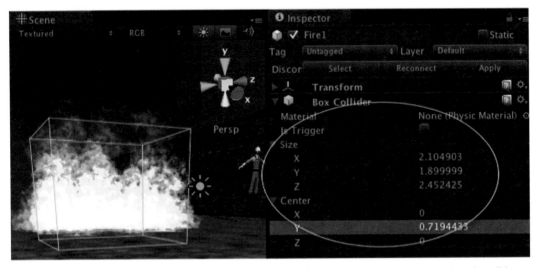

FIG 6.15 Adding a box collider to a particle system.

Step 46. Create a new tag called *fire* and set this to the tag for Fire1.
Step 47. Open *pickup.js* and add an OnTriggerStay() function as shown in Listing 6.17 to continually reduce the player's health while standing in the fire.

Listing 6.17 Using a Trigger to Determine When a Game Object Is Inside Another's Collider

```
...
function Start()
{
      //first held object
      currentObj = GameObject.Find("wrench");
}
function OnTriggerStay (other : Collider)
{
      if(other.gameObject.tag == "fire")
      {
            Camera.main.GetComponent("gui").health =
                  Camera.main.GetComponent("gui").health
                      - 1;
      }
}
function OnControllerColliderHit (hit : ControllerColliderHit)
{
...
```

Step 48. To heal the player you can add an object or another particle system that increases their health while standing inside its collider. To achieve this, add the Sparkle Rising particle system to the Scene and give it a Box Collider with IsTrigger checked. Create a tag for it called *heal*.

Step 49. The player's health can be increased while the player stands inside the sparkles by adding the code shown in Listing 6.18 to the *pickup.js* file.

Listing 6.18 Adding Another Type of Trigger and Capping the Health

```
function OnTriggerStay (other : Collider)
{
    if(other.gameObject.tag == "fire")
    {
        if(Camera.main.GetComponent("gui").health > 0)
        {
        Camera.main.GetComponent("gui").health =
            Camera.main.GetComponent("gui").health - 1;
        }
    }
    else if(other.gameObject.tag == "heal")
    {
        if(Camera.main.GetComponent("gui").health < 100)
        {
        Camera.main.GetComponent("gui").health =
            Camera.main.GetComponent("gui").health + 1;
        }
    }
}
```

Step 50. Play. You will find that health decreases in the fire and increases in the Sparkles. The extra if statements cap the health between 0 and 100.

Step 51. You can complete the scenario by adding a main menu and a game over screen, and placing keys, fires, and sparkles at a variety of locations in the maze.

6.5 Teleportation

Teleportation is a player mechanic often used to move the player's character very quickly to different locations in a map. It can happen explicitly via actual teleportation devices placed in a game environment, such as they are in *Quake*, which make it obvious that the player's location has changed or inexplicitly by which teleportation is the developer's trick for loading another game level or another part of a map. Inexplicit teleportation can occur when very large game environments need to be divided up into workable chunks the computer's processor can handle. If you play the original *Halo* you will experience this transition. When the player reaches the physical boundary of a game mesh, a shimmer falls over the screen and the next part of the map is loaded. The same type of teleportation can occur when a character reaches the exterior door of a building and the game needs to load the inside map of the building so the player can enter it and continue playing.

Both types of teleportation are examined in the next workshop.

6.5.1 Implicit Teleports

⊙ **Hands On**

Teleportation

Step 1. Download *Chapter Six/teleport.zip* from the Web site. Open the project in which you will find two scenes inside a folder called _Scenes, one called *outside* and the other *sewerScene*. The one with the sewer model is an original project downloaded from the Unity Web site. The other is a simple terrain. Open the *outside* scene.

Step 2. Play. You will have control over a first person character and be able to move around on a terrain in which there is a large factory and a door with a light above it.

Step 3. Add a cube game object to the scene. Transform, rotate, and scale the cube until it sits neatly in front of the factory door, as shown in Figure 6.16.

Step 4. Select the cube in the Hierarchy, and in the Inspector turn off the Mesh Renderer and check the IsTrigger for its box collider. This will make the cube invisible and leave just the collider as a trigger.

Step 5. Create a new tag called *toSewer* and set this as the tag for the cube.

Step 6. Create a new JavaScript file named *teleport,* add the script in Listing 6.19, and attach it to the First Person Controller.

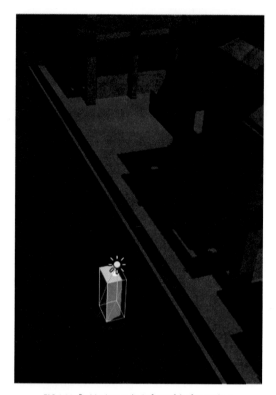

FIG 6.16 Positioning a cube in front of the factory door.

Listing 6.19 Using a Trigger Event to Teleport to Another Scene

```
function OnTriggerEnter (obj : Collider)
{
     if(obj.gameObject.tag == "toSewer")
     {
          Application.LoadLevel("sewerScene");
     }
}
```

Step 7. Select File > Build Settings from the main menu and add the *outside* and *sewerScene* scenes to the *Scenes in Build* box by dragging them from the Project.

Step 8. Play. Walk up to the factory door and you will be teleported into the sewer room. You could add any number of doors in this way to your game by giving each one its own tag and sending the player to a different scene using if statements in the OnTriggerEnter() function.

Step 9. To get back from the sewer room to the outside scene you need to replicate the previous task. Double-click on sewerScene in the Project to open it. There is a first person controller in this scene too. Note that it is not the same first person controller as the outside scene and therefore does not have the teleport code attached.
Step 10. Create a cube like the previous one and place it in front of the door at the top of the sewer room. Tag it with *toOutside*.
Step 11. Create a JavaScript file named *teleportOutside* and add the code from Listing 6.19, except replace *toSewer* with *toOutside* and change the scene name from *sewerScene* to *outside*.
Step 12. Attach teleportOutside to the First Person Controller.
Step 13. Play. You will now be able to teleport back and forth between the outside scene and the inside scene.

6.5.2 Explicit Teleports

Explicitly transporting from one location to another in the same scene works in a similar way. Now we are going to create a set of particle systems that teleport the player from one location to another.
    Step 1. Import the particles package used in the previous workshop into the current project.
    Step 2. Place a Sparkle Rising particle system on the ground near the door.
    Step 3. Add a box collider to the particle system and resize to fit around the particles.
    Step 4. Rename the particle system in the Hierarchy to Sparkle1.
    Step 5. Duplicate Sparkle1 and rename Sparkle2.
    Step 6. Place Sparkle2 somewhere else in the game environment, for example, on the roof of the factory.
    Step 7. Create a JavaScript file named *teleportTo* and add the code from Listing 6.20.

Listing 6.20 Script to Reposition a Colliding Game Object at the Position of Another Game Object

```
var to: GameObject;
function OnTriggerEnter(obj: Collider)
{
    obj.gameObject.transform.position = to.transform.
      position;
    obj.gameObject.transform.position.x =
    obj.gameObject.transform.position.x + 1;
}
```

Attach this script to Sparkle1 and Sparkle2. Any game object with a collider attached that enters Sparkle1 will automatically be teleported to the position of Sparkle2. This not only includes the player's character, but any game object that might be thrown into it. *Think portal.*

The position the player is transported to should be slightly outside the collider of the destination teleport, as otherwise the player will get stuck in an endless loop between transporters. This is why the *x* position has 1 added to it in Listing 6.20, although you could also modify the *z* position as needed.

> ● **Note**
>
> If the player falls through the floor or ground plane after teleporting it will be because the position he is teleporting to is below the ground plane. Always ensure that the teleportation object sits above the ground plane it is meant to be on.

Step 8. Select Sparkle1 in the Hierarchy, and in the Inspector set the *to* variable in the *teleportTo* script to Sparkle2 as shown in Figure 6.17.

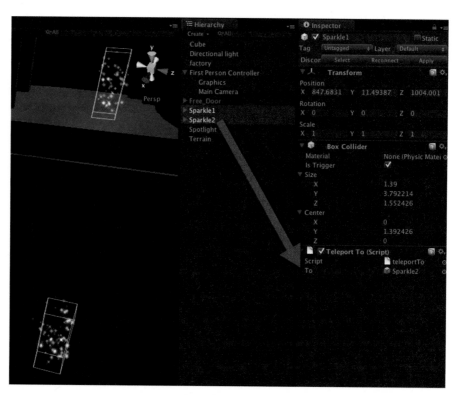

FIG 6.17 Setting objects up for teleportation.

Step 9. Now do the same for Sparkle2 except set its *to* variable to Sparkle1.
Step 10. Play. You will be able to teleport back and forth between the sparkles.

6.6 Summary

This chapter examined the parts of games impacting directly on players: user interface and interaction with the game environment. From a design point of view, user interfaces borrow many principles from the domain of graphic art. What looks good and how someone perceives visual elements in two dimensions have been studied and disseminated in art and visual communication long before computer games, and these realms hold much valuable knowledge that we can transform into digital interfaces.

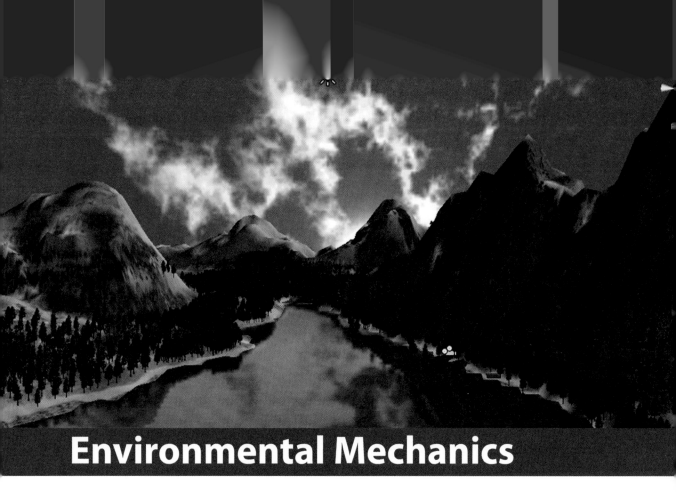

Environmental Mechanics

Environments are not just containers, but are processes that change the content totally.

Marshall McLuhan

7.1 Introduction

Probably one of the most exciting tasks in creating art assets for a game is in the designing of the game world. From moulding mountains and placing trees on a terrain to designing a high-quality building interior the task can seem enormous and daunting at first. But before diving into the design, sometimes it is a good idea to sit back and examine the way things are in the real world—how shadows fall on the ground, how natural vegetation grows, what clouds look like, and all the little details inside buildings from stains on the carpet to the emergency exit sign.

When a player is in your game environment it should be the things that aren't missing that they don't notice that will make it more believable. For example, a hospital is not a series of corridors painted gray. There are so many little details, such as posters on the walls, rubbish bins, seating areas, and clocks on the wall that make the location feel like a hospital. One of the most difficult game environments for newbies to create is an outdoor landscape. At first trees can look clumped together and awkwardly positioned, mountains impossibly steep and oddly shaped, and a lack of correct shading and shadows.

This chapter is primarily about observing how things are and applying the rules of nature and architecture to develop game environments. It begins by examining fundamental map design, followed by terrain design, using camera effects for professional-looking scene rendering, and finishes up with the creation of some simplistic but highly effective weather systems.

7.2 Map Design Fundamentals

Map design for game levels is a sizable area of discussion and rules, and opinions on the best approach differ between genre and game developers. In this section, numerous ideas have been gathered from single-player and multiplayer 3D environments. Many of these suggestions have been taken from online discussions of designers at Valve, Ubisoft, Bungie, and a variety of other blogs and postings.

7.2.1 Provide a Focal Point

In a vast map it is a good idea to provide a focal point. This will act as the player's goal location. If the terrain is rather desolate, like that shown in Figure 7.1, the player's eye will be drawn to the dominating tower. In addition, because there are no other structures or objects in the area, the player will have no choice but to go toward the tower.

In a rather busy map, a large focal object that can be seen from most places in the level will assist the player with orientation. In *Crysis*, the player is placed in a thick jungle environment with many ridges. A crumbling and trembling massive mountain is shown in the distance as the obvious goal destination. Although at times the player can become disorientated among the trees, the mountain is visible from many positions, guiding and beckoning the player toward it.

7.2.2 Guide and Restrict the Player's Movement

Although many game maps, whether they be outdoor terrains or inner city streetscapes, may seem endless, they are not. They are designed cleverly to draw a player along a certain path and restrict them access to parts of the map that aren't actually there. For example, racing games such as *Split Second* blatantly guide the player along a path—the racing circuit! The player cannot jump the barriers along the sides of the road and drive off into the distance because there is no distance. What can be seen in the distance

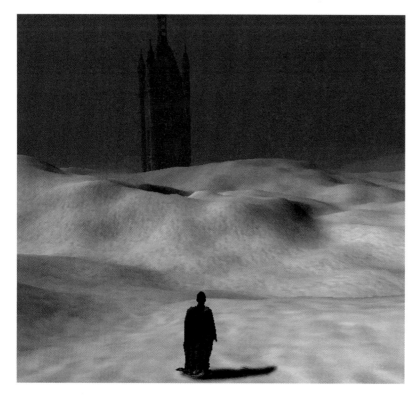

FIG 7.1 A large map terrain
with focal point.

are billboards and 3D objects with very low polycounts. As the player can
never get anywhere near these objects, having them in high definition
is a pointless waste of computer memory.

Terrain maps, such as those encountered in *Halo*, subtly guide the player
along a path where the sides are defined by steep inclines, vast drops, or
endless water.

Enemy and reward placement also push the player into moving in a certain
direction. Players of first person shooters know that they are moving toward
their goal as the number of enemies increases. If there are nonplayer
characters in a certain location, they are obviously guarding something
important and the player feels the need to investigate. Even in children's
games where there aren't such gruesome enemies, placing power-ups
or extra point pickups along the path will keep them moving in the right
direction.

7.2.3 Scaling

A recurring mistake newbie map designers make is in the scaling and
detail of an environment and the objects within it. While some people are
naturally talented at being able to create realistic-looking scenes, others

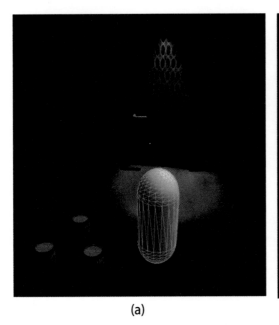
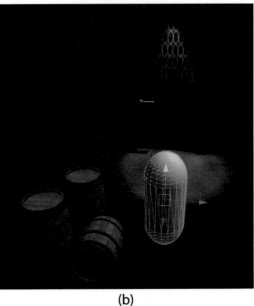

(a)　　　　　　　　　　　　　　　　(b)

FIG 7.2 A scene with barrels of different sizes.

have to work at it. The most common error is to create a huge building, terrain, or city and place tiny little objects in it.

Don't be afraid to resize an original asset. Look at the real world and the proportions of objects within it. Figure 7.2 demonstrates the unnatural-looking proportions of the barrels (a) and how they are better matched to the size of the player's character (b). If there is a door in the scene, make sure it has correct proportions with respect to the player's character. The same goes for stairs, furniture, trees, cars, and anything else in the scene.

7.2.4 Detail

As they say, "the devil is in the detail." With this in mind, the same observational prowess used for proportions should be applied to map details. Wherever you are look around at the details that make the real world seem … well … real! Have a look at the way trees intersect with the ground. They don't just look as though they are sitting on top of a pole driven into the ground. The terrain at the base is undulated from the tree's roots, the grass is higher near the base where the gardener couldn't fit the lawn mower, and there might be other interesting weeds or rocks scattered about. Even a pole that has been driven into the ground will eventually get taller grass growing at its base.

If you get a chance to look at a mountain or river view take note of where the trees and grasses are positioned and the color of the dirt. Mountains have a tree line beyond which trees do not grow because it is too cold. At this point you might find rockier ground and snow. Nearer the water

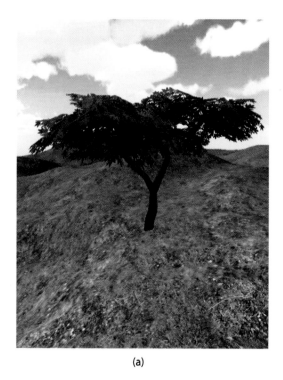

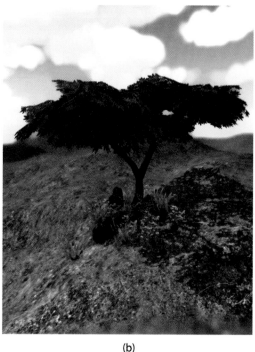

(a)   (b)

FIG 7.3 Two trees on a terrain (a) with no detail and (b) with detail.

you will find taller reeds and grasses. There is a reason why nature looks the way it does, and if you want your maps and terrain to be convincing you need to notice the little things.

Figure 7.3 contains a screen capture of two trees in a Unity scene: (a) just the tree added to a terrain and (b) the tree surrounded by detail with shadowing and other camera effects added. Note how the tree in Figure 7.3b is more convincingly part of the landscape than the one in Figure 7.3a. The idea is to strategically position objects and use special effects to remove the harsh boundary where one object meets another.

If you are creating a map based on a real-world landscape or building, go to that building. Sit and observe. Take photographs. If you're mapping the inside of a hospital, go and have a look at all the things in a hospital that make it look and feel like a hospital. The colors, charts on the walls, trolleys, exit signs, and markings on the floor, to name a few, are all symbolic things that will keep the player immersed in your game environment.

7.2.5 Map Layout

Physical map layout differs dramatically according to the restrictions of perspective, narrative, and genre. Sometimes the logical structure of the story and the game play paths from start to end match with the analytical structure of the game environment and sometimes they don't. For example, a game that is a simple *from start to end* consists of a linear story in which the player is moving through a story like an actor in a movie. Instead of being a key decision maker, the player will have a very linear game map in which the player moves from some starting position to an ending position. The level may convince the player that he has some control over his destiny with smatterings of game play; however, in the end, the real options are that the player dies or moves on at each challenge. Other open-type simulations such as *SimCity* have an evolving narrative that in no way at all dictates the physical layout of the map.

With this in mind, we examine several game-level design structures and discuss how the player's journey through the story and the actual game world are related. While each of the ones presented illustrate a single game progression strategy, it is more the case for real games to use a hybrid of the ones presented to make for a more engaging player experience. Their generalization, illustrated in Figure 7.4, herein is for academic purposes only.

Open

A truly open game map will have multiple starting positions and ending positions with numerous unordered challenges in between, as shown in Figure 7.4a. From a narrative point of view, *The Sims* is this type of game,

FIG 7.4 Game level design structures.

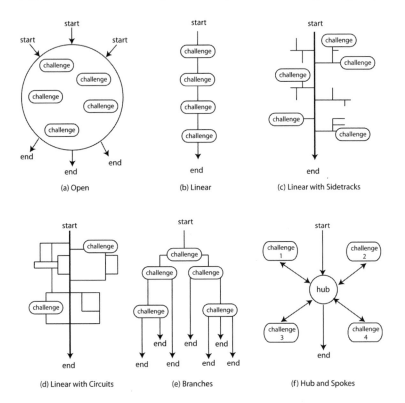

(a) Open

(b) Linear

(c) Linear with Sidetracks

(d) Linear with Circuits

(e) Branches

(f) Hub and Spokes

as you can start with any character you like, end the game when you like, and take on whatever challenges take your fancy along the way. The game environment of *The Sims* is also quite open in the way by which players can decide on the look, personality, and goals of their avatars and the layout and furnishing of their houses. The city map, however, is not open. It is physically a network structure with fixed positions of housing blocks and city buildings.

Physically speaking, the *EVE Online* maps are open with a variety of starting positions, numerous ways of traveling from one location to another, many unordered challenges, and multiple places to end/complete your journey. The players' choices in these types of games are vast. Of course the game map isn't one large infinite mesh, as it would be too big to process, but a series of minimaps cleverly linked together to give the impression of immeasurable universes.

Linear

Most games based around a story are linear; that is, they have a start, a journey, and an end (shown in Figure 7.4b). Players typically accompany their character, the hero, through a series of carefully crafted challenges to the end. The start is always the same, the journey is always the same, and the end is always the same. In terms of a map it means a game environment in which there is only one path to travel to get from the starting position to the end. Along the way there may be puzzles, barriers, and enemies to battle, but the path is always the same.

To add some interest to the linear map, sidetracks (shown in Figure 7.4c) can be added that can take players down a dead end path but provide extra bonuses or clues to aid in their progression along the main path. The danger here is that players could choose to skip an entire sidetrack unless encouraged to go down it because they have no other choice; for example, the main path might contain a locked door and the key is down a sidetrack.

Even more complexity is created when circuits (shown in Figure 7.4d) are added off the main path. These provide players with opportunities to bypass parts of the main path. They can also disorient players and send them back to the beginning. *Dungeons and Dragons* and other maze-type games are created with both circuits and sidetracks. These maze games align perfectly with the narrative and map structures, as it is the sidetracks and circuits that dictate the maze's physical layout.

Racing games are another example of a linear path with a circuit. The circuit takes the player from the start, around a track, and back to the start. The player's journey is one that evolves according to the player's racing skills; however, in the end, the game remains linear, as the start position, end position, and goal always remain the same.

Any game that has a linear story line similar to that in books and movies will require a linear map to ensure that players play through the story and live out the full life of their character. If the physical map has sidetracks and circuits, players will require a motivational story by which to choose to explore them. This can be achieved by placing side rooms or corridors off the main path that reward players' exploration with extra ammunition, health, or other items that can assist their game progress.

Branching

A level with branching has the one starting position and multiple ending positions, as shown in Figure 7.4e. Narratively speaking, this means a story that starts in the same place but has multiple outcomes depending on the player's game choices. These are difficult narratives to write, as a new story needs to be written for each branch. In addition, extra branches require extra artwork with respect to map designs. While a fork in the road might not literally represent a branch, it could mean that the player travels to another map or enters through a one-way door into another world.

If branching is used in physical terms in a game map it will mean that players can skip over a lot of game play and be content on their way to the end. On the other side, players can replay the game and take a different journey each time until they have explored all branches.

Spoke and Hub

Last but not least is the spoke and hub structure. This provides a progressive set of challenges by which the player must achieve challenge 1 to unlock challenge 2, complete challenge 2 to unlock challenge 3, and so forth. After each challenge, the player returns to the same central hub state. The single player path in *Starcraft II* is very much like this in which the player is located on a spaceship representing his home base; however, he must leave this hub to take on challenges. After each challenge, the player, if successful, has accumulated money and points and can upgrade his armada, weapons, and troops before proceeding to new unlocked challenges.

This level design structure requires numerous maps or map areas in which the challenges take place. Because of the progressing unlocking nature of the design, the player will eventually explore and experience all the game play and maps, unlike in a branching scenario.

As mentioned previously, today's games are far more complex than the preceding level structures; however, they do include elements of one or more. What is important to keep in mind is that the game does not start with the game art or map levels. It must start with a conceptual design and story, as otherwise you might find yourself developing a lot of art assets that never see the light of day.

7.2.6 Other Considerations

Player Starting Position

How often have you loaded a game level and had your character looking at a wall or the ground? Can't remember? Never? There is a reason why. The first thing players want to do when entering a game environment is to start the game. If they are facing a strange unexpected direction they will have little idea where to go next. It might be that they need only to turn around to see the door they need to go through or the corridor they need to walk down. But it is just a neater way of introducing the player to your level.

Flow

Flow in level design refers to the way in which players move from the beginning of the level to their goal. It is the level designer's job to make the environment flow as best he can to challenge players, keep them moving toward their goal, and keep them engaged. Flow is mostly dictated by the physical layout of the map as described in Section 7.2.5.

Although in the end we all know the designer is herding the player down a certain path, this need not be revealed to the player immediately. Providing players with numerous paths to take allows them to make decisions in their game play about the way they traverse the map. This creates an illusion of freedom where there is none.

Game developers, Valve, and others use a variety of methods to control the flow through the game. In some areas you will want the player to run, in others to walk. Breaking the map into narrow areas that make the player feel confined, thus increasing tension in the game play, creates *narrow flow*.

Side rooms are another common technique in 3D environments. They give the map extra areas of interest but are dead ends. The player's reward for exploring these areas is by way of extra weapons, power-ups, and other useful items. Side paths without reward don't encourage the player to explore, and thus the exercise of creating these areas in the map becomes pointless and just extra work for the artists.

Trapping

Blocking the exit of a dead end after the player has entered is another way to create tension and panic. You could use this partway through a map or at the goal location. It should be obvious that if you do trap a player in part of the level he is able to get out. Most seasoned players would expect that if they become trapped it is the end of the level, they have some puzzle to solve, or very soon they will die or be rescued.

Use the 3D Dimension

Three-dimensional environments have height as well as depth and width. A map with various height levels allows for the player to get from one place to another via alternate routes. In addition, if players can see that there are multiple heights to a building or terrain they will expect to be able to get to these heights that could be used as resting or attacking positions.

Vantage Points

Ensure that your map has multiple vantage points where the player can hide or use as an attacking position. Some might be in better locations than others and will provide players with choice and variety in the way they choose to approach the game play.

If you are designing for a multiplayer environment, then multiple vantage points will ensure that play does not become predictable and ultimately boring. In the original *Halo* multiplayer mode, there is one map in which players can teleport between two spacecraft and shoot at each other across the void. There is a nice little nook off to the side of one of the ships with a cloaking shield in it. The same location looks out across the void and is also perfect for using the sniper rifle on your opponent when they are on the other ship. The cloaking field only starts a short time, and therefore it is wise to stand near the cloaking shield until your opponent comes into view on the other ship, pick up the cloak, and start shooting. As you cannot move and use the zoom on the sniper rifle at the same time, having played the map a few times, this strategy fails as your opponent knows where you are shooting from even when he can't see you.

It is unavoidable that players will eventually explore and use up all the vantage points in a multiplayer map; however, the more variety provided, the longer the game play potential.

Map and level design are challenging for even the seasoned game developer and there are many books devoted to the topic. If you are interested in reading up on game and level design, start by reading some books dedicated to the subject, such as *Fundamentals of Game Design*, 2nd edition, by Ernest Adams.

7.3 Terrain

Terrains are meshes that make up the ground in an outdoor scene. They usually undulate in height and sport a variety of surface textures to make them look like a real outdoor desert, mountain, and even alien world scenes. The more detailed a terrain, the more polygons from which it will be made as additional vertices are required to give them a real-world smooth appearance. Because large elaborate terrains require a lot of processing, numerous tricks are employed to make the terrain look more detailed.

While there are many available tools for creating terrains, making them look real can be quite a challenge. The best examples come from nature.

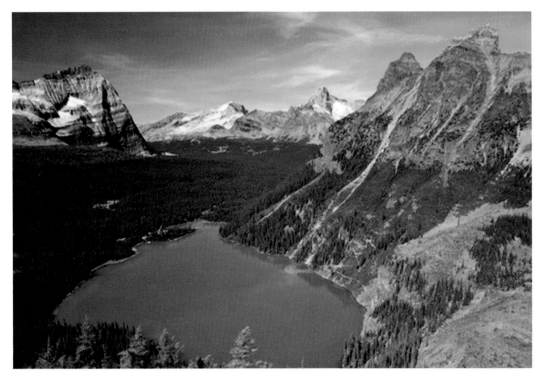

FIG 7.5 Lake Louise.

7.3.1 Drawing a Terrain

As you will find in the next section, although a terrain can be computer generated, the most detailed and realistic terrains are best created by hand. Throughout this chapter we work with the same terrain, adding differing effects to make it feel as realistic as possible. The terrain will be modeled on a photograph of Canada's Lake Louise, as shown in Figure 7.5.

⦿ Unity Hands On

Creating a Terrain

    Step 1. Open Unity and create a new project.

    Step 2. From the main menu select Terrain > Create Terrain. A large flat plane will appear in the scene.

    Step 3. Add a directional light. When creating the terrain, a directional light helps show up the definition.

    Step 4. To sculpt the terrain, select the terrain in the Hierarchy. A toolset will appear in the Inspector. The operation of the buttons is defined in Table 7.1.

TABLE 7.1 Terrain editor tools

#	Tool icon	Use
1		Raise and lower the terrain. The selected brush shape is used to emboss the terrain. Each stroke in the same place lifts the terrain.
2		Set the terrain height. This allows for the exact altitude of any part of the terrain to be set. A height of 0 is the same level as the default terrain plane.
3		Smooth the terrain. This brush allows you to smooth terrain heights between differing levels to get a smoother effect from jagged surfaces.
4		Add a texture to the terrain. This brush allows you to paint the terrain with the texture of your choice.
5		Place trees. Places trees on the surface of the terrain under the brush location.
6		Place flowers, small plants, and rocks. This brush performs the same action as the tree planting brush; however, it places smaller multiple models on the surface of the terrain
7		Controls the overall settings for the terrain. In this area you can set distances for level of detail and when trees are rendered as billboards instead of 3D objects. These settings are for optimizing the performance of the terrain in the game.

Step 5. For sculpting, select Tool 1. The brush size will affect the area of ground you can sculpt in one stroke and the opacity of the strength. A higher opacity will cause more of the terrain to be lifted in one stroke.

Step 6. Hold down the left mouse button over the terrain to start lifting the surface. At this stage begin with a basic outline of the Lake Louise area based on Figure 7.5, as shown in Figure 7.7. To lower the terrain, hold down the shift key with the mouse stroke.

● Note
You might find it easier to replicate a real-world image if you place it on a plane inside the Editor to use as a reference, as shown in Figure 7.6.

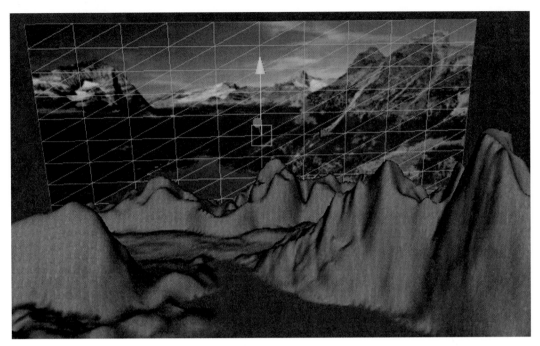

FIG 7.6 Inserting a reference photo into the Scene while editing.

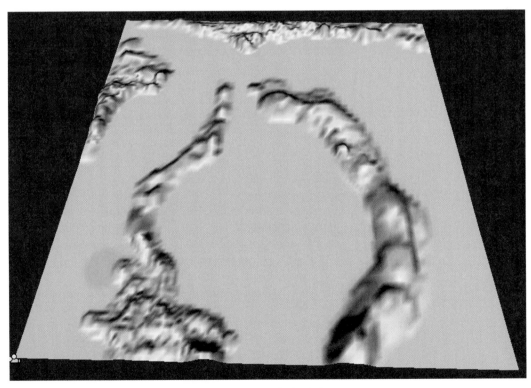

FIG 7.7 A basic terrain plan for Lake Louise.

375

Step 7. Using a combination of Tools 1, 2, and 3, sculpt and smooth the terrain into an approximate representation of the Lake Louise landscape as shown in Figure 7.8.

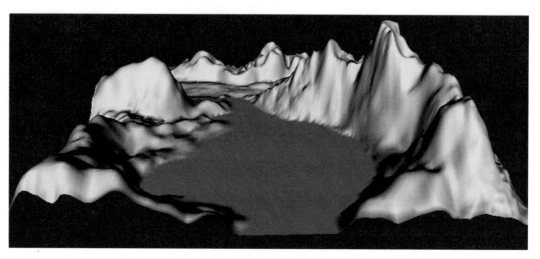

FIG 7.8 A terrain sculpted to represent Lake Louise.

Step 8. Once the basic terrain is constructed it can be textured. For texturing, seamless images are required. These images must be placed in the Project. Acquire these textures by searching online. An excellent seamless texture pack is available at http://aeonicdesign.ca/Textures/Textures/AeonicTexturePack.zip.

Step 9. Click on Tool 4 to select the terrain painting brush. Before you can start coloring the terrain, the images need to be loaded as terrain textures. Select the Edit Textures button as shown in Figure 7.9 and select Add Texture. A pop-up window will allow you to select the image and its tile size. The larger the tile size, the more terrain a single copy of the image will cover.

Step 10. Select a texture to be the first and click on Apply to add it to the terrain texture list. Because the first texture added will cover the entire terrain automatically, picking an image that represents the most common surface color saves a lot of texturing work later.

Step 11. Add more images to the texture list and use the brush size, opacity, and target strength settings to paint the terrain. The opacity value sets how much of the underneath texture mixes with the newly added texture, and the target strength is how much of the added texture is placed on the surface. A low opacity will allow a lot of the underneath color to show through. A low target strength will add very little of the current texture to the surface. Experiment with these values to get the effect right. If you make a mistake it is simple enough to recolor over the mistakes.

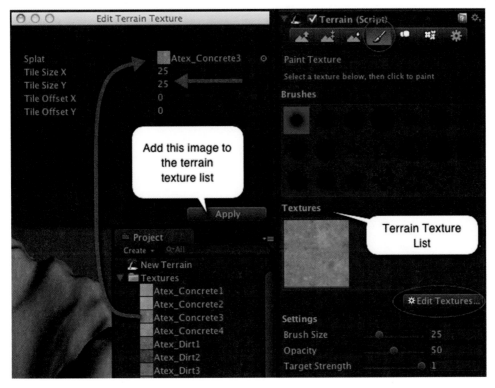

FIG 7.9 Adding a terrain texture.

Wherever trees will be placed, think about the final effect. If you want the trees to look lush and forest like, a ground color similar to the trees will make it look denser than it is. An example of the painted terrain is shown in Figure 7.10.

Step 12. Trees can also be painted onto the surface using Tool 5. Currently, there are no trees in the Project. Download the terrain assets package available at http://unity3d.com/support/resources/assets/terrain-assets and import into your project.

Step 13. Trees are added to the tree brush in the same way images are added to the textures. Add a couple of appropriate trees.

Step 14. Examine the photograph of Lake Louise. Note how the trees do not cover the entire landscape? Obviously they will not be in the lake area but they are thickest near the water and thin out to a distinct level after which the odd tree is found. In the real world, elevation and soil content at heights make it inhospitable for trees. Therefore, mimicking nature in this way makes the terrain look better.

Step 15. In the picture of Lake Louise there is also a thin line of sand around the edge of the lake. Once you have added the trees, take a small texture painting brush, select a light sand color, and add this

FIG 7.10 An example of a painted terrain.

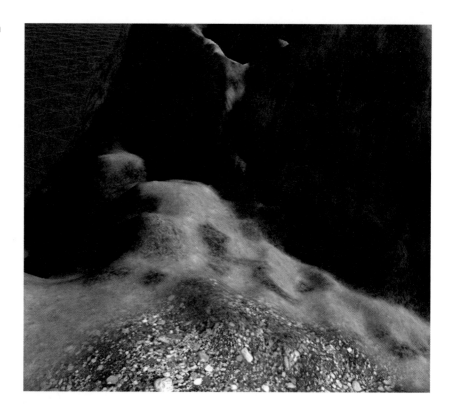

detail. It will lift the tree line and create shore for the water of the lake as shown in Figure 7.11.

Step 16. From the main menu select Assets > Import Package > Water. Choose the Pro version if you have it; otherwise Basic will do.

Step 17. Locate the Daylight Water prefab. It will be in the Standard Assets folder in the Project. Drag it onto the terrain. At first it will appear as a small blue circle. Select it in the Hierarchy. Press R to resize and drag the resizing axes in the Scene to make the water the same size as the lake area. It is okay if the water intersects with the terrain. If the water is at the exact same y position as the terrain there will be a rendering conflict between the ground of the map and the water. Lift the water up slightly in the y direction to eliminate this.

Step 18. Import the Character Controller package.

Step 19. Add a First Person Controller to the Scene. Play and you will be able to walk around and take a first-hand look at your handiwork. At this level you may notice a lot of little details you've missed.

Step 20. When playing, if you cannot see the background mountains increase the Main Camera's Far Clipping Plane to 5000. As you want to portray a feeling of vastness to the player in this environment, having the background mountains pop in and out of view as the player moves spoils this effect.

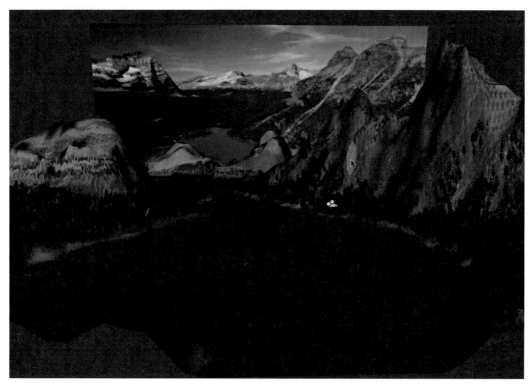

FIG 7.11 Trees and shoreline added to Lake Louise terrain.

Step 21. Lake Louise is a vibrant blue color. The water you've added might not be quite right. To change this, select the Water in the Hierarchy and change its Reflective Color to a more suitable blue as shown in Figure 7.12.

Step 22. Last but not least, import the Skybox package.

Step 23. Select Edit > Render Settings from the main menu and set the Skybox Material variable in the Inspector to the skybox of your choice as shown in Figure 7.13.

Step 24. Remove the plane containing the real photograph of Lake Louise and play to enjoy your new creation. An example is shown in Figure 7.14.

Step 25. One final step to perform is to create shadows on the surface of the terrain. Ensure that you have at least one directional light in the scene. Select Window > Lightmapping from the main menu.

A lightmap is a generated texture laid over the terrain like a cloth that contains black spots where shadows should appear. It is generated based on the location of the lights in the scene and how rays cast from them hit (or don't hit) the terrain. Objects in the way of the light rays cause black spots on the lightmap.

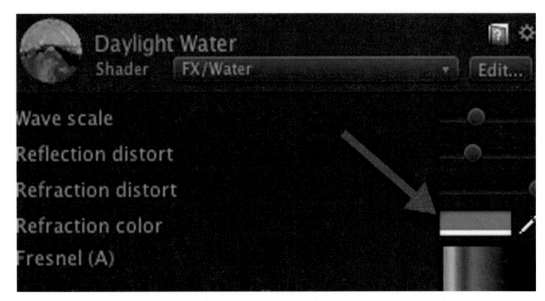

FIG 7.12 Changing water colors.

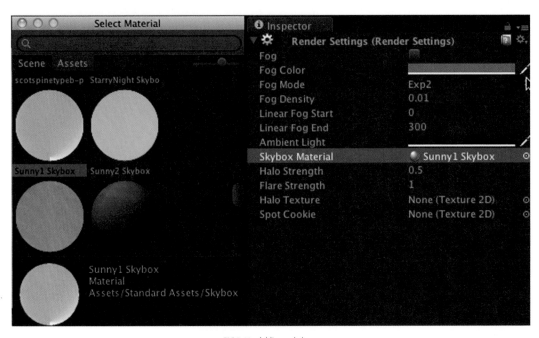

FIG 7.13 Adding a skybox.

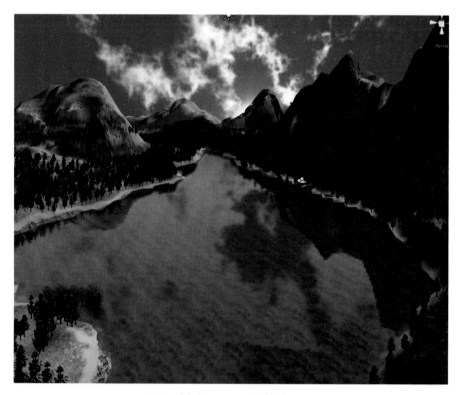

FIG 7.14 Lake Louise as interpreted by the author.

Step 26. Select the directional lights in the environment and ensure that they have the value for Shadow Type set to Hard or Soft Shadows in the Inspector.

Step 27. In the Lightmapping window with the Object tab selected, click on a directional light in the Hierarchy to add.

Step 28. Select the Bake tab and click on the Bake button.

The term *baking* in games and computer graphics refers to creating a texture of an image and adding it to a mesh in cases where sometimes the texture might be dynamically created. For example, dynamic shadows that are generated and therefore can change in the game environment as it plays are not baked. Shadows that are baked into the environment have become part of the environment's textures and therefore cannot change during game play.

The terrain baking procedure may take some time. A progress bar will appear in Unity. At this time it is best to go and make a cup of coffee. The baking screen is shown in Figure 7.15.

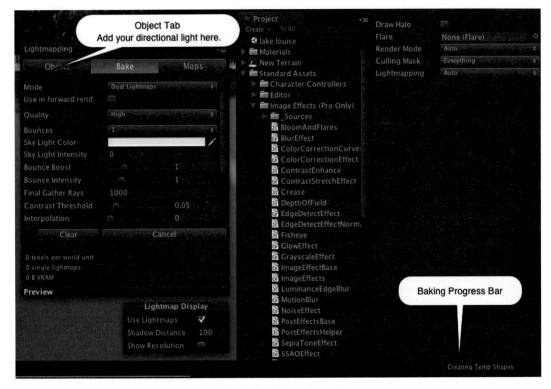

FIG 7.15 Creating a lightmap for a terrain.

⊙ On the Web

For more information on lightmapping in Unity, visit http://unity3d.com/support/documentation/Manual/Lightmapping.html. Lightmapping before and after images of the Lake Louise terrain are shown in Figure 7.16. Note how the trees now cast shadows.

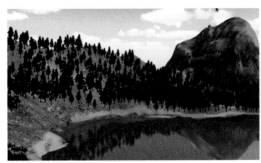

Before Lightmapping

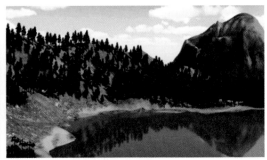

After Lightmapping

FIG 7.16 Lake Louise terrain before and after lightmapping.

7.3.2 Procedural Terrain

Procedural terrain is that generated by a computer algorithm. Most of the methods are based on fractals. A program is written that defines the vertices of a mesh and recursively raises and lowers the points to create altitude. One simple terrain producing method is the midpoint displacement algorithm.

This algorithm works starting with a flat surface. It divides it in half and then raises or lowers the middle point. Then each half is halved and the midpoint of these is raised or lowered. A 2D representation of this progression is illustrated in Figure 7.17.

Another popular procedural terrain generation algorithm is the Diamond Square method illustrated in Figure 7.18. Starting with a square mesh with a power of 2 + 1 number of vertices in width and height,[1] for example, 257,

FIG 7.17 Midpoint displacement on a 2D line.

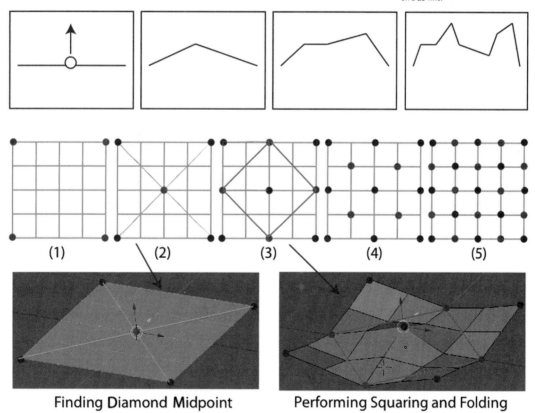

(1) (2) (3) (4) (5)

Finding Diamond Midpoint

Performing Squaring and Folding

FIG 7.18 The Diamond-Square algorithm.

---

[1] We need to add an extra vertex along the sides so that there is an odd number of vertices, allowing for an exact middle one to be located.

513, 1025, all four corners are set to the same initial height [Figure 7.18 (1)]. The second step, the diamond step, locates the central vertex where the diagonals from the initial vertices intersect. Step 3 creates squares between the central point and previous initial points. Now imagine fold lines between the red points and the height values assigned to the blue points shown in green in Figure 7.18. Blue points determine height, and green lines are where the mesh is allowed to fold.

The Diamond-Square method continues creating diamonds to find midpoints and squares for lowering and raising until all points in the grid have height values associated with them.

◁ **Unity Specifics**

Unity has a terrain editor plugin that employs the Diamond-Square algorithm for creating realistic-looking terrains without all the hard work of sculpting and painting. You can check it out by downloading the package from http://unity3d.com/support/resources/unity-extensions/terrain-toolkit.

Perlin Noise is another popular algorithmic way to generate landscapes. It is used in the next workshop to produce a natural-looking terrain from a plane object in Unity.

◉ **Unity Hands On**

Generating a Terrain Procedurally

Step 1. Create a new Unity project and import the Character Controller package.

Step 2. Add a plane to the scene and a first person controller (FPC). Position the FPC just above the plane and add a directional light as shown in Figure 7.19. Scale the plane's *x* and *z* size to 10.

◉ **Note**

If you want a smoother, more detailed terrain, you will need to use a plane with more vertices than the one supplied with Unity. To do this, using Blender or your favorite 3D modeling program, create a plane and apply subdivisions to give it the number of polygons you desire.

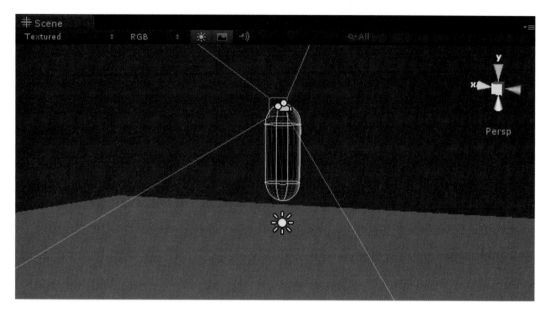

FIG 7.19 A plane and FPC for starting the project.

Step 3. Select the plane in the Hierarchy and remove its Mesh Collider component in the Inspector. We will add a new one shortly after its terrain heights have been modified.

Step 4. Create a JavaScript file called *makeTerrain.js*. Add the code shown in Listing 7.1.

Listing 7.1 Script to Create Random Height Values on a Mesh

```
function Start()
{
     var mesh: Mesh = this.GetComponent(MeshFilter).mesh;
     var vertices: Vector3[] = mesh.vertices;
     for (var v = 0; v < vertices.Length; v++)
     {
          vertices[v].y = Random.Range(0,10);
     }
     mesh.vertices = vertices;
     mesh.RecalculateBounds();
     mesh.RecalculateNormals();

     this.gameObject.AddComponent(MeshCollider);
}
```

Step 5. Attach the script to the plane.

Step 6. Play. The terrain will have random heights across its surface. Note that the Mesh Collider is added after the heights have been set. This will ensure that the FPC does not fall through.

After the mesh vertices are modified in the *y* direction for height, the bounding volume and normals are recreated. The bounding volume is used by the game engine to improve the processing of geometrical operations such as collision detection and overlap. The reason being that in the first instance, computing overlapping volumes is easier than lower level collision detection. Before exact collisions are calculated, determining if there might be a collision between two objects is more efficient with bounding volumes.

In addition, the plane's normals are also recalculated. Because the plane's mesh has changed shape, the normals must be adjusted for the new vertex values for the mesh to be shaded and shadowed correctly.

Using a random function to determine height is not a realistic way to produce rise and fall in a terrain, as the height can change erratically with each vertex. At small height values it might look all right, but try changing the random range from 0 to 50 and the surface of the plane will become very jagged.

Step 7. To create smoother rises and falls in a surface, a mathematical curve such as Sine or Cosine can be used. Modify *makeTerrain.js* to reflect the changes shown in Listing 7.2.

Listing 7.2 Using a Sine Function to Set the Terrain Height

```
. . .
for (var v = 0; v < vertices.Length; v++)
{
        vertices[v].y = Mathf.Sin(vertices[v].x * 10);
}
. . .
```

Step 8. Play. The shape of the sine wave will be visually evident. The terrain will be smooth, but too uniform to replicate a natural landscape.

Another way to create a landscape procedurally is to use Perlin Noise, a pseudo-random mathematical algorithm that provides smooth gradients between points. This is the method used for landscape generation in *Minecraft*.

Step 9. Downloand *Chapter Seven/Perlin.js* from the Web site. Add the file to your Project inside a new folder called *Plugins*.

Step 10. Modify *makeTerrain.js* to that shown in Listing 7.3.

Listing 7.3 Using Perlin Noise to Generate Terrain Height

```
function Start()
{
    var surface : Perlin = new Perlin();

    var mesh: Mesh = this.GetComponent(MeshFilter).mesh;
    var vertices: Vector3[] = mesh.vertices;

    for (var v = 0; v < vertices.Length; v++)
    {
        vertices[v].y = surface.Noise(
                    vertices[v].x * 2 + 0.1365143,
                    vertices[v].z * 2 + 1.21688) * 10;
    }

    mesh.vertices = vertices;
    mesh.RecalculateBounds();
    mesh.RecalculateNormals();

    this.gameObject.AddComponent(MeshCollider);
}
```

● Note

Perlin Noise

Perlin Noise is the same algorithm used in Photoshop for generating the Render Clouds filter. The image created by Perlin Noise is grayscale, where black indicates the lowest altitude and white the highest, as shown in Figure 7.20a.

In fact, you can create a procedurally generated terrain in Unity (shown in Figure 7.20b) by (1) adding a terrain, (2) getting the flat terrain texture with Terrain > Export Heightmap, (3) opening this texture with Photoshop, (4) applying Photoshop's Render Clouds filter, (5) saving the texture in the same raw format, and (6) selecting Terrain > Import Heightmap in Unity to load the heights.

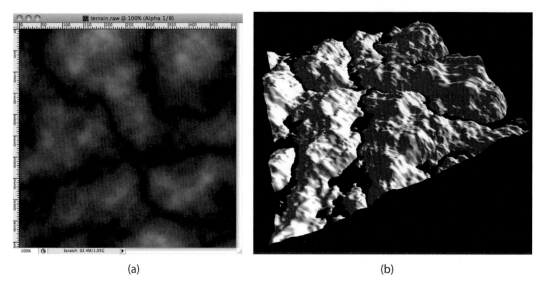

(a)   (b)

FIG 7.20   (a) A texture created with Photoshop's Difference Clouds Filter. (b) A Unity Terrain with the same texture used as a heightmap.

The difference in using a random number for the height and Perlin Noise is illustrated in Figure 7.21.

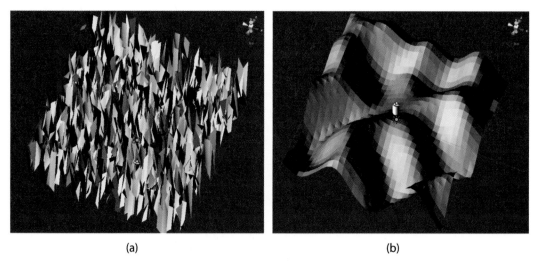

(a)   (b)

FIG 7.21   (a) A terrain with random height values. (b) A terrain with Perlin Noise height values.

7.3.3 Procedural Cities

Generating realistic cities with code is more challenging than landscapes. While terrain can reuse trees, rocks, grass, and dirt textures, reuse of the same building or random street structures can look unrealistic. In the same way that fractals can be used for generating terrain and layout, they too can be used to create objects on the terrain such as trees and buildings.

A Lindenmayer system or L-system is a fractal algorithm used commonly for generating trees as it has a natural branching structure. An L-system is constructed from a string representing drawing commands. The string is built through an iterative process where parts of the string are replaced with other strings. An L-system begins with an axiom and a set of rules thus:

$$F \rightarrow F+F$$

Starting with the axiom as the original string, each character in the string matching a rule is replaced with the rules string. Therefore, after one iteration, the aforementioned becomes:

$$F+F$$

Then, each F in the new string is replaced by the rule in the next iteration, thus:

$$F+F+F+F$$

Note that only the character F is replaced, and with F + F, the already existing + carries over to the next string. This is illustrated in Figure 7.22.

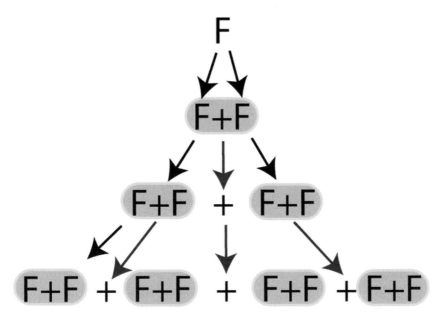

FIG 7.22 L-system rewriting.

After numerous iterations, a string such as F + F + F + F is then interpreted by a drawing algorithm in which the letters represent lines and the + a turn to the right (if − is used it means turn to the left). It is reminiscent of turtle graphics in which a cursor on the screen is given commands to draw a line, turn right, draw another line, etc. The turn angle is preset. Let's say F represents draw a straight line and + represents turn 90°. The drawn result would be a square as shown in Figure 7.23.

In addition to drawing and turning, an L-system can contain push and pop points. These are represented by square braces ([,]). When the drawing algorithm encounters these points it remembers its location on a [, keeps drawing, and then returns to the remembered location when it encounters a]. For example, F[+F]F where + is 45° would produce the L-system shown in Figure 7.24.

L-systems become more complex with the addition of extra rules such as the one shown in Figure 7.25. This is a famous fractal called the Sierpinski triangle.

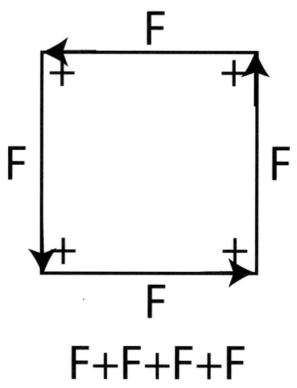

FIG 7.23 An L-system that draws a square.

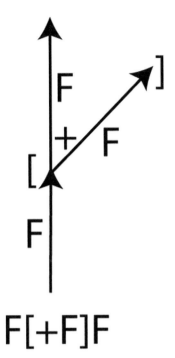

F[+F]F

FIG 7.24 An L-system with remembered locations.

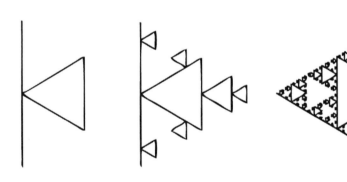

2 iterations   4 iterations   7 iterations

Axiom: F
Rule 1: F-> A-F-A
Rule 2: F-> F+A+F
+, - :   60 degrees

FIG 7.25 Sierpinski triangle.

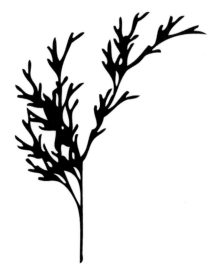

Axiom: X
Rule 1: X-> F-[[X]+X]+F[+FX]-X
Rule 2: F -> FF
Angle : 25 degrees

FIG 7.26 An L-system tree.

Natural and familiar shapes can be created with L-systems (as shown in Figure 7.26).

To produce a procedural map, at least two types of L-systems are required: one for drawing the map layout with the transportation routes and one for creating the buildings. Figure 7.27a illustrates a simple street map using the same L-system as the one for the tree in Figure 7.26 with the angle set to 90°. Figure 7.27b shows how an L-system can be used to create buildings. Simple lines are replaced with 3D blocks. The result in the three iterations shown hints at how compelling a fully finished building could look.

● **On the Web**
Procedural City Generator
The aforementioned techniques for generating a city procedurally come from the research work of Muller and Parish. Their approach has been packaged into the CityEngine software—a 3D modeling package built purposely to generate vast city landscapes. A free trial can be downloaded from http://procedural.com/.

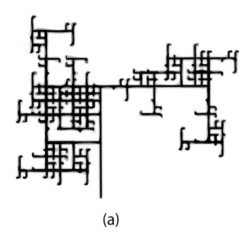

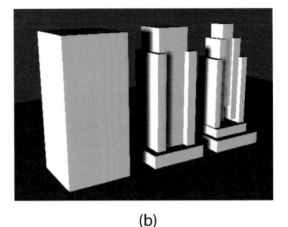

(a)

(b)

Although the programming of an algorithm to build a 3D L-system city is beyond the scope of this book, it is possible using Perlin Noise and existing building models to generate a city. This is the topic of the next workshop.

Unity Hands On

Procedural Cities

Step 1. Create a new Unity project and import the Character Controller package.

Step 2. Add a plane to the scene and an FPC. Position the FPC just above the plane and add a directional light as shown in Figure 7.19. Scale the plane's *x* and *z* sizes to 10.

Step 3. Download *Chapter Seven/Perlin.js* from the Web site. Add the file to your Project inside a new folder called *Plugins*.

Step 4. Create a JavaScript file named *makeCity* and reuse the code from Listing 7.3.

Step 5. Play. What you should have is the heightened terrain from the previous example. Now instead of heights we will add buildings.

Step 6. If you put a print statement inside the for loop in *makeCity .js* and print out the height values being assigned to the plane, you'll notice they range between −4 and 4. We will use these values to assign buildings instead of terrain heights. Go to Turbosquid and download eight models of various types of houses and buildings. You will also find eight building models already downloaded from Turbosquid on the Web site as *Chapter Seven/buildings.zip*.

Step 7. Add the buildings to the Project.

Step 8. Add each building into the Scene and position them on the plane. Because different artists created them, their scaling will be different. Resize and rotate each building as you see fit such that they have reasonable relative sizes and orientations.

Step 9. Create eight prefabs in the Project—one for each building. Drag each building out of the Hierarchy and onto its own prefab.

Step 10. Modify *makeCity.js* to that in Listing 7.4.

Listing 7.4 Using Building Prefabs to Create a City Based on Perlin Noise Height Values

```
var buildings: GameObject[];
function Start()
{
    var surface : Perlin = new Perlin();

    var mesh: Mesh = this.GetComponent(MeshFilter).mesh;
    var vertices: Vector3[] = mesh.vertices;
    var scalex = this.transform.localScale.x;
    var scalez = this.transform.localScale.z;

    for (var v = 0; v < vertices.Length; v++)
    {
        var perlinValue = surface.Noise (
                          vertices[v].x * 2 + 0.1365143,
                          vertices[v].z * 2 + 1.21688) * 10;
        perlinValue =
            Mathf.Round((Mathf.Clamp (
                perlinValue,0,buildings.length)));
        print(perlinValue);
        Instantiate(buildings[perlinValue],
            Vector3(vertices[v].x * scalex,
            vertices[v].y,
            vertices[v].z * scalez),
            buildings[perlinValue].transform.rotation);
    }

    mesh.vertices = vertices;
    mesh.RecalculateBounds();
    mesh.RecalculateNormals();

    this.gameObject.AddComponent(MeshCollider);
}
```

Step 11. Select the plane in the Hierarchy and find the makeCity script in the Inspector. Set the size of Buildings to 8 and drag and drop each building prefab onto the exposed building array elements in the script. Note that you can have any number of buildings and the code will adjust for it.

Step 12. Play. The result will be a small city as illustrated in Figure 7.28.

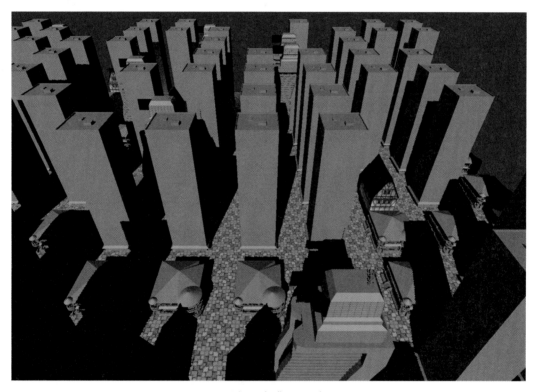

FIG 7.28 A procedurally generated city.

● Note

As Perlin Noise creates smooth regions that graduate between white and black when drawn as a grayscale, you can use these values to determine the city density at these locations. For example, white might represent high density and black low or no density. Where the map is densest use the skyscraper type building models and where it is lower use small houses. This will create a relatively realistic city.

7.3.4 Infinite Terrain

Infinite terrain or endless terrain is a form of procedurally generated landscapes. It uses a mathematical equation and the player's current position to create the landscape as the player moves. Small parts of the map are created as needed based on the player's visible distance. Any map outside the visible range is not generated and therefore not a load on computer memory.

To create undulation of a terrain, a mathematical formula is used for determining the height based on the x and z positions on the terrain for which there will always be a y value no matter the x and z values. For example, the sine or cosine functions can produce values for infinite values of x and/or z and the result used as the y value.

The beauty of using a formula is that the result of y for any x and z values is always going to be the same, thus assuring us that if we return to a previous location on the map that was destroyed after we left but recreated on our return, the height remains the same. In addition, the terrain can be infinitely large, generated entirely by the computer. This means a human artist is not required to constantly churn out more and more of the landscape. Terrain textures, trees, rocks, and other model objects are used over and over again.

Perlin Noise makes for a good choice in infinite terrain generation applications as it produces a random yet smooth undulating surface.

⦿ On the Web
An Infinite Terrain Generator
Developing an infinite terrain generator is a tricky business and as such is beyond the scope of this book. However, a generous Unity forum member going by the name of *Quick Fingers* posted a package for one on the Unity Web site. For this book, the code has been modified to use Perlin Noise and places trees and different textures on the terrain at varying heights. You can download the project from the Web site as *Chapter Seven/InfiniteTerrain.zip*.

On opening the Infinite Terrain scene, you will find a Terrain Generator object in the Hierarchy. Select this to modify the terrain's parameters in the Inspector. You will notice that different terrain textures are used for different altitudes. When rendered, the contrast between the textures is evident. They are not blended in the same way as the Unity paint on textures in the Unity Terrain Editor. This is because they are placed on the mesh live as the game is playing and the mesh is generated. While a blending algorithm could blend the textures to make them fit together better, it would slow down the generation of the terrain.

As you move around the map watch the action in the Scene. Only the parts of the map that are within sight of the player's camera are generated and drawn. As you move around, as parts of the map become out of sight, they are destroyed. This keeps the memory usage low and allows you to move infinitely in any direction totally oblivious to the small mesh your character is standing on.

A view of the infinite landscape is shown in Figure 7.29.

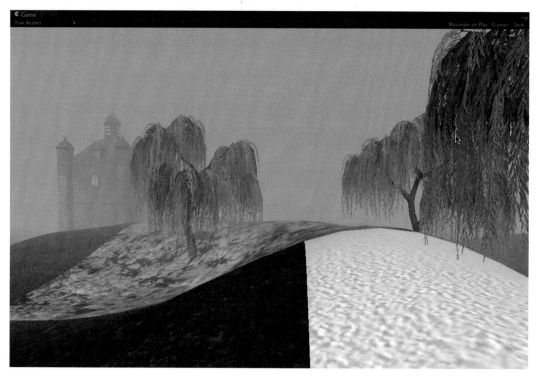

FIG 7.29 An infinite landscape generated in Unity.

7.4 Camera Tricks

Cameras are the player's eyes into the game environment. What the camera sees is projected onto the computer screen. Before each pixel is drawn the game developer can add special treatments to the properties and colors of the pixels by attaching scripts to the camera. This allows for the creation of many different visual effects. For example, a blur effect can be added to the camera when the player is underwater to give the illusion water is in the player's eyes or the scene can be rendered in sepia to make it look like an old-time movie.

Many of the following effects come from the domain of image processing and photographic postproduction and can be found readily as filters in Adobe

Photoshop. They have found their way into gaming as a way of enhancing the player's visual perception of the environment. Some of the wide ranges of camera effects available in Unity are shown in Figure 7.30.

FIG 7.30 A sample of the camera effects available in Unity.

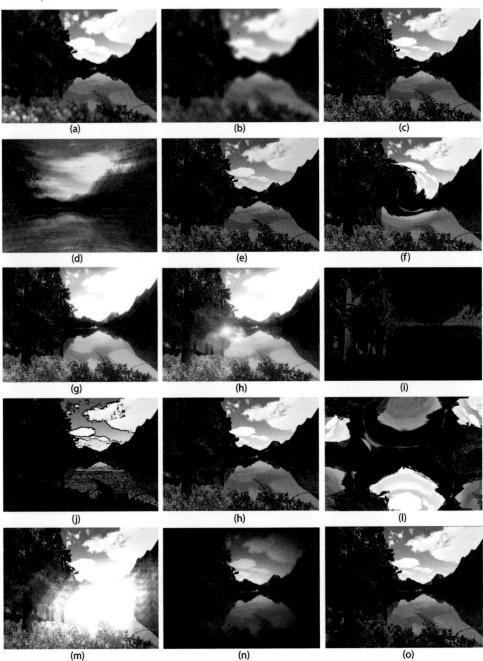

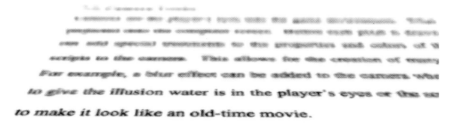

FIG 7.31 A shallow depth of field.

7.4.1 Depth of Field

Depth of field is the term used to describe how an optical lens focuses on the surrounding environment. It describes the distance between the closest and the farthest objects in view that appear in sharp focus. A shallow depth of field has items only nearest the middle of the view in focus as shown in Figure 7.31.

As the human eye is a lens it also projects an image with a depth of field. Unlike in a straightforward virtual terrain where all objects are in focus, for humans, our real world tends to become fuzzy in the distance and sometimes close up. Adding a depth of field effect to the game view camera gives the scene a higher feel of realism, quality, and 3D effect. The depth of field effect in Unity is shown in Figure 7.30.

7.4.2 Blur

Blur is an effect that makes the entire image look out of focus. It can be used effectively to simulate the look of being underwater.

Setting a pixel's color to the average color of its neighbors creates a blur effect. Within a certain radius all pixel colors are sampled, added together,

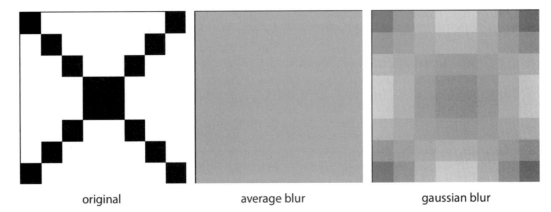

| original | average blur | gaussian blur |

FIG 7.32 Average blur versus Gaussian blur.

and then divided by the number of pixels. Each pixel is then given the same average value. Another familiar blur is Gaussian blur. It adds the pixel colors together to determine an average; however, pixel colors in the center of the selection are given more weight and therefore the blur appears to radiate outward. The difference in the effects is illustrated in Figure 7.32.

The blur effect in Unity is shown in Figure 7.30.

7.4.3 Grayscale

Grayscale reduces colored images down to variations of gray such that it looks like a black and white photograph. The simplest method for creating grayscale from color is the *average* method that takes the red, green, and blue components of a pixel and divides by three. This new value is reassigned to the original pixel. The *lightness* method sets a pixel value to the average of its highest and lowest color components. For example, if a pixel had an RGB value of 255,45,60, the highest value 255 and the lowest value 45 would be added together and divided by two. The final method, called *luminosity*, gives the best grayscale result by cleverly weighting the green value to account for human eye sensitivity. The luminosity algorithm is 0.21 R + 0.71 G + 0.07 B.

Unity's blur effect is illustrated in Figure 7.30.

7.4.4 Motion Blur

Motion blur is an effect used to make something look like it is moving rapidly or to give the player a dreamy view of the environment. The pixels appear to streak across the page in the direction of the motion. In addition, objects can have ghosting effects surrounding them. The effect is achieved by partially leaving the previous frame on the screen while rendering the next one. This effect is also useful in persuading players that their character is disorientated as a result of being drugged or in a dream state. Motion blur is illustrated in Figure 7.30. Motion blur is often used in racing games when the scenery is moving past the camera quickly and in first and third person games when the character is moving quickly.

7.4.5 Sepia Tone

Sepia tone is the brownish tinge seen on old photographs and film. It is achieved using an algorithm similar to that used for grayscale. The red, green, and blue values of a pixel are reset based on the addition of percentages of their original color components thus:

> Sepia Red = R × 0.393 + G × 0.769 + B × 0.189
> Sepia Green = R × 0.349 + G × 0.686 + B × 0.168
> Sepia Blue = R × 0.272 + G × 0.534 + B × 0.131

You may have seen sepia tone used in the cut scenes of games where an event is taking place in the past or in actual environments when the game is set in the past. *The Sims Medieval* uses sepia tones for its world map and storytelling still shots.

Sepia tone applied in Unity is demonstrated in Figure 7.30.

7.4.6 Twirl

The twirl effect takes a portion of the screen pixels and wraps them around a whirlpool-type motion as shown in Figure 7.30. This effect is usually seen in film footage or cut scenes when one scene is crossing into another. A similar effect can be found in vintage Batman animated cartoons (and other similar productions) where the bat insignia was circled in and out in between acts.

7.4.7 Bloom

Bloom is the glow effect seen around light sources that extend into the environment. It makes an image look overexposed and the colors washed out. It is more prominent the stronger the light source and the dustier the environment.

An example of the bloom effect being used in Unity is shown in Figure 7.30.

7.4.8 Flares

Flares are bursts of reflected and refracted light. The most commonly known flare is a lens flare, which causes a series of translucent, rainbow, bright circles on an image from light passing through a camera lens as shown in Figure 7.30. It is often used in games to give the player the illusion they are looking into the sun when facing skyward.

Flares can also be caused by bright light passing through partially transparent materials such as glass or reflected off shiny surfaces such as polished metal and water.

7.4.9 Color Correction

Color correction does as its name suggests. It takes certain colors occurring in an image and changes them to another color. For example, a hill covered in green grass could be made to look like a hill of dead brown grass by replacing the color green with brown.

In games, color correction can be used for rendering night vision effects, changing most of the colors to green as shown in Figure 7.30. Each R, G, B value is matched with a replacement R, G, B value. At any time, color correction, as with all these effects, can be turned off. Using this method you could simulate the well-known Splinter Cell game play where the main character can use his night vision goggles in dark environments, which changes what the player sees on the screen at a press of a button.

7.4.10 Edge Detection

An edge detection algorithm scans an image for areas where pixels in close proximity contrast in color. Because the difference between individual pixels would produce erratic effects, the algorithm must determine if a pixel is on the edge of an area of similar color by looking at its surrounding pixels. This creates a picture that looks like a sketched outline.

The optimal approach to edge detection is the Canny edge detection algorithm. Further technical details about it can be found at http://pages.drexel.edu/~weg22/can_tut.html.

The edge detection algorithm in Unity outlines all objects with a black line as shown in Figure 7.30.

7.4.11 Crease

Creasing is a nonphotorealistic effect that increases the visibility of game world objects by drawing a line around the silhouette, much like in comic book images. In a busy game environment with many objects, such as buildings and trees, drawn from similar colors and tones, objects can become difficult to distinguish. By applying creasing at differing depths, the line can distinguish between near and far objects.

The example from Unity shown in Figure 7.30 has drawn a line around the top edge of the mountains, thus distinguishing them even more from the skybox.

7.4.12 Fish Eye

The fish eye effect produces an image as seen in a spherical mirror or through a wide-angle lens. The image produced is hemispherical in nature. Depending on the amount of curvature in the image, it can look completely distorted and inside out as the one from Unity in Figure 7.30. When used in a less exaggerated manner, the effect widens the field of view, showing more of the scene than is in the camera's normal range. However, to fit in the extra parts of the image, at the outer edges the scene starts to bend with the effect, becoming more exaggerated the farther it is from the center.

7.4.13 Sun Shafts

Sun shafts are produced by a bright light source being partially occluded and viewed when passing through atmospheric particles. For example, sun shafts are prominent after a sun shower when the sun is partially blocked by clouds and the air is heavy with moisture. You might also imagine sun shafts coming through a dusty attic window or in between the trees in a rainforest.

This effect as produced in Unity is shown in Figure 7.30.

7.4.14 Vignette

Vignetting is an effect used to focus the viewer's attention on an object in an image by darkening and/or blurring the peripheries. The start of each James Bond movie provides an example where the viewer is looking down the barrel of a gun. The view is restricted to a small circle in the middle of the screen and the supposed inside of the gun barrel sets the outside to black. Vignetting need not be this dramatic. Instead of the edge darkening abruptly, it might fade to black instead.

In a game view, a vignette can focus the player's attention on an area of the game environment or be used to restrict the player's view. Unity's vignette script is illustrated in Figure 7.30.

7.4.15 Screen Space Ambient Occlusion (SSAO)

The SSAO effect approximates shadowing in from ambient light based purely on the image produced by the camera. As it is a postproduction effect, it does not rely on a light source or on information about an object's materials to calculate shadows. It works with the image to emphasize holes, creases, and areas where objects meet. For example, without any lighting in a game environment to provide dynamic or baked shadows, trees stand on the terrain but somehow look disconnected and not in contact. SSAO provides a dusting of shadow around these connection points such that these types of intersections don't appear unnatural.

The use of SSAO in Figure 7.30 brings more depth and natural effect to the image, providing shadowing in and under the rocks and grass and between the leaves of the tree.

This section examined a variety of camera effects. These are added to the rendering postproduction after the camera has determined the scene. As such they can require a great deal of computer processing and are not recommended for use on platforms without sufficient graphics processing capability (like many mobile devices).

As Unity only provides these effects with the Pro version, they have not been fully elucidated here. However, the interested reader is encouraged to read Unity's own documentation found at http://unity3d.com/support/documentation/Components/comp-ImageEffects.html.

7.5 Skies

There are a number of ways to create skies for a 3D game environment. The easiest way is to set the background color of the camera to blue. Alternatively, if you want to include fog, setting the fog color to the background color gives the illusion of a heavy mist and provides for landscape optimization as discussed in Chapter Two.

To get clues as to what a game environment sky should look like, we can just look up. Our sky is more than a blue blanket covering the earth. Its colors change throughout the day with the position of the sun, the quality of the air, the weather, and the longitude and latitude.

The daytime sky appears blue due to a phenomenon known as *Rayleigh scattering* (named after a physicist of the same name). As sunlight enters the earth's atmosphere, it interacts with the air and dust particles, which bend the light and scatter the different colors across the sky. The color that is scattered the most is blue. At sunset, the sun's rays enter the atmosphere at different angles relative to the viewer and cause more yellow and red light to be scattered. Rayleigh scattering is caused by particles smaller than the wavelength of light.

Particles that are comparable or larger than the wavelength of light also scatter it. This effect is described by the *Mie theory*, developed by physicist Gustav Mie. The theory explains how particles such as water droplets affect the scattering of light. The Mie theory elucidates why clouds are different shades of gray and white.

Another factor influencing the look of the sky is *turbidity*. Turbidity describes the amount of suspended solid particles in a fluid. In the sky, turbidity relates to the number of dust, ash, water, or smoke particles in the air. The density of these particles affects both Rayleigh scattering and the Mie theory as it also adds to light scattering. For example, when the earth experiences a large volcanic event, which spews tons of dust and ash into the air, sunsets appear to last longer and have more vivid colors.

The following sections examine two ways to create skies: one that uses a simple texture and the other that considers the physical theories of light and air interaction described earlier.

7.5.1 Skyboxes

The most common method of creating a sky with cloud textures is to use a skybox. This is essentially an inside-out cube placed over the camera with seamless images of the sky rendered on it. Because it only requires six planes and six textures, it is a relatively cost-effective way to create a convincing-looking sky. The six textures are referred to by their position on the cube: up, down, front, back, left, and right. An example skybox is shown in Figure 7.33.

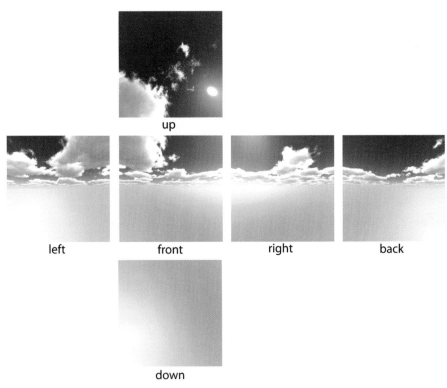

FIG 7.33 The six textures making up a skybox.

Unity Specifics
Skyboxes

Unity comes with a number of skyboxes. To use these, you must import the skybox package by selecting Asset > Import Package > Skyboxes.

To apply a skybox to a scene, select the Main Camera and location of the Camera component in the Inspector. Set the Clear Flags value to Skybox. Select Edit > Render Settings from the main menu and, in the Inspector, set the Skybox Material to the one you want. In the Game, the chosen skybox will display.

To use your own skybox, create a folder on your computer containing each of the skybox textures. Name the textures after the folder name and suffix with their position. For example, if your folder were called *sunset*, then each of the images would be sunset_up.jpg, sunset_down.jpg, sunset_front.jpg, sunset_back.jpg, sunset_left.jpg, and sunset_right.jpg. Drag and drop this folder into the Project. Your custom skybox will now be available in the Render Settings.

7.5.2 Sky Domes

A sky dome, as the name suggests, is a dome mesh placed over the environment with a sky texture stretched across the inside surface as shown in Figure 7.34.

The sky dome is attached to the player's camera, like an oversized helmet, such that it moves everywhere with the player. Unlike a real helmet, it does not rotate as the camera looks around—it just translates, ensuring that it is always projecting a sky with the player at the center. This ensures that the player never sees the edges of the dome. If the dome is not big enough, as terrain and scenery come into view, they will pop through the dome edges. Strategic sizing and positioning of the dome are critical to ensure that this does not occur.

Because the UVs of the sky dome are inline in arcs across the sky mesh, it's simple to scroll textures across the mesh in the same way the textures are scrolled across a plane in Chapter Two. This makes it easy to add cloud textures to the dome and move them across the sky.

In the next workshop, a sky dome package created by Unity Developer Martijn Dekker[2] will be used to place a sky, complete with moving clouds and a sun, around a first person controller. Dekker has taken into consideration Rayleigh scattering and the Mie Theory to produce a truly exceptional sky dome.

---

[2]Slightly modified by the author to suit the purposes of the workshop.

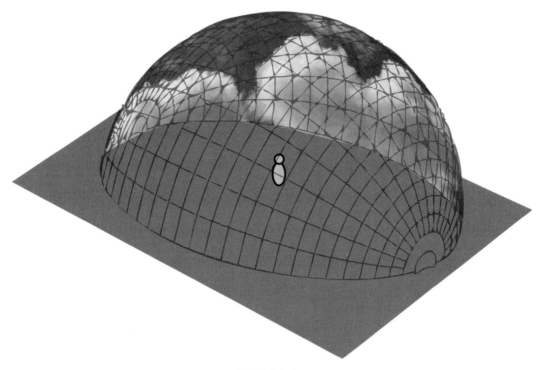

FIG 7.34 A sky dome.

⊙ Unity Hands On
Sky Domes

    Step 1. Create a new Unity Project. Import the Character Controller and Terrain Assets.

    Step 2. In the scene add a Terrain. Style and texture as you see fit.

    Step 3. Add a First Person Controller to the Scene. Position the player over the terrain.

    Step 4. Because the sky dome object you are about to add generates its own sun, you do not need to add a directional light; however, you will need to change the light type to Directional. Modify *skyDomeScript.js* with that in Listing 7.5.

Listing 7.5 Set the Sun's Light Type to Directional

```
...
void Start ()
     {
        sunLight = new GameObject("Sun");
        sunLight.AddComponent("Light");
        sunLight.light.type = LightType.Directional;
}
...
```

Step 5. Play to ensure that the player isn't falling below the terrain. Reposition the player as necessary.

Step 6. Download *Chapter Seven/SkyDome.unitypackage* from the Web site and import into Unity.

Step 7. From the skydome folder created in Project, after the import, drag and drop the SkyDome prefab into the Hierarchy. The SkyDome will appear as a large white sphere in the Scene.

Step 8. Select the SkyDome object in the Hierarchy. Locate the Skydome Script component in the Inspector and set the Player attribute to the First Person Controller as shown in Figure 7.35.

FIG 7.35 The Skydome Script component and setting the Player attribute.

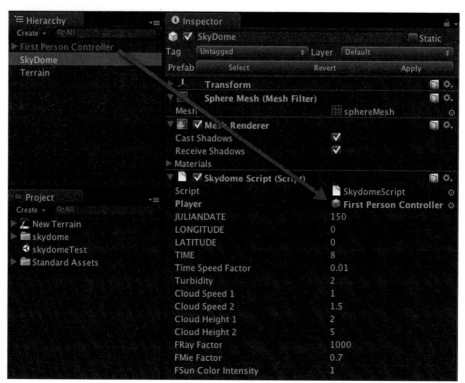

Step 9. Play. A sky dome with clouds will fill the sky. The sky dome has an internal clock, which will cause the sun to move across the sky, making for a day, sunset, night, and sunrise cycle. There are two layers of clouds whose settings are independent.

In the SkyDome Script settings in the Inspector, you can modify the specific sky dome properties for a variety of effects. These include:

- JULIANDATE: Sets the day of the year (with January 1st being day 1)
- LONGITUDE and LATITUDE: Player's position coordinates on the surface
- TIME: The time of day where 0 is midnight
- Time Speed Factor: The speed at which time passes
- Turbidity: The amount of scattering particles in the air. The higher the turbidity, the longer the sunsets and sunrises last.
- Cloud Speed 1 & 2: The speed at which the clouds move across the sky
- Cloud Height 1 & 2: The relative distance the clouds appear to be from the player
- FRay Factor: The affect of Rayleigh scattering, which determines how blue the sky appears. With a setting of 0 there is no blue (the sky remains black).
- FMie Factor: The effect of the Mie Theory with respect to the brightness of the clouds
- FSun Color Intensity: The brightness of the sun

For example, if you set the LONGITUDE to 18, the LATTITUDE to 65, and the JULIANDATE to 1, which would position the player somewhere in Iceland on the 1st of January (winter), you'll notice that the days are very short and that the sun stays pretty much in the same position in the sky when it is up. If you set the Turbidity to 10, the sunrise and sunset will be longer and the sun's glare will appear brighter.

7.5.3 Clouds

The previous two sections examined skies with clouds. Clouds on the skybox were fixed and did not change position or color. Clouds on the sky dome moved across the sky and exhibited turbulence. While the sky dome method includes layers of clouds, giving the perception of depth, the player can never get above or in among them. When you want to portray clouds in a 3D fashion such that you could more around them, you need to examine techniques for generating volumetric fog.

Volumetric fog is a more complex technique than the fog used previously. Whereas the stock standard fog used in computer graphics applies a faded out effect over all 3D assets in a scene, volumetric fog is contained within a 3D space. This makes it more processor intensive to render. However, this is not a real issue on today's consoles and desktop machines.

The types of natural effects that can be achieved with volumetric fog include low-lying clouds, mist, and dust as shown in Figure 7.36. You use it whenever you want to look at clouds from above or move through a variety of fog densities. Whereas the default fog gives a set density, in volumetric fog the player can walk through dense patches and then light patches.

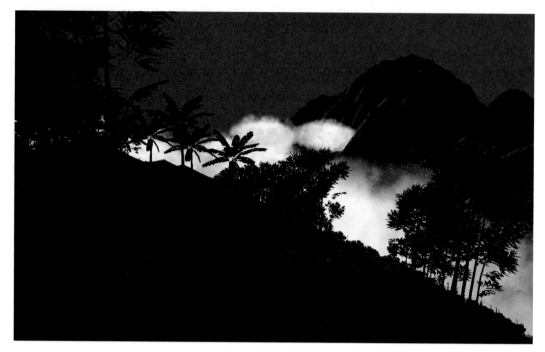

FIG 7.36 Volumetric clouds.

One method for producing volumetric clouds is to use mass instances of billboards with cloud textures on them. The system used to produce the image in Figure 7.36 was developed by Unity developer Julian Oliden and is available for download from http://jocyf.com/utilsEnglih.html. It is also included in the starter project file in the next workshop.

⚙ **Unity Hands On**
Volumetric Clouds

    Step 1. Download *Chapter Seven/VolumeClouds.zip*. Open the project in Unity.
    Step 2. Locate the CloudsToy Mngr prefab in the Project under the Volumetric Clouds prefab.
    Step 3. Drag and drop this prefab into the Scene. You won't be able to see it yet as it requires a Terrain to align itself.
    Step 4. Add a Terrain to the scene.
    Step 5. Sculpt the terrain or import a height map. Paint the terrain as you like.
    Step 6. Add a directional light.

Step 7. Select the CloudsToy Mngr in the Hierarchy. Press play. In the Scene you will be able to see the volume of the clouds over the terrain as shown in Figure 7.37. The CloudsToy Mngr sizes itself correctly to cover the terrain.

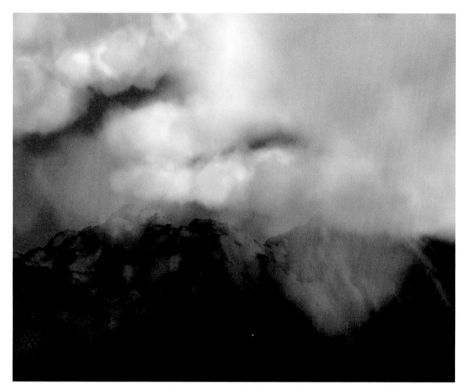

FIG 7.37 The Unity CloudsToy package in use.

Step 8. Add a first person controller to the Scene. Delete the original main camera.
Step 9. Play.
Step 10. If you have a mountainous terrain, you might like to lower the CloudsToy Mngr object such that it sits with the mountains poking out of the yellow bounding box in the Scene. This will create clouds that the player can walk through and above.

Settings for the CloudsToy Mngr can be changed through the Inspector by selecting the CloudsToy Mngr object in the Hierarchy. Settings begin with Cloud Presets, which allow you to select from Stormy-, Sunrise-, and Fantasy-looking clouds. These are useful to give you an idea of what the package can do as well as recovering to a more realistic-looking cloud type should you modify the other settings to the point of no return and end up with pinpoint clouds or no clouds at all.

Of particular note in the settings are the Cloud Creation Size and Disappear Multiplier. The Cloud Creation Size sets the size of the blue box displayed in the Scene. This box is the area in which clouds are spawned. The Disappear Multiplier determines the size of the yellow box. This is the area to which clouds will travel from the yellow box, but beyond they fade away.

Further down in the settings are cloud colors, sizes, and velocity.

The CloudsToy Mngr can be integrated into your own projects by importing the Chapter Seven/CloudsToy v1.2.unitypackage available from the Web site.

7.6 Weather

The weather affects the look and feel of our environment dramatically. Although players won't be able to feel the cold of virtual snow in a game environment, the correct lighting, coloring, and special effects will make them feel like they are there and add an extra dimension to your scene.

7.6.1 Wind

Wind is one of these elements. Although you can't see it, it moves environmental objects around. It looks especially good in a 3D world when acting on cloth, trees, and grass.

◁ **Unity Specifics**
Terrain Wind Element
A terrain in Unity can have wind applied through the setting of the bend factor of trees and using a wind zone. To do this, select a tree in the Terrain Editor and click on Edit Trees. In the pop-up window you will find a value for bend as shown in Figure 7.38. Set this to a value other than zero to make the trees sway in the breeze. Add a wind zone by selecting GameObject > Create Other > Wind Zone and then move the object near the First Person Controller. Play to see the trees move in the wind.

Grass and flower objects will sway automatically with the terrain breeze. The wind settings for this are found in the settings panel of the Terrain Editor as shown in Figure 7.39.

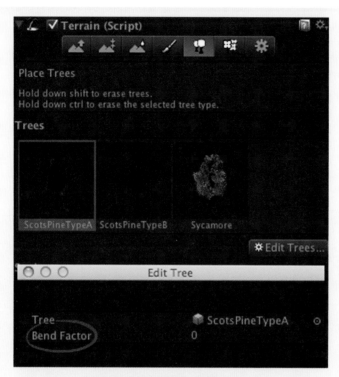

FIG 7.38 Adding a bend factor to terrain trees.

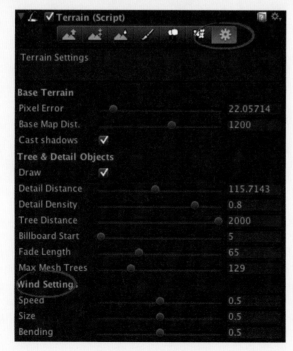

FIG 7.39 Setting the terrain wind.

◉ Unity Hands On

Flying the Flag

In this workshop you will learn how to add wind effects with the Unity physics system.

> **Step 1.** Create a new Unity Project. Add a cube and resize to the shape of a long flagpole.
>
> **Step 2.** Add a Cloth by selecting GameObject > Create Other > Cloth. Rotate the cloth and resize to fit at the top of the flagpole. Add a texture to the cloth. One side of the cloth should be embedded in the flagpole cube as shown in Figure 7.40.

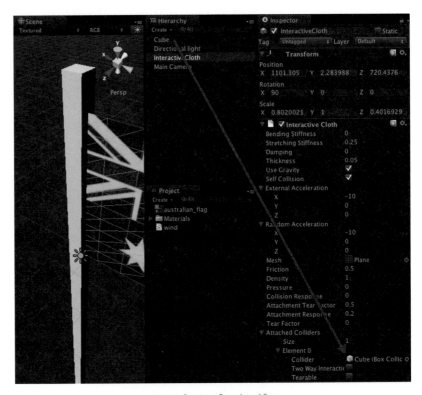

FIG 7.40 Creating a flagpole and flag.

> **Step 3.** Select the Cloth in the Hierarchy and locate the Interactive Cloth component. Set the Size of the Attached Colliders to 1 and drag and drop the cube object (which is the flagpole) onto the Collider value (see Figure 7.40).
>
> **Step 4.** Set the Interactive Cloth component's value for External Acceleration and Random Acceleration to a vector parallel with the flag. In the given example, in Figure 7.40, this is (−10,0,0).

Step 5. Play. The flag will flap under the physics of its own weight and the acceleration values. While the external acceleration is constant, the random one will add extra boost now and then. This gives an effect similar to a real flag in a breeze.

Step 6. Beneath the flag add a plane to act as the ground.

Step 7. Next to the flagpole, above the ground, add a sphere. To the sphere add a rigidbody.

Step 8. Play. Ensure that the sphere falls to the ground.

Step 9. Select the sphere in the Hierarchy and select Component > Physics > Constant Force to add a force to the sphere. Set the value of Force for this to the same value as the Cloth's External Acceleration, for example, (−10,0,0).

Step 10. Play. The sphere will now fall but in an arc. When it hits the ground it will roll off in the direction the constant force is pushing it.

Step 11. Create a new JavaScript file called *windControls*. Add the code in Listing 7.6.

Listing 7.6 A Scrollbar That Controls the Wind

```
var cloth: GameObject;
var sphere: GameObject;
var vScrollbarValue : float;
function OnGUI ()
{
     vScrollbarValue = GUI. VerticalScrollbar (
          Rect (25, 25, 100, 100),
          vScrollbarValue, 0.0, 100.0, 0.0);
     cloth.GetComponent(InteractiveCloth).externalAcceleration =
          new Vector3(-vScrollbarValue,0,0);
     sphere.GetComponent(ConstantForce).force =
          new Vector3(-vScrollbarValue,0,0);
}
```

Step 12. Attach this code to the Main Camera. Select the Main Camera and locate the script in the Inspector. Set the values for cloth to the InteractiveCloth and sphere to the Sphere objects in the Hierarchy.

Step 13. Play. The scrollbar will control the amount of wind force on the objects.

7.6.2 Precipitation

Rain and snow add yet another dimension to the game environment. Not only do they look good but they add atmosphere and can be used to impair the vision of the player strategically. Precipitation falls into a category of computer graphics special effects called *particle systems*. They rightly deserve a category of their own and as such will be dealt with in the next section.

7.7 Particles

Particle systems are objects constructed from the mass generation of animated billboards. Each billboard represents a single particle. They are used most commonly in games to generate fluidic and fuzzy phenomena such as rain, snow, dust, fire, smoke, and explosions. The CloudsToy implemented previously and the Detonator objects used in other chapters' workshops are examples of particle systems.

A particle system consists of an emitter that spawns the particles at a specific location. As they are created, each particle is given a velocity, size, and life length. The particle begins its life, is scaled to the given size, and travels off at the set velocity for the length of its life. At the end of its life the particle is destroyed. For extra effect, a particle can be given a rotational velocity, an animated color change, and size changes throughout its life. Several example particle systems are illustrated in Figure 7.41.

FIG 7.41 Particle systems: (a) a uniform system with all particles having a vertical velocity; (b) a vertical system with random *x* and *y* velocities, expanding size and changing color; (c) a fire made with three systems—one for inner glow, one for flames, and one for smoke; and (d) a water fountain.

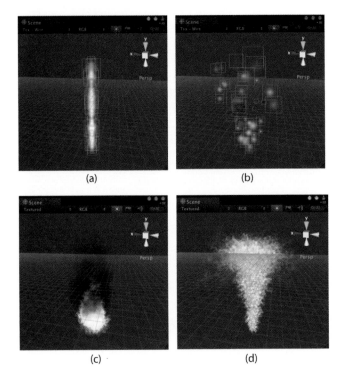

(a)   (b)

(c)   (d)

Particle systems can be very processor intensive as they can require hundreds or thousands of particles to simulate the desired effect. However, having each particle represented as a 2D billboard helps lower overheads (somewhat).

A number of prefab particle systems are included in Unity packages; however, the best way to get an understanding of their intricacies is to create them from scratch.

Unity Hands On
A Snowy Retreat

Step 1. Download *Chapter Seven/Particles.zip*. Open the SnowyRetreat scene in Unity.

Step 2. Select GameObject > Create Object > Particle System to add a particle system into the scene. While selected, the particle system runs even if the game is not. The default particle system is shown in Figure 7.42.

FIG 7.42 Unity's default particle system.

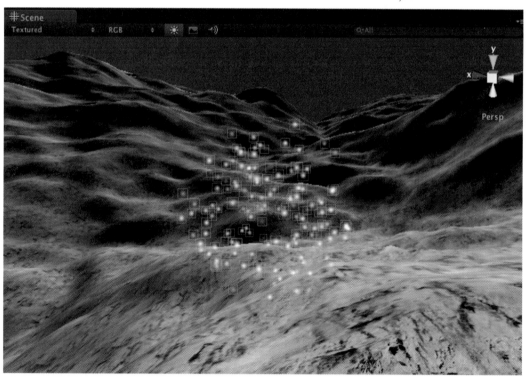

Step 3. Rename the particle system *Smoke* and reposition it in the top of the chimney of the log cabin.

Step 4. Select Smoke in the Hierarchy and locate the Ellipsoid Particle Emitter component in the inspector. This is the object spawning the particles.

Step 5. Set the World Velocity *y* value to 2. Note how the particles start to move upward.

Step 6. Change the Min Size to 3 and the Max Size to 4. This is the range of sizes between which particles will be scaled.

Step 7. Modify the Min Energy to 5 and the Max Energy to 15. This is the range of lifetime given to individual particles. Note how the particles go farther up. This is because they are living longer than before.

Step 8. Change the *x* and *z* values for Rnd Velocity to 0.5. This will give each particle a random *x* and *z* value added on top of any world or local velocity. In this case it will make the particles go up and slightly out.

Step 9. Below in the Particle Animator component set the *x* value for force to 0.5. This will apply a constant force in the *x* direction to each particle. It will cause them to rise up out of the chimney and start to move off at an angle as if blown by a slight wind.

Step 10. Set the Rnd Force's *x* and *y* values to 1. This will add an extra force to the particles between −0.5 and 0.5 in the *x* and *y* directions. In some cases it will add to the constant force and other times counteract it. This will make for more random smoke movement while still keeping it blowing away into the distance.

Step 11. Change the Animate Colors to alternate colors of white and gray. This will give the smoke more character and depth. These colors are the colors the particle will cycle through during its lifetime, starting at color 0 and finishing at color 4.

Step 12. Play. By now you should have a nice smoking particle effect coming from the chimney as shown in Figure 7.43.

Step 13. Next we are going to make it snow. Add a new particle system to the scene and call it Snow. Position it above the cabin.

Step 14. Set the World Velocity *y* value to −5. This will make the particles fall.

Step 15. Change the Min and Max Energy to 20 and 50, respectively. The particles need enough time to fall to the ground before being destroyed.

Step 16. Increase the Min and Max Emission to 200 and 500, respectively, to create more particles. For denser snow you can increase these values later.

Step 17. Set the Particle Emitter's Ellipsoid size to (50,1,50). This will increase the area in which particles are created in the *x* and *z* directions, meaning that they will be created at the same *y* position but cover a larger area. By now the particles should be looking like snow.

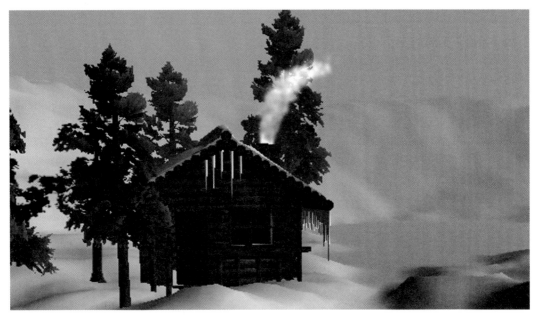

FIG 7.43 A particle system simulating chimney smoke.

Step 18. If you'd rather have bigger snowflakes, increase the Min and Max Sizes of the particles.

Step 19. Add the First Person Controller to the Scene and place it just outside the cabin. It may need to be resized to fit the scene.

Step 20. Delete the old Main Camera.

Step 21. Select the First Person Controller camera and set the Background color to that of the fog.

Step 22. Play. Watch the snow falling.

The only problem with the current snow is that it is a very isolated system. If you walk your character down the road a little, you will walk out of the snow zone. You could increase the size of the emitter ellipsoid to cover a larger area, but this would mean increasing the number of falling particles to get the same density. Unfortunately, the more particles, the more strain on the processing of your game and the slower it will run. However, we can employ a simple trick to make it look as though it is snowing everywhere on the terrain.

Step 23. Select the Snow in the Hierarchy and drag and drop it onto the First Person Controller to attach. Now it will move everywhere the player does. Select the Snow object once attached and set its position to (0,10,0). This will ensure that the snow emitter is always directly above the player.

Step 24. Depending on how fast the player can move, you may need to increase the ellipsoid size a little so that the player never outruns new particles. In this example, if you set the ellipsoid's size to (100,1,100) and the Min and Max Emissions to 500 and 100, respectively, it gives good snow coverage that can keep up with the player's maximum speed.

Step 25. Finally, we are going to add little snow splats on the ground when the snowflakes hit the ground. Create a new particle system and call it Splat.

Step 26. Set the Min and Max Sizes to 0.1 and 0.3, the Min and Max Energies to 0.3 and 0.3, the Min and Max Emissions to 10 and 10, the World Velocity y value to 1, the Rnd Velocity to (1,1,1), and the Ellipsoid to (0,0,0). Tick the One Shot box.

The emitter ellipsoid size of 0 will cause all particles to originate from the same location, and One Shot will make the emitter shoot out all particles at once instead of releasing them randomly. This creates a little puff effect.

Step 27. Create a new prefab from the Splat and remove the Splat object from the Hierarchy.

Step 28. Select the Snow particle system attached to the First Person Controller in the Hierarchy. From the main menu select Component > Particles > World Particle Collider. At this instance you will notice a change in the behavior of the snow. It will start to bounce off everything!

Step 29. Create a JavaScript file called *particlehit* and add the code in Listing 7.7.

Listing 7.7 Script to Detect Individual Particle Collisions and Instantiate Another Particle System

```
var splat: Transform;
function LateUpdate ()
{
      var theParticles = particleEmitter.particles;
      for (var i = 0; i < particleEmitter.particleCount; i++ )
      {
            if(theParticles[i].energy > particleEmitter.
maxEnergy)
            {
                  var splatObj: Transform =
                        Transform.Instantiate(splat,
                                    theParticles[i].position,
                                    Quaternion.identity );
                        theParticles[i].energy = 0;
                        Destroy(splatObj.gameObject, 0.3);
            }
      }

      particleEmitter.particles = theParticles;
}
```

Step 30. Attach this script to the Snow object.

Because individual particles do not exist to attach script to, this code attaches to the particle emitter and loops through all its particles. When it detects a particle's individual energy value has become larger than the emitter's maximum energy setting, it instantiates a splat. The trick now is to cause the particle's energy to spike when it collides as this doesn't happen automatically.

Step 31. Select the Snow object and locate the World Particle Collider component in the Inspector. Set the Collision Energy Loss to −100. This will boost the energy (a.k.a. life) of the particle by 100, which is far greater than the emitter maximum of 50. When this happens, the attached particle script test will become true and a splat obj will be instantiated.

Step 32. Before playing, set the Splat value of the Particle Hit script attached to the Snow to the Splat prefab created before. This is illustrated in Figure 7.44.

Step 33. Play. The snowflakes will now create small puffs when they hit the ground. The final scene is shown in Figure 7.45.

The very same particle system can be used to create rain. The only difference would be the size of the particles and the splashes.

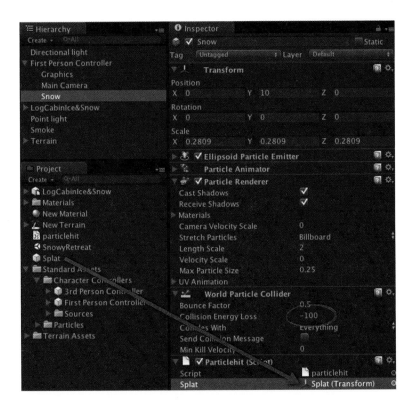

FIG 7.44 Setting the snow particle system up to detect particle collisions and create a splat.

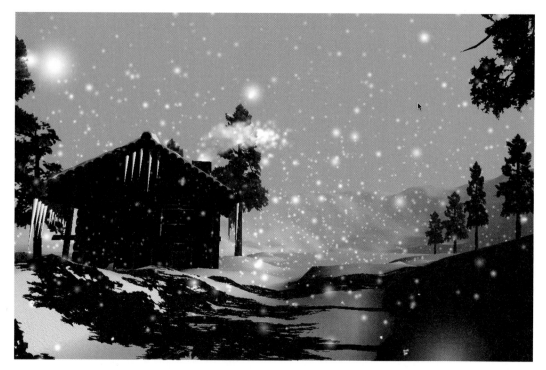

FIG 7.45 The final snow scene.

7.8 Summary

This chapter examined the artistic and scientific aspects of the real world in order to recreate similar environments as game environments. So many of the physics and mathematics of the real world translate into virtual environments, and an understanding of these assists us in making the virtual look and feel as real as possible for a player.

Only through observing the world around us, the types of vegetation, the shapes of rocks, the colors in the sky, and the way things move can we gain a deeper appreciation of the articulation of what can turn a virtual environment into something believable. This chapter has only scratched at the surface of what is possible in developing the aesthetics of a game environment, although it is hoped that you've gained enough knowledge and confidence to go in search of new techniques that you can incorporate in your games to make them look that much more professional and polished.

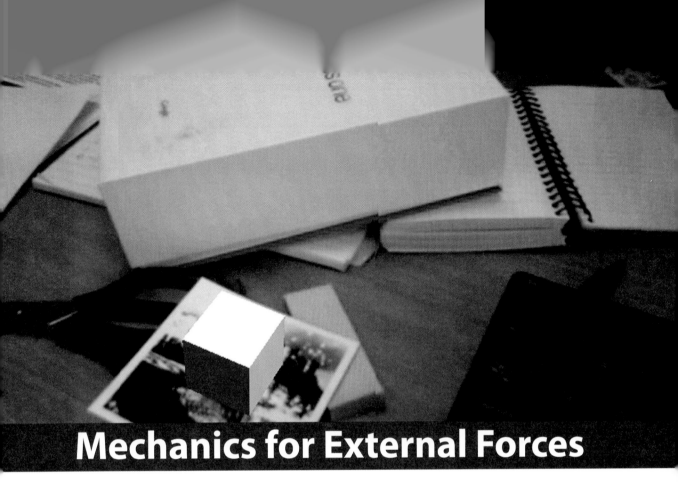

Mechanics for External Forces

The Force will be with you. Always.

Obi-Wan Kenobi

8.1 Introduction

Designing games is challenging now more than ever. In addition to high-end gaming consoles and high-powered desktop graphics cards, there are also low-powered mobile devices for which to cater. Of course, if you're designing a game for a mobile device it is not likely it will be released on a console. In addition to considering the different ways in which art assets are delivered, the designer also has the challenge of coming up with a really unique gaming experience.

The flood of mobile devices in the pockets of almost every consumer over 9 years of age has recently seen many small and independent game studios pop up—each battling for the casual gamer's attention.

Human–computer interaction (HCI) technology that once only existed in science fiction is now forefront in the designer's mind. Whether it be the tapping and dragging of a finger across a tablet screen or the tracking of waving arms and legs in front of a screen, the opportunity to create truly unique user experiences has never been more achievable.

Furthermore, if the challenge of designing for multiple platforms and a diversity of HCI methods weren't enough, multiplayer modes have almost become a necessity. Thanks to Twitter, Facebook, and others, today's players want to share their gaming experience with their friends, even if it is just to tell them they beat the other's high score.

This chapter examines the issue of new technologies with relation to game design and development. It examines how to integrate interactive devices, mobile devices, and social networking with your own games at the technical level. Workshops for integrating Unity with Twitter, Facebook, mobile devices, and more are featured throughout.

8.2 Up and Running on a Mobile Device

One of the best ways to investigate as many of the new HCI features used in games as possible is to deploy an application to a mobile device. Unity supports both Android and iOS development with the purchase of an extra plugin. If your version of Unity is still in its trial period you will have up to 30 days to explore these platforms.

The next workshop demonstrates deployment to the Android platform as the process is far simpler than for iOS.

◉ Unity Hands On
Your First Android Application
You will need Unity Android and an Android mobile device to create this project. A 30-day trial version comes with the Unity Indy download.

Step 1. Download and install the Android SDK from http://developer .android.com/sdk/index.html.
Step 2. Open Unity and create a new project.
Step 3. From the main menu select File > Build Settings.
Step 4. In the Platform box click on Android.
Step 5. At the bottom click the Switch Platform button.
Step 6. Plug in the Android device with the USB cable to the computer.
Step 7. Turn on the device.
Step 8. If it is the first time the device has been turned on, skip over all the tutorial and settings checks and setup (you can do this later).
Step 9. The main screen will look something like that shown in Figure 8.1.
Step 10. Press on the menu settings icon on the device. This will bring up a menu.

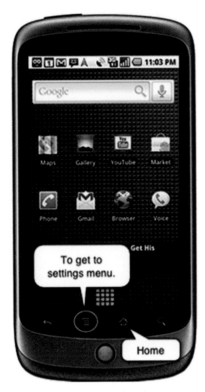

FIG 8.1 The Android interface.

Step 11. Select Settings.

Step 12. Select Applications.

Step 13. Select Development.

Step 14. Check the USB debugging and Stay awake options.

Step 15. Press the little house button to go to the home screen.

Step 16. Return to Unity.

Step 17. Go back to the Build Settings window.

Step 18. Click on the Player Settings button.

Step 19. In the Inspector, locate the Bundle Identifier field in the Other Settings area. Type a value in here of the format com.yourname .TestApplication as shown in Figure 8.2.

Step 20. At the top of the Inspector enter a Product Name. This will be the name under the icon for the game on the phone.

Step 21. Back in the Build Settings window click on the Build And Run button.

Step 22. Unity will want a name for the build file: "test" will do for now. If this is the first time you have created an Android build, Unity will also want to know the location of your Android SDK folder.

Step 23. The application will build and be pushed to the phone.

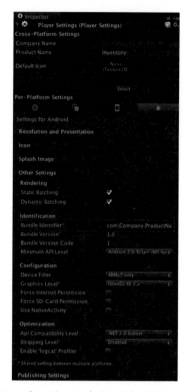

FIG 8.2 Essential settings for Unity Android deployment.

Step 24. It will run automatically and you will get the Unity splash screen followed by a blue screen. This is an empty game project. The one you just created and it is successfully running on the mobile device.

◉ Note

If Unity returns the error "No Android Device" when trying to build, unplug the phone and plug in again. Windows may want you to install new software. Allow it to find the software and install it. It will require drivers for the "Android Composite ADB Interface."

◉ On the Web

For detailed instructions on setting up Unity and Android, watch the author's tutorial at http://vimeo.com/17919196.

Step 25. Return to Unity. In the Game, change the aspect to Nexus One Tall or another mobile resolution to suit your device as shown in Figure 8.3.

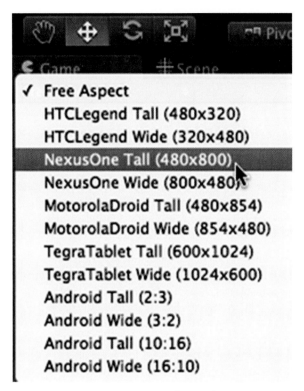

FIG 8.3 Selecting the screen display resolution of a mobile device in the Unity Editor.

Step 26. Download *Chapter Eight/Google Android.3ds* and add to the Project.

Step 27. Drag the Google Android from the Project into the Scene.

Step 28. Double-click on the Google Android in the Hierarchy. The Scene view will zoom in on it.

Step 29. If the axis gizmo in the top of the Scene is set to ISO, click on it to set it to Perspective.

Step 30. Select the Main Camera in the Hierarchy. From the main menu select GameObject > Align with View. This will match the camera to the Scene orientation. The 3D model will appear in the small camera preview window.

Step 31. Add a directional light.

Step 32. Select File > Build & Run to send the app to your mobile.

8.3 Integrating Haptics and External Motion into Games

The word *haptic* derives from the Greek meaning "a sense of touch." In addition to touching a screen, keyboard, controller, or mouse, computer games suffer from a lack of touch. Console controllers introduced haptics to games through vibration. Today this is still the most commonly used touch feedback. Some of the first game-related peripherals to include vibration as a game feedback include the Nintendo 64 Rumble Pak and Sony PlayStation's Dual Shock analog controller.

◁ Unity Specifics
Vibration
You can make an iOS and Android device (with the required capability) vibrate by executing the code iPhoneUtils.Vibrate();

In 2003, Sony released the EyeToy for PlayStation 2. This is essentially a webcam that attaches to the gaming console. Through the processing of the image taken by the camera, computer vision and gesture recognition algorithms can estimate the movements of a player.

Although the Nintendo Wii took game haptics to a new level with its Wii Remote, it was Microsoft that broke new ground by releasing the Kinect in 2010. Although players are not feeling the game environment with a sense of touch, they are still interacting with it kinesthetically and therefore experiencing a level of immersion not before experienced in preceding games. The Kinect provides full-body 3D motion capture through the use of a continually projecting infrared laser out in front of the screen in a pixel grid. Depth data are gathered from a monochrome sensor gathering information about the reflections of the laser. Currently the Kinect is capable of tracking six people simultaneously. The Kinect is also able to perform facial and voice recognition tasks.

The Kinect differs from the PlayStation Move, a game controller wand with built-in accelerometers and light on top, by sensing actual 3D data. The Move released also in 2010 uses a combination of motion sensing with visual recognition from the PlayStation Eye (the successor of the EyeToy) to recognize player movements.

Numerous groups are attempting to make access to the Kinect open source and cross platform. These include OpenKinect (http://openkinect.org/wiki/Main_Page) and OpenNI (http://openni.org/).

OpenKinect is a community of developers bringing free programming interfaces for the Kinect to Windows, Linux, and Mac such that independent application developers and researchers can implement their own Kinect-based games and applications. Links to their source code and tutorials for installation and use can be found on their Web site.

OpenNI is a not-for-profit organization driven by industry to promote the use of natural HCI in applications and games. Their OpenNI framework is open source and helps developers to integrate low-level vision and audio sensors and high-level computer vision and tracking algorithms for use in products that deliver third-party middleware solutions to be used by others.

Succeeding the technology of the Kinect are systems such as the Stage System by Organic Motion (http://organicmotion.com/). Currently used for real-time motion capture, this system has the potential to make games that are projected onto all the walls of a room where the player is positioned right in the center of the action. The Stage System has the ability to capture true full-body 3D-surround motion and structure with the use of its six cameras. It differs from the Kinect in that the Kinect only captures distances from the device itself to whatever is in front of it and tracks for key human features such as hands, feet, and head. Technologies such as these are driving games toward full-body immersive systems reminiscent of Star Trek's Holodeck.

8.4 Accessing Mobile Hardware Features

Believe it or not, mobile phones weren't originally designed for playing games. However, as games have become more popular on the platforms and their hardware and screens have advanced, games taking advantage of all the devices have to offer have grown in numbers. Primarily these include interacting with touch screens, inbuilt motion sensors, and location-based services.

This section explains these features and how to access them from within Unity.

8.4.1 Accelerometer

Accelerometers are electromechanical devices that measure acceleration forces. A circuit board, no bigger than a fingernail, can measure its angle of tilt by detecting the downward force of gravity and how fast it is traveling by sensing motion and vibration. Modern mobile devices have a microelectromechanical systems accelerometer integrated. These consist of a simple cantilever beam attached to a seismic mass sealed in a gas pocket. The beam acts as a bendable needle that moves under accelerative forces. Imagine the pendulum of a grandfather clock on the back of a truck and how it would move as the truck accelerates. The accelerometer is, in principle, the same. The movement of the beam is measured and reported as acceleration.

These same type of accelerometers are also found in the Nintendo Wii Remote and its Nunchuk and the PlayStation 3 Dual Shock 3 controller.

Data from accelerometers can be used in games to change the screen orientation, for example, turning a controller on its side, giving movement commands such as bowling or batting in Wii Sports games, or moving a character around in an environment, to name a few. The iPhone version of *Spore Origins*, for example, allows players to navigate their creature around in the primordial slime by tilting and rotating the device.

The accelerometer reports movement in 3D. In the case of Android, holding the device in an upright portrait with the screen facing you, an *x* acceleration will be registered if you tilt the phone forward and back, a *y* acceleration will be registered as the phone is swiveled around its vertical midpoint, and *z* acceleration is registered when the phone is brought toward and away from you. This is illustrated in Figure 8.4.

FIG 8.4 Acceleration axes of the Google Nexus One HTC mobile.

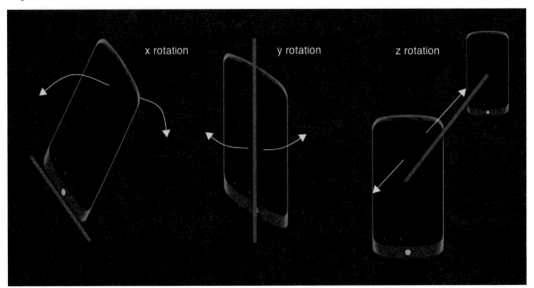

⊲ **Unity Specifics**
Measuring Acceleration
To access a device's acceleration data from within Unity, the Input class is used. When played on an iOS- or Android-enabled device (with an accelerometer), Input.acceleration will return the device's acceleration as a Vector3 value. The code in Listing 8.1 can be added to its own JavaScript, attached to the Main Camera, and deployed to a mobile device to display current acceleration values on the screen. The *x*, *y*, and *z* values obtained in this example could be used to change transform data of a game object and thus its position in the game world. Be careful though! The X, Y, and Z of the device do not automatically match the X, Y, and Z of your game world.

Listing 8.1 Unity JavaScript to Report on Mobile Device Acceleration

```
var speed = 10.0;
var dir: Vector3 = Vector3.zero;
function OnGUI()
{
    GUI.Label (Rect (10, 10, 100, 20), "x: " + dir.x);
    GUI.Label (Rect (10, 30, 100, 20), "y: " + dir.y);
    GUI.Label (Rect (10, 50, 100, 20), "z: " + dir.z);
}
function Update ()
{
    if(Mathf.Abs(Input.acceleration.x) > 1)
        dir.x = Input.acceleration.x;
    if(Mathf.Abs(Input.acceleration.y) > 1)
        dir.y = Input.acceleration.y;
    if(Mathf.Abs(Input.acceleration.z) > 1)
        dir.z = Input.acceleration.z;
}
```

8.4.2 Orientation

As revealed previously, the accelerometer in a device also measures its orientation. As the accelerometer is fixed with respect to the device, it is assumed that its orientation is the same. A device can register one of six orientations: facing up, facing down, upright portrait, upright landscape, upside-down portrait, and upside-down landscape.

◁ **Unity Specifics**
Measuring Orientation
As in the previous section, device orientation can be gathered from the Input class. The orientation value is found in Input .deviceOrientation. Each of the six orientation positions is catered for with the values DeviceOrientation.FaceDown, DeviceOrientation .FaceUp, DeviceOrientation.PortraitUpsideDown, DeviceOrientation .LandscapeLeft, DeviceOrientation.LandscapeRight, and DeviceOrientation .Portrait. These orientations relate to the Google Nexus One HTC mobile as shown in Figure 8.5.

Adding the script in Listing 8.2 to a new JavaScript file, attaching it to the Main Camera, and deploying the application to a mobile device will illustrate the reporting of orientation from within Unity. The orientation can then be used to move characters and/or flip the player's view.

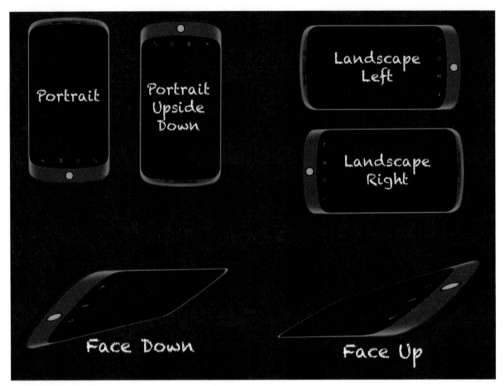

FIG 8.5 Orientations of a Google Nexus One HTC mobile phone.

Listing 8.2 Unity JavaScript to Report on Device Orientation

```
private var orientString = "Unknown";
private var pivotPoint = Vector2(200,200);
private var rotAngle = 0;
function OnGUI()
{
     if (Input.deviceOrientation == DeviceOrientation.FaceDown)
     {
          orientString = "Face Down";
          rotAngle = 0;
     }
     if (Input.deviceOrientation == DeviceOrientation.FaceUp)
```

```
    {
        orientString = "Face Up";
        rotAngle = 0;
    }
    if (Input.deviceOrientation == DeviceOrientation.Portrait)
    {
        orientString = "Portrait";
        rotAngle = 0;
    }
    if (Input.deviceOrientation ==
            DeviceOrientation.PortraitUpsideDown)
    {
        orientString = "Portrait Upside Down";
        rotAngle = 180;
    }
    if (Input.deviceOrientation ==
            DeviceOrientation.LandscapeLeft)
    {
        orientString = "Landscape Left";
        rotAngle = 90;
    }
    if (Input.deviceOrientation ==
            DeviceOrientation.LandscapeRight)
    {
        orientString = "Landscape Right";
        rotAngle = -90;
    }

    GUI.BeginGroup (Rect (Screen.width / 2 - 200,
                          Screen.height / 2 - 200, 400, 400));
    GUIUtility.RotateAroundPivot (rotAngle, pivotPoint);
    GUI.Label (Rect (0, 0, 400, 400), orientString);
    GUI.EndGroup ();
}
```

8.4.3 Web Services

Access to the Internet is another feature integrated into mobile devices.
People use them to surf the Web and send and receive email. This
functionality can be exploited in games to send emails from within a game
or obtain data from a Web site. For example, extra game information may
be obtained from a Web site on an as needed basis. This occurs in *Parallel
Kingdom* when the player wants to look up further information
on a monster or item.

Calling and Retrieving URLs
Unity provides a WWW() function that can make a URL request retrieving data. As data can be sent and retrieved in any format, it makes it quite a powerful feature. For calls to Web sites, data are collected in raw HTML. You cannot display the webpage as it appears, but rather gather its HTML code. XML and HTML Unity parser packages can be purchased from the Unity Store should you wish to display a Web site inside a Unity application.

The following workshops demonstrate simple methods for sending emails. In the latter exercise where a Web server is employed, the code could be modified to support the sending of user data to a game server for a multiplayer game. However, WWW calls are notoriously slow with respect to a game server and this method would not be recommended for live-action games, such as real-time car racing.

◉ **Unity Hands On**
Sending Mail with Device Mail Client
> **Step 1.** Create a JavaScript file named *interface* and add the code shown in Listing 8.3.

Listing 8.3 Sending a Simple Email Message from a Unity Application

```
function OnGUI()
{
      if(GUI.Button(Rect(10,10,180,30),"Send"))
      {
            Application.OpenURL(
"mailto:test@email.com?subject=Test Email&body=from Unity App");
      }
}
```

> **Step 2.** Attach this code to the Main Camera.
> **Step 3.** This code won't work in the Unity Editor. Build and push the app to a mobile phone.
> **Step 4.** Run the app. When you push the Send button, the email client installed on the device will open with the subject and body lines already included.
> **Step 5.** To send more information from the app to email client, modify *interface.js* to that in Listing 8.4.

434

Listing 8.4 Prepopulating Email Data in a Unity Application Before Sending

```
private var toEmail = "test@email.com";
private var nameField = "My Name";
private var messageField = "Message";
function OnGUI()
{
    GUI.Label(Rect(10,10,50,50),"To");
    toEmail = GUI.TextField (Rect (100, 10, 200, 50), toEmail);

    GUI.Label(Rect(10,60,50,50),"Name");
    nameField = GUI.TextField (Rect (100, 60, 200, 50),
                nameField);
    GUI.Label(Rect(10,120,120,50),"Message");
    messageField = GUI.TextArea(Rect(100, 120, 200, 200),
                messageField);
    if(GUI.Button(Rect(50,350,180,50),"Send"))
    {
        Application.OpenURL("mailto:" + toEmail + "?" +
                "subject=Test Email&" +
                "body=From: " +
                nameField + "\n" + messageField);
    }
}
```

Step 6. Play. An email form will be created in the Unity app as shown in Figure 8.6. When send is pressed the information entered will be sent to the user's email client.

⬤ **Note**

The format for a mailto string should be mailto:email_address?email _information. The question mark always separates the email address of the recipient with extra data, which are divided into a number of headers separated by ampersands. Each header has a name and its own value set with an equals sign. The headers can include:

- subject—the text that will appear in the subject line
- body—the email message
- cc—the email address of others to send a copy of the message
- bcc—the email address of others who will receive the email but not appear in the send email message of the original

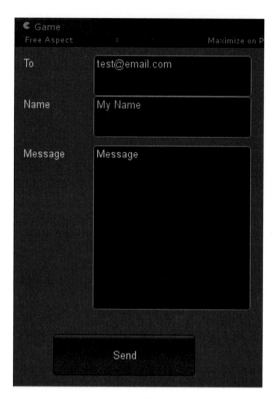

FIG 8.6 A simple email form screen in Unity.

⊙ Unity Hands On
Sending Mail via a Web Server

This method of sending an email from your app may be preferred as the application will not close to open the mail app. Data are sent straight from the app to the server. You can also use this method for passing other information to a Web server.

Step 1. Create a new Unity Project.

Step 2. Create a JavaScript file called *emailViaServer* and add the code shown in Listing 8.5. Note that the server URL is shown in bold in the code. This is where you put the URL of your own server.

Listing 8.5 Sending Data from a Unity App to a Web Server for the Purpose of Emailing

```
private var toEmail = "test@email.com";
private var nameField = "My Name";
private var messageField = "Message";
private var showWebMessage = false;
```

```
private var emailSuccessful = 1;
function webMessageScreen()
{
      GUI.BeginGroup (Rect (Screen.width / 2 - 50,
Screen.height / 2 - 50, 100, 100));
      GUI.Box (Rect (0,0,100,100), "Email Message");

      if(emailSuccessful == 1)
            GUI.Label(Rect(10,20,100,50),"Sending...");
      if(emailSuccessful == 2)
            GUI.Label(Rect(10,20,100,50),"Email Sent");
      else if(emailSuccessful == 3)
            GUI.Label(Rect(10,20,100,50),"Email Failed");

      if (GUI.Button (Rect (10,50,80,30), "Ok"))
      {
            showWebMessage = false;
      }
      GUI.EndGroup ();
}

function sendEmail()
{
      emailSuccessful = 1;
      showWebMessage = true;
      var msgBody = "From: " + nameField + "\n" + messageField;
      var form = new WWWForm();
      form.AddField("to", toEmail);
      form.AddField("subject", "Email Subject");
      form.AddField("body", msgBody);
      var www = new WWW("http://someweb.com/emailer.php", form);
  yield www;
  if (www.error != null)
  {
    emailSuccessful = 3;
  }
  else
  {
    emailSuccessful = 2;
  }
}

function OnGUI()
{
      GUI.Label(Rect(10,10,50,50),"To");
      toEmail = GUI.TextField (Rect (100, 10, 200, 50), toEmail);

      GUI.Label(Rect(10,60,50,50),"Name");
      nameField = GUI.TextField (Rect (100, 60, 200, 50), nameField);

      GUI.Label(Rect(10,120,120,50),"Message");
```

```
        messageField = GUI.TextArea (Rect (100, 120, 200, 200),
                                      messageField);

        if(GUI.Button(Rect(50,350,180,50),"Send"))
        {
                sendEmail();
        }
        if(showWebMessage)
        {
                webMessageScreen();
        }
}
```

Step 3. Attach this code to the Main Camera. You can test this application in the Unity Editor as it does not require your mail program. It will send data to a server and the server will send the email. Remember to check your spam folder for the test email.

Step 4. The server code is written in php. The code is very simple. In this case, emailer.php is given in Listing 8.6.

Listing 8.6 php Web Emailer

```php
<?php
$to = $_POST["to"];
$subject = $_POST["subject"];
$body = $_POST["body"];
$headers = 'From: mobileEmailTester@someweb.com' . "\r\n" .
  'Reply-To: no-reply@someweb.com' . "\r\n" .
  'X-Mailer: PHP/' . phpversion();
 if (mail($to, $subject, $body, $headers))
 {
 echo("<p>Message successfully sent!</p>");
 } else
 {
 echo("<p>Message delivery failed...</p>");
 }
?>
```

If you have access to a php-enabled Web server, try creating your own php server file with this code and redirect your mobile app to it. The full URL of emailer.php should appear in the sendEmail() function of Listing 8.5.

8.4.4 Global Positioning System (GPS)

Today's smart phones and tablets come with GPS receivers. These devices calculate their position on the earth by bouncing signals off the satellites of the global positioning system. The GPS was conceived by the American Department of Defense (DOD) in 1973 with the first satellites being launched in 1978. In 1993 the DOD decided to make it free for civilian use. The official name of the system is NAVSTAR (Navigation System for Timing and Ranging).

The GPS consists of 30 satellites orbiting the earth within a distance of 20,200 kilometers. The satellites are solar powered and circle the globe two times each day. The configuration of the satellites is such that at any location on the Earth's surface at least four are visible in the sky.

The GPS receiver in a mobile device calculates its position through analysis of the high-frequency, low-power radio signals emitted by the satellites. It determines its distance from any four of the satellites it is able to detect and works out its position. The process is called *trilateration*.

Trilateration finds the intersection of a number of circles or spheres. In the case of 3D space and the GPS system, for each detected satellite a sphere can be imagined around each with a radius equal to the distance to the satellite calculated by the GPS device. The location of each satellite is known, as the DOD monitors them constantly to ensure that they are aligned. With this information from four satellites and including the earth itself as another sphere in the equation, the location of the GPS device can be restricted to the area in which all spheres intersect. This process is illustrated in Figure 8.7 with just two spheres. The typical accuracy of GPS in mobile devices is around 10 meters.

Possibly the largest GPS-based game is *Geocaching*. It's a worldwide treasure hunt involving the hiding and locating of small boxes of items placed all around the globe. The GPS positions of *geocaches* are registered on the Web. Using a GPS navigation system, people scour the earth, arriving at the correct coordinates and then searching in the vicinity for a box, canister, or jar hidden cleverly under a pile of sticks, behind a brick, or even inside hollow fence poles. When found, the person records his or her presence on the log book inside and leaves a small token or gift. More details about the geocaching phenomenon can be found at http://geocaching.com.

The general genres of games that include geocaching are known as location-based games. Most are in the format of real-world scavenger hunts, such as visiting locations for points or virtual artifacts. *Tourality* (http://tourality .com/) is one such game; see Figure 8.8. The goal is to reach as many predefined GPS locations (stored in game sets) in the shortest amount of time. *Tourality* generates game sets based on the location of the player. It is possible to play in single player or multiplayer mode.

FIG 8.7 Satellite trilateration with two satellites.

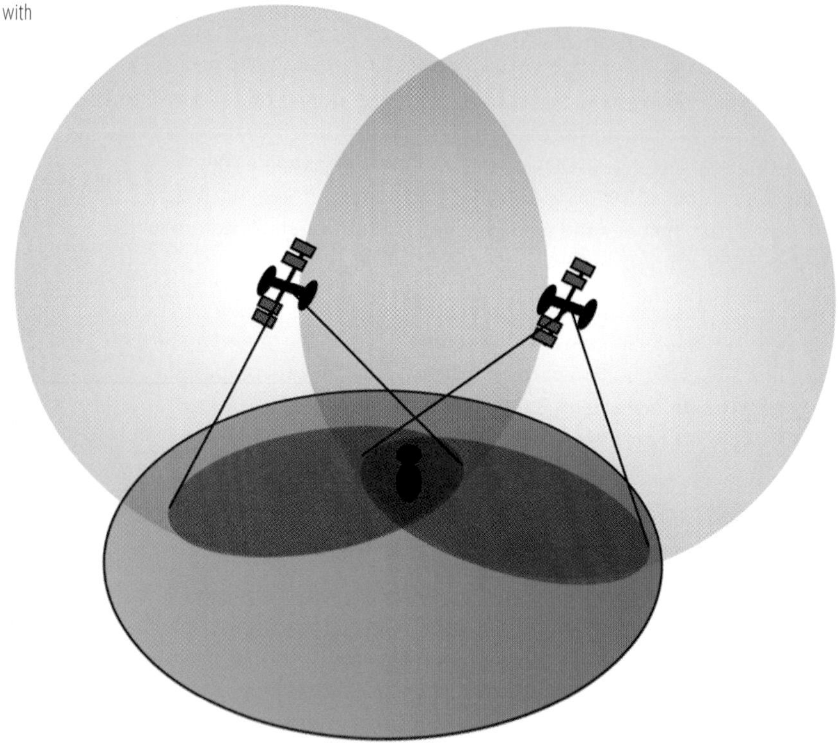

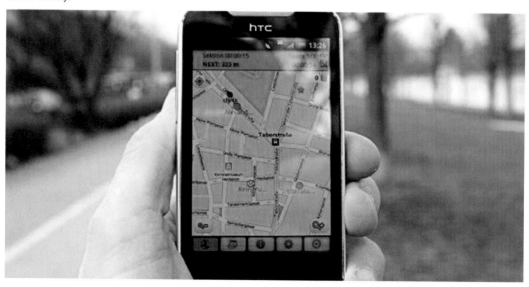

FIG 8.8 *Tourality*.

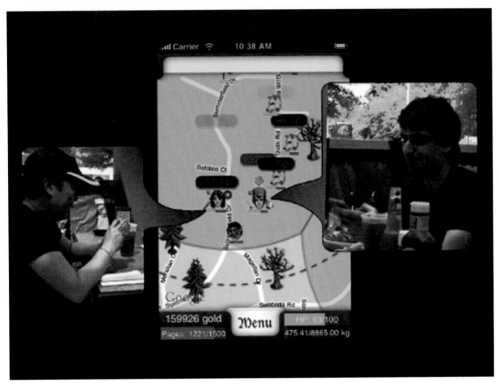

FIG 8.9 *Parallel Kingdom.*

Parallel Kingdom by PerBlue is the first location-based mobile massively multiplayer online role-playing game played in the real world (http://parallelkingdom.com/). It uses a player's GPS location to superimpose an imaginary fantasy world over the top of a Google Map as shown in Figure 8.9. The player can move around an approximate 1.3-mile radius on the map by tapping on the mobile screen. To move farther afield, the player has to physically go to another location in the real world. As with other role-playing games, players fight monsters and collect items while exploring their environment for experience points and leveling up their skills.

My Grove, by Kranky Panda (http://krankypanda.com/mygrove/), is another location-based multiplayer game that creates a virtual world over a map of the real world as shown in Figure 8.10. Players move from one geographical location to another with the goal being to plant and maintain virtual fruit trees to offset carbon emissions. Players compete against each other to be the top fruit producers in their area. They can also help other players tend to their trees or sabotage them!

You too can use GPS coordinates in your own games. The next workshop shows you how to obtain a player's location in Unity iOS and Android.

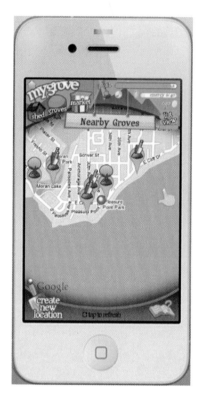

FIG 8.10 *My Grove.*

◎ Unity Hands On
GPS

Step 1. Create a new Unity project. Set it to build for iPhone or Android depending on the device you have.

Step 2. Create a new JavaScript file called *getGPS*. Add the code shown in Listing 8.7.

Listing 8.7 Obtaining GPS Coordinates

```
var locationFound: boolean;
function Start ()
{
     locationFound = false;
     iPhoneSettings.StartLocationServiceUpdates();

     var maxWait : int = 10;
     while (iPhoneSettings.locationServiceStatus ==
       LocationServiceStatus.Initializing && maxWait > 0) {
       yield WaitForSeconds(1);
       maxWait--;
     }
```

```
    if (maxWait < 1)
        {
        return;
        }

    if (iPhoneSettings.locationServiceStatus ==
                        LocationServiceStatus.Failed)
        {
        return;
        }
    else
        {
    locationFound = true;
    }

    iPhoneSettings.StopLocationServiceUpdates();
}
function OnGUI()
{

    if(locationFound)
    {
        GUI.Label(Rect(10,10,200,30),"Latitude: " +
                    iPhoneInput.lastLocation.latitude);
        GUI.Label(Rect(10,30,200,30),"Longitude: " +
                    iPhoneInput.lastLocation.longitude);
        GUI.Label(Rect(10,50,200,30),"Altitude: " +
                    iPhoneInput.lastLocation.altitude);
        GUI.Label(Rect(10,70,200,30),"Accuracy: " +
                    iPhoneInput.lastLocation.
                                horizontalAccuracy);
        GUI.Label(Rect(10,90,200,30),"Time: " +
                    iPhoneInput.lastLocation.timestamp);
    }
    else
    {
        GUI.Label(Rect(10,10,200,30),
                    "Could not initialise location services.");
    }
    if(GUI.Button(Rect(10,110,80,50),"Quit"))
    {
        Application.Quit();
    }
}
```

Step 3. Play. If your mobile device can access satellite data, the screen will contain details of your GPS location.

8.4.5 Augmented Reality (AR)

Although AR technology has been available since 1968, it has only been since 2006 or so that applications have become increasingly popular. This is due primarily to the availability of webcams with desktop and laptop computers and cameras, coupled with increased processing power in handheld devices and mobile phones. Technology from the domain of three-dimensional gaming is particularly key with respect to augmented reality as it allows efficient and seamless integration of high-quality animated virtual objects with AR applications.

In recent times, AR has slowly been creeping into the field of computer games. Some interactive applications of note include the Sony PlayStation Eye Toy and the EyePet and the Ninendo DS3D Nintendogs. In these games, players see their real world streamed via a camera onto the screen and superimposed with virtual game characters. The characters are positioned such that they appear to be existing in the real world. Players almost feel like they can reach out and touch them.

Augmented reality is a multidisciplinary field based in computer science with the goal of providing a viewer with an environment containing both real and virtual objects. With the use of mobile devices with cameras, computer-generated images are projected on top of the physical environment. To ensure correct positioning of virtual objects in the real world, hardware and software are required to determine accurately the viewer's location and orientation (point of view, POV). The POV can be matched with the location of a camera in a virtual model of the physical location and augmented objects and information projected onto the real-world image. Alternatively, a visual symbol in the real world known as a *fiduciary marker* can have its position relative to the POV determined and used as the location and orientation of a virtual object. This latter AR technique is examined in this section as such applications can be created easily for Android mobile devices with Unity and the Qualcomm Augmented Reality SDK.

☉ Unity Hands On
Augmented Reality in Unity on Android Device

Step 1. Visit https://ar.qualcomm.com/qdevnet/sdk and download the QualComm Unity Extension. Install on your computer as per the instructions on the Web site.

Step 2. Create a new Unity project and import the QCAR-1.0.unitypackage. Set the project for the Android platform.

Step 3. In the Project open the Qualcomm Augmented Reality > Prefabs folder and drag and drop the ARCamera into the Scene. Delete the original Main Camera.

Step 4. Download *Chapter Eight/marker.unitypackage* and import into the project. This package contains AR tracking marker data.
Step 5. Drag and drop Image Target prefab into the Scene from the Qualcomm Augmented Reality > Prefabs folder in the Project. Set the Image Target of this to tracker as shown in Figure 8.11.

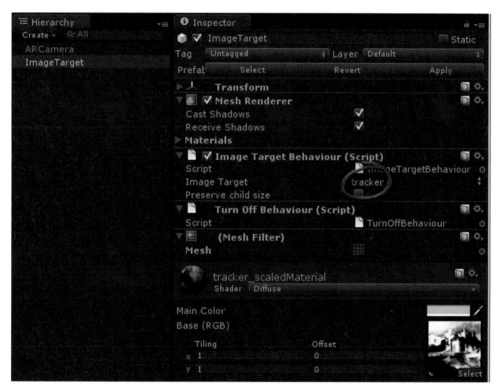

FIG 8.11 Setting the AR marker.

Step 6. Add a cube to the Scene. Resize the cube and position it on top of the marker as shown in Figure 8.12. This will be the size and position of the cube relative to the marker in the AR application.
Step 7. Download the marker from *Chapter Eight/marker.jpg* and print out (if you are unable to print, you can also simply open the image and point your device at your screen).
Step 8. Select File > Build and Run from main menu. The camera will open on the Android device. Point it at the marker and the cube will appear as shown in Figure 8.13.

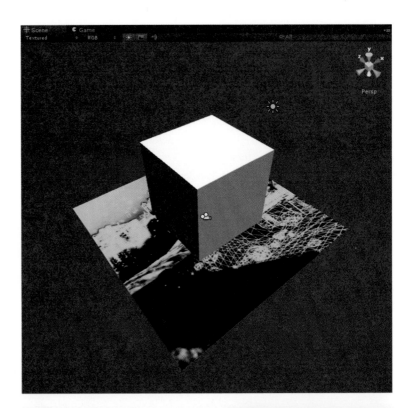

FIG 8.12 A cube positioned on the marker.

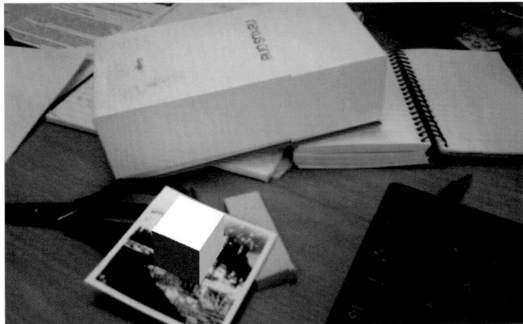

FIG 8.13 A simple AR application with Unity running on Android.

8.5 The Social Mechanic

Whether you are playing a game on a mobile device, desktop computer, or console, nowadays it is difficult to escape the social element. From creating personalized 3D avatars on Xbox live to inviting friends to farm virtual pastures on Facebook, the opportunity to boast about your fortunes (or misfortunes) in computer games now expands much farther than your immediate family and friends. Most computer games proudly display the Twitter, Facebook, MySpace, OpenFeint, and other icons on their menu screens—encouraging you to share your gaming experiences with the wider community.

As online social networks have been developed by other parties, it's not always an easy process to integrate your game with their system. Fortunately, many developers provide application programming interfaces (APIs) for you to use in your own code. These are plug-and-play functions that you can call in your script to access their system's functionality.

This section looks at two popular social network APIs and how they integrate with Unity.

8.5.1 Twitter

Twitter is a Web service allowing people to post a message 140 characters long to a Web site. The message isn't for anybody in particular, although Twitter allows other subscribers to follow the messages of another. In a way it is a method for posting your thoughts at any time into cyberspace for nobody or everybody to read about. The Twitter.com Web site was founded by Jack Dorsy and was launched in July 2006. Since then it has grown to over 200 million users posting around 200 million messages (called tweets) a day.

Twitter has its own API allowing other applications to retrieve twitter data. This API can be run as a URL typed into a Web site. For example, at the time of writing, typing http://twitter.com/statuses/user_timeline/aplusk.json?count=2 into a Web browser will return the text shown in Listing 8.8—the last two tweets by Ashton Kutcher, supposedly the most followed person.

Listing 8.8 Data about the Last Two Tweets Posted by Ashton Kutcher

```
[{"truncated":false,"user":{"profile_use_background_
image":true,"protected":false,"location":"Los Angeles,
California","is_translator":false,"profile_background_
color":"9AE4E8","name":"ashton
kutcher","follow_request_sent":false,"statuses_
count":6789,"profile_background_image_url":"http:\/\/
a1.twimg.com\/profile_background_images\/189603515\/
6a00d83451f25369e2012877a0864a970c.jpg","url":"http:\/\/
```

facebook.com\/Ashton","following":true,"verified":true,
"utc_offset":-18000,"created_at":"Fri Jan 16 07:40:06
+0000 2009","profile_text_color":"333333",
"description":"I make stuff, actually I make up stuff,
stories mostly, collaborations of thoughts, dreams,
and actions. Thats
me.","id_str":"19058681","profile_sidebar_fill_
color":"DDFFCC","default_profile":false,"listed_
count":70202,"geo_enabled":false,"profile_background_
tile":true,"favourites_count":82,"notifications":false,
"id":19058681,"show_all_inline_media":false,"profile_link_
color":"8f000e","profile_image_url":"http:\/\/a3.twimg.com\/
profile_images\/1263338441\/Photo_on_2010-11-
30_at_20.36__3_normal.jpg","lang":"en","friends_
count":638,"profile_sidebar_
border_color":"BDDCAD","default_
profile_image":false,"contributors_
enabled":false,"time_zone":"Eastern Time (US
& Canada)","followers_count":6989941,"screen_
name":"aplusk"},"in_reply_to_user_id":null,"in_reply_to_
status_id":null,"text":"The cost of 1 nuke for a year
= 99,000 sq ft of solar panels. Nukes serve no purpose-
#cutnukes not clean energy!
http:\/\/t.co\/ecdJaG4","geo":null,"favorited":false,
"created_at":"Tue Jun 21 00:46:40 +0000
2011","in_reply_to_status_id_str":null,"id_
str":"82972670613929984","in_reply_to_screen_
name":null,"in_reply_to_user_id_str":null,"id":82
972670613929984,"contributors":null,"retweeted":
false,"source":"web","coordinates":null,"retweet_
count":45,"place":null},{"truncated":false,"user":
{"is_translator":false,"default_profile":false,"profile_
use_background_image":true,"protected":false,"loc
ation":"Los Angeles, California","follow_request_
sent":false,"statuses_count":6789,"profile_background_
color":"9AE4E8","name":"ashton
kutcher","profile_background_image_url":"http:\/\/
a1.twimg.com\/profile_background_images\/189603515\/6a
00d83451f25369e2012877a0864a970c.jpg","url":"http:\/\/
facebook.com\/Ashton","contributors_enabled":
false,"following":true,"verified":true,"utc_offset":-
18000,"created_at":"Fri Jan 16 07:40:06 +0000
2009","profile_text_color":"333333","description":"
I make stuff, actually I make up stuff, stories mostly,
collaborations of thoughts, dreams, and actions. Thats
me.","id_str":"19058681","listed_count":70202,"profile_
sidebar_fill_color":"DDFFCC","profile_background_
tile":true,"favourites_count":82,"friends_count":638
,"notifications":false,"id":19058681,"profile_link_

```
color":"8f000e","profile_image_url":"http:\/\/a3.twimg.
com\/profile_images\/1263338441\/Photo_on_2010-11-
30_at_20.36__3_normal.jpg","default_
profile_image":false,"show_all_inline_
media":false,"lang":"en","geo_enabled":false,"profile_
sidebar_border_color":"BDDCAD","time_zone":"Eastern
Time (US & Canada)","followers_count":6989945,"screen_
name":"aplusk"},"in_reply_to_user_id":null,"in_reply_
to_status_id":null,"text":"Joey Roth's stuff is legit
http:\/\/t.co\/pGQbtuX via
@Fab","geo":null,"favorited":false,"created_at":"Mon Jun
20 20:32:47 +0000
2011","in_reply_to_status_id_str":null,"id_
str":"82908775849267200","in_reply_to_screen_
name":null,"in_reply_to_user_id_str":null,"id":829
08775849267200,"contributors":null,"retweeted":fal
se,"source":"\u003Ca href=\"http:\/\/twitter.com\/
tweetbutton\"rel=\"nofollow\"\u003ETweet
Button\u003C\/a\u003E","coordinates":null,"retweet_
count":46,"place":null}]
```

Data returned are in a format called JSON (JavaScript Object Notation). It was designed as a human-readable text data interchange standard. Although it's difficult to make immediate sense of it by just looking at Listing 8.8 (because it is standardized), computer algorithms can be written to extract data into a more meaningful format. Messages in JSON are in the format *key : data*. To find messages typed in by Ashton among the other text, the key "*text*" is searched for and the following text in double quotes is the actual message. For the reader's benefit, the key "*text*" has been typed in bold in Listing 8.8 after which you will find the message.

Posting messages to Twitter on behalf of a user is much more complex. There are three authentication steps to which you need to adhere. The first step is to send Twitter a message from your application asking for permission to access the user's account. The user's Web browser then opens, asking them if it is ok for the application they are using to access the Twitter account. If the user permits this access he or she receives a PIN number. The user enters this PIN number into the application. Following this, the application sends another message to Twitter telling it that it has the PIN. Once Twitter determines that this PIN is correct, it sends personalized authority tokens back to the application. These tokens can be stored inside the application so that the user doesn't have to go through the authorization process again. With the tokens, the application can post tweets to the user's Twitter account.

The authorization process and sending tweets from a Unity application are examined in the next workshop.

Tweeting Unity

Step 1. Go to https://dev.twitter.com/apps/new and register your application. This will give you a number of keys and authorization values for your application. You can do this even if your application is only for the personal testing purposes of this tutorial. After you submit the application you will receive personalized codes for your app. They will look something like this:

API key:

`MpYzjvyhPZJe8Qyiitigfw`

Consumer key:

`SpMzjvyjKOJe5Xyiitigfw`

Consumer secret:

`LKJ5ddZzJOwaQghWRRmzR3YU4tOEypqASDf93Ge98`

Keep these values handy as you will require them soon. Note that the ones listed here are not real and will not work in your application.

Step 2. Create a new Unity project with a new Scene called TwitterPosting.

Step 3. Download and add *Chapter Eight/PostTweet.js* to the Project.

Step 4. Create a new folder in the Project called *Plugins*. Download and add *Chapter Eight/TwitterHelpers.js*. The reason the .cs files go in the Plugins folder is that we want Unity to compile them first—that way the functions inside are ready for use by the PostTweet code.

Step 5. Attach PostTweet to the Main Camera.

Step 6. Modify the PostTweet code to include the OnGUI function given in Listing 8.9.

Listing 8.9 A GUI Interface to Handle Twitter Authorization and Sending Tweets

```
function OnGUI()
{
     //if they are authenticated show a tweeting box
     if(Connected)
     {
          GUI.BeginGroup (Rect (Screen.width / 2 - 200,
                    Screen.height / 2 - 60, 400, 120));
          GUI.Box (Rect (0,0,400,120), ScreenName +
                                    " Send Your Tweet");
          Tweet = GUI.TextField(Rect(10,30,380,30), Tweet);
          GUI.Label(Rect(310,70,80,30),"Chars = " + Tweet.length);
```

```
            //if tweet too long blank out send button
            if(Tweet.length < 140)
            {
                    if (GUI.Button(Rect(10,70,80,30), "Submit"))
                    {
                            tweetSuccessful = false;
                            SubmitTweet();
                    }
            }

            GUI.Label(Rect(100,70,150,30),tweetSentMessage);

            GUI.EndGroup ();
            return;
    }

    //if not authenticated go through the authorisation process
    GUI.BeginGroup (Rect (Screen.width / 2 - 50,
                    Screen.height / 2 - 60, 100, 120));
    GUI.Box (Rect (0,0,100,120), "Access Twitter");
    if(!Authorized)
    {
            GUI.Label(Rect (10,30,80,50),
                    "Authorizing with Twitter. Stand by!");
    }
    else if(!Connected)
    {
            GUI.Label(Rect (10,30,80,50),"Pin:");
            AccessPIN = GUI.TextField(Rect(10,50,80,30), AccessPIN);
            if (GUI.Button(Rect(10,80,80,30), "Submit"))
    {
            SubmitPIN();
    }

    }

    GUI.EndGroup ();
}
```

The code in Listing 8.9 displays the box for entering the user's
PIN after they have received it from Twitter. If they are already
connected with Twitter the text field for submitting tweets is
displayed instead.

Step 7. Next you'll want to store the tokens once the user has been
authenticated so that the next time they use your program they
don't need to go through the authentication process again. To
do this we will use the PlayerPrefs functions to set and get these
values.

Step 8. Modify the Start() function of PostTweet to that shown in Listing 8.10.

Listing 8.10 Retrieving Previously Stored User Twitter Authentication Tokens

```
function Start()
{
        //Get any saved user twitter authentication information
        AuthToken = PlayerPrefs.GetString("AUTHTOKEN");
        AuthTokenSecret = PlayerPrefs.GetString("AUTHTOKENSECRET");
        UserId = PlayerPrefs.GetString("USERID");
        ScreenName = PlayerPrefs.GetString("SCREENNAME");
        //user hasn't connected to Twitter and allowed access
        if(UserId == "" && ScreenName == "")
        {
                AuthenticateTwitter();
        }
        else
        {
                Connected = true;
        }
}
```

Step 9. After the user has submitted the PIN for the first time and has been authenticated successfully, you'll want to set the PlayerPrefs. To do this, modify the SubmitPIN() function of PostTweet to that in Listing 8.11.

Listing 8.11 Saving User Twitter Authentication Values for the Application

```
function SubmitPIN()
{
        ...
        var emptyBody: byte[] = new byte[1];
        emptyBody[0] = 0;

        var authStep2 = new WWW(AccessTokenURL, emptyBody, headers);
        yield authStep2;

        //remember player tokens and details for posting
        //so next time they use the app you don't have to
        //authenticate with Twitter again
        AuthToken = TwitterHelpers.GetAuthToken(authStep2.text);
```

```
    AuthTokenSecret =
        TwitterHelpers.GetAuthTokenSecret(authStep2.text);
    UserId = TwitterHelpers.GetUserId(authStep2.text);
    ScreenName = TwitterHelpers.GetScreenName(authStep2.text);
    PlayerPrefs.SetString("AUTHTOKEN", AuthToken);
    PlayerPrefs.SetString("AUTHTOKENSECRET", AuthTokenSecret);
    PlayerPrefs.SetString("USERID", UserId);
    PlayerPrefs.SetString("SCREENNAME", ScreenName);

    Connected = true;
}
```

Step 10. Take the keys obtained in Step 1 and add them into the strings at the top of PostTweet for the API_KEY, CONSUMER_KEY, and CONSUMER_SECRET.

Step 11. Play. As soon as the application starts running the Web browser will open and take you to your Twitter account. Log in if you aren't already. An authorization page will open asking to give the Unity application access to your Twitter account as shown in Figure 8.14.

Step 12. After pressing Authorize App, Twitter will present you with a PIN number as shown in Figure 8.15. Copy the PIN number and return to your Unity application.

Authorize UnityTweeter to use your account?

This application will be able to:

- Read Tweets from your timeline.
- See who you follow, and follow new people.
- Update your profile.
- Post Tweets for you.
- Access your direct messages.

Authorize app   **No, thanks**

This application **will not be able to**:

- See your Twitter password.

UnityTweeter
By Aardbei Studios
www.holistic3d.com

An example use of Unity and the Twitter API for use in the book "Holistic Game Development with Unity"

FIG 8.14 Twitter's application access authorization form.

You've granted access to UnityTweeter!

Next, return to UnityTweeter and enter this PIN to complete the authorization process:

5222856

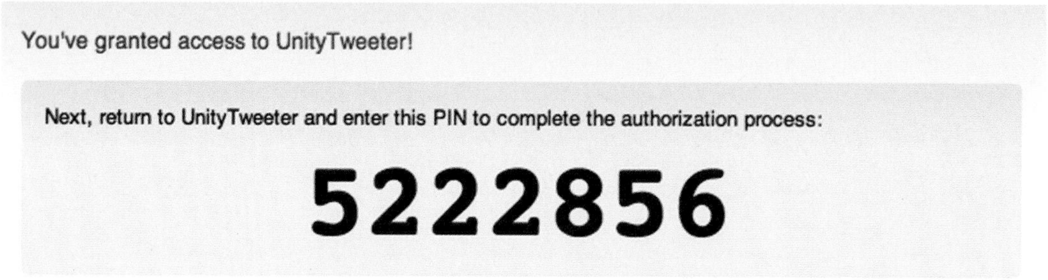

FIG 8.15 Authorization PIN number from Twitter.

Step 13. The screen in Unity will now be waiting for the PIN number as shown in Figure 8.16. Type the Twitter PIN into the text field and press Submit.

Step 14. If all has gone to plan, the Unity application will display a window for you to enter tweets. This is illustrated in Figure 8.17. Type in a message and hit the Submit button. Tweets only allow a maximum of 140 characters. Therefore, when the text field is too large, the Submit button will disappear.

FIG 8.16 Unity awaiting Twitter PIN.

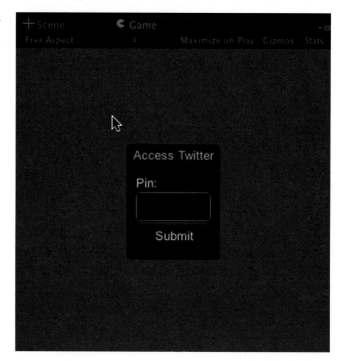

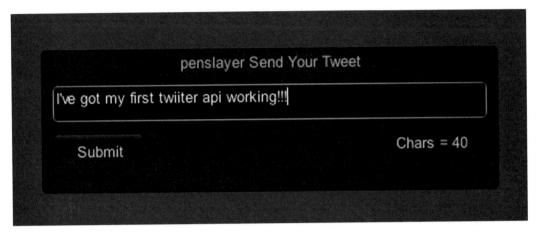

FIG 8.17 A simple Twitter posting form.

Step 15. Log into your Twitter account and check that your message has gone through.

Step 16. You can use this very method in your games to send automatic tweets on behalf of players about their status in the game, including current score, items they may have purchased, when their character has died, or when they unlock a level.

⊙ Unity Hands On

Twitter Data in 3D

Performing a search on Twitter data is far easier than authenticating for a single user. You can use the Twitter API to search for any keywords. For example, http://search.twitter.com/search.json?q=Unity will return JSON data with tweets mentioning Unity. In this workshop you will use the Twitter API to get the last tweet posted by a specific user and display their tweet text and profile image in the Unity 3D environment.

Step 1. Download *Chapter Eight/JSON.zip* from the Web site. Open the 3DTweets scene.

Step 2. Play. A male character will be standing on a large plane with a rocky texture.

Step 3. The tweet and user profile is going to appear on a board above the character's head. This board is the prefab called Tweeter. Drag this object into the Scene and position near the character as shown in Figure 8.18.

Step 4. Create a new JavaScript called *UserTweets*. Add the code from Listing 8.12. The JSON parser referred to in the code is already in the project in the Plugins folder.

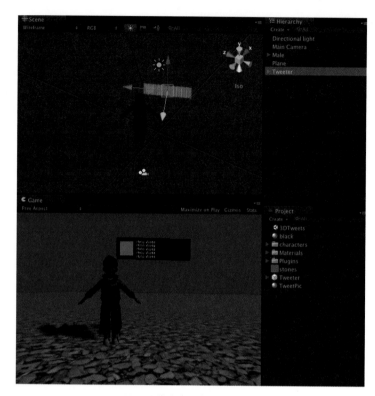

FIG 8.18 A 3D object to display Twitter data.

Listing 8.12 Script to Get the Last Tweet for a Specific User in Twitter and Draw with 3D Text

```
private var twitterTextURL: String =
  "http://twitter.com/statuses/user_timeline/aardbeistudios.
  json?count=1";
private var twitterPictureURL: String =
  "http://a2.twimg.com/profile_images/739029753/" +
        "aardbei3300x259_reasonably_small.jpg";
var userImage: GameObject;
var lastTweet: TextMesh[];
function DivideLines(lineLength : int, original: String)
{
  //empty all lines before starting
  for(var j = 0; j < lastTweet.length; j++)
    lastTweet[j].text = "";
```

```
    //copy character by character into the 3D lines
    //look for spaces to break sentence
    var lineCount = 0;
    for(var i = 0; i < original.length; i++)
    {
        if((lastTweet[lineCount].text.length +
                    (original.IndexOf(" ",i)-i)) <
                    lineLength ||
                    (lastTweet[lineCount].text.length >=
                            lineLength &&
                            original[i] != " "))
        {
            lastTweet[lineCount].text += original[i];
        }
        else
        {
            lineCount++;
            lastTweet[lineCount].text += original[i];
        }
        //if we've run out of lines quit writing
        if(lineCount >= lastTweet.length)
            return;
    }
}

function Start()
{
    //get users last message
    var www : WWW = new WWW (twitterTextURL);
    //wait for data from twitter
    yield www;

    var hash=JSON.ParseJSON(www.text);

    for (var item : DictionaryEntry in hash)
    {
        DivideLines(25, item.Value["text"]);
    }

    //get users profile image
    var www1 : WWW = new WWW (twitterPictureURL);
    //wait for data from twitter
    yield www1;

    //put profile image onto plane
    serImage.renderer.material.mainTexture = www1.texture;
}
```

Step 5. Attach the UserTweets.js script to the Tweeter object in the Hierarchy. Expand the Tweeter object. Select it and locate the UserTweets component. Add the TweetProfilePic and the TweetText objects to the script as shown in Figure 8.19.

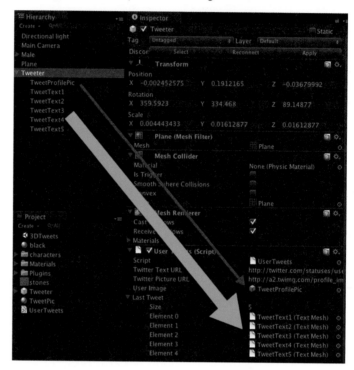

Step 6. Play. The plane above the character's head will display the last tweet from, in this case, the user called *aardbeistudios*, and their profile image.

Step 7. To get others or your own tweets, simply replace the Twitter user name in the Twitter Text URL of the UserTweets script with another as shown in Figure 8.20.

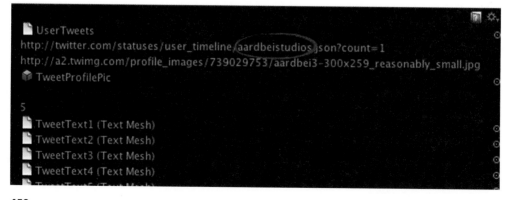

Step 8. To change the profile image, modify the Twitter Picture URL. You can get this by browsing to the Twitter user of your choice, right-clicking on the profile picture, selecting Open Image In New Tab or the equivalent, and getting the image URL from the URL displayed in the new tab.

8.5.2 Facebook

The process of user authentication with Facebook is similar to that of Twitter. Facebook also supplies programming interfaces in C++ and C# for XCode and Visual Studio programming.

The process of authorizing the player's account is done through a series of Web-based calls as is the case with Twitter. Facebook, however, is a far bigger beast and the amount of data you can obtain is very large. These data are organized into the Facebook Graph. In brief, it is a data network that links your own profile with that of your friends and their friends and their friends.

Facebook, like Twitter, returns JSON-formatted data. The URLs to call to get access to these data are documented at http://developers.facebook.com/docs/reference/api/. We will take a look at some of these calls and data they return in the following workshop.

◉ Unity Hands On
Accessing Facebook

Accessing data in Facebook requires extra code to be created that returns an authorization number to you. This code needs to be hosted on a Web server and registered with Facebook as a Facebook app. As this is slightly out of the scope of this book, we will be using one already created by Unity developer Paul Price. The inspiration, Facebook API, and JSON code come from his Web site at http://ifc0nfig.com/accessing-facebook-within-unity/.

Note that this is but one way to get your Unity application to talk to Facebook.

> **Step 1.** Download *Chapter Eight/Facebook.zip*. Open the project in Unity and select the ConnectToFacebook scene.
> **Step 2.** Play. A small GUI box with a Connect to Facebook button will appear in the Game, as shown in Figure 8.21.
> **Step 3.** Click on this button. Your browser will open. If you aren't logged into Facebook you will be asked to do so. In the end a window with your authentication token will appear. This is shown in Figure 8.22.

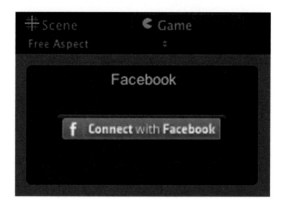

FIG 8.21 Connect to Facebook button in Unity.

FIG 8.22 The Magic Token needed by the Unity application to retrieve data from Facebook.

YOUR MAGIC TOKEN

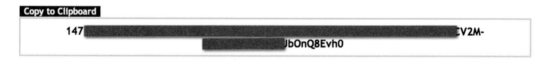

Please copy and paste this token into the game window.

Step 4. This token is unique to you. You need to enter it into the Unity application so that Unity can communicate with your account. To do this, modify interface.js to the code shown in Listing 8.13.

Step 5. Play. After the Magic Token appears in your browser, copy and paste it into the Magic Token box, shown in Figure 8.23, which will appear in the Unity application after you hit the Connect button.

Step 6. Select Authenticate to Save. The code also saves the Magic Token in the player preferences for later use. This saves you typing it in every time the program runs.

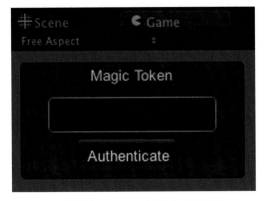

FIG 8.23 A GUI element to enter the Facebook Magic Token.

Listing 8.13 Code to Switch over to a Magic Token Entering Box after Facebook Connection Is Made

```
...
function OnGUI()
{
     if(!showTokenBox)
     {
          GUI.BeginGroup (Rect (10, 10, 200, 100));
          GUI.Box (Rect (0,0,200,100), "Facebook");
          if(GUI.Button (Rect (25,40,150,30), t))
          {
               Application.OpenURL(
                 "https://graph.facebook.com/oauth/authorize" +
                 "?client_id=147305235313757&redirect_uri=" +
                 "http://ifcOnfig.com/Facebook/UnityGame/" +
                 "&type=user_agent&display=page");

               showTokenBox = true;
          }
          GUI.EndGroup ();
     }
     else if(showTokenBox)
     {
          GUI.BeginGroup (Rect (10, 10, 200, 100));
          GUI.Box (Rect (0,0,200,100), "Magic Token");
          MagicToken = GUI.TextField (Rect (25, 30, 150, 30),
                                      MagicToken, 120);
          if(GUI.Button(Rect( 50, 65, 90, 30), "Authenticate"))
```

```
          {
               UFacebook.MagicToken = MagicToken;
               PlayerPrefs.SetString("FACEBOOKTOKEN", MagicToken);
          }
          GUI.EndGroup ();
     }
}
```

Step 7. To make use of this connection with your Facebook account, modify the interface.js code to return the details from your profile as given in Listing 8.14.

Listing 8.14 Displaying Information from Facebook

```
var t: Texture2D;
var MagicToken = "";
...

function RequestUserDetails()
{
     if(MagicToken != "")
     {
          UFacebook.MagicToken = MagicToken;
          UFacebook.GetUserProperty("me", "link");
     }
     return null;
}

function Start()
{
     MagicToken = PlayerPrefs.GetString("FACEBOOKTOKEN");
     RequestUserDetails();
}

function OnGUI()
{
     if(!showTokenBox)
     {
          GUI.BeginGroup (Rect (10, 10, 200, 100));
          GUI.Box (Rect (0,0,200,100), "Facebook");
          if(GUI.Button (Rect (25,40,150,30), t))
          {
               Application.OpenURL(
               "https://graph.facebook.com/oauth/authorize" +
               "?client_id=147305235313757&redirect_uri=" +
```

```
                       "http://www.ifcOnfig.com/Facebook/UnityGame/" +
                       "&type=user_agent&display=page");

                       showTokenBox = true;
               }
        GUI.EndGroup ();

  }
  else if(showTokenBox)
  {
        GUI.BeginGroup (Rect (10, 10, 200, 100));
        GUI.Box (Rect (0,0,200,100), "Magic Token");
        MagicToken = GUI.TextField (Rect (25, 30, 150, 30),
                                            MagicToken, 120);

        if(GUI.Button(Rect( 50, 65, 90, 30), "Authenticate"))
        {
               UFacebook.MagicToken = MagicToken;
               RequestUserDetails();
               PlayerPrefs.SetString("FACEBOOKTOKEN",
        MagicToken);
        }
        GUI.EndGroup ();
  }

  scrollViewVector = GUI.BeginScrollView
                       (Rect(250,10, 400, 400),
                       scrollViewVector,
                       Rect (0, 0, 600, 600));
  UFacebook.LastRequest = GUI.TextArea
                              (Rect (0, 0, 600, 600),
                       UFacebook.LastRequest);
  GUI.EndScrollView();
}
```

Step 8. Play. A scrollbox will now display with information obtained
from your Facebook profile. The RequestUserDetails() function
does all the work, calling functions in the existing C# code in the
Project's Plugins direction. Using your Magic Token it calls one of
the Facebook Graph API URLs. In this case, https://graph.facebook
.com/me.

Step 9. Your profile picture is available by calling http://graph
.facebook.com/YOUR_USERNAME/picture. The user name can be
obtained from previous data and placed in the URL with code as
shown in Listing 8.15. Note that the picture is downloaded in the
same way as images in the Twitter workshop.

Listing 8.15 Displaying Your Profile Picture in Unity

```
var t: Texture2D;
var MagicToken = "";
...

function RequestUserDetails()
{

    if(MagicToken != "")
    {

        UFacebook.MagicToken = MagicToken;
        UFacebook.GetUserProperty("me", "link");
        GetDisplayPicture();
    }

    return null;
}

...

function OnGUI()
{

    ...
    scrollViewVector = GUI.BeginScrollView
                        (Rect (250,10,400, 400),
                        scrollViewVector, Rect
                        (0, 0, 600, 600));
    UFacebook.LastRequest = GUI.TextArea
                            (Rect (0, 0, 600, 600),
                        UFacebook.LastRequest);
    GUI.EndScrollView();

    if(profilePic != null)
        GUI.Button (Rect (10,155, 100, 100), profilePic);
}

function GetDisplayPicture()
{
    var username = UFacebook.username;
    if( username != "")
    {

        var www : WWW = new WWW ("http://graph.
                            facebook.com/" + username +
                            "/picture");
        yield www;
        profilePic = www.texture;
    }
}
```

Step 10. To get data from other Facebook Graph APIs, more functions can be added into the Facebook UFacebook.cs file in Projects > Plugins. This file is in C# so unless you know what you are doing, it is recommended that you don't change this file.

However, for illustrative purposes, a function called GetUserFriends() has been added. This calls the Facebook Graph API that returns the current user's friends. The URL to achieve this is shown at http://developers.facebook.com/docs/reference/api/ and is https://graph.facebook.com/me/**friends**?access_token=... "friends" in this case is the keyword for data retrieval. Note that in the API documentation you can get data for anything from news feeds, likes, and photos. All you would need to do is copy the GetUserFriends() function in the C# file, give it another name, and change the word "friends" for something else such as "groups." As an example, the C# function for GetUserGroups() would be

```
public static string GetUserGroups(string user)
{
        try
        {
                FacebookAPI api = new FacebookAPI(MagicToken);
                Facebook.JSONObject request = api.Get("/" + user +
                                                "/groups");
                LastRequest = request.ToDisplayableString();

                return request.ToDisplayableString();
        }
        catch
        {
                return null;
        }
}
```

Step 11. To call the GetUserFriends() function and display the information in the text field, modify the interface.js code to reflect Listing 8.16.

Listing 8.16 Requesting a User's Friend List from Facebook

```
var t: Texture2D;
...

function RequestUserFriends()
{
        if(MagicToken != "")
        {
```

```
            UFacebook.MagicToken = MagicToken;
            UFacebook.GetUserFriends("me");
        }
        return null;
    }

function OnGUI()
{
        ...
        if(GUI.Button(Rect (10,120,100,30),"Get Friends"))
        {
            RequestUserFriends();
        }
        if(profilePic != null)
            GUI.Button (Rect (10,155, 100, 100), profilePic);
    }
...
```

Step 12. Play. You will now be able to access a listing of your friends from inside Unity.

In addition to accessing Facebook data, you can also embed a Unity game into a Facebook page for others to play, like, and rate. For this you need to build a Web platform version of your game and have a Web server where you can host it.

◉ Unity Hands On
Embedding a Unity Game into Facebook

Step 1. Create a Unity game. In Build Settings, build it for the Web Player Platform. It will save into a folder with two files: HTML and Unity. Rename the HTML one to *index.html*.

Step 2. Upload these to a Web server. You should be able to browse to the game in a Web browser just by using the folder URL. For this example the game is in http://aardbeistudios.com/facebook/Asteroids/.

Step 3. Visit https://facebook.com/developers/. Login and press the "+Set Up New App" button in the top right corner of the page.

Step 4. Enter an App name, agree to the terms, and click Create App.

Step 5. On the next page enter some basic information—for now just type in an Application Name and Description.

Step 6. Select the Facebook Integration tab.

Step 7. Enter a name for your app in the Canvas Page settings. It must be unique and does not need to be the same as the name of your Unity project.

Step 8. Enter a Canvas URL. This is the location on the Web where you have uploaded your Unity Web project.

Step 9. Click on Save Changes.

Step 10. You can now see your game embedded in Facebook using the Canvas Page, for example, http://apps.facebook.com/holistic_asteroids/ as shown in Figure 8.24.

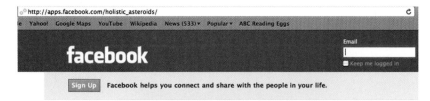

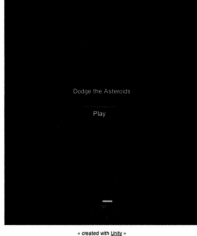

FIG 8.24 A Unity game embedded in Facebook.

● **Note**

Games embedded in Web pages will take a while to load. The larger the Unity file, the longer a player will have to wait for it. Casual gamers don't like to wait. Keep your game small and neat.

8.5.3 OpenFeint

OpenFeint is a social networking platform created especially for mobile games. It was launched in 2009 for iOS on the iPhone and iPad and is now available for Android-supporting devices. It provides a set of easy-to-use APIs that allow developers to integrate functionality such as leaderboards, forums, live chat, rewards, beat the highest score, and play with friends.

As with Twitter and Facebook, your game talks to OpenFeint with authorization tokens. To obtain these tokens, visit the OpenFeint developers' site at https://api.openfeint.com/dd. Here you create a login and then begin registering your game. On entering the Application Information tab you will be given a Client Application ID, Product Key, and Product Secret as shown in Figure 8.25. This information is entered into your programming code to provide your game with access to the OpenFeint features.

FIG 8.25 Obtaining authorization tokens for OpenFeint.

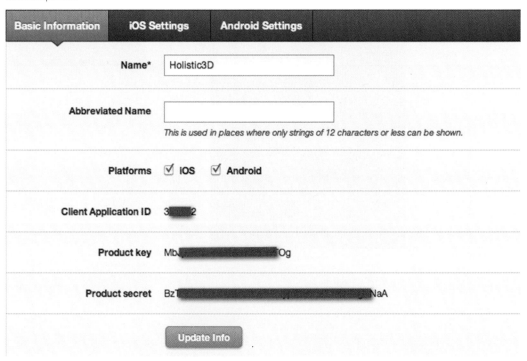

On the OpenFeint Web site you will find assistance for developers and downloads of APIs for iOS and Android. There is even a beta version of one for Unity.

Integrating OpenFeint with Your Unity Game

Step 1. Create a login at the OpenFeint developer site as discussed
in the previous section (https://api.openfeint.com/dd).

Step 2. Login and Add a New Game. Give your game a name and
select the Android development platform. Click on save.

Step 3. Select Application Information. Record the Client Application
ID, Product Key, and Product Secret.

Step 4. Create a new Unity Android Project.

Step 5. Download *Chapter Eight/OpenFeint-UnityAndroid
.package*.

Step 6. Import the package into your project.

Step 7. Download *Chapter Eight/OpenFeintController.cs* and add into
the Project > Plugins folder.

Step 8. Select GameObject > Create Empty from the main menu.
A new game object will be added to the Hierarchy. Rename it
OFObject.

Step 9. Drag and drop the OpenFeintController script from Project >
Plugins onto the OFObject.

Step 10. Create a new JavaScript file in the root of the Project called
OFInterface. Add the code shown in Listing 8.17.

Listing 8.17 Initializing OpenFeint

```
var OF;

function Start()
{
      OFObject = GameObject.Find("OFObject");
      if(!OFObject) //if not found one must be added
      {
            print("Create an OFObject before proceeding");
      }
      else
      {
            OF = (OFObject.GetComponent
                  ("OpenFeintController") as
                  OpenFeintController);
      }
}

function OnGUI()
{
      if (GUI.Button(new Rect(10,10,300,80), "Initialize
        OpenFeint"))
      {
```

```
            OF.Init();
        }
    }

function Update ()
{
}
```

Step 11. Attach OFInterface to the Main Camera.

Step 12. In *OpenFeintController.cs* insert your Application Name, Product Key, Product Secret, and Client Application ID in the corresponding empty quotes from the OpenFeint Web site, respectively.

Step 13. Play to see how your button is aligned on the screen in the Editor. Note that the button will not function in the Editor; you must build and deploy the app to an Android device.

Step 14. Build and Run to push the application to an attached Android device.

Step 15. Press the button and OpenFeint will open. Do not log into OpenFeint at this point.

Step 16. Return to Unity and select File > Build Settings. On the Build Settings pop up select Player Settings to bring up the Android configuration values in the Inspector. Give your application a name, icon, and bundle identifier.

Step 17. Open the AndroidManifest file in the Plugins > Android folder in the Project. Edit the package name string to match your bundle identifier as shown in Figure 8.26.

Step 18. Return to the OpenFeint developers' site and select the Application Information for your game title. On this page select Android Settings as shown in Figure 8.27. You will need to supply the package name created in the previous step, an icon, description, and at least two screen captures. Select Save.

Step 19. Before you can activate your game in OpenFeint it will require at least one leaderboard and one achievement. To add this, select the Features tab in the top right of the webpage. A leaderboard keeps track of players and high scores, and achievements reward players for reaching specific game play status such as bronze, silver, and gold medals or unlocking new levels. Achievements can be unlocked relative to in-game scores. The achievement scores obtained in OpenFeint set the players' overall level across all their playing of OpenFeint-enabled games. For a single game you can allocate up to 1000 bonus OpenFeint points with a maximum of 200 points per achievement.

Once you have added these items, return to the Overview page for your app and select the orange *Enable Android* button. This will place your OpenFeint game linkage *Under Review*.

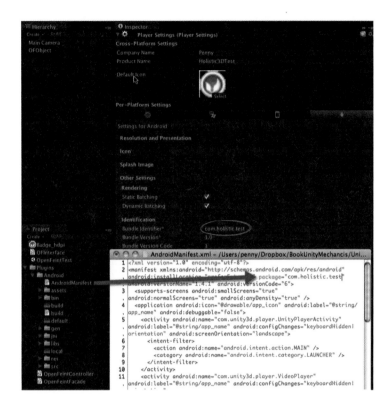

FIG 8.26 Setting the Android bundle identifier and package.

FIG 8.27 Completing the OpenFeint information for your app.

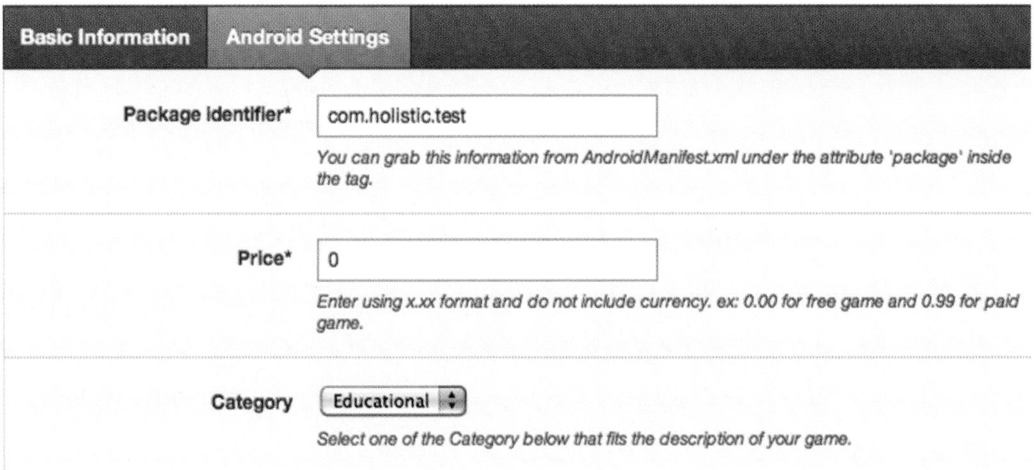

Basic Information | Android Settings

Package Identifier* `com.holistic.test`

You can grab this information from AndroidManifest.xml under the attribute 'package' inside the tag.

Price* `0`

Enter using x.xx format and do not include currency. ex: 0.00 for free game and 0.99 for paid game.

Category `Educational ⬍`

Select one of the Category below that fits the description of your game.

Note that you can still use and test your OpenFeint interface without its having completed the review process. As long as you have all the IDs and keys you are ready to go.

Ensure that you take note of the leaderboard and achievement IDs as you will need these in the code to send scores to the leaderboard and unlock achievements.

Step 20. To explore further the functionality of the OpenFeint interface, modify the OFInterface script to that in Listing 8.18. Remember to replace the three leaderboard IDs and achievement ID with your own.

Listing 8.18 Integrating Further OpenFeint Features into an App

```
var OF;
var score: int = 0;
var scoreStyle: GUIStyle;
private var medal = false;
function Start()
{

    ...

}

function OnGUI()
{
    GUI.Label(new Rect(200,10,200,80),"Score: " + score,
                          scoreStyle);
    if(!OF.isInitialised())
    {
        if (GUI.Button(new Rect(10,10,150,50),
                          "Initialise OpenFeint"))
        {
            OF.Init();
        }
    }
    else if (!OF.isUserLoggedIn())
    {
        GUI.Button(new Rect(10,10,150,50), "Initialising...");
    }
    else
    {
        if (GUI.Button(new Rect(10,70,150,50), "Leaderboard"))
```

```
            {
                  OF.LaunchLeaderboardDashboard("796236");
            }
            if (GUI.Button(new Rect(10,130,150,50),
                  "Achievements"))
            {
                  OF.LaunchAchievements();
            }
            if (GUI.Button(new Rect(10,190,150,50),
                  "Get Scores"))
            {
                  OF.GetHighScores ("796236");
            }
            if (GUI.Button(new Rect(10,250,150,50),
                  "Submit Score"))
            {
                  OF.SubmitScore("796236",score);
            }
      }
}

function Update ()
{
      if(Mathf.Abs(Input.acceleration.x) > 1 ||
            Mathf.Abs(Input.acceleration.y) > 1 ||
            Mathf.Abs(Input.acceleration.z) > 1)
      {
            iPhoneUtils.Vibrate();
            score++;
            if(score > 400 && !medal)
            {
                  OF.UnlockAchievement(1052482);
                  OF.Message("You've achieved a Gold Medal!");
                  medal = true;
            }
      }
}
```

Step 21. Build and Run. Screen displays are shown in Figure 8.28. When the application first opens it will display a score and Initialize OpenFeint button (Figure 8.28a). On pressing this, the OpenFeint linkage will log you in (Figure 8.28b). When logged in this button will disappear and the other buttons will be displayed (Figure 8.28c).

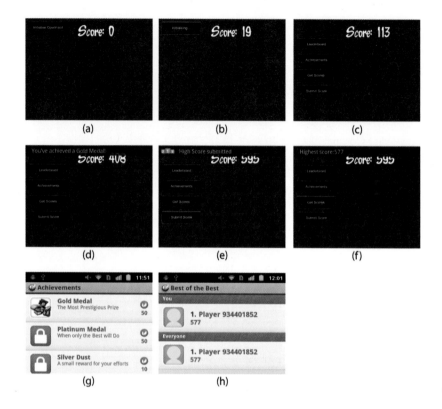

FIG 8.28 **FIG 8.28** An OpenFeint integration within a Unity game playing in Android.

Shake the phone to increase your score. The script also unlocks an achievement when the score goes over 400. An achievement unlock message is sent to OpenFeint using achievement's ID and it is unlocked (Figure 8.28d).

At any time you may press the Submit Score button to register your score with OpenFeint (Figure 8.28e). You can review your highest score by pressing the Get Score button (Figure 8.28f).

Unlocked and locked achievements for the game can be viewed by pressing the Achievement's button (Figure 8.28g).

The Leaderboard button takes you to the OpenFeint leaderboard for the game (Figure 8.28h). The game can have numerous leaderboards. You must identify them with their ID.

This workshop has covered most of the OpenFeint functionality allowed by the Unity integration package. The package for this tutorial was taken from http://support.openfeint.com/dev/unity3d/. It is still in beta so expect it to have changed by the time this book is published. There is an iOS version available but it is still very buggy. The author recommends keeping an eye on this site for more details as they become available.

8.6 Platform Deployment: App Store, Android Market, and Consoles

In the past, publishing a game was an exercise in self-publicity and tenacity. Small independent developers would have to approach the big publishing houses with their dreams of grandeur, convince the publishers to invest in their game, and then stick to strict milestones and release deadlines for, in the end, what might amount to 7% royalties. While this situation is still possible nowadays and could lead a small development company to much fame and fortune via the publishers' vast network of marketing resources, small independent developers do have many more options available to them.

8.6.1 Publishing for the App Store and Android Market

The App Store delivers developers games directly to the consumer, cutting out the middleman. Applications for iOS and Mac OSX+ are listed in the store that buyers can purchase over the Internet and download directly to their desktop computer or mobile device.

Applications written for the AppStore must be developed with an XCode component. For example, Unity builds its code via XCode when pushing the application to the iPhone or iPad.

Developers wishing to put content in the AppStore or on iOS devices must register as an Apple Developer. At the time of writing, this costs $99 per year. For this, the developer gets access to the Apple Development Network, beta releases of Mac operating system updates, and authentication protocols to build and push applications for testing to their mobile devices.

Once a game is ready for deployment it is submitted to Apple for approval. This process can take up to 2 weeks. Apple has a checklist of the things it looks for when approving an application and it is prudent to check these off yourself before submitting. If there is something wrong with your application, you will have to fix it and resubmit for approval.

Apple has a fixed pricing scale for all apps. Fees taken by Apple are different in different countries, but equate to approximately 30%.

For the latest information on the exact procedures, visit http://developer.apple.com/.

The Android Market has a more relaxed approach to app publishing. It currently requires a Gmail account and a small once off fee of $25 to start selling apps. To get started, visit http://developer.android.com/index.html.

You will require the Android SDK to build applications. It is being updated constantly for new versions of Android; to ensure that your applications are compatible, it is best to update frequently.

To create an Android game, Unity functions in the same way as for the iOS. The game is created in the Unity editor and the final product is built via the Android SDK on its way to the mobile.

Android allows the developer to put any price on their app. A transaction fee of 30% is paid to Google for each app sold. This is detailed here at https://google.com/support/androidmarket/developer/bin/answer .py?&&answer=112622.

If you completed the workshop in Section 8.2, you're 95% on your way to placing an app in the Android Market.

8.6.2 Console Publishing

The different game console providers, including Microsoft, Nintendo, and Sony, have a variety of rules and regulations as to who can and can't publish on their platforms. In the case of Nintendo, a games studio must complete an application form to be authorized as an official developer (http://warioworld.com/).

Microsoft supplies the free XNA Game Studio development kit for the creation of Xbox and Windows 7 desktop and mobile games. Independent developers can submit their game to the AppHub (http://create.msdn.com/) for listing in the Xbox Live Marketplace. Access to the AppHub costs $99 per year. All games submitted are peer reviewed, and those listed and sold receive 70% of the revenue.

To become an official developer for PlayStation or Xbox (which means your titles get published on DVD and marketed by the respective publishers) is quite a big hurdle. The application process involves proving to the publishers that you have a quite experienced team and around five AAA published titles under your belt. The development kits start from around $10,000 each.

For the reader interested in pursuing console development, here are some URLs worth checking out:

- Microsoft: http://xbox.com/en-US/Developers/Home
- Sony Playstation: http://scedev.net/
- Nintendo: http://warioworld.com/apply/

8.6.3 Download Direct to Player

Last but not least there is the option to self-publish and make your desktop playable game available for download on your own Web site or via a download client such as Steam or Direct2Drive.

A download client allows players to search through a multitude of titles online and purchase, download, and install directly onto their computer, much in the same way the App Store and Android Market work.

Steam is a platform consisting of a software client that runs on desktop computers and manages distribution, management rights, and multiplayer functionality. It was developed by Valve Corporation (the famous developers of the Half-Life games series) and released in 2003. Steam currently manages 1250 titles and has over 30 million active users. It manages games for both large publishing houses and small independent developers. Information on Steam readying your game can be found at https://partner.steamgames.com/.

Direct2Drive is one of a number of online game stores with their own download clients. They are always looking to list and manage new game titles, even from small unknown developers. They provide a digital shop front in numerous countries and manage player purchases. Like Steam, they too retain purchase records so players can download their game at any time. This is a useful service that means the player isn't misplacing DVDs and jewel cases with serial numbers on them. It's all stored online and available as needed. Details of distributing with them are available from http://direct2drive.com/staticpage .aspx?topic=publisher_contact.

8.7 Summary

This chapter examined some of the external mechanics and forces that drive game development in certain directions. If you are an independent developer, there has never been a better time to get your game out into the world on a desktop computer, on a mobile device, or in the Xbox Live Marketplace. Relatively inexpensive high-quality tools, such as Unity, are bringing power to the people, allowing small inexperienced teams to take their first steps. And online stores are cutting out the publisher, allowing a more direct line to the consumer. While publishing someday with one of the big three might be your dream, there is no reason why your baby steps can't start now.

In addition, the availability of software development kits and game engines that access all the hardware functionality features of new mobile and peripheral devices means, as a game designer, that you can let your mind run wild. Finding clever new ways to interact kinesthetically with the virtual world could just give you the next big thing in computer games.

Whichever path you decide to take, know that the face of game design and development has taken the biggest turn in the past 5 years than it ever did in the previous 40, and you don't need to be a computer scientist anymore to work with the technology and create really amazing and visually exciting games.

Index

Note: Page numbers followed by *b* indicates boxes, *f* indicates figures and *t* indicates tables.